ACCA

Strategic Professional

Advanced Taxation (ATX – UK) FA2020

Workbook

For exams in June 2021, September 2021, December 2021 and March 2022

BPP LEARNING MEDIA

First edition 2020

ISBN 9781 5097 3492 4

ISBN (for internal use only): 9781 5097 3342 2

e-ISBN 9781 5097 3292 0

British Library Cataloguing-in-Publication Data

A catalogue record for this book is available from the British Library.

Published by

BPP Learning Media Ltd

BPP House, Aldine Place

142–144 Uxbridge Road

London W12 8AA

learningmedia.bpp.com

Printed in the United Kingdom

Contains public sector information licensed under the Open Government Licence v3.0.

We are grateful to the Association of Chartered Certified Accountants for permission to reproduce past examination questions and extracts from the syllabus. The suggested solutions in the practice answer bank have been prepared by BPP Learning Media Ltd, except where otherwise stated.

A note about copyright

Dear Customer

What does the little © mean and why does it matter? Your market-leading BPP books, course materials and e-learning materials do not write and update themselves. People write them on their own behalf or as employees of an organisation that invests in this activity. Copyright law protects their livelihoods. It does so by creating rights over the use of the content.

Breach of copyright is a form of theft – as well as being a criminal offence in some jurisdictions, it is potentially a serious breach of professional ethics.

With current technology, things might seem a bit hazy but, basically, without the express permission of BPP Learning Media:

- Photocopying our materials is a breach of copyright
- Scanning, ripcasting or conversion of our digital materials into different file formats, uploading them to Facebook or emailing them to your friends is a breach of copyright

You can, of course, sell your books, in the form in which you have bought them – once you have finished with them. (Is this fair to your fellow students? We update for a reason.) Please note the e-products are sold on a single user licence basis: we do not supply 'unlock' codes to people who have bought them second-hand.

And what about outside the UK? BPP Learning Media strives to make our materials available at prices students can afford by local printing arrangements, pricing policies and partnerships which are clearly listed on our website. A tiny minority ignore this and indulge in criminal activity by illegally photocopying our material or supporting organisations that do. If they act illegally and unethically in one area, can you really trust them?

Contents

Helping you to pass

BPP Learning Media – ACCA Approved Content Provider

As an ACCA Approved Content Provider, BPP Learning Media gives you the opportunity to use study materials reviewed by the ACCA examining team. By incorporating the examining team's comments and suggestions regarding the depth and breadth of syllabus coverage, the BPP Learning Media Workbook provides excellent, ACCA-approved support for your studies.

These materials are reviewed by the ACCA examining team. The objective of the review is to ensure that the material properly covers the syllabus and study guide outcomes, used by the examining team in setting the exams, in the appropriate breadth and depth. The review does not ensure that every eventuality, combination or application of examinable topics is addressed by the ACCA Approved Content. Nor does the review comprise a detailed technical check of the content as the Approved Content Provider has its own quality assurance processes in place in this respect.

BPP Learning Media do everything possible to ensure the material is accurate and up to date when sending to print. In the event that any errors are found after the print date, they are uploaded to the following website: www.bpp.com/learningmedia/Errata.

The PER alert

Before you can qualify as an ACCA member, you not only have to pass all your exams but also fulfil a three-year practical experience requirement (PER). To help you to recognise areas of the syllabus that you might be able to apply in the workplace to achieve different performance objectives, we have introduced the 'PER alert' feature (see the section below). You will find this feature throughout the Workbook to remind you that what you are learning to pass your ACCA exams is equally useful to the fulfilment of the PER requirement. Your achievement of the PER should be recorded in your online My Experience record.

Chapter features

Studying can be a daunting prospect, particularly when you have lots of other commitments. This Workbook is full of useful features, explained in the key below, designed to help you to get the most out of your studies and maximise your chances of exam success.

Key term

Central concepts are highlighted and clearly defined in the Key terms feature. Key terms are also listed in bold in the Index, for quick and easy reference.

Formula to learn

This boxed feature will highlight important formula which you need to learn for your exam.

Formula provided

This will show formula which are important but will be provided in the exam.

PER alert

This feature identifies when something you are reading will also be useful for your PER requirement (see 'The PER alert' section above for more details).

Illustration

Illustrations walk through how to apply key knowledge and techniques step by step.

Activity

Activities give you essential practice of techniques covered in the chapter.

Essential reading

Links to the Essential reading are given throughout the chapter. The Essential reading is included in the free eBook, accessed via the Exam Success Site (see inside cover for details on how to access this).

At the end of each chapter you will find a Knowledge diagnostic, which is a summary of the main learning points from the chapter to allow you to check you have understood the key concepts. You will also find Further study guidance which contains suggestions for ways in which you can continue your learning and enhance your understanding. This can include: recommendations for question practice from the Further question practice and solutions, to test your understanding of the topics in the Chapter; suggestions for further reading which can be done, such as technical articles and ideas for your own research. The Chapter summary provides more detailed revision of the topics covered and is intended to assist you as you prepare for your revision phase.

Introduction to the Essential reading

The digital eBook version of the Workbook contains additional content, selected to enhance your studies. Consisting of revision materials and further explanations of complex areas (including illustrations and activities), it is designed to aid your understanding of key topics which are covered in the main printed chapters of the Workbook.

To access the digital eBook version of the BPP Workbook, follow the instructions which can be found on the inside cover; you'll be able to access your eBook, plus download the BPP eBook mobile app on multiple devices, including smartphones and tablets.

A summary of the content of the Essential reading is given below.

Chapter		Summary of Essential reading content
1	Ethics, tax avoidance schemes	• Detail on the fundamental principles, the conceptual framework that requires ACCA members to identify, evaluate and address threats to compliance with the fundamental principles, and ethical dispute resolution • Detail on direct tax and VAT avoidance schemes
2	The income tax computation	• Further detailed revision of the income tax computation from TX
3	Pensions and other tax-efficient investment products	• Further detailed revision of pensions from TX
4	Employment income	• Detailed revision of the calculation of employment income from TX, including benefit calculations and the rules for allowable deductions
5	Property income	• More detailed revision of the calculation of property income from TX • Further depth regarding furnished holiday lets • Further depth regarding rent a room relief
6	Personal tax planning	There is no essential reading for this chapter
7	Capital gains tax computation	• Detail on the treatment of disposals between connected persons • Loss, damage and destruction of assets – election to avoid part disposal computation • Further depth regarding negligible value claims
8	Shares and securities, CGT reliefs	• Share disposals – illustration of a share disposal following a rights issue • Detail of capital distributions on liquidation • Illustration of takeovers involving shares and cash • Details of the interaction of takeovers with business asset disposal relief and investors' relief • Detailed revision of private residence relief, gift relief and rollover relief from TX • Detail on altering dispositions made on death
9	Overseas personal taxation	• Illustrations of split year treatment • Illustrations of deemed domicile • Detail on the remittance basis • Detail on the taxation of non-resident individuals •

Chapter		Summary of Essential reading content
		• Detail on use of capital losses by non-domiciled individuals
		• Availability of CGT reliefs for non-UK resident individuals and non-UK assets
		• Illustration of gains chargeable on an individual who is temporarily non-UK resident
		• Detail on the OECD model double taxation agreement

10	Personal tax administration	• Detailed revision from TX of the following areas:
		   - Penalties for failure to notify chargeability
		   - Filing dates for tax returns
		   - Penalties for late filing
		   - Amendments to tax returns
		   - Payments on account
		   - HMRC powers
		   - Appeals

11	Inheritance tax computation	• Details on exceptions to the IHT charge • Detailed revision of IHT basics from TX, including the lifetime exemptions, illustrations of the computation of lifetime IHT, death IHT on a lifetime gift and the death estate • Valuation rules for quoted and unquoted shares, unit trusts and life assurance policies • Further depth regarding business and agricultural property reliefs • Illustration of grossing up death gifts
12	Inheritance tax: further aspects	• Further depth on the IHT implications of trusts • Detail on IHT administration and penalties
13	Capital tax planning	There is no essential reading for this chapter

14	Sole traders	• Detailed revision of topics from TX including numerical activities where relevant covering:
		   - Badges of trade
		   - Adjustments to profit
		   - Capital allowances
		   - Basis periods
		 • Numerical illustration of the cash basis
		 • Detail about the impact of trade losses on Class 4 NICs

15	Sole trader losses and partnerships	• More detailed revision of trade losses from TX with activities • Numerical illustration highlighting how trade losses are used differently for Class 4 NIC purposes • More detailed revision of partnerships from TX with activities
16	Corporation tax for single companies	• Detailed revision of corporation tax for single companies, including accounting periods, long

Chapter		Summary of Essential reading content
		periods of account, and the elements of taxable total profits (TTP)
		• Treatment of income and expenses on non-trade intangible assets
		• Illustrations of basic chargeable gains and share matching for companies
		• Reorganisation rules and takeovers as they apply to corporation tax
		• Rollover relief illustration
		• Revision of corporation tax administration from TX, including notification of chargeability, filing returns, compliance checks and record-keeping
17	Losses for single companies	• Illustrations of trading loss relief to non-12 month accounting periods and of terminal loss relief for companies
		• Detail of circumstances where carried forward trading losses are used only against trading profits
18	Owner-managed business tax planning	There is no essential reading for this chapter
19	Corporate groups and consortia	• Activity to revise identifying group relationships from TX
		• Group definition for sharing the AIA
		• Activity to identify available profits and losses for group relief
		• Detail of the implications of the transfer of intangible assets within chargeable gains groups
20	Administration, winding up and purchase of own shares	• Illustrations of accounting periods in administration, and of going from administration to liquidation and vice-versa
		• Details of the implications of making distributions outside a formal winding-up
21	Close companies and investment companies	• Interest payable and receivable from HMRC on close company penalty tax charges
22	Overseas aspects of corporation tax	• Implications of overseas companies trading in the UK
		• Illustration of the overseas branch exemption election
		• Implications of incorporating an overseas PE into a non-resident subsidiary
		• Details of relief available for overseas PE losses
		• Detailed definition of a controlled foreign company (CFC)
23	Value added tax	• Further detailed revision of VAT from TX including:
		- Basic principles of VAT
		- VAT registration and deregistration
		- Deduction of input VAT
		- Accounting for VAT
		- Valuation of supplies

Chapter		Summary of Essential reading content
		- Administration - Overseas VAT • Activity regarding the flat rate scheme • Further illustrations about the partial exemption
24	Stamp taxes	There is no essential reading for this chapter
25	Corporate tax planning	There is no essential reading for this chapter

Introduction to Advanced Taxation (ATX)

Overall aim of the syllabus

The aim of the syllabus is to apply relevant knowledge and skills and exercise professional judgement in providing relevant information and advice to individuals and businesses on the impact of major taxes on financial decisions and situations.

Brought forward knowledge

The Advanced Taxation (ATX) syllabus covers almost every topic that was included in Taxation (TX), with a few minor exceptions. Since tax law changes every year, this text includes all the topics covered at Taxation (TX) again, updated to the latest Finance Act. This material is often summarised in the main chapter with more detailed revision contained in the essential reading, available in Appendix 2 of the digital edition of this workbook.

The syllabus

The broad syllabus headings are:

A	Knowledge and understanding of the UK tax system through the study of more advanced topics within the taxes studied previously and the study of stamp taxes
B	The impact of relevant taxes on various situations and courses of action, including the interaction of taxes
C	Minimising and/or deferring tax liabilities by the use of standard tax planning measures
D	Communicating with clients, HM Revenue and Customs and other professionals

Main capabilities

On successful completion of this exam, you should be able to:

A	Apply further knowledge and understanding of the UK tax system through the study of more advanced topics within the taxes studied previously and the study of stamp taxes
B	Identify and evaluate the impact of relevant taxes on various situations and courses of action, including the interaction of taxes
C	Provide advice on minimising and/or deferring tax liabilities by the use of standard tax planning measures
D	Communicate with clients, HM Revenue and Customs and other professionals in an appropriate manner

Links with other exams

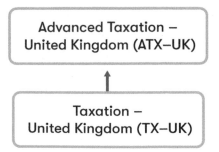

The diagram shows where direct (solid line arrows) and indirect (dashed line arrows) links exist between this exam and other exams preceding or following it.

The Advanced Taxation (ATX) syllabus assumes knowledge acquired in Taxation (TX – UK) and develops and applies this further and in greater depth.

Achieving ACCA's Study Guide Learning Outcomes

This BPP Workbook covers all the Advanced Taxation (ATX) syllabus learning outcomes. The tables below show in which chapter(s) each area of the syllabus is covered.

A	Knowledge and understanding of the UK tax system through the study of more advanced topics within the taxes studied previously and the study of stamp taxes	
A1	Income and income tax liabilities in situations involving further overseas aspects and in relation to trusts, and the application of additional exemptions and reliefs	**Chapters 2, 3, 4, 5, 9, 14, 15**
A2	Chargeable gains and capital gains tax liabilities in situations involving further overseas aspects and in relation to closely related persons and trusts, and the application of additional exemptions and reliefs	**Chapters 7, 8, 9**
A3	Inheritance tax in situations involving further aspects of the scope of the tax and the calculation of the liabilities arising, the principles of valuation and the reliefs available, transfers of property to and from trusts, overseas aspects and further aspects of administration	**Chapters 11, 12**
A4	Corporation tax liabilities in situations involving overseas and further group aspects and in relation to special types of company, and the application of additional exemptions and reliefs	**Chapters 16, 17, 19, 20, 21, 22**
A5	Stamp taxes	**Chapter 24**
A6	Value added tax, tax administration and the UK tax system	**Chapters 10, 16, 23**

B	The impact of relevant taxes on various situations and courses of action, including the interaction of taxes	
B1	Taxes applicable to a given situation or course of action and their impact	**Chapters 6, 13, 18, 25**
B2	Alternative ways of achieving personal or business outcomes may lead to different tax consequences	**Chapters 6, 13, 18, 25**
B3	Taxation effects of the financial decisions made by businesses (corporate and unincorporated) and by individuals	**Chapters 6, 13, 18, 25**
B4	Tax advantages and/or disadvantages of alternative courses of action	**Chapters 6, 13, 18, 25**
B5	Statutory obligations imposed in a given situation, including any time limits for action and the implications of non-compliance	**Chapters 10, 16, 23**

C	Minimising and/or deferring tax liabilities by the use of standard tax planning measures	

C1	Types of investment and other expenditure that will result in a reduction in tax liabilities for an individual and/or a business	Chapters 6, 13, 18, 25
C2	Legitimate tax planning measures, by which the tax liabilities arising from a particular situation or course of action can be mitigated	Chapters 6, 13, 18, 25
C3	The appropriateness of such investment, expenditure or measures, given a particular taxpayer's circumstances or stated objectives	Chapters 6, 13, 18, 25
C4	The mitigation of tax in the manner recommended, by reference to numerical analysis and/or reasoned argument	Chapters 6, 13, 18, 25
C5	Ethical and professional issues arising from the giving of tax planning advice	Chapter 1
C6	Current issues in taxation	All chapters

D	**Communicating with clients, HM Revenue and Customs and other professionals**	
D1	Communication of advice, recommendations and information in the required format	Chapters 6, 13, 18, 25
D2	Presentation of written information, in language appropriate to the purpose of the communication and the intended recipient	Chapters 6, 13, 18, 25
D3	Conclusions reached with relevant supporting computations	Chapters 6, 13, 18, 25
D4	Assumptions made or limitations in the analysis provided, together with any inadequacies in the information available and/or additional information required to provide a fuller analysis	Chapters 6, 13, 18, 25
D5	Other non-tax factors that should be considered	Chapters 6, 13, 18, 25

The complete syllabus and study guide can be found by visiting the exam resource finder on the ACCA website: www.accaglobal.com/gb/en.html.

The Exam

Computer-based exams

With effect from the March 2020 sitting, ACCA have commenced the launch of computer-based exams (CBEs) for this exam with the aim of rolling out into all markets internationally over a short period. BPP materials have been designed to support you, whether you sit the exam as a CBE or paper-based examination (PBE). For more information on these changes, when they will be implemented and to access Specimen Exams in the Strategic Professional CBE software, please visit the ACCA website. Please note that the Strategic Professional CBE software has more functionality than you will have seen in the Applied Skills exams.

www.accaglobal.com/gb/en/student/exam-support-resources/strategic-professional-specimen-exams-cbe.html

Approach to examining the syllabus

The Advanced Taxation (ATX) syllabus is assessed by a 3 hour 15 minute exam. The pass mark is **50%**. All questions in the exam are **compulsory**.

The questions will be scenario-based and may involve consideration of more than one tax, some elements of planning and the interaction of taxes.

Throughout the exam, you will be expected to identify issues, as well as demonstrate detailed knowledge of the tax system. In line with this emphasis on practicality, questions may require you to address 'the UK tax consequences' of a given situation without indicating which particular taxes to consider. It is up to you to identify the relevant taxes, and the issues in respect of those taxes, before beginning your answer.

Calculations are normally only required in support of explanations and advice, and not in isolation. Again, it is often up to you to decide what calculations to produce in order to do this in the most efficient manner. Advice on how to approach a given problem may be provided in the question.

You will be expected to undertake both calculation and narrative work. There is no specific allocation of numerical calculation versus narrative balance within Taxation (TX) and Advanced Taxation (ATX). However, in practice, TX is mainly computational, whereas ATX is mainly narrative. In both exams, your ability to explain your treatment of tax issues and to present your opinions is vital. It is important to note that this does not mean that you need to have perfect grammar or spelling; it means that you need to make yourself understood.

Tax rates, allowances and information on certain reliefs will be given in the exam. You should familiarise yourself with the information provided so that you know how to find it quickly in the exam.

Format of the exam		Marks
Section A	Two compulsory case-study questions. Question 1 has 35 marks and Question 2 has 25 marks. Question 1: • Includes four professional marks • In order to gain the professional marks, it is first necessary to satisfy the requirement in relation to the style and format of the document requested (eg report, letter, memo or meeting notes) and then to provide clear explanations and coherent calculations Both questions: • Require you to analyse the information provided and use any guidance given to help address the requirements • Because they are relatively large, require careful time management using the number of marks allocated to each requirement to determine how much time to spend on each part • Are likely to deal with a number of different taxes	60 (incl. four professional marks)

Format of the exam		Marks
	• May have coverage of technical taxation topics new in Advanced Taxation (ATX), such as international aspects, stamp taxes, tax planning and interaction of taxes • Usually also include application of technical aspects from Taxation (TX) One question will have five marks on ethical issues.	
Section B	Two compulsory 20-mark questions Both questions: • Contain an introductory paragraph, which outlines the technical areas within the question • Have concise structured information and sub-headings to make them easier to assimilate and navigate • Can cover both business and personal tax issues • May deal with more specialist topics such as advanced corporation tax (eg, dealing with close companies or advising on the tax effects of purchase of own shares by a company), advanced personal tax (eg, advising on tax advantaged share schemes) or advanced capital taxes (eg, dealing with trusts), as well as application of technical aspects from Taxation (TX – UK)	40
		100

Analysis of past exams

The table below provides details of when each element of the syllabus has been examined in the ten most recent sittings and the question number in which each element was examined. Section A questions are Questions 1 and 2, Section B questions are Questions 3 and 4 (and, before June 2018, Question 5). Note that in exams before June 2018 there were three questions in Section B (of which two had to be answered) so five questions in total are referenced.

Chapter		Mar 2020	Sep/Dec 2019	Mar/Jun 2019	Dec 2018	Sep 2018	Mar/Jun 2018	Sep/Dec 2017	Mar/Jun 2017	Sep/Dec 2016	Mar/Jun 2016
	ETHICS										
1	Ethics, tax avoidance schemes		1(a)	2(c)	1(d)	1(b)	1(iii)	2(c)	2(d)	1(c)	2(c)
	PERSONAL TAX										
2	The income tax computation	1(d)		1(a)	1(c)	2(a) 3(c)	1(ii)	2(a) 5(b)	1(i)		2(b) 5(a) 5(b)
3	Pensions and tax efficient investment products	3(d) 4(c)			4(c)	2(c)	4(c)	2(a) 5(b)	1(iii)		
4	Employment income			1(a) 3(c) 4(a)	4(a)	3(c)	1(ii) 4(a)	2(a) 3(c)	1(i) 4(a)	4(a) 4(b)	2(b) 3(c) 5(b)

Chapter		Mar 2020	Sep/Dec 2019	Mar/Jun 2019	Dec 2018	Sep 2018	Mar/Jun 2018	Sep/Dec 2017	Mar/Jun 2017	Sep/Dec 2016	Mar/Jun 2016
5	Property income	4(b)		B		B					
6	Personal tax planning			1(a)	4(c)			3(c) 5(b)		4(a) 4(b)	
	CAPITAL TAX										
7	Capital gains tax computation	1(b) 2(a) 3(d)		1(b) 4(a)	3(a)	2(b)	1(i)	2(a)	4(b)	2(a)	1(b) 3(a)
8	Capital gains tax – shares and reliefs	1(b) 2(a)	2(b)	1(b)	3(a) 3(b) 4(b)	3(b) 4(a)	3(a) 3(c)	2(a) 5(a)	1(iii) 3(b) 4(b)	2(a)	1(b) 3(a) 4(a)
9	Overseas personal taxation	1(a) 1(b)	2(a) 2(c)				3(a) 3(b)		3(b)	2(a) 2(b) 2(c) 4(c)	
10	Personal tax administration										1(a)
11	Inheritance tax computation	1(c)	2(b)	1(b)	1(a)	2(b) 4(a)	1(i) 3(a)	2(b) 5(a)	1(ii) 3(a)	3(a)	1(b) 3(b)
12	Inheritance tax: further aspects	4(a)	2(b)			2(b)	3(a)		1(ii) 3(a)	2(c)	
13	Capital tax planning	1(c)		1(b)	1(a) 3(a)	2(b)	1(i) 3(c)	2(b) 5(a)	3(a)	3(a) 4(c)	2(b) 3(a)
	OWNER-MANAGED BUSINESS TAX										
14	Sole traders	3(a) 3(b)			1(c)		1(ii)	4(a)	1(i)	2(a) 3(b)	1(a) 5(a)
15	Sole trader losses and partnerships		4(b)	4(b)	1(c)	3(a)	4(b)	4(b)	1(i)		
16	Corporation tax for single companies	2(b)	3(a) 3(c)	1(a) 3(b)	1(c) 2(a)	4(b)	2(a) 2(c)	1(a) 1(c) 3(a) 3(b)	2(a) 5(a) 5(c)	1(a) 5(a)	2(a) 4(b)
17	Losses for single companies			1(a)	1(c)		2(c)			5(b)	4(b)
18	Owner-managed business tax planning	3(a) 3(b)	1(b) 4(a)	4(b)	1(c)	3(c)	1(ii) 4(b)	2(a) 3(b)	1(i) 4(b) 4(c)	2(a) 3(b)	1(a) 2(a) 2(b)
	CORPORATE TAX										

Chapter		Mar 2020	Sep/Dec 2019	Mar/Jun 2019	Dec 2018	Sep 2018	Mar/Jun 2018	Sep/Dec 2017	Mar/Jun 2017	Sep/Dec 2016	Mar/Jun 2016
19	Corporate groups and consortia	2(b)	3(c)	2(a)	2(a)	1(a)	2(a)	1(a) 1(b)	2(a) 2(b) 5(c)	1(a)	2(a)
20	Administration, winding up, purchase of own shares								4(b)	5(a)	4(a)
21	Close companies and investment companies		1(c)							4(b)	
22	Overseas aspects of corporation tax	2(c)	3(b)	2(a)	2(b)		2(c)				
23	Value added tax	2(b) 3(c)	1(c) 4(c)	2(b) 3(a)	1(b) 2(c)	1(a) 3(d)	1(ii) 2(b)	1(d) 4(c)	2(c) 5(d)	1(b) 5(b)	1(a) 4(c)
24	Stamp taxes							1(a)	2(b)		
25	Corporate tax planning			2(a)	2(a)	1(a)	2(a) 2(d)	1(i) 1(ii)	2(a) 2(b)	1(a) 5(a)	3(b)

IMPORTANT! The table above gives a broad idea of how frequently major topics in the syllabus are examined. It should **not** be used to question spot and predict, for example, that Topic X will not be examined because it came up two sittings ago. The examining team's reports indicate that they are well aware that some students try to question spot. They avoid predictable patterns and may, for example, examine the same topic two sittings in a row, particularly if there has been a recent change in legislation.

Essential skills areas to be successful in Advanced Taxation

We think there are three areas you should develop in order to achieve exam success in Advanced Taxation (ATX – UK):

(a)   Knowledge application

(b)   Specific ATX skills

(c)   Exam success skills

These are shown in the diagram below.

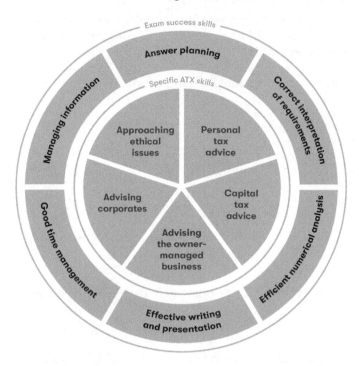

Specific ATX skills

These are the skills specific to ATX that we think you need to develop in order to pass the exam.

In this Workbook, there are five **Skills Checkpoints** which define each skill and show how it is applied in answering a question. A brief summary of each skill is given below.

Skill 1: Approaching ethical issues

The consideration of ethical issues will be mostly new to you in ATX, although some of the underlying principles were mentioned in TX, such as the difference between tax avoidance and tax evasion.

There will always be five marks in Section A on ethical issues.

Questions will often involve identifying, evaluating and addressing threats to compliance with the five fundamental principles which should underlie all ACCA members' professional behaviour. Given that ethics will feature in every exam, it is essential that you master the appropriate technique for approaching ethical issues in order to maximise your mark.

BPP recommends a step-by-step technique for approaching questions on ethical issues:

Step 1	Work out how many minutes you have to answer the question.
Step 2	Read the requirement(s) and think what format will be required.
Step 3	Read the scenario and highlight and/or make notes of the information that will enable you to answer the requirement(s).

| Step 4 | Prepare an answer plan, eg linking the fundamental principles to the scenario and dealing with other issues such as money-laundering and tax-avoidance. |
| Step 5 | Write up your answer. |

Skills Checkpoint 1 covers this technique in detail through application to three typical exam-standard questions on ethics.

Skill 2: Personal tax advice

Personal tax advice is a fundamental aspect of the ATX exam.

The basic approach BPP recommends for approaching personal tax advice questions is similar in structure to approaching ethical dilemmas; it only differs because these questions will be longer and may well involve calculations as well as explanations.

Step 1	Look at the mark allocation and calculate the amount of time available for the question.
Step 2	Read the requirement(s) and analyse them.
Step 3	Read the scenario and highlight and/or make notes of the information that will enable you to answer the requirement(s).
Step 4	Then make a plan of the points that you need to cover in your answer, including what supporting calculations you will need to do. Use key words from the requirements as headings.
Step 5	Write up your answer using key words from the requirements as headings.

Skills Checkpoint 2 covers this technique in detail through application to an exam-standard question.

Skill 3: Capital tax advice

The ATX exam could require you to deal with capital taxes: capital gains tax (CGT) and/or inheritance tax (IHT).

In a Section A question, you may be presented with a complex personal tax scenario of which capital taxes are a part.

Capital taxes may also appear in a Section B question in a slightly more structured way. Both Section A and Section B questions may involve considering more than one tax (typically CGT and IHT) for one transaction.

A step-by-step technique for approaching these types of questions is outlined below.

Step 1	Work out how many minutes you have to answer the question.
Step 2	Read the requirements and analyse them.
Step 3	Read the scenario and highlight and/or make notes of the information that will enable you to answer the requirements, making sure you identify the different taxes involved.
Step 4	Prepare an answer plan.
Step 5	Write your answer. Use sub-headings for each tax to show which you are writing about.

The question extract we will be looking at in Skills Checkpoint 3 is a good example of the Section B style.

Skill 4: Owner managed business advice

You could also have a question which will focus on an owner managed business (OMB). This could be either a sole trader, a partnership, or an individual running their business through a company (as a director-shareholder).

As there is such a wide variety of potential scenarios and such a range of tax implications for OMBs, it is important that we use our exam technique skills to successfully interpret the requirement and apply our knowledge to the specifics from the scenario when we answer the question.

A step-by-step technique for attempting these questions is outlined below.

Step 1	Look at the mark allocation and calculate the amount of time available for the question.
Step 2	Read the requirements and analyse them.
Step 3	Read the scenario and highlight and/or make notes of the information that will enable you to answer the requirements.
Step 4	Then make a plan of the points that you need to cover in your answer, including what supporting calculations you will need to do.
Step 5	Write up your answer using key words from the requirements as headings.

Skills Checkpoint 4 covers this technique in detail through application to an exam-standard question.

Skill 5: Corporate tax advice

The ATX exam could also contain a question involving a company or group of companies, that has either carried out or is considering a range of transactions. Your task will be to analyse the taxation implications of those transactions, in a set of structured requirements.

This may involve more than one tax (for example, VAT and stamp taxes issues may well arise on corporate transactions, and companies may also need to consider employment taxes). It is important to be methodical in dealing with corporate questions; to be able to analyse the information given to determine the relevant syllabus areas and to identify any tax planning opportunities that may arise.

A step-by-step technique for attempting these questions is outlined below. It is similar to the structure we have seen for our other Skills.

Step 1	Look at the mark allocation and calculate the amount of time available for the question.
Step 2	Read the introduction to the question, then read the requirements and think how you might answer them.
Step 3	Now go back to the scenario in the question and highlight the information that will enable you to answer the requirements. Highlight important facts such as dates of transactions and ownership percentages.
Step 4	Make a plan of the points that you need to cover in your answer, including what supporting calculations you will need to do. A group structure diagram may help you to understand the group relationships and their relevance to the scenario.
Step 5	Write your answer.

Skills Checkpoint 5 covers this technique in detail through application to an exam-standard question.

Exam success skills

Passing the ATX exam requires more than applying syllabus knowledge and demonstrating the specific ATX skills; it also requires the development of excellent exam technique through question practice.

We consider the following six skills to be vital for exam success. The Skills Checkpoints show how each of these skills can be applied in the exam.

1 Exam success skill 1

Managing information

Questions in the exam will present you with a lot of information. The skill is how you handle this information to make the best use of your time. The key is determining how you will approach the exam and then actively reading the questions.

Advice on developing Managing information

Approach

The exam is 3 hours 15 minutes long. There is no designated 'reading' time at the start of the exam, however, one approach that can work well is to start the exam by spending 10–15 minutes carefully reading through all of the questions to familiarise yourself with the exam paper.

Once you feel familiar with the exam paper consider the order in which you will attempt the questions; always attempt them in your order of preference. For example, you may want to leave to last the question you consider to be the most difficult.

If you do take this approach, remember to adjust the time available for each question appropriately – see Exam success skill 6: Good time management.

If you find that this approach doesn't work for you, don't worry – you can develop your own technique.

Active reading

You must take an active approach to reading each question. Focus on the requirement first, underlining/ highlighting key verbs such as 'prepare', 'comment', 'explain', 'discuss', to ensure you answer the question properly. Then read the rest of the question, underlining/highlighting and annotating important and relevant information, and making notes of any relevant technical information you think you will need.

2 Exam success skill 2

Correct interpretation of the requirements

The active verb used often dictates the approach that written answers should take (eg 'explain', 'discuss', 'evaluate'). It is important you identify and use the verb to define your approach. The **correct interpretation of the requirements** skill means correctly producing only what is being asked for by a requirement. Anything not required will not earn marks.

Advice on developing correct interpretation of the requirements

This skill can be developed by analysing question requirements and applying this process:

Step 1	**Read the requirement** Firstly, read the requirement a couple of times slowly and carefully and highlight the active verbs. Use the active verbs to define what you plan to do. Make sure you identify any sub-requirements and any topics which you are specifically told you do not need to cover in your answer.
Step 2	**Read the rest of the question** By reading the requirement first, you will have an idea of what you are looking out for as you read through the scenario and any exhibits in Section A. This is a great time saver and means you don't end up having to read the whole question in full twice. You should do this in an active way – see Exam success skill 1: Managing Information.

Step 3	Read the requirement again
	Read the requirement again to remind yourself of the exact wording before starting your written answer. This will capture any misinterpretation of the requirements or any requirements that are missed entirely. This should become a habit in your approach and, with repeated practice, you will find the focus, relevance and depth of your answer plan will improve.

3 Exam success skill 3

Answer planning: Priorities, structure and logic

This skill requires the planning of the key aspects of an answer which accurately and completely responds to the requirement.

Advice on developing Answer planning: Priorities, structure and logic

Everyone will have a preferred style for an answer plan. For example, it may be a mind map, bullet-pointed lists or simply annotating the question paper if you are attempting a paper-based exam. Choose the approach that you feel most comfortable with, or, if you are not sure, try out different approaches for different questions until you have found your preferred style.

For most questions, especially question 1, simply highlighting the on-screen text is likely to be insufficient. It would be better to draw up a separate answer plan in the format of your choosing (eg a mind map or bullet-pointed lists). You will want to remind yourself of key facts from the scenario to avoid having to re-read the question - you should at the very least make a few notes including vital information such as the following key factors:

- Nature of the taxpayer: is it an individual or a company?
- For individuals: their age, any family relationships, their residence and domicile status, whether they're a basic, higher or additional rate taxpayer, and whether they've used their CGT annual exempt amount /IHT exemptions
- For companies: their ownership structure and group relationships
- Relevant dates: the date you need to assume in the question (stated at the start of each question), any year end(s) of businesses, dates of actual or proposed transactions, the date that a business started, dates of gifts (or death!) for IHT

The March 2020 Examiner's report stated that 'weak students did not spend enough time thinking before they started writing. This meant that they produced an unstructured answer which, in the case of an explanatory or discursive answer, did not include sufficient relevant points and/ or they wasted time providing information that had not been asked for, and in the case of a comprehensive computational answer, often led to illogical, difficult to follow computations.' This emphasises the importance of planning.

4 Exam success skill 4

Efficient numerical analysis

This skill aims to maximise the marks awarded by making clear to the marker the process of arriving at your answer. This is achieved by laying out an answer such that, even if you make a few errors, you can still score subsequent marks for follow-on calculations. It is vital that you do not lose marks purely because the marker cannot follow what you have done.

Advice on developing Efficient numerical analysis

This skill can be developed by applying the following process:

Step 1	Use a standard proforma working where relevant
	If answers can be laid out in a standard proforma then always plan to do so. This will help the marker to understand your working and allocate the marks easily. It will also help you to work through the figures in a methodical and time-efficient way. However, the ATX exam is unlikely to award huge amounts of marks for calculations: don't waste time performing full tax computations when you can 'work at the margin' - we

	look at this skill in the Personal Tax Planning chapter.
Step 2	**Show your workings** Keep your workings as clear and simple as possible and ensure they are cross-referenced to the main part of your answer. Where it helps, provide brief narrative explanations to help the marker understand the steps in the calculation. This means that if a mistake is made you do not lose any subsequent marks for follow-on calculations.
Step 3	**Keep moving!** It is important to remember that, in an exam situation, it is difficult to get every number 100% correct. The key is therefore ensuring you do not spend too long on any single calculation. If you are struggling with a solution then make a sensible assumption, state it and move on.

5 Exam success skill 5

Effective writing and presentation

Written answers should be presented so that the marker can clearly see the points you are making, presented in the format specified in the question. The skill is to provide efficient written answers with sufficient breadth of points that answer the question, in the right depth, in the time available.

Advice on developing Effective writing and presentation

Step 1	**Use headings** Using the headings and sub-headings from your answer plan will give your answer structure, order and logic. This will ensure your answer links back to the requirement and is clearly signposted, making it easier for the marker to understand the different points you are making. Underlining your headings will also help the marker.
Step 2	**Write your answer in short, but full, sentences** Use short, punchy sentences with the aim that every sentence should say something different and generate marks. Write in full sentences, ensuring your style is professional.
Step 3	**Do your calculations first and explanation second** Questions often ask for an explanation with supporting calculations. The best approach is to prepare the calculation first then add the explanation before the calculation. Performing the calculation first should enable you to explain what you have done.

6 Exam success skill 6

Good time management

This skill means planning your time across all the requirements so that all tasks have been attempted at the end of the 3 hours 15 minutes available and actively checking on time during your exam. This is so that you can flex your approach and prioritise requirements which, in your judgement, will generate the maximum marks in the available time remaining.

Advice on developing Good time management

The exam is 3 hours 15 minutes long, which translates to 1.95 minutes per mark. Therefore a 10-mark requirement should be allocated a maximum of 20 minutes to complete your answer before you move on to the next task. At the beginning of a question, work out the amount of time you should be spending on each requirement and write the finishing time next to each requirement on your exam paper. If you take the approach of spending 10–15 minutes reading and planning at the start of the exam, adjust the time allocated to each question accordingly; eg if you allocate 15 minutes to reading, then you will have 3 hours remaining, which is 1.8 minutes per mark.

The March 2020 Examiner's report said weaker students had poor time management. 'It appeared that these students spent a disproportionate amount of time on some question parts, such that they did not have sufficient time to complete all questions. Students are reminded once again of the need to consider the number of marks available for each question part, and allocate their time accordingly.'

Keep an eye on the clock

Aim to attempt all requirements, but be ready to be ruthless and move on if your answer is not going as planned. The challenge for many is sticking to planned timings. Be aware this is difficult to achieve in the early stages of your studies and be ready to let this skill develop over time.

If you find yourself running short on time and know that a full answer is not possible in the time you have, consider recreating your plan in overview form and then add key terms and details as time allows. Remember, some marks may be available, for example, simply stating a conclusion which you don't have time to justify in full.

Question practice

Question practice is a core part of learning new topic areas. When you practice questions, you should focus on improving the Exam success skills – personal to your needs – by obtaining feedback or through a process of self-assessment.

1

Ethics, tax avoidance schemes

Learning objectives

On completion of this chapter, you should be able to:

	Syllabus reference no.
Remember the material covered in Taxation (TX – UK) under the heading: 'the overall function and purpose of taxation in a modern economy'	A6(b) A1
Understand the statutory obligations imposed in a given situation, including any time limits for action and advise on the implications of non-compliance	B5
Be aware of the ethical and professional issues arising from the giving of tax planning advice	C5
Be aware of and give advice on current issues in taxation	C6

Exam context

There will be five marks awarded in Section A for your comments on ethical matters.

You need to know the fundamental principles of the ACCA's code of conduct, and when presented with a scenario you should quickly review these to make sure that they are not compromised. If there is a threat then consider how serious it is and how you should respond.

You may also be required to describe procedures to prevent money laundering. These consist of client identification and reporting of suspicions of money laundering.

You need to be aware of the difference between tax evasion and tax avoidance. However, even if a particular scheme constitutes tax avoidance, rather than tax evasion, it may still be scrutinised by HM Revenue and Customs (HMRC) who may use anti-avoidance legislation to combat it. This is a rapidly developing area of tax law and you will be expected in ATX – UK to be aware of current issues in taxation.

Chapter overview

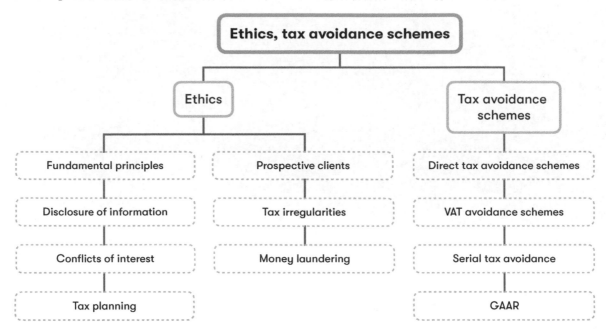

1 Ethics

1.1 Fundamental principles

The ACCA *Code of Ethics and Conduct* details the following fundamental principles which should underlie all members' professional behaviour:

- Integrity
- Objectivity
- Professional competence and due care
- Confidentiality
- Professional behaviour

Essential reading

See Chapter 1 of the Essential reading for more detail on the fundamental principles, the conceptual framework that requires ACCA members to identify, evaluate and address threats to compliance with the fundamental principles, and ethical dispute resolution.

The Essential reading is available as an Appendix of the digital edition of the Workbook.

1.2 Disclosure of information

The fundamental principle of **confidentiality** means that, in relation to information acquired as a result of professional and business relationships, you should not:

- Disclose such information acquired, nor
- Use it for your own advantage or that of third parties such as other clients

This duty continues even after the end of relationship between you and your client or employer.

However, you **may disclose confidential information if:**

- Disclosure is **permitted by law** and is authorised by the client or your employer
- Disclosure is **required by law**, such as under anti-money laundering legislation
- There is a **professional duty or right to disclose when not prohibited by law**, such as under a quality review

You may also **use experience and expertise gained from advising clients to advise other clients.**

1.3 Conflicts of interest

1.3.1 Threat to fundamental principles

You should take **reasonable steps to identify circumstances that could pose a conflict of interest** which may pose a threat to the fundamental principles. For example:

- Acting for both spouses/civil partners in a settlement on the breakdown of the relationship
- Acting for both a company and its directors and/or shareholders in a personal capacity
- Acting for both parties on the sale of a business

1.3.2 Safeguards

Safeguards you should take to **avoid a conflict of interest** include:

- **Notifying the relevant parties** that there may be a conflict of interest
- Obtaining **consent** of the relevant parties to act for them

If consent is refused, then you must not continue to act for the parties in the matter that has given rise to the conflict of interest.

The following **additional safeguards** should also be considered:

- The use of **separate engagement teams**
- **Procedures to prevent access to information** (eg, strict physical separation of such teams, confidential and secure data filing)
- **Clear guidelines** for members of the engagement team on issues of security and confidentiality
- The use of **confidentiality agreements** signed by employees and partners of the firm
- **Regular review of the application of safeguards** by a senior individual not involved with relevant client engagements

Where a conflict of interest poses a threat to one or more of the fundamental principles, that cannot be eliminated or reduced to an acceptable level through the application of safeguards, you should conclude that it is not appropriate to accept a specific engagement, or that resignation from one or more conflicting engagements is required.

Activity 1: Conflict of interest

You have acted for Robenick Ltd for several years, and also for the three directors and shareholders, Rob, Ben and Nick.

Recently, Rob has had a disagreement with Ben and Nick over the direction of the company.

Required

1 Explain the safeguards that you would have put in place when you started to act for both the company and its director/shareholders.

2 Outline the ethical issue that has now arisen and the actions that you should take.

Solution

1.4 Tax planning

PER alert

One of the competencies you require to fulfil Performance Objective 17 Tax planning and advice of the PER is to advise clients responsibly about the differences between tax planning, tax avoidance and tax evasion. You can apply the knowledge you obtain from this chapter of the Workbook to help demonstrate this competence.

When you are providing tax planning advice to a client you are fully responsible for the advice you give. The fundamental principle of **professional competence and due care** is relevant here.

Anything you recommend must be **legal**. You should understand **the basic distinction** between **tax avoidance** (tax mitigation through legal means) and **tax evasion** (illegal, such as failure to disclose relevant information or providing false information).

You may suggest arrangements which HMRC might disagree with your conclusion as to the tax consequences. You need to explain to the client that full details must be given to enable HMRC to consider the matter, and you should warn them that any negotiations with HMRC will take time and incur expense.

Make sure that you know the time limits for any claims that need to be made and that such claims are made within the limits.

1.5 Prospective clients

1.5.1 Threat to fundamental principles

Before **accepting a new client**, you should **consider whether acceptance of the client or the particular engagement would create any threats to compliance with the fundamental principles**.

Threats to **integrity** or **professional behaviour** may be created from questionable issues associated with the client, for example, if they have engaged in tax evasion.

Threats to **professional competence** and **due care** may be created if the engagement team does not possess the necessary skills to carry out the engagement.

Where it is not possible to implement safeguards to reduce the threats to an acceptable level, you should decline to enter into the relationship.

1.5.2 Contacting existing accountants

You should **contact the existing accountants** to ascertain if there are **any matters you should be aware of** when deciding whether to accept the appointment or not.

The existing accountants are bound by **confidentiality**. This means the extent to which a client's affairs may be discussed with a prospective accountant will depend on the nature of the engagement and on whether the client's permission has been obtained.

If the **client refuses permission**, the **existing accountants should inform you of this refusal**. You should then inform the client that you are **unable to accept the appointment**.

Activity 2: Existing accountants

You have acted for Trystan but have discovered a serious tax irregularity which Trystan has refused to correct. You have advised Trystan that you can no longer act for him.

You receive a letter from other ACCA accountants advising you that they have been asked to act for Trystan.

Trystan has forbidden you to divulge any information about him.

Required

1   Explain what action you should take in response to the letter.

2   Explain what action the other ACCA accountants should take as a result of your action.

Solution

1.5.3 Money laundering

You should also consider the rules relating to **money laundering** before accepting a new client. These are dealt with in the money laundering section below.

1.6 Tax irregularities

1.6.1 Tax evasion

The **evasion or attempted evasion of tax** is a threat to the fundament principles of **integrity** and **professional behaviour.** It may be also the subject of **criminal charges** under both **tax law** and **money laundering legislation**.

You have the following responsibilities:

(a) If the client fails to provide any information requested by you, for example in preparing returns or computations, you need to consider whether you can continue to act for the client.

(b) You should advise clients to make full disclosure to HM Revenue & Customs (HMRC), or to authorise you to do so if errors exist in information already submitted to HMRC. If the client refuses then you can no longer act for them. You must inform HMRC that you are no longer acting for the client but you are not under an obligation to explain why, as this would be a breach of confidentiality.

Whether or not you feel able to continue to act for the client, you are still under a professional duty to ensure the client understands the seriousness of offences against HMRC.

Activity 3: Tax evasion

You are a tax manager in a firm of accountants. You are preparing the tax return for Sonia, and amongst her papers you find a bank statement for a new account resulting in interest of £2,500 in the tax year. Sonia says that the interest should not be put on her tax return. You have advised her that it should be included on her tax return.

Required

Outline the actions you should take if Sonia continues to refuse to allow you to put the interest on her tax return

Solution

1.6.2 Errors by HMRC in the taxpayers' favour

Problems may arise if **HMRC makes an excessive repayment of tax** in error to a taxpayer, even though HMRC has received full disclosure of the facts. This is a threat to **the fundamental principle** of **integrity**.

If the repayment is made directly to the client, you should tell them to refund the excess sum to HMRC as soon as possible. Failure to correct the error may be a civil and/or criminal offence by the client.

If the client refuses you must consider whether you should continue to act for the client. If you cease to act, you must notify HMRC that you no longer act for the client, but you are under no duty to give HMRC any further details. It may be necessary to consider whether a report should be made under the money laundering rules.

If the repayment is made to you on the client's behalf, you must notify HMRC. Failure to do so could involve both you and client in a civil and/or criminal offence.

1.7 Money laundering

> **Money laundering:** The process by which criminals attempt to conceal the true origin and ownership of the proceeds of their criminal activity. This can include **tax evasion**.

1.7.1 General principles

You are bound by legislation to **implement preventative measures**, including **client identification procedures**, and to **report suspicions** to the appropriate authority. Failure to follow these legislative requirements is a criminal offence, which could lead to a fine and/or imprisonment.

1.7.2 Client identification procedures

Where a new client is taken on, you should **verify their identity by reliable and independent means**. This could include:

(a) Where the client is an individual: by obtaining **independent evidence**, such as a passport, driving licence, HMRC document such as a notice of coding, and proof of address.

(b) Where the client is a company: by obtaining **proof of incorporation**; by establishing the primary business address; by identifying the shareholders and directors of the company; and by establishing the identities of those persons instructing you on behalf of the company and verifying that those persons are authorised to do so.

If satisfactory evidence cannot be obtained, no work should be undertaken.

You should **retain all client identification records for at least five years** after the end of the client relationship, together with records of all work carried out for the client.

1.7.3 Suspicion of money laundering

When you **take on a new client** you should **review their activities** to **satisfy yourself** that they are **not engaged in money laundering**.

During the course of the engagement, you should regularly review the client's actions to satisfy yourself that they are consistent with the client's usual activities.

If you have suspicions, a money laundering report should be made either to your firm's money laundering officer or, if you are not in a firm, directly to the National Crime Agency.

You should not inform a client that a money laundering report has been made. This is known as **'tipping off'** and is a criminal offence.

2 Tax avoidance schemes

2.1 Direct tax avoidance schemes

Promoters of tax avoidance schemes relating to direct taxes (income tax, national insurance contributions, capital gains tax, corporation tax, inheritance tax and stamp taxes) **have disclosure obligations**. There is also an obligation on taxpayers to disclose details of schemes in certain cases.

Notification is required from a promoter of arrangements or proposed arrangements, the main benefit of which is to enable any person to obtain an advantage in relation to tax.

A tax advantage is defined as relief or increased relief from tax, repayment or increased repayment of tax, avoidance or reduction of a charge to a tax.

Any person that **fails to comply with any of the disclosure provisions is liable to a penalty** not exceeding £600 per day running from the date the failure to disclose occurred. Where a disclosure notice has been issued, but not complied with within 10 days, the maximum daily penalty is £5,000.

Essential reading

See Chapter 1 of the Essential reading for more detail on direct tax avoidance schemes and the disclosure of tax avoidance schemes (DOTAS) regime

The Essential reading is available as an Appendix of the digital edition of the Workbook.

2.2 Value added tax (VAT) avoidance schemes

Promotors of VAT avoidance schemes also have disclosure obligations similar to those for direct taxes explained above.

Penalties for failure to disclose include an initial penalty of up to £600 per day, but a higher penalty of up to £1 million may be set in some circumstances.

Essential reading

See Chapter 1 of the Essential reading for more detail on VAT avoidance schemes and the disclosure of tax avoidance schemes for VAT and other indirect taxes (DASVOIT) regime.

The Essential reading is available as an Appendix of the digital edition of the Workbook.

2.3 Serial tax avoidance

Taxpayers who use more than one tax avoidance scheme which has been defeated on or after 6 April 2017 may be classed as serial tax avoiders by HMRC.

A defeated scheme is one for which either:

- The taxpayer has reached an agreement with HMRC so the tax advantage that would have been expected under the scheme is not available; or
- HMRC has obtained a favourable court or tribunal ruling about its assessment of the scheme.

Such taxpayers will be issued with a **serial tax avoidance warning notice which has effect for five years** that requires them to submit additional information to HMRC about their tax affairs annually, for example their use of tax avoidance schemes.

Sanctions against serial tax offenders include:

- **Penalties** if further tax avoidance schemes are entered into during the notice period increasing with the number of such schemes entered into
- Being **publicly named as a serial tax avoider**
- **Restrictions on direct tax reliefs for up to three years**

2.4 General anti-abuse rule (GAAR)

The aim of the GAAR is to deter taxpayers from entering into abusive 'tax arrangements' and to deter would-be promoters from promoting such arrangements. The main purpose of 'tax arrangements' is to obtain a tax advantage, rather than, for example, having a genuine commercial purpose.

Examples of abusive arrangements include those that result in:

- Significantly less income, profits or gains
- Significantly greater deductions or losses, or
- A claim for the repayment or crediting of tax (including foreign tax) that has not been, and is unlikely to be paid

HMRC can counteract tax advantages by simply increasing the taxpayer's liability, on a just and reasonable basis.

A penalty will also be imposed if the taxpayer enters into arrangements which are countered by the GAAR. The **penalty is equal to 60% of the tax advantage gained**.

Chapter summary

Ethics, tax avoidance schemes

Ethics

Fundamental principles
- Integrity
- Objectivity
- Professional competence and due care
- Confidentiality
- Professional behaviour

Disclosure of information
- Do not disclose or use for advantage
- Unless:
  - Permitted by law and authorised by client
  - Required by law
  - Under professional duty or right to disclose

Conflicts of interest
- Identify circumstances
  - Spouses/civil partners on relationship breakdown
  - Company and shareholders/directors
  - Both parties on sale of business
- Safeguards
  - Notifying parties
  - Obtaining consent of parties
  - Additional safeguards
- Do not act if threat cannot be managed

Tax planning
- Responsible for advice
  - Tax avoidance, not tax evasion
  - HMRC may disagree, so costly negotiations
  - Time limits for claims must be met

Prospective clients
- Consider threat to fundamental principles
  - Integrity/professional behaviour
  - Professional competence and due care
  - Do not accept client if threat cannot be managed
- Contacting existing accountants
  - Matters to be aware of
  - If client refuses contact, do not accept client
- Money laundering

Tax irregularities
- Tax evasion
  - Disclosure by client to HMRC
  - Cease to act if no disclosure, tell HMRC but not why
- Errors in taxpayers' favour
  - Refund to HMRC
  - Cease to act if no refund, tell HMRC but not why

Money laundering
- Concealment of proceeds of criminal activity
- Client identification procedures
- Suspicions of money laundering

Tax avoidance schemes

Direct tax avoidance schemes
- Promoters must disclose, sometimes taxpayers
- Main benefit of scheme is obtaining advantage in relation to tax
- Penalties for non-disclosure initially up to £600 per day

VAT avoidance schemes
- Promoters must disclose
- Penalties for non-disclosure initially up to £600 per day

Serial tax avoidance
- Taxpayer has used more than one defeated scheme
- Serial tax avoidance warning notice
- Sanctions
  - Penalties
  - Public naming
  - Restrictions on tax reliefs

GAAR
- Deter taxpayers from entering into abusive tax arrangements
  - Significantly less income, profits or gains
  - Significantly greater deductions or losses
  - Claim for the repayment or crediting of tax not paid
- HMRC can increase taxpayer's liability
- Penalty up to 60% of tax advantage

Knowledge diagnostic

1. Fundamental principles

The five fundamental principles of ethics should underlie all your professional behaviour.

2. Disclosure of information

You should not disclose confidential information acquired as a result of your professional and business relationships unless permitted by law, required by law, or if there is a professional duty or right to disclose.

3. Conflicts of interest

A conflict of interest is a commonly met threat to compliance with the fundamental principles and you should take safeguards against it.

4. Tax planning

You must distinguish between tax evasion (illegal) and tax avoidance (legal) when giving tax planning advice.

5. Prospective clients

When accepting a new client, you should consider any threat to the fundamental principles, contact existing accounts, and consider the money laundering rules.

6. Tax irregularities

If you discover that a client has misled HMRC in order to evade tax, you have a duty to consider your position in relation to both the client and HMRC.

7. Money laundering

Money laundering rules require you to implement preventative measure and report suspicions to the appropriate authority.

8. Tax avoidance schemes

- There are disclosure requirements for promoters of direct tax avoidance schemes (DOTAS). Businesses may be required to disclose use of VAT avoidance schemes (DASVOIT).
- Serial tax avoiders may have to provide additional information to HMRC for five years. Sanctions against serial tax avoiders include penalties, public naming and restrictions on direct tax reliefs.
- There is a general anti-abuse rule (GAAR) to enable HMRC to counteract tax advantages gained from abusive tax arrangements.

Further study guidance

Question practice

Now try the following from the Further question practice bank (available in the digital edition of the Workbook):

- Tilly
- Royce
- Donald

Activity answers

Activity 1: Conflict of interest

1   When you commenced acting for both the company and Rob, Ben and Nick, you should have advised each that you were acting for the others and obtained their consent to act.

Providing there were no areas where the interests of the clients conflicted, there is no reason why you should not have acted for all the clients, although it may be advisable to have ensured that, for example, separate engagement teams were responsible for each client and that these teams observed guidelines on security and confidentiality.

2   Now that there has been a disagreement between Rob and the other clients, the situation has changed and there is a conflict of interest, which is a threat to the fundamental principle of objectivity.

It is most likely that it would be inappropriate to continue to act for all the clients, and you will need to cease to act, either for Rob, or for Ben, Nick and the company.

Activity 2: Existing accountants

1   You should advise the other ACCA accountants that Trystan has not given you permission to divulge any information.

2   The other ACCA accountants should inform Trystan that they are unable to act.

Activity 3: Tax evasion

If Sonia still refuses to enter the interest on her return you should advise her that you can no longer act for her, and you must also advise HMRC that you no longer act. You are not obliged to disclose the reason to HMRC.

You should explain to Sonia the seriousness of her failure to provide the information to HMRC.

At this stage you have a suspicion that a tax offence may be committed, and you should discuss this with your firm's money laundering officer.

The income tax computation

Learning objectives

On completion of this chapter, you should be able to:

	Syllabus reference no.
Remember the material studied in Taxation (TX – UK) under the headings:	
'Property and investment income'	A1(a) B4
'The comprehensive computation of taxable income and the income tax liability'	A1(a) B5
'The use of exemptions and reliefs in deferring and minimising income tax liabilities'	A1(a) B7
Advise on the tax implications of jointly held assets	A1(e)(i)
Recognise the tax treatment of savings income paid net of tax	A1(e)(ii)
Understand the allocation of the personal allowance to different categories of income	A1(f)(i)
Advise on the income tax position of the income of minor children	A1(f)(ii)

Exam context

You may be asked to prepare an income tax computation in the examination or, for example, you may be asked to calculate the after-tax income that would be derived from a new income source. It is therefore vital that you understand how the income tax computation is prepared. When considering how income tax will change due to a change in income do not overlook the effect of an increase in income on the amount of the personal allowance.

The chapter also introduces tax planning concepts. Note the treatment of joint income of spouses/civil partners and the anti-avoidance rules that apply if a parent gives funds to a minor child.

Chapter overview

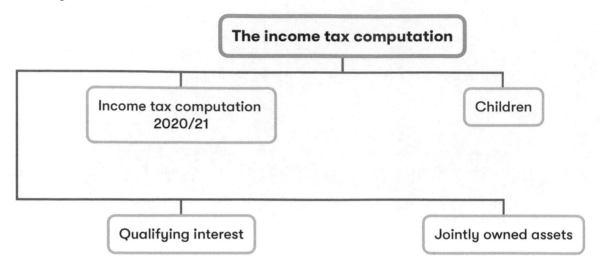

1 Income tax computation 2020/21

The income tax computation is assumed knowledge from your Taxation (TX – UK) studies. An income tax pro-forma is included here to remind you of the basic computation.

	Non-savings income (NSI)	Savings income (SI)	Dividend income (DI)
	£	£	£
Trading income (Chapter 14)	X		
Employment income (Chapter 4)	X		
Overseas property business income (Chapter 9)	X		
Interest from o/seas securities (Chapter 9)		X	
Dividends from o/seas securities (Chapter 9)			X
Bank interest received		X	
Interest on gilts/bonds etc		X	
Dividends received			X
Discretionary trust income (× 100/55)	X		
Interest in possession trust income			
– From NSI or SI (× 100/80)	X	X	
– From DI (× 100/92.5)			X
UK property business income (Chapter 5)	X	–	–
Total income	X	X	X
Less qualifying interest	(X)	bal (X)	bal (X)
Net income before losses	X	X	X
Losses	(X)	bal (X)	bal (X)
Net income (NI)	X	X	X
Less personal allowance (PA)	(X)	bal (X)	bal (X)
Taxable income	X	X	X
Income tax on NSI (20/40/45%)			X
Income tax on SI (0/20/40/45%)			X
Income tax on DI (0/7.5/32.5/38.1%)			X
Annual allowance charge on excess pension contributions (Chapter 3)			X
Less tax reducers:			
– EIS/SEIS/VCT, (Chapter 3)			
– Marriage allowance			
– Property business income finance costs (Chapter 5)			(X)
Less DTR (Chapter 9)			(X)
IT liability			X
Less tax deducted at source (PAYE)			(X)

	Non-savings income (NSI)	Savings income (SI)	Dividend income (DI)
	£	£	£
IT payable			X
			=

Formula provided

For 2020/21 the personal allowance is £12,500.

The savings income nil rate band is £1,000 for basic-rate taxpayers, £500 for higher-rate taxpayers and £0 for additional-rate taxpayers.

The dividend nil rate band is £2,000 for all taxpayers.

When calculating the income tax liability the tax bands are:

	NSI	SI	DI
Additional-rate band (>£150,000)	45%	45%	38.1%
Higher-rate band (>£37,500)	40%	40%	32.5%
Basic-rate band	20%	20% 0% *	7.5%

*The 0% savings starting rate applies to savings income only in the first £5,000 of taxable income.

Essential reading

See Chapter 2 of the Essential reading for more detail on the income tax computation basics.

The Essential reading is available as an Appendix of the digital edition of the Workbook.

2 Children

Children are taxed on any income they receive after allowing for the deduction of their own personal allowance.

Income from a minor child received from funds provided by a parent (not grandparents) is deemed to be the parent's income if the amount of income received exceeds £100 (gross) a year. This includes income from trusts created by a parent in favour of a child.

3 Qualifying interest

Qualifying loan interest payments are **deductible** in an individual's income tax computation.

Interest will be qualifying interest if the loan concerned is used for qualifying purposes. These include:

(a) Purchase of an interest in a partnership or an employee-controlled company or a cooperative.

(b) Purchase of ordinary shares in, or loan of money to, a close trading company (includes companies resident in the European Economic Area (EEA) which would be close if resident in the UK). Relief is not available if Enterprise Investment Scheme (EIS) relief is claimed on the shares (see later in this Workbook).

(c) Purchase by a partner or employee of plant and machinery used in the business or used in the performance of duties. Interest is allowed for three years from the end of the tax year in which the loan was taken out and is apportioned if the asset is used partly for private use.

4 Jointly owned assets

Income from property owned jointly by spouses and civil partners is split 50:50 unless the couple make a joint declaration to HMRC specifying the actual proportions they are each entitled to. In Chapter 6 we will consider spouse/civil partner tax planning points.

Activity 1: Income tax computation

Holly receives £100,000 salary each year (PAYE £27,500). She also received £6,000 dividend income, and £12,500 bank deposit interest in 2020/21. Her expenses for the year included a qualifying interest payment of £2,000 and she pays £12,000 into her personal pension plan.

Required

Calculate her income tax payable for 2020/21.

Solution

Chapter summary

```
┌──────────────────────────────────────┐
│     The income tax computation       │
└──────────────────────────────────────┘
                    │
┌──────────────────────────────────────┐
│     Income tax computation 2020/21   │
└──────────────────────────────────────┘
```

	Non-savings income (NSI)	Savings income (SI)	Dividend income (DI)
	£	£	£
Trading income (Chapter 14)	X		
Employment income (Chapter 4)	X		
Overseas property business income (Chapter 9)	X		
Interest from o/seas securities (Chapter 9)		X	
Dividends from o/seas securities (Chapter 9)			X
Bank interest received		X	
Interest on gilts/bonds etc		X	
Dividends received			X
Discretionary trust income (× 100/55)	X		
Interest in possession trust income			
— From NSI or SI (× 100/80)	X	X	
— From DI (× 100/92.5)			X
UK property business income (Chapter 5)	X		
Total income	X	X	X
Less qualifying interest	(X)	bal (X)	bal (X)
Net income before losses	X	X	X
Losses	(X)	bal (X)	bal (X)
Net income (NI)	X	X	X
Less PA	(X)	bal (X)	bal (X)
Taxable income	X	X	X
Income tax on NSI (20/40/45%)			X
Income tax on SI (0/20/40/45%)			X
Income tax on DI (0/7.5/32.5/38.1%)			X
Annual allowance charge on excess pension contributions (Chapter 3)			X
Less tax reducers			
— EIS/SEIS/VCT, (Chapter 3)			
— marriage allowance			
— property business income finance costs (Chapter 5)			(X)
Less DTR (Chapter 9)			(X)
IT liability			X
Less tax deducted at source (PAYE)			(X)
IT payable			X

```
                    ┌──────────────────────────────────┬───────────────────────────┐
              ┌───────────┐              ┌──────────────────┐           ┌────────────────────┐
              │ Children  │              │ Qualifying interest │        │ Jointly owned assets │
              └───────────┘              └──────────────────┘           └────────────────────┘
```

Children

- Taxed on their own income after PA deducted
- Income of > £100pa from parent is taxed on parent

Qualifying interest

- Qualifying loan interest payments are deductible in the IT computation
- Common examples include interest on loan to
  – buy interest in partnership
  – buy shares in, or loan money to, a close company
  – purchase by a partner or employee of plant and machinery used in business/ duties

Jointly owned assets

- Income split 50:50 unless joint declaration specifying actual proportions

Knowledge diagnostic

1. Calculation of taxable income

- In a personal income tax computation, bring together income from all sources, splitting the sources into non-savings, savings and dividend income.
- Most savings income is received without the deduction of tax. Dividends are also received gross. There are a number of sources of exempt income.
- Qualifying interest is deducted from total income to compute net income.
- All persons are entitled to a personal allowance. It is deducted from net income in a manner such as to save most tax. This is often against non-savings, then savings then dividend income but is not always the case. The personal allowance is reduced by £1 for every £2 that adjusted net income exceeds £100,000 and can be reduced to nil.
- Qualifying interest and the personal allowance are deducted to maximise the tax savings.

2. Calculation of income tax payable

- Income tax is worked out on taxable income. First tax non-savings income, then savings income and then dividend income. There are nil rate bands for savings and dividend income.
- Tax reducers reduce tax on income at a set rate of relief.
- From tax liability, deduct any income tax suffered at source to arrive at tax payable. The tax suffered at source can be repaid.

3. Spouses, civil partners and children

Spouses, civil partners and children are all separate taxpayers. There are special rules to prevent parents from exploiting a child's personal allowance. Income from married couples/civil partners is split 50:50 unless the couple elect otherwise.

Further study guidance

Question practice

There are no questions in the Further question practice bank which relate solely to the material in this chapter. In the following chapters covering more detail on different aspects of the income tax computation you will find many questions which will test the income tax computation.

Activity answers

Activity 1: Income tax computation

	Non-savings income	Savings income	Dividends
	£	£	£
Employment income	100,000		
Bank interest		12,500	
Dividends			6,000
Less			
Interest	(2,000)		
Net income	98,000	12,500	6,000
PA (W1)	(11,750)	-	-
Taxable income	86,250	12,500	6,000

Tax		
NSI	52,500 @ 20% (W3) =	10,500
	33,750 @ 40% =	13,500
SI	500 @ 0% savings income nil rate band (HRTP)	0
	12,000 @ 40% =	4,800
DI	2,000 @ 0% dividend nil rate band	0
	4,000 @ 32.5% =	1,300
Income tax liability		30,100
Less tax @ source		
	PAYE	(27,500)
Income tax payable		2,600

Workings

1 **Personal allowance**

	£
Personal allowance	12,500
Less ½ (101,500 (W2) – £100,000)	(750)
Abated personal allowance	11,750

2 **Adjusted net income**

	£
Net income (£98,000 + £12,500 + £6,000)	116,500
Less gross personal pension contribution (£12,000 × 100/80)	(15,000)

	£
ANI	101,500

3 *Basic rate band extension*

	£
Basic-rate band	37,500
Gross personal pension contribution	15,000
Extended basic-rate band	52,500

Skills checkpoint 1

Approaching ethical issues

Chapter overview

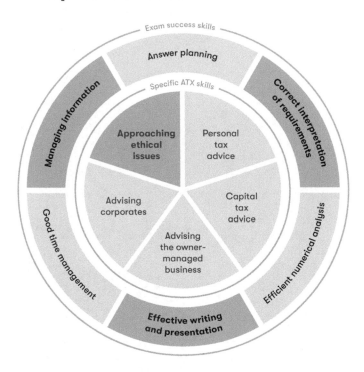

Introduction

The consideration of ethical issues will be mostly new to you in ATX – UK, although some of the underlying principles were mentioned in TX – UK, such as the difference between tax avoidance and tax evasion.

There will always be five marks in Section A on ethical issues.

Questions will often involve identifying, evaluating and addressing threats to compliance with the five fundamental principles which should underlie all ACCA members' professional behaviour. These are:

- Integrity
- Objectivity
- Professional competence and due care
- Confidentiality
- Professional behaviour

You may also be expected to deal with aspects of money laundering and tax avoidance for all or some of the five marks available for ethical issues.

This Skills Checkpoint looks at three typical questions on ethics so that you can see how they should be approached in the exam.

We will focus on three general exam success skills and the specific ATX-UK skill on approaching ethical issues. Once you are familiar with these skills, you can then use them to tackle further ethical issue questions.

Skills checkpoint 1: Approaching ethical issues

ATX – UK approaching ethical issues

The key steps in applying this skill are outlined below. They will be explained in more detail in the following sections, and illustrated by answering requirements of adapted past exam questions.

STEP 1 Work out how many minutes you have to answer the question.

STEP 2 Read the requirement(s) and think what format will be required.

STEP 3 Read the scenario and highlight and/or make notes of the information that will enable you to answer the requirement(s).

STEP 4 Prepare an answer plan, eg linking the fundamental principles to the scenario and dealing with other issues such as money-laundering and tax-avoidance.

STEP 5 Write your answer.

Exam success skills

The following illustrations are based on adapted extracts from three past exam questions: Snowdon (Mar/Jun 18), Opus Ltd group (06/14), and Grand Ltd group (09/18).

These three exam success skills are particularly important for answering questions on ethical issues:

- **Managing information.** As ethical issues are examined in a Section A question, you will have to extract the relevant information from the scenario. Make sure that you take account of any information you are given which restricts your answer, such as matters which have already been dealt with.

- **Correct interpretation of requirements.** Again, since ethical issues will be examined in a Section A question, you will have to extract the requirements from the scenario. The requirement at the end of the question will only be a summary of the work you have to undertake. You must make sure you only deal with the issues raised.

- **Effective writing and presentation.** Some Section A questions may require you to use a specific format such as a letter, a memorandum or notes. Whatever format is required you should make your points clearly and succinctly. Avoid making general statements: always relate your comments to the specific scenario.

Skill activity 1 – Snowdon

STEP 1 Work out how many minutes you have to answer the question.

Consider spending about up to a third of your time on reading and planning and the rest of the time writing up your answer.

For an ethical issues question of 5 marks you will have approximately 10 minutes. This time should be split approximately as follows:

- Reading the question – 1 minute
- Planning your answer – 2 minutes
- Writing your answer – 7 minutes

Required

Prepare the memorandum as requested in the email from your manager.

5 marks

STEP 2 Read the requirement(s) and think what format will be required.

Required

Prepare the memorandum[1] as requested in the email from your manager[2].

5 marks

> [1] A memorandum is a formal report which provides information about the matters raised.

> [2] Can assume that they know about the idea of the fundamental principles.

STEP 3 Read the scenario and highlight and/or make notes of the information that will enable you to answer the requirement(s).

Your manager has had a meeting with Snowdon, a potential new client[3]. Snowdon requires advice[4] in respect of a cottage he has purchased from his sister Coleen, who has since died, and his unincorporated business 'Siabod' which he started on 1 July 20XX and intends to expand.

> [3] Vital information – don't waste time writing about procedures for existing clients.

> [4] Key point: does your firm have expertise in these areas of tax?

An extract from an email from your manager detailing the work you are required to do is set out below.

Please prepare a memorandum for Snowdon's client file covering a summary of the procedures[5] we should follow before we agree to become Snowdon's tax advisers.

> [5] Suggests using a list of points rather than a continuous narrative.

STEP 4 Prepare an answer plan.

Here we have produced a bullet-point list but you could use a spider diagram if you prefer.

- Fundamental principles:
    - Integrity
    - Professional Behaviour
    - Professional competence
- **Threats** to fundamental principles and how to manage them (**safeguards**)
- Contacting existing accountants
- Money laundering
    - Identification procedures
    - Review activities

STEP 5 Write your answer.

Procedures we should follow before we agree to become Snowdon's tax advisers

- We must have regard to the fundamental principles of professional ethics[6]. This requires us to consider whether becoming tax advisers to Snowdon would create any threats[7] to compliance with these principles in particular:

> [6] State they are relevant but don't waste time on general discussion about them.

> [7] Key word you should be using.

- **Integrity** [8] **and professional behaviour**[9]: we must consider the appropriateness of Snowdon's attitude to complying with the law and the disclosure of information to HM Revenue & Customs (HMRC).

- **Professional competence and due care**[10]: we must ensure that we have the skills and competence necessary to be able to deal with the matters which may arise in connection with Snowdon's affairs in relation to inheritance tax and the expansion of his business.

If any such threats are identified, we should not accept the appointment unless the threats can be reduced to an acceptable level via the implementation of safeguards[11].

- We should contact Snowdon's existing tax adviser(s)[12] in order to ensure that there has been no action by Snowdon which would preclude the acceptance of the appointment on ethical grounds.

- We must obtain evidence of Snowdon's identity[13] (for example, his passport) and his address to comply with money laundering requirements.

- We must carry out a review in order to satisfy ourselves that Snowdon is not carrying on any activities which may be regarded as money laundering.

[8] Being straightforward and honest in professional and business relationships.

[9] Avoiding any action that may bring discredit to the profession, eg by being associated with client involved in tax evasion.

[10] Maintain professional knowledge and skill to provide competent professional service. Relate to scenario.

[11] Key word you should be using.

[12] Procedure to be followed.

[13] Money-laundering procedure.

Examining team's comments and mark scheme – Snowdon

Examining team's comments:

This appeared to be a question for which most candidates were well prepared, and most scored well. Those that didn't tended to be too general in their comments, such as talking about the need to ensure adherence to ACCA's fundamental ethical principles, without identifying which of these principles is/are particularly relevant in this scenario. It is always important in an ethics requirement to relate your answer specifically to the (potential) client, and the scenario in the question.

Mark scheme	Marks
Fundamental principles	3
Contact existing tax advisers	1
Identity checks	1
Money laundering review	1
Max	5

Skill activity 2 – Opus Ltd group

STEP 1 Work out how many minutes you have to answer the question.

Consider spending about up to a third of your time on reading and planning and the rest of the time writing up your answer.

For a six-mark question you have about 12 minutes. This time should be split approximately as follows:

- Reading the question – 2 minutes

- Planning your answer – 2 minutes

- Writing your answer – 8 minutes

Required

Carry out the work required as set out in the email from your manager relating to the error in the corporation tax return of Binni Ltd.

Note. You are not required to calculate the amount of interest payable or to consider any penalty which may be charged.

6 marks[14]

[14] This question also requires you to consider tax administration which is commonly related to ethical issues. There will still be at least 5 marks available on ethical issues.

STEP 2 Read the requirement(s) and think what format will be required.

Required

Carry out the work required as set out in the email from your manager relating to the error in the corporation tax return of Binni Ltd.

Note. You are not required[15] to calculate the amount of interest payable or to consider any penalty which may be charged.

6 marks

[15] So don't write about these issues – there are no extra marks available for them even if your answer is correct.

STEP 3 Read the scenario and highlight and/or make notes of the information that will enable you to answer the requirement(s).

Binni Ltd is a member of the Opus Ltd group of companies. All of the companies in the group, including Binni Ltd, have always paid corporation tax by instalments[16].

[16] Relevant to interest issue below.

The following is an extract of an e-mail from your manager:

Error in the corporation tax return of Binni Ltd

A detailed review of the results of Binni Ltd for the year ended 31 May 20XX has revealed that no adjustment was made in respect of an amount of disallowable expenditure. As a result of this, the company's corporation tax liability for the year was understated by £8,660. I have told the company that there may be interest and penalties in respect of this error.

Explain[17] how the interest on the underpaid tax[18] will be calculated and state[19] the matters which would need to be considered if the company were unwilling[20] to disclose the error to HM Revenue & Customs (HMRC).

[17] ACCA verb - To make an idea clear.

[18] Tax administration issue.

[19] ACCA verb - Explain precisely so focus on exact scenario.

STEP 4 Prepare an answer plan.

Here we have produced a bullet-point list but you could use a spider diagram if you prefer.

[20] Don't waste time in considering the scenario where they agree to disclose.

- Interest on underpaid tax runs from instalment dates
- Tax evasion identification
- Fundamental principles
  - Integrity
  - Professional behaviour
- Threats to fundamental principles, cannot be managed by safeguards so must cease to act
- Impact for client including criminal prosecution
- Tell HMRC ceased to act but not why
  - Fundamental principle: Confidentiality
- Money laundering:
  - Reporting
  - Criminal prosecution

STEP 5 Write your answer.

Error in the corporation tax return of Binni Ltd

Interest on underpaid tax[21]

Binni Ltd will be regarded as having underpaid corporation tax on each of the four payment dates[22] for the year ended 31 May 20XX. Accordingly, interest may be charged from 14 December in the previous year and 14 March, 14 June and 14 September in the same year on any amounts of underpaid corporation tax.

[21] Use sub-headings to show which part of the question you are answering.

[22] Interest runs from each instalment due date.

Disclosure of the error

The error is tax evasion as it is a failure to disclose relevant information. This is a threat[23] to our compliance with the fundamental principles of integrity[24] and professional behaviour[25].

The directors of Binni Ltd must be advised to make full disclosure of the error or authorise our firm to make such disclosure, without delay. If they refuse, we must advise the directors that we can no longer act for the company since we cannot safeguard[26] against these threats. Even if we cease to act for Binni Ltd, we are still under a professional duty[27] to ensure that the directors understand the seriousness of offences against HMRC, including the possibility of criminal prosecution under tax law.

We must also inform HMRC that we have ceased to act for the company. We should not, however, advise HMRC of the error unless the directors consented to such disclosure as this would be a breach of the fundamental principle of confidentiality[28].

Tax evasion may also constitute money laundering and we are also bound by legislation to report suspicions to the appropriate authority. Again, this may lead to criminal prosecution under money laundering legislation.

[23] Key word you should be using.

[24] Being straightforward and honest in professional and business relationships.

[25] Avoiding any action that may bring discredit to the profession.

[26] Key word you should be using.

[27] Aspect of Integrity.

[28] Disclosing confidential information outside the firm without proper and specific authority. There is no legal or professional right or duty to disclose details to HMRC.

Examining team's comments and mark scheme – Opus Ltd group

Examining team's comments:

This was a standard question and an opportunity for all candidates to earn some straightforward marks.

Unfortunately, a minority of candidates decided to address the penalties aspect of the question in great detail without thinking about the other relevant issues.

Stronger candidates recognised the need to consider the importance of disclosing the error from the point of view of tax evasion, money laundering and the acceptability of continuing to act for the company. These stronger candidates were able to score well on this part of the question.

Mark scheme	Marks
Interest on underpaid tax	2
Action required	
Necessary to disclose	2
Implications of failure to disclose	3½
Max	6

Skill activity 3 – Grand Ltd group

STEP 1   Work out how many minutes you have to answer the question.

Consider spending about up to a third of your time on reading and planning and the rest of the time writing up your answer.

For an ethical issues question of 5 marks you will have approximately 10 minutes. This time should be split approximately as follows:

- Reading the question – 1 minute

- Planning your answer – 2 minutes

- Writing your answer – 7 minutes

Required

Prepare the notes[29] as requested in the email from your manager.

5 marks

[29] Notes are less formal than a memorandum but still need to be clear and concise.

STEP 2   Read the requirement(s) and think what format will be required.

Required

Prepare the notes as requested in the email from your manager[30].

5 marks

[30] So you can assume knows about relevant legislation.

STEP 3   Read the scenario and highlight and/or make notes of the information that will enable you to answer the requirement(s).

Your manager has had a meeting with Bryce, the managing director of Grand Ltd.

The following is an extract of an email from your manager following the meeting:

Tax evasion and tax avoidance

Bryce and his daughter (who is a tax expert[31] in the field of capital allowances) have drawn up a plan which they claim will enable a company to claim a tax deduction of 180%[32] of the cost of new machinery. The plan is complicated in that it involves the creation of a new, wholly-owned subsidiary[33] and a series of contracts[34] involving the leasing and sub-leasing of the machinery between the two companies.

I have not looked at the plan in detail because, even if it would appear to have the intended tax effect, I am sure that it would fall within the general anti-abuse rule (GAAR).

Please prepare notes which:

- Distinguish between tax evasion and tax avoidance[35] and state[36] the purpose of the GAAR.

- Explain[37] why the GAAR is likely to apply to this particular plan[38].

STEP 4   Prepare an answer plan.

Here we have produced a bullet-point list but you could use a spider diagram if you prefer.

- Tax evasion
- Tax avoidance
- GAAR: counteract avoidance
- Why GAAR applies:
    - Tax advantage
    - Tax arrangements
    - Abusive

STEP 5   Write your answer.

Tax evasion and tax avoidance and purpose of the general anti-abuse rule (GAAR)

- Tax evasion: illegal[39], involves the provision of false information or the withholding of information in order to evade tax.

- Tax avoidance: legal[40], use of legal methods in order to reduce the amount of tax payable.

[31] So you can assume knows about relevant legislation.

[32] Exceeds cost of machinery so effectively making a profit on its acquisition.

[33] Identify tax arrangements.

[34] Suggests not commercial reasons, just tax avoidance, so abusive tax arrangements.

[35] Brief description of what constitutes each and whether illegal or legal.

[36] ACCA verb - Explain precisely.

[37] ACCA verb - To make an idea clear.

[38] Not just a general description, deal with specific scenario.

[39] Important to state this.

[40] Again, important to state this in relation to GAAR.

- GAAR: intended to counteract tax advantages, obtained via what would otherwise be legal tax avoidance methods, where the arrangements can be considered to be abusive.[41]

[41] Important word you should be using.

Why the GAAR is likely to apply to the plan drawn up by Bryce and his daughter

- The tax advantage[42] obtained would be a tax deduction in excess of the cost of the machinery.

[42] Use this terminology.

- The tax arrangements[43] would be the formation of the subsidiary and the series of leasing contracts which are intended to obtain the tax advantage.

[43] Identify.

- The arrangements are likely to be regarded as abusive[44] because they appear to have been designed to give rise to additional tax deductions rather than for genuine commercial reasons.

[44] Key point as arrangements in themselves would otherwise be acceptable.

Examining team's comments and mark scheme – Grand Ltd group

Examining team's comments:

This was clearly an area candidates were prepared for, and was generally done very well, with most candidates scoring at least four of the five available marks. A few candidates produced an exceptionally long answer, and, while they probably scored full marks, these could also have been obtained with a much more concise answer, leaving more time for other parts of the exam. It may be tempting to write at length on a topic with which a candidate is very familiar, and confident, but attention should always be paid to the maximum number of marks available.

Mark scheme	Marks
Tax evasion, tax avoidance and the purpose of the GAAR	4
Application to plan	3
Max	5

Exam success skills diagnostic

Every time you complete a question, use the diagnostic below to assess how effectively you demonstrated the exam success skills in answering the question. The table has been completed below for Grand Ltd group to give you an idea of what questions to ask to complete the diagnostic.

Exam success skills	Your reflections/observations
Good time management	Did you spend too long on the question? If so, perhaps you wrote too much on GAAR.
Managing information	Did you pick up all the information you required to satisfactorily answer the requirements. For example, did you spot that the tax

Exam success skills	Your reflections/observations
	deduction on the purchase of the new machinery was 180%?
Correct interpretation of requirements	Did you restrict your answer to the second part of the question to the particular plan? Or did you answer more generally?
Answer planning	Did you leave out any aspect in your plan, for example tax evasion?
Effective writing and presentation	Did you present your answer in a logical order? Or was it muddled up between the different parts? Did you repeat yourself?
Efficient numerical analysis	Not relevant
Most important action points to apply to your next question	

Summary

This Skills Checkpoint has shown you how to approach ethical issues using the specific ATX – UK skill. You need to be prepared to state the fundamental principles and apply them to the specific scenario. Don't forget to address money laundering issues. The Grand Ltd question also shows that you may need to discuss issues relating to tax evasion and tax avoidance, including GAAR.

We also focused on three exam success skills. Managing information requires you to extract the relevant information from the scenario and also any information you are given which restricts your answer. Correct interpretation of requirements requires you also to extract the requirement from the scenario and only deal with the issues raised. Effective writing and presentation may involve using a specific format and always includes making your points clearly and succinctly and related to the scenario.

Using these skills will help you become a successful student so make sure you use them when you attempt further questions on ethical issues.

Pensions and other tax-efficient investment products

Learning objectives

On completion of this chapter, you should be able to:

	Syllabus reference no.
Remember the material studied in Taxation (TX – UK) under the headings: 'Explain and compute the relief given for contributions to personal pension schemes, and to occupational pension schemes' (This is the relevant TX syllabus outcome within ATX B7)	A1(a) B7
The threshold level of income below which tapering of the pensions annual allowanced does not apply	A1(g)(iii)
Understand and apply the rules relating to investments in the seed enterprise investment scheme and the enterprise investment scheme	A1(g)(i)
Understand and apply the rules relating to investments in venture capital trusts	A1(g)(ii)

Exam context

In your exam you may well find that you are advising a high net worth individual. That individual may be looking to invest their money in a tax-efficient way and so could be considering a pension contribution or investment in a tax-efficient investment product such as an EIS/SEIS or VCT investment. All of these will trigger tax relief based on the amount invested and can therefore reduce the individual's tax liability and some will have other tax advantages that you may need to explain or apply to information given in the scenario.

Chapter overview

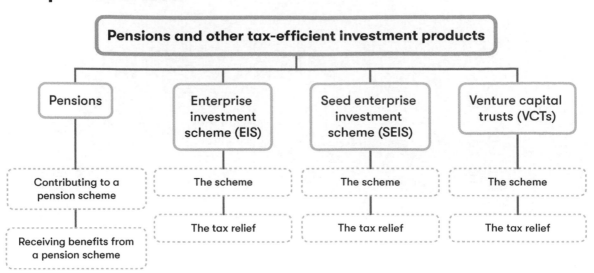

1 Pensions

1.1 Contributing to a pension scheme

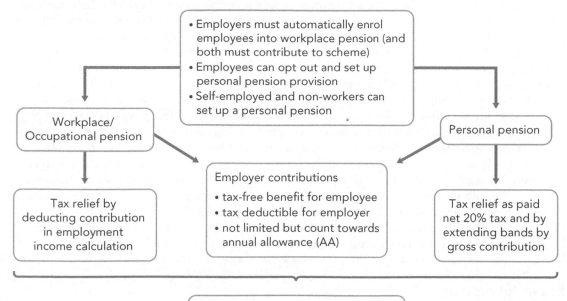

- Employers must automatically enrol employees into workplace pension (and both must contribute to scheme)
- Employees can opt out and set up personal pension provision
- Self-employed and non-workers can set up a personal pension

Workplace/ Occupational pension

Personal pension

Tax relief by deducting contribution in employment income calculation

Employer contributions
- tax-free benefit for employee
- tax deductible for employer
- not limited but count towards annual allowance (AA)

Tax relief as paid net 20% tax and by extending bands by gross contribution

---

Two methods of capping tax relief on contributions:

1 Tax relief for individual available on higher of:
- relevant earnings
- £3,600

If more paid, relief capped at maximum. Relevant earnings-employment income, trade income, income from a furnished holiday let.

2 Compare

Total gross (tax relievable) contributions by everyone in the tax year   vs   Annual allowance (AA) available → £40,000

If total contributions > AA there is an AA charge on the excess subject to IT at the individual's marginal rate of tax (NSI rates).

- Abated to a minimum of £4,000 if the individual is a higher earner (see * below)
- If AA isn't used in a tax year it can be carried forward three tax years provided the individual was a member of a pension scheme in that year
- Use current year AA first then brought forward unused AA on a FIFO basis

---

* If an individual has adjusted income > £240,000 their AA is reduced.
AA reduced by 1/2 (adjusted income −£240,000)
Once adjusted income > £312,000 the minimum AA of £4,000 is available.

Adjusted income
For self-employed = net income
For employed = net income + pension contributions to workplace pensions + all employer pension contributions

The reduction only applies where threshold income > £200,000
Threshold income = net income − gross personal pension contributions

Exam focus point

Question 4 Pedro in the March 2020 exam asked students to calculate the reduction in a taxpayer's income tax liability as a result of making a large contribution into their personal pension. Students were also asked to explain the amount of personal allowance available. In the scenario students were told that the taxpayer's employer already made a contribution to an occupational pension scheme on behalf of taxpayer and that the taxpayer wanted to make a large contribution to a personal pension scheme. The examining team said 'there were few very good answers to this question, although many managed to score half marks. Weaker students were clearly very confused about the rules for pension contributions relief and produced some very muddled answers. It appeared that quite a few students adopted a scattergun approach, including calculations, presumably as they occurred to them, which proved difficult to follow, and to mark, in some cases. It is important to adopt a logical approach to this sort of question, working through the income tax computation line by line, thinking through one stage at a time. Additionally some students wasted time by calculating the individual's income tax liability prior to their pension contribution, when this was given in the question. Others wrote a detailed explanation of some of the rules, instead of, or as well as, calculations. The only explanation required was in respect of the amount of personal allowance available to the taxpayer. Other explanations, sadly, didn't score marks.'

Essential reading

See Chapter 3 of the Essential reading for more detail on contributing to a pension scheme as this is assumed knowledge from Taxation (TX – UK).

The Essential reading is available as an Appendix of the digital edition of the Workbook.

Formula provided

The annual allowance, minimum allowance, threshold income limit, income limit and the £3,600 maximum contribution for relief without earnings are all given to you in the Tax rates and allowances available in the exam.

1.2 Receiving benefits from a pension scheme

On retirement there are a number of common ways that an individual can receive benefits from their pension. One is flexi-access drawdown where the individual usually takes a **tax-free lump sum of 25% of the pension fund**. The **rest of the pension fund is then reinvested to provide taxable pension income** as required by the individual.

However, an individual is not allowed to build up an indefinitely large pension fund. There is a **maximum value of a pension fund** which is called the **lifetime allowance** and it is currently **£1,073,100**. It is only when an individual comes to take benefit from the pension fund that the fund value is compared to the lifetime allowance. In most situations, the pension fund will not exceed the lifetime allowance and there are no additional tax consequences. **If, however, the fund value exceeds the lifetime allowance then there will be an income tax charge on the excess value of the fund.**

The rate of tax which applies to the excess value of the fund depends on the type of benefit to be taken from the excess funds. If the funds are to provide:

- a **lump sum** the **excess** is charged to income tax at **55%**
- **pension income** the **excess** is charged to income tax at **25%**.

The lower rate of tax on the funds providing pension income is due to the fact that as the individual then draws the pension income further income tax will be due based on the individual's marginal rate of tax as they draw the benefit.

Formula provided

The lifetime allowance will be given to you in the Tax Rates and Allowances available in the exam.

Activity 1: Lifetime allowance exceeded

Amy retired on 1 July 2020 and decided to start taking her pension benefits from that date. She has a money purchase fund which was valued at £1,800,000 at 1 July 2020. Amy took the maximum tax-free lump sum and the balance of her lifetime allowance she used to provide pension income by flexi-access drawdown. The excess of the fund over the lifetime allowance was taken as a lump sum.

Required

Explain how much Amy receives on 1 July 2020 after tax.

Solution

1.3 Enterprise investment scheme (EIS)

1.3.1 The scheme

KEY
TERM

Enterprise investment scheme: A scheme designed to support individuals investing in **small, unlisted trading companies**. These types of companies find it hard to raise finance and so individuals are encouraged to **subscribe for shares in these companies in return for tax breaks**.

In order to benefit for tax reliefs, certain conditions regarding the investment need to be made:

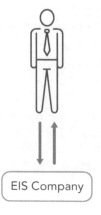

Subscribes in cash for newly issued ordinary shares which are irredeemable and fully paid up

Investor must not be connected with company. Connection through employment or owning > 30% of the share capital.

The investor cannot hold other shares in the company at the time the investment is made (except when existing holdings are only EIS/SEIS shares).

EIS Company

The company will be a small unquoted trading company meeting certain conditions.
The details of the conditions are excluded from the Advanced Taxation (ATX-UK) syllabus.

1.3.2 The tax reliefs

There are three types of relief available to the individual:

1. Income tax (IT) relief	2. Capital gains tax (CGT) relief	3. EIS reinvestment relief
IT relief is available as a tax reducer on subscriptions **of up to £1,000,000** in any tax year. The relief is the **lower** of: • **30% of the amount subscribed** (up to a maximum of £1,000,000) • the individual's **income tax liability for the year.** The investment must be in **new issues of ordinary shares** in an **unquoted trading company** to **unconnected persons**. A claim for EIS IT relief must be made by the fifth anniversary of the normal self-assessment filing date for the tax year of investment. (ie by 31 January 2027 for an investment in 2020/21). The investor can claim to have all or some of the shares treated as issued in the previous tax year. **If the shares are held for three or more years the benefit of the IT relief is kept.** If, however, the shares are **sold within three years then some or all of the relief is withdrawn.** • If the shares are sold at a gain or the transaction is	Provided the **shares are held for three or more years any gain on the sale of shares will be exempt.** If the shares are held **for less than three years, the gain will be taxed normally.** If the shares are sold at a **capital loss this capital loss will always be allowable. However, in the calculation of the loss the cost is reduced by the net EIS relief not withdrawn.** The capital loss may be relieved against general income in the same way as a trading loss (see Chapter 15).	A **deferral relief** is available where an individual disposes of any chargeable asset and **reinvests in qualifying EIS shares within the one year before and three years after the disposal of the chargeable asset.** (This relief will be covered in Chapter 8.)

1. Income tax (IT) relief	2. Capital gains tax (CGT) relief	3. EIS reinvestment relief
not at arm's length then all the relief is withdrawn • If the shares are sold at a loss then the amount withdrawn = proceeds × 30% (or original % relief if lower) This is illustrated in Activity 2.		

Dividends received from an EIS company are taxable as normal dividends.

Activity 2: Enterprise investment scheme

Mr Big has earned income for 2020/21 of £51,000. He subscribes £60,000 for 30,000 new £1 ordinary shares in an EIS qualifying company and these shares are issued to him in November 2020. He sells the shares in January 2022 for their market value of £10,000.

Required

1   Calculate Mr Big's 2020/21 income tax liability.

2   Show how much of the previous income tax relief is withdrawn in 2021/22.

3   What is his capital gains tax position in 2021/22?

Solution

1.4 Seed enterprise investment scheme (SEIS)

1.4.1 The scheme

KEY TERM

> **Seed enterprise investment scheme (SEIS):** A similar scheme to the EIS but gives **more generous tax reliefs** to investors in **smaller start-up trading companies.**

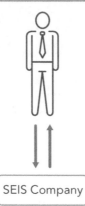

Investor must not be connected with company.
Connection through employment or owning > 30% of the share capital. While an employee is connected being a director does not exclude relief.

Subscribes in cash for newly issued ordinary shares which are irredeemable and fully paid up

SEIS Company

The company will be a very small start-up unquoted trading company meeting certain conditions. The details of the conditions are excluded from the Advanced Taxation (ATX-UK) syllabus.

1.4.2 The tax reliefs

The SEIS scheme also has three tax reliefs available:

1. Income tax (IT) relief	2. Capital gains tax (CGT) relief	3. SEIS reinvestment relief
IT relief is available as a tax reducer on **subscriptions of up to £100,000** in any tax year. The relief is the **lower** of: • **50% of the amount subscribed** (up to a maximum of £100,000) • the **individual's income tax liability** for the year. The features of the SEIS IT reducer are then the same as we saw for EIS relief. All or part of the investment can be treated as if made in the previous year. **If the shares are sold within three years some or all of the IT relief will be withdrawn** in the same was as we have seen for EIS relief.	The **same rules as for EIS CGT relief apply.** Provided the shares are held for three or more years any gain on the sale of shares will be exempt. If the shares are held for less than three years, the gain will be taxed normally. If the shares are sold at a capital loss this capital loss will always be allowable. However, in the calculation of the loss the cost is reduced by the net SEIS relief not withdrawn. The capital loss may be relieved against general income in the same way as a trading loss (see Chapter 15).	An **exemption relief** is available where an individual disposes of any chargeable asset and **reinvests in qualifying SEIS shares during the same tax year.** (This relief will be covered in Chapter 8).

1.5 Venture capital trusts (VCTs)

1.5.1 The scheme

> **Venture capital trust (VCT): Listed companies which invest in unquoted trading companies and meet certain conditions.** They are different to EIS and SEIS companies in that the investor can spread their risk via the VCT investing in many smaller unquoted trading companies whereas under an EIS or SEIS investment the entire investment is made in one company.

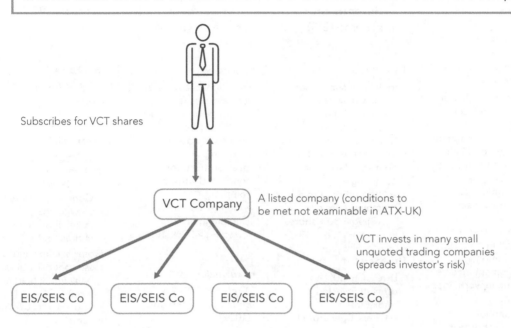

Subscribes for VCT shares

VCT Company — A listed company (conditions to be met not examinable in ATX-UK)

VCT invests in many small unquoted trading companies (spreads investor's risk)

EIS/SEIS Co   EIS/SEIS Co   EIS/SEIS Co   EIS/SEIS Co

1.5.2 The tax reliefs

The VCT scheme also has three tax reliefs:

1. Income tax (IT) relief	2. Capital gains tax (CGT) relief	3. VCT dividend income is tax-free income
IT relief is available as a tax reducer on **subscriptions of up to £200,000** in any tax year. The relief is the **lower** of: • **30% of the amount subscribed** (up to a maximum of £200,000) • the **individual's income tax liability** for the year. The **IT relief is clawed back in the same way as for EIS relief** if the VCT shares are disposed of within **five** years.	**Gains on disposal of both secondary purchases or new issues of VCT shares are exempt from CGT.** **Losses are not allowable.** There is **no minimum holding requirement** for this treatment.	Dividends received from VCT shares are tax-free income.

Note. There is no VCT equivalent to the reinvestment reliefs we saw for EIS and SEIS investments.

If an individual is entitled to more than one of these IT reducers then the VCT reducer is deducted first, then the EIS reducer and then finally the SEIS reducer.

Chapter summary

Pensions and other tax-efficient investment products

Pensions

Contributing to a pension scheme

- Tax relief on higher of £3,600 and relevant earnings
  - tax relief via payment being net of 20% tax and extending bands of tax by gross contribution for personal pension scheme
  - tax relief via deducting contribution in employment income working in workplace scheme
- Excess annual allowance charge if total contributions by everyone to the scheme in the tax year exceed the annual allowance available
- Annual allowance £40,000
- Reduced if adjusted income > £240,000 to minimum of £4,000
- Any unused AA is carried forward 3 years on a FIFO basis
- Annual allowance charge is on excess contributions over AA at the individual's marginal rate of tax using NSI rates

Receiving benefits from a pension scheme

- Maximum value of fund is £1,073,100
- Tax excess on retirement at 25% (if used to provide pension income) or 55% (if taken as a lump sum)

Enterprise investment scheme (EIS)

The scheme

- Individual subscribes for newly issued ordinary shares in small unquoted trading company
- Investor must not be connected with the company
  - Connection through employment or owning > 30% shares

The tax relief

- IT relief @ 30% on amount invested (max £1m)
  - Cannot generate IT repayment
  - Relief clawed back if shares sold < 3 years
- CGT exempt if gain and keep shares > 3 years
  - Losses always allowable (cost reduced by net EIS relief not withdrawn)
- EIS reinvestment relief
  - Defers gain on sale of any asset if reinvest in EIS shares 1 year before/ 3 years after

Seed enterprise investment scheme (SEIS)

The scheme

- Individual subscribes for newly issued ordinary shares in very small start up unquoted trading company
- Investor must not be connected with the company
  - Connection through employment or owning > 30% shares

The tax relief

- IT relief @ 50% on amount invested (max £100k)
  - Cannot generate IT repayment
  - Relief clawed back if shares sold < 3 years
- CGT exempt if gain and keep shares > 3 years
  - Losses always allowable (cost reduced by net SEIS relief not withdrawn)
- SEIS reinvestment relief
  - Exempts gain on sale of any asset where reinvest in SEIS shares in same tax year

Venture capital trusts (VCTs)

The scheme

Individual invests in VCT shares

The tax relief

- IT relief @ 30% on amount invested (max £200k)
  - Cannot generate IT repayment
  - Relief clawed back if shares sold < 5 years
- Gains exempt and losses not allowable (no minimum holding period)
- VCT dividends tax-free income

BPP
LEARNING
MEDIA

Knowledge diagnostic

1. Pensions

An employee should be entitled to join to join their employer's workplace/ occupational pension scheme. Both employees and the self-employed can take out a personal pension with a financial institution such as a bank or building society.

An individual can make tax relievable contributions to their pension of up to the higher of their earnings and £3,600. Contributions to personal pension schemes are made net of basic rate tax. Employers normally operate net pay arrangements in respect of payments into workplace pension schemes.

Employers will make pension contributions to workplace pension schemes and these are tax deductible for the employer and a tax-free benefit for the employee.

The annual allowance is the limit on the amount that can be paid into a pension scheme each year. If this limit is exceeded there is an income tax charge on the excess contributions. The annual allowance is reduced if an individual has adjusted net income in excess of £240,000. Unused annual allowance can be carried forward for up to three years.

An annual allowance charge arises if tax-relievable contributions exceed the available annual allowance.

An individual can start to receive pension benefits from the age of 55. Under flexi-access drawdown, a tax-free lump sum of 25% of the pension fund can be taken and the remained reinvested to give taxable pension income as required.

The maximum value that can be built up in a pension fund is known as the lifetime allowance.

2. Enterprise investment scheme

The enterprise investment scheme encourages individuals to invest in small unquoted trading companies by providing then with three tax incentives:

- An IT reducer of 30% × amount invested (subject to max £1 million)
- Gains on EIS shares exempt if shares kept for > 3 years. Losses always allowable.
- EIS Reinvestment relief allows any gain to be deferred where EIS shares are subscribed for in the one year before/ 3 years after the disposal.

3. Seed enterprise investment scheme

The seed enterprise investment scheme also encourages individuals to invest in very small start-up style unquoted trading companies by providing three tax incentives:

- An IT reducer of 50% × amount invested (subject to max £100,000)
- Gains on SEIS shares exempt if shares kept > 3 years. Losses always allowable.
- SEIS Reinvestment relief allows all/ part of any gain to be exempted if SEIS shares are subscribed for in the same tax year.

4. Venture capital trusts

Venture capital trusts are listed companies who invest in small EIS/ SEIS type companies. They allow an investor to invest in these types of company while allowing risk diversification. Investment is encouraged by offering three tax incentives:

- An IT reducer of 30% × amount invested (subject to max £200,000)
- Gains on sale of VCT shares are exempt and losses not allowable (no minimum holding period.)
- Dividends from VCT received tax free

Further study guidance

Question practice

Now try the following from the Further question practice bank (available in the digital edition of the Workbook):

*   Eric and Melanie
*   Lee and Harry

Activity answers

Activity 1: Lifetime allowance exceeded

The maximum tax-free lump sum Amy can take is 25% × £1,073,100 = £268,275.

The balance of the lifetime allowance £804,825 will be taxable on Amy as she draws the pension income in the future at her marginal rate of tax.

The excess value of the fund over the lump sum is £726,900 (£1,800,000 − £1,073,100). As this is drawn as a lump sum it will be taxed at 55% meaning that Amy will keep 45% or £327,105 (45% × £726,900).

Amy will thus receive £595,380 after tax (£268,275+ £327,105).

Activity 2: Enterprise investment scheme

1 2020/21 Income tax liability

	Non-savings income
	£
Employment income	51,000
Less PA	(12,500)
	38,500
Tax thereon:	
37,500 × 20%	7,500
1,000 × 40%	400
38,500	7,900
Less tax reducers	
EIS relief	
60,000 × 30% = 18,000	*(7,900)
IT liability	Nil

* (restricted to tax liability)

Note. Note that a claim could be made to have the remaining £10,100 of relief in the previous tax year. (The rest of the answer assumes this claim has not been made).

2 The shares are sold within three years at a loss.

IT relief withdrawn/ clawed back = proceeds × 30% (or original % relief if lower) (W)

$$= £10,000 × 13.2\%$$

$$= £1,320$$

Working

Original Rate of EIS relief = £7,900/£60,000

$$= 13.2\%$$

3   The shares are sold within three years at a loss.

Losses are always allowable, however, the cost is reduced by the net EIS relief not withdrawn.

		£
Proceeds		10,000
Cost	60,000	
(7,900 – 1,320)	(6,580)	
		(53,420)
Allowable loss		(43,420)

4

Employment income

Learning objectives

On completion of this chapter, you should be able to:

	Syllabus reference no.
Remember the material covered in Taxation (TX – UK) under the headings:	
'Income from employment'	A1(a) B2
'National insurance contributions for employed persons'	A1(a) B6
Identify personal service companies and advise on the tax consequences of providing services via a personal service company	A1(c)(iii) A4(b)(vi)
Advise on the tax treatment of lump sum receipts	A1(c)(ii)
Advise on the tax treatment of share option and share incentive schemes	A1(c)(i)

Exam context

In the exam you may well find yourself advising an employee about their remuneration package. They may be asking you to consider their after-tax income from a package or to be comparing the after-tax income of two alternative packages. As well as considering the marginal tax on the benefit provided or foregone, remember to take into account other costs. For example, an employee who chooses to receive a higher salary and use his own car for business will have to bear the running costs of the car as well as the capital depreciation. Also don't forget to consider the national insurance costs!

You may find that a client in the exam is suggesting a business structure which will fall foul of the personal service company anti-avoidance legislation. It is vital that you understand the proposed structures which will be caught out by this legislation and that you can explain to your client what the consequences of this will be.

Lump sums are commonly paid on the termination of an employment. You may be required to discuss which elements of a termination package are tax free, and the consequences of the ongoing provision of a benefit.

Share incentives and share options may well feature in a question about employees. You may be required to advise the employer about which incentive scheme would meet their needs. You need to know the different conditions for each scheme – you will not get any marks for recommending an enterprise management incentive scheme to a company whose gross assets exceed £30 million.

Chapter overview

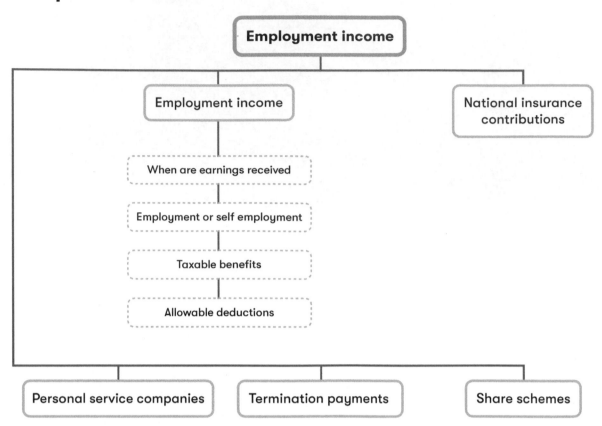

1 Employment income

Employment income includes income arising from employment under a contract of service and includes salaries and bonuses, benefits and pensions. An individual is generally assessed on the amounts **received** during the tax year.

The standard employment income pro-forma, which you will have covered in Taxation (TX – UK) is:

Employment income	£
Salary	X
Bonus	X
Benefits	X
	X
Allowable deductions	(X)
Employment income	X

You are expected to remember the detail of this pro-forma including the rules on benefits and allowable deductions from Taxation (TX – UK).

Essential reading

See Chapter 4 of the Essential reading for more detail revising the calculation of employment income.

The Essential reading is available as an Appendix of the digital edition of the Workbook.

2 National insurance contributions

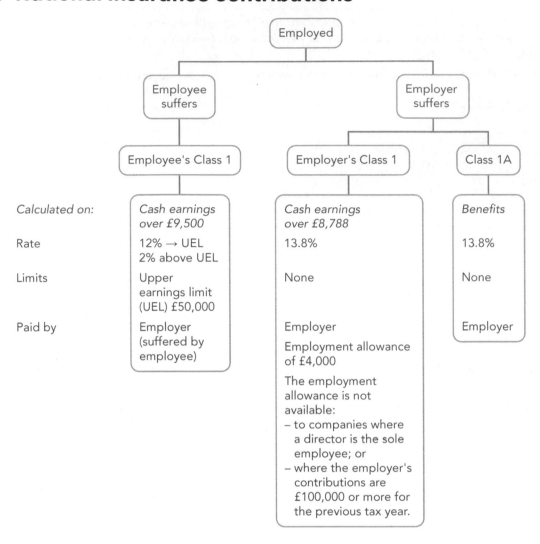

The diagram shows:

Employed branches into **Employee suffers** and **Employer suffers**.

Employee suffers → **Employee's Class 1**

Employer suffers → **Employer's Class 1** and **Class 1A**

Calculated on:	Employee's Class 1	Employer's Class 1	Class 1A
	Cash earnings over £9,500	Cash earnings over £8,788	Benefits
Rate	12% → UEL 2% above UEL	13.8%	13.8%
Limits	Upper earnings limit (UEL) £50,000	None	None
Paid by	Employer (suffered by employee)	Employer; Employment allowance of £4,000. The employment allowance is not available: – to companies where a director is the sole employee; or – where the employer's contributions are £100,000 or more for the previous tax year.	Employer

Essential reading

See Chapter 4 of the Essential reading for more detail revising the detail of national insurance calculations for employees.

The Essential reading is available as an Appendix of the digital edition of the Workbook.

3 Personal service companies

Individuals generally pay less tax if they are taxed as self-employed than they would if they were taxed as an employee. This is due to more generous rules regarding the deductibility of expenses for self-employed individuals and lower rates of national insurance. This meant that some individuals who were normally classed as employees started making arrangements to make their relationship with their employer look more like a self-employed relationship to access lower tax bills. Consider the typical employer-employee relationship and the tax due as illustrated in the left side of the diagram below. Employees would resign from their employer, set up an intermediary and then start to immediately contract with their previous employer through the intermediary thus receiving a fee into the intermediary rather than a salary. The individual would then extract the profits from the intermediary via a dividend rather than a salary thus gaining lower rates of income tax and saving national insurance.

The diagram below shows the typical employer-employee relationship on the left-hand side and then the new arrangement on the right-hand side.

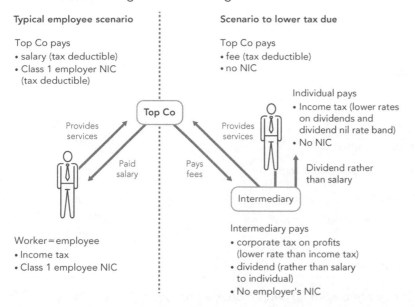

Typical employee scenario

Top Co pays
- salary (tax deductible)
- Class 1 employer NIC (tax deductible)

Provides services

Paid salary

Worker = employee
- Income tax
- Class 1 employee NIC

Scenario to lower tax due

Top Co pays
- fee (tax deductible)
- no NIC

Provides services

Pays fees

Individual pays
- Income tax (lower rates on dividends and dividend nil rate band)
- No NIC

Dividend rather than salary

Intermediary pays
- corporate tax on profits (lower rate than income tax)
- dividend (rather than salary to individual)
- No employer's NIC

HMRC set up **anti-avoidance legislation** to prevent this perceived abuse of the **self-employed vs employed rules**. This anti-avoidance legislation applies to those who have set up companies to offer their services rather than be employed. It can be referred to as **personal service company** legislation or **IR35**.

KEY TERM

> **Personal service company:** The name given to a company caught by anti-avoidance legislation which catches those who have set up companies to offer their services rather than to be employed.

In order to determine whether the anti-avoidance legislation applies or not, HMRC will look through the intermediary and look at the relationship between the Top Co and the individual. Using the **employed vs self-employed factors** HMRC will decide whether, in **substance**, the individual is an **employee** of the Top Co. These factors are covered in further detail in the Essential reading section of this chapter; they include consideration of:

- Contract of/ for services
- Control of work
- Provision of own equipment
- Hire helpers
- Financial risk
- Integral position
- Opportunity to profit
- Number of employers

If HMRC conclude that, in **substance**, the individual is an **employee** of the Top Co then the **personal service company (IR35) legislation applies**. This has the effect of changing the way that the situation is taxed.

A **deemed salary** needs to be calculated and the individual will be taxed on this deemed salary rather than on the dividends they receive from the intermediary. Thus, the individual will pay both income tax and class 1 employee NIC on the deemed salary. For the intermediary the deemed salary is an allowable trading expense. Class 1 employer's NIC is also payable which is also an allowable trading expense.

In calculating the 'deemed salary' we take all payments from the client (Top Co) to the intermediary (known as **relevant engagements**) and we deem them to be salary to the extent they have not already been paid as a salary. The following pro-forma will allow you to compute the deemed salary.

	£
Income from relevant engagements	X
Less statutory 5% deduction	(X)
	X
Less salary/benefits paid to worker	(X)
Less employer's NIC on actual payments	(X)
Less expenses allowable under employment income	(X)
Gross amount of deemed payment	G
Employer's NIC (note) on gross deemed payment (G × 13.8/113.8)	(X)
Actual deemed payment to worker	X

Note. The employment allowance (if available) cannot be used to reduce the employer's NIC on this deemed payment.

In order to avoid a double charge to tax note that if dividends have been drawn from the intermediary they are not taxed on the individual as a dividend as they form part of the deemed salary on which the individual is taxed.

The deemed salary is taxed as if it is paid to the individual on the last day of the tax year.

> **Exam focus point**
>
> The exam will often test a scenario where you are required to spot that the personal service company rules will be likely to apply. You must also be able to calculate and explain the deemed salary on which an individual will be taxed if caught under these rules.

Activity 1: Personal service company

Alan is currently employed by Farringdon Ltd and is paid a salary of £70,000 per year. He has no other income for the tax year.

Alan is planning to resign from Farringdon Ltd and form Alan Ltd (a personal service company). Alan Ltd will provide services to Farringdon Ltd and to other companies. The services will be carried out by Alan personally.

All of Alan Ltd's income will be in respect of relevant engagements and therefore subject to the personal service company (IR35) legislation. Alan will be a director, and the only employee of Alan Ltd.

Alan Ltd estimated income and outgoings for a full tax year

	£
Gross income	85,000
Salary paid to Alan	52,000
Administrative expenses	3,000
Travel expenses reimbursed to Alan	1,500
Dividend paid to Alan	18,000

The travel expenses are those which will be necessarily incurred by Alan in performing the work for Farringdon Ltd and the other customers of Alan Ltd.

Required

Prepare calculations to determine the effect on Alan's annual income, after deduction of all taxes of working for Alan Ltd rather than Farringdon Ltd.

Solution

---

4 Termination payments

```
                          ┌─────────────────────┐
                          │ Termination payments │
                          └─────────────────────┘
```

┌──────────────────────────┐ ┌──────────────────────────┐ ┌──────────────────────────┐
│ • For death, injury and │ │ • Payment as reward for │ │ • Other ex-gratia payments│
│   disability   │ │   services (past or future),│ │   such as compensation for│
│ • Approved lump sum   │ │   eg terminal bonuses or │ │   loss of office (non-   │
│   on retirement   │ │   golden handshakes   │ │   contractual and no   │
│ • Legal costs recovered │ │ • Compensation for loss of│ │ expectation)   │
│   by employee from   │ │   office which is contractual│ │ • Any benefits (eg, use of│
│   employer following   │ │   or there was reasonable │ │   company car) after   │
│   legal action to recover│ │   expectation of payment │ │   termination   │
│   compensation for loss │ │   (including payment in lieu│ │ • Some payments in respect│
│   of employment   │ │   of notices (PILONs))   │ │   of notice period (referred│
└──────────────────────────┘ │ • Post-employment notice │ │   to as non-PENP) (see next│
                              │   pay (PENP)(see next   │ │   section)   │
                              │   section)   │ └──────────────────────────┘
           │   └──────────────────────────┘
           ▼   │   │
┌──────────────────────────┐   ▼   ▼
│ Fully exempt from   │ ┌──────────────────────────┐ ┌──────────────────────────┐
│ income tax and NIC   │ │ Taxed in year of receipt │ │ • The first £30,000 is received│
└──────────────────────────┘ │ as normal employment   │ │   tax free (IT and NIC). │
                              │ income with Class 1   │ │ • If statutory redundancy pay│
                              │ (employee and employer NICs)│ │ (SRP) is received this   │
                              └──────────────────────────┘ │   reduces the £30,000   │
                                                            │   exemption available.   │
                                                            │ • The excess over £30,000 is│
                                                            │   taxable as specific   │
                                                            │   employment income in the│
                                                            │   year received and is taxed│
                                                            │   as the top slice of income│
                                                            │   (NS rates).   │
                                                            │ • Class 1A NIC will be due on│
                                                            │   the excess.   │
                                                            └──────────────────────────┘

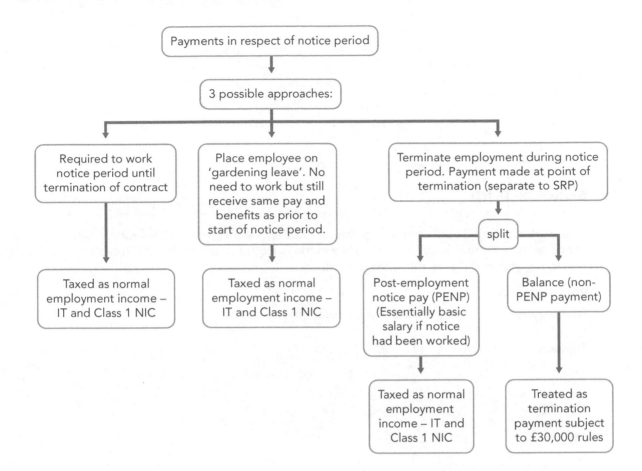

 Exam focus point

The application of termination payment tax rules to specific scenarios is frequently examined in ATX.

 Activity 2: Termination payment

Ban was made redundant from UpTempo Ltd on 1 May. His employment contract entitled him to two months' notice which he worked. His annual salary was £30,000. He was also given £1,300 in statutory redundancy pay and a £34,500 non-contractual (and non-expected) lump sum as a gesture of goodwill.

Required

Explain how Ban's payments received will be taxable.

Solution

Activity 3: PENP

Piotr worked for Apple Ltd earning a salary of £72,000. He resigned on 1 February 2021 and Apple Ltd asked him to leave without notice. They made him a payment of £32,000. Piotr's employment contract stated a three-month notice period.

Required

Explain how the payment of £32,000 is treated for tax and NIC.

Solution

5 Share schemes

5.1 Introduction

In order to incentivise its staff, an employer may offer its employees the opportunity to **buy shares in their employer at a discount** on current market value or may offer that they can **acquire shares through a share option scheme**.

If the employee is **given shares**, or is sold shares at less than their market value, they are treated as receiving specific employment income of **the difference between the market value and the amount (if any) which the employee pays for the shares**. In this situation, when the base cost of the shares is calculated for capital gains tax purposes any amount charged to income tax is added to the acquisition cost of the shares. In addition, if the shares are 'readily convertible assets' then an amount equal to that charged to income tax is treated as 'earnings' for NICs meaning Class 1 NICs will be due. A share will be a 'readily convertible asset' if it can be sold on a stock exchange.

If the employee is offered shares through a share option scheme there are different tax considerations which are covered below.

KEY TERM

> **Share schemes:** Schemes whereby a company gives/sells shares to its employees, often as part of a remuneration package. This will have tax consequences. A typical share option scheme will be set up as follows:
>
> - **Grant** – this is the date that the employee is given **the right to buy shares at a future date at a price set now**.
> - **Exercise** – this is the date where the employee decides to **take up the rights and buy the shares**.
> - **Disposal** – once the employee owns the shares they can then choose when to go on and **sell** the shares.

The tax at each of these dates will depend on whether the share scheme is **tax advantaged or not**. A share scheme is **tax-advantaged** if it complies with certain conditions. It is therefore **less flexible** than a non-advantaged share scheme as it is restricted by having to comply with conditions. However, a tax-advantaged share scheme will have a **preferential tax treatment**.

This table outlines the normal tax rules which will apply whether a share scheme is tax advantaged or not, although there follows more information about tax-advantaged share schemes.

	Non-advantaged share schemes	Tax-advantaged share schemes
Grant	No tax	No tax
Exercise	Income tax (and NIC if listed shares)	No tax
	MV at exercise X	
	Exercise price (X)	
	Taxable X	
Disposal	CGT	CGT
	Proceeds X	Proceeds X
	MV at exercise (X)	Cost (X)
	Gain X	Gain X

Note. That the rules regarding whether NIC will be due on shares involves considering whether the shares are **readily convertible assets** eg if they can be sold on a stock exchange.

There are four types of tax-advantaged share scheme on the Advanced Taxation (ATX – UK) syllabus and each one is now considered below in more detail. Note that costs of setting up a tax-advantaged share scheme are tax deductible for the company.

5.2 Tax-advantaged share schemes

5.2.1 Save as you earn (SAYE) share option schemes

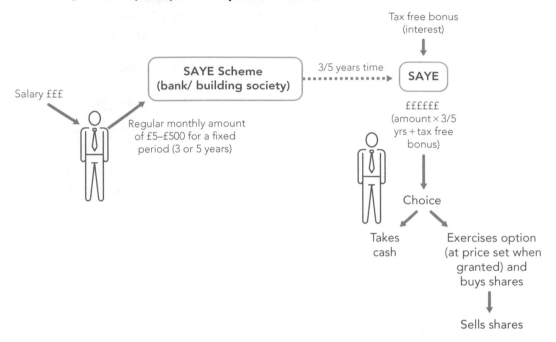

Essential reading

See Chapter 4 of the Essential reading as to what makes a SAYE scheme qualify as tax-advantaged.

The Essential reading is available as an Appendix of the digital edition of the Workbook.

Where the scheme meets the conditions to be tax-advantaged there are the following tax consequences:

- There is **no income tax or national insurance** when the share options are **granted or exercised**.
- On **sale** of the shares any gain is subject to **capital gains tax**. The cost of the shares in the gain calculation is the price the employee paid for the shares.
- There is **no income tax or national insurance** if the employee chooses to take the **cash**.

5.2.2 Company share option plan (CSOP)

Under a CSOP scheme, which can be restricted to selected employees and full-time directors, an employee is granted options to buy shares. Options must be exercised between three and ten years from grant to achieve the beneficial tax treatment (see below). An employee can be granted options over shares up to the value of £30,000 (at the date of grant).

Essential reading

See Chapter 4 of the Essential reading for details as to what makes the CSOP qualify as tax advantaged.

The Essential reading is available as an Appendix of the digital edition of the Workbook.

Provided these conditions are met:

- There is **no income tax or national insurance on grant or exercise** of the option.
- On **sale** of the shares any gain is subject to **capital gains tax**. The cost of the shares in the gain calculation is the option price paid by the employee to acquire the shares.

Essential reading

See Chapter 4 of the Essential reading for further detail about tax if the options are exercised before three years or after 10 years after grant.

The Essential reading is available as an Appendix of the digital edition of the Workbook.

5.2.3 Enterprise management incentives (EMI)

The EMI scheme is intended to help smaller, higher risk companies recruit and retain employees who have the skills to help them grow and succeed. They are also a way of rewarding employees for taking a risk by investing their time and skills to help small companies achieve their potential. Employees must spend a certain amount of time working for the company each week to be eligible to be given EMI options, but the company can choose to which of the eligible employees it grants such options. Therefore, the EMI scheme is **particularly useful if a company wishes to reward its key employees.**

EMIs are similar to CSOPs, as an employee is granted options to buy shares. Specific features of the EMI scheme include the following:

- A qualifying company can grant each of its employees options over shares worth up to £250,000 at the time of grant, subject to a maximum of £3m in total.
- The company may set a target to be achieved before an option can be exercised. The target must clearly be defined at the time the option is granted.
- Options can be granted at a discount below the market value at the date of grant, although there are tax consequences of this (see below).

Some of these features make the EMI a more attractive scheme than a CSOP, but there are restrictions, in particular regarding which companies can operate EMI schemes.

Essential reading

See Chapter 4 of the Essential reading for more detail on the conditions regarding what specifically makes a scheme tax-advantaged under EMI.

The Essential reading is available as an Appendix of the digital edition of the Workbook.

Key points are that the company must have **gross assets not exceeding £30 million** and must **have less than 250 full-time equivalent employees** when the options are granted. There is also a limit that at any one time an employee may only hold EMI options over shares with a value of up to £250,000 at the date of grant.

Provided the conditions are met:

- There is **no income tax or national insurance at grant**.
- There is **no income tax or national insurance at exercise unless the shares are issued at a discount** to market value at grant. At exercise there will be an income tax charge (and possibly a national insurance charge) based on the lower of:
  (i) The discount (ie the difference between market value at grant and the price paid (exercise price)).
  (ii) The difference between the market value at exercise and the price paid (exercise price).
- On **sale** of the shares any gain is subject to **capital gains tax**. The cost of the shares in the gain calculation is the amount paid for the shares plus any discount taxed as earnings described above. In order to determine whether any gain will be eligible for business asset disposal relief the usual conditions are relaxed as set out in Chapter 8.

5.2.4 Share incentive plans (SIP)

Here a company sets up a trust (SIP) and gives the SIP money. The **SIP then buys shares and holds them on behalf of employees**. Thus, SIPs are different to the other types of share options we have seen in that the individuals aren't granted options but are given the shares. All full or part-time employees must be eligible to participate in the scheme.

Essential reading

See Chapter 4 of the Essential reading for more detail on conditions for a SIP to qualify as tax advantaged.

The Essential reading is available as an Appendix of the digital edition of the Workbook.

There are four ways that shares can be acquired by members of a SIP:

(a) **Free shares** can be given up to £3,600 per year to each employee.

(b) The employee can purchase **partnership shares** at any time in the year. The amount to be paid is deducted from the employee's pre-tax salary up to the lower of £1,800 and 10% of salary in any tax year.

(c) The employer can also award **matching shares** free to employees who purchase partnership shares at a maximum ratio of 2:1.

(d) Dividends on the shares in the SIP are tax free if the dividends are used to acquire more shares.

Essential reading

See Chapter 4 of the Essential reading for more detail on the ways shares can be acquired and features of a SIP.

The Essential reading is available as an Appendix of the digital edition of the Workbook.

The income tax treatment depends on how long the shares are kept in the SIP and then there will be capital gains tax to consider when the individual eventually sells the shares. For free and matching shares the tax treatment is outlined below:

- There is **no income tax (IT) or national insurance (NIC)** when the shares are **given to the employees** (and put into the SIP).
- If the shares are held in the **SIP >5 years**:
  - There is **no IT or NIC when the shares are taken out of the plan.**
- If the shares are held in the **SIP 3–5 years**:
  - There is an **IT and NIC charge** based on the **lower** of the **market value at award** and **market value at withdrawal.**
- If the shares are held in the **SIP <3 years**:
  - There is an **IT and NIC charge** based on the **market value at withdrawal**.
- There is **no charge to CGT on shares taken out of the plan and sold immediately**. A charge to CGT will arise on sale to the extent the shares increase in value after they are withdrawn from the plan.

Activity 4: Share options

Fred is granted options over 10,000 shares on XYZ plc at a price of £1.50, their current market value. They are exercisable in six years' time when the market value of the shares is expected to be £4. Fred will then dispose of the shares after a further two years, for their new market price of £5.50.

Required

Show the tax implications if the scheme is either advantaged or non-advantaged.

Solution

Exam focus point

Share schemes are frequently examined in ATX and you must ensure that you understand, and can apply to particular scenarios, the tax rules for both non tax-advantaged and tax-advantaged share schemes. You must also be able to recommend the most suitable type of tax-advantaged share schemes for a particular company.

Chapter summary

Employment income

Employment income

Employment income	£
Salary	X
Bonus	X
Benefits	X
	X
Allowable deductions	(X)
Employment income	X

When are earnings received

Earlier of time of payment and time become entitled to payment

Employment or self-employment

- Employment – contract of service
- Self-employment – contract for services

Taxable benefits

- Pro rate for part availability
- Deduct employee contribution (except fuel)
- Accommodation benefit
  - Greater of (1) annual value and (2) Rent paid by employer
  - Additional charge = % × (cost – £75,000) if cost > £75,000
  - Exempt if job related accommodation (customary, necessary, security)
- Use of asset – 20% × MV of asset
- Gift of asset
  - Greater of (1) MV at gift and (2) MV at acquisition less benefit already taxed
- Beneficial loans
  - Interest at ORI less interest actually paid
  - Only if loans > £10,000
- Medical insurance – cost of providing
- Use of car
  - CO_2 % × list price of car
  - Add 4% if diesel not meeting RDE2 standard, max % 37%
- Private fuel – £24,500 × CO_2% (no deduction for partial reimbursement)
- Van £3,490 (Private fuel £666)
- Remember exempt benefits

Allowable deductions

- Workplace pension scheme contributions
- Fees and subscriptions to professional bodies
- Statutory mileage deductions
- Qualifying travel expenses
- Payroll deduction scheme
- Other expenses wholly, exclusively and necessarily incurred in performance of duties

National insurance contributions

- Class 1 employee
  - Cash earnings over £9,500
  - 12%: £9,500–£50,000
  - 2%: >£50,000
- Class 1 employer
  - Cash earnings over £8,788
  - 13.8%: >£8,788 (No UEL)
  - Employment allowance max £4,000
  - No employment allowance if:
    (1) company has only one director employee; or
    (2) employer's contributions are £100,000 or more for previous tax year
- Class 1A
  - Paid by employer
  - 13.8% × benefits

Personal service companies

- Apply where individual would be employee of Top Co but for the intermediary (use employed vs self-employed rules to determine)
- Treat payments from Top Co to Intermediary (relevant engagements) as deemed salary to extent income is not actually paid as salary.

	£
Income from relevant engagements	X
Less statutory 5% deduction	(X)
	X
Less salary/benefits paid to worker	(X)
Less employer's NIC on actual payments	(X)
Less expenses allowable under employment income	(X)
Gross amount of deemed payment	G
Employer's NIC on gross deemed payment	
Note that the employment allowance (if available) cannot be used to reduce the employer's NIC on this deemed payment.	(X)
Actual deemed payment to worker	X

Termination payments

- Exempt
  - For death, injury and disability
  - Approved lump sum on retirement
- Taxable (IT and Class 1 NICs)
  - Reward for past/future services
  - PILONs (contractual or reasonable expectation)
  - PENP
- Partially taxable
  - Genuine compensation for loss of office (non-contractual and no expectation)
  - Statutory redundancy pay
  - Continued provision of benefits
  - Non-PENP
  - First £30,000 exempt (IT and NIC), excess taxable (IT as top slice and Class 1A NICs only)
- Payments in respect of notice period
  - If work notice – IT and Class 1 NIC
  - Gardening leave – IT and Class 1 NIC
  - Terminate during notice period with payment
    ◦ PENP taxed IT and Class 1 NIC
    ◦ Non-PENP subject to £30,000 exemption rules

Share schemes

- Save as you earn (SAYE)
  - All employees
  - £5 min/£500 max per month
  - Max discount at grant = 20% of MV of shares
  - 3 or 5 year contributions
  - No IT on grant or exercise
  - CGT on sale
- Company share option plan (CSOP)
  - Selected employees
  - No discount at grant of option
  - Value of shares over which employee holds options = max £30,000
  - Exercisable between 3 and 10 years from grant
  - No IT on grant or exercise
  - CGT on sale
- Enterprise management incentives (EMI)
  - Key employees (must be full time: 25 hours per week and < 30% if own shares)
  - Company has gross assets ≤ £30 million and < 250 full time equivalent employees
  - Max £250,000 options per employee (max £3m in total)
  - No IT on grant
  - No IT on exercise unless issued at discount when charged IT on lower of (1) discount and (2) MV at exercise – price paid
  - CGT on sale
- Savings incentive plan (SIP)
  - All employees (full/part time)
  - Free shares (up to £3,600 pa), partnership shares (up to £1,800), matching shares (max 2:1) and dividend shares
  - Held for >5 years: no IT/NIC
  - Held 3–5 years: IT/NIC on lower of value at award or value at withdrawal
  - Held <3 years: IT/NIC on value at withdrawal

Knowledge diagnostic

1. Employment income

General earnings are taxed in the year of receipt. Money earnings are generally received on the earlier of the time payment is made and the time entitlement to payment arises. Non-money earnings are generally received when provided.

Employment involves a contract of services whereas self-employment involves a contract for services.

Employees are taxed on benefits under the benefits code. The amount of a taxable benefit is reduced by any amount paid by the employee to the employer (except private fuel) by 6 July following the end of the tax year.

The benefit in respect of accommodation is its annual value. There is an additional benefit if the property cost the employer more than £75,000.

Employees who have a company car are taxed on a % of the car's list price which depends on the car's CO_2 emissions. The same % multiplied by £24,500 determines the benefit where private fuel is also provided. Statutory approved mileage allowances can be paid tax free to employees who use their own vehicle for business journeys.

Taxable cheap loans are charged to tax on the difference between the official rate of interest and any interest paid by the employee.

20% of the value of assets made available for private use is taxable.

Workplace childcare is an exempt benefit.

There is a residual charge for other benefits, usually equal to the cost of the benefits.

Some benefits are exempt from tax such as removal expenses and the provision of sporting facilities (subject to certain limits).

To be deductible, expenses must be for qualifying travel or wholly, exclusively and necessarily incurred.

2. National Insurance contribution

National Insurance contributions are divided into four classes.

Employees pay employee's class 1 NICs. Employees pay the main employee's rate between the employee's threshold and upper earnings limit and the additional rate on earnings above the upper earnings limit. Employers pay employer's Class 1 NICs above the employer's threshold. For employers there is no upper earnings limit.

NICs are based on earnings periods.

The employment allowance enables employers to reduce its total Class 1 employer's contributions by up to £4,000 per tax year.

Employers pay Class 1A NIC on most taxable benefits.

3. IR35/Personal service companies

The IR35 provisions prevent avoidance of tax by providing services through a company.

IR35 treats any payments from relevant engagements to be taxed as a deemed salary to the extent they've not actually been paid as a salary and IR35 applies if, in substance, the individual is an employee.

4. Termination payments

Payments made on the termination of employment may be fully taxable, partially exempt or exempt.

5. Share options

Where shares or share options are provided to an employee, income tax and/or national insurance contributions may be payable.

BPP
LEARNING
MEDIA

There are a range of tax-advantaged share schemes under which an employer may be able to give employees a stake in the business.

A Save As You Earn (SAYE) share option scheme allows employees to save regular monthly amounts for a fixed period and use the funds to take up options to buy shares free of income tax and NIC. Alternatively they can simply take the cash saved.

There is no income tax or NIC on the grant of a company share option plan (CSOP) option. There is also no income tax or NIC on an exercise taking place between three and ten years after the grant. Only CGT will apply to the profit on disposal of the shares.

No income tax or NIC is chargeable on either the grant or exercise of options under the enterprise management incentive (EMI) scheme provided the exercise takes place within 10 years of the grant and the exercise prices is at least equal to the market value of the shares at the date of grant.

Employees may be given £3,600 of free shares a year under a share incentive plan (SIP). In addition, they can purchase up to £1,800 worth of partnership shares a year and employers can provide up to £3,600 worth of matching shares. Once the shares have been held for five years there is no income tax or NIC when shares are taken out of the plan.

Further study guidance

Question practice

Now try the following from the Further question practice bank (available in the digital edition of the Workbook):

- Taker
- Poster plc
- Envirotech plc

Activity answers

Activity 1: Personal service company

The answer can either be calculated by comparing Alan's annual income as an employee of Farringdon Ltd and as an employee of Alan Ltd and then comparing the two figures or by producing a marginal calculation looking at how Alan's income and tax changes. Both options are shown below.

Two computations:

	Employee of Farringdon Ltd	IR35 (Employee of Alan Ltd)
Salary	70,000	52,000
Dividend		18,000
Less income tax (W1), (W3)	(15,500)	(15,782)
Less employee's NIC (W2), (W5)	(5,260)	(5,274)
Net income	49,240	48,944

Alan's net income is £296 lower if he becomes an employee of Alan Ltd (IR35 applies) (£49,240–48,944).

Workings

1 **Alan's income tax if he remains an employee of Farringdon Ltd**

	£
Salary	70,000
Less personal allowance	(12,500)
Taxable income	57,500
NSI: £37,500 × 20%	7,500
£20,000 × 40%	8,000
Income tax due	15,500

2 **Alan's employee's NIC if he remains an employee of Farringdon Ltd**

	£
(£50,000 − £9,500) × 12%	4,860
(£70,000 − £50,000) × 2%	400
Employee's NIC	5,260

3 **Alan's income tax if employed by Alan Ltd and IR35 applies**

	£
Salary (£52,000 + £18,706) (W4)	70,706
Less personal allowance	(12,500)
Taxable income	58,206
NSI: £37,500 × 20%	7,500

	£
£20,706 × 40%	8,282
Income tax due	15,782

4 Calculation of deemed salary if IR35 applies

	£
Income from relevant engagements	85,000
Less 5% statutory deduction	(4,250)
Less travel expenses	(1,500)
Less salary	(52,000)
Less employer's NIC on actual salary (£52,000 − £8,788) × 13.8%)	(5,963)
(no employment allowance as Alan is sole employee of company)	
	21,287
Less employers' NIC on deemed payment 13.8%/113.8% × £21,287	(2,581)
Deemed employment income	18,706

5 Alan's employee's NIC if IR35 applies

	£
(£50,000 − £9,500) × 12%	4,860
(£70,706 − £50,000) × 2%	414
Employee's NIC	5,274

A marginal calculation:

Effect on Alan's income if he works for Alan Ltd instead of Farringdon Ltd

	£
Reduction in salary (£70,000 − £52,000)	(18,000)
Add:	
IT on salary not payable (40% × £18,000)	7,200
NIC on salary not payable (2% × £18,000)	360
Additional dividend receivable	18,000
Less:	
Tax on dividend (Note)	0
Tax on deemed employment income (W)	(7,482)
NIC on deemed employment income (W)	(374)
Net decrease in Alan's annual income	(296)

6 Deemed employment income

	£
Income from relevant engagements	85,000
Less 5% statutory deduction	(4,250)

	£
Less travel expenses	(1,500)
Less salary	(52,000)
Less employer's NIC on actual salary (£52,000 – £8,788) × 13.8%)	(5,963)
(no employment allowance as Alan is sole employee of company)	
	-
	21,287
Less employers' NIC on deemed payment 13.8%/113.8% × £21,287	(2,581)
Deemed employment income	18,706
Income tax on deemed employment income 40% × £18,706	7,482
NIC on deemed employment income 2% × £18,706	374

Note. Because Alan is treated as receiving deemed employment income from the company the dividend received from the company is not also subject to income tax.

You would not need to prepare both types of calculation in your examination. The two alternative methods have been shown here to show you different ways you could approach this type of question. The two calculation approach is certainly easier to follow however it is more time consuming. The marginal approach is more time efficient however you would need to be careful not to make numerical mistakes.

Activity 2: Termination payment

	Taxable in full	First £30,000 tax free
Payment for working notice 2/12 × 30,000	5,000	
Lump sum (34,500 + (30,000 -1,300))		5,800
	5,000	5,800

The £5,000 for working Ban's notice will be taxable as normal employment income. It will be subject to income tax and Class 1 employer and employee NICs.

The first £28,700 of the £34,500 non-contractual non-expected goodwill payment will be received free of income tax and NIC (the statutory redundancy pay uses up £1,300 of the £30,000 exemption). The excess of £5,800 will be chargeable to income tax as Ban's top slice of income (non-savings rates) and will be liable to Class 1A NICs only.

Activity 3: PENP

The PENP of £18,000 (3/12 × £72,000) will be subject to income tax and class 1 employee NIC on Piotr and Class 1 employer NIC on Apple Ltd.

The remaining £14,000 (£32,000-£18,000) is an ex-gratia termination payment qualifying for the £30,000 exemption and so is not subject to income tax or NIC.

Activity 4: Share options

	Non-advantaged	Tax-advantaged
Benefit on exercise:		
MV	4.00	
Cost	(1.50)	
Benefit for one share	2.50	

	Non-advantaged		Tax-advantaged
× 10,000	£25,000		0

Capital gain on disposal:

	Non-advantaged		Tax-advantaged
Proceeds	5.50	Proceeds	5.50
MV (exercise)	(4.00)	Cost	(1.50)
Gain for one share	1.50	Gain for one share	4.00
Total gain (× 10,000)	£15,000	Total gain (× 10,000)	£40,000

5

Property and trust income

Learning objectives

On completion of this chapter, you should be able to:

	Syllabus reference no.
Remember the material studied in Taxation (TX – UK) under 'property and investment income'	A1(a)B4
Understand the income tax position of trust beneficiaries	A1(e)(iii)

Exam context

The computation of income from a UK property business is generally a straightforward matter, but you need to look out for the special areas of lease premiums, furnished holiday lettings and rent a room relief. The rules on finance costs are also highly examinable.

Although you are not required to know how to calculate the income tax liability of trustees, you need to know how the trust income is taxed in a beneficiary's hands.

Chapter overview

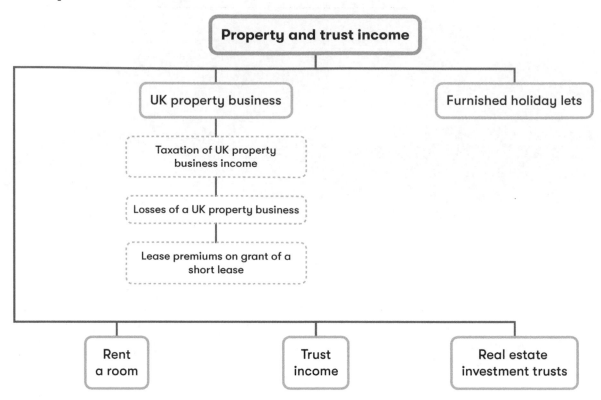

1 Taxation of UK property business profits

1.1 Overview of UK property business profits

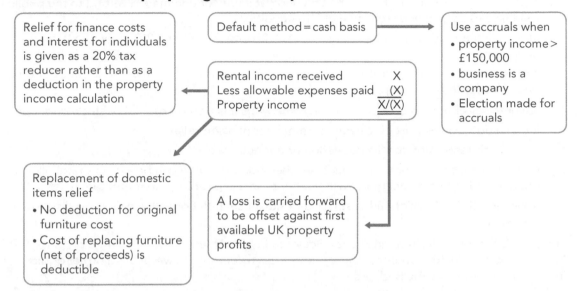

Relief for finance costs and interest for individuals is given as a 20% tax reducer rather than as a deduction in the property income calculation

Default method = cash basis

Use accruals when
- property income > £150,000
- business is a company
- Election made for accruals

Rental income received	X
Less allowable expenses paid	(X)
Property income	X/(X)

Replacement of domestic items relief
- No deduction for original furniture cost
- Cost of replacing furniture (net of proceeds) is deductible

A loss is carried forward to be offset against first available UK property profits

Essential reading

See Chapter 5 of the Essential reading for more detail on property income.

The Essential reading is available as an Appendix of the digital edition of the Workbook.

1.2 Grant of a short lease

A new tenant often pays both annual rental and a one-off premium. If the **lease granted is for less than 50 years, part of the premium** is treated as **rent received in advance** and increases the landlord's property income assessment for the year in which the premium falls due.

The **rental income assessment** is calculated as:

	£
Premium	A
Less 2% × (n – 1) × A	(X)
	X

(n = no. of years on lease)

Where a trader has **paid** a premium for the granting of a short lease he may **deduct the following amount against his trading profit, in addition to any rent paid.**

Amount deductible (per annum) = Amount taxed as rent on landlord / No of years of lease

Essential reading

See Chapter 5 of the Essential reading for more detail on this calculation.

The Essential reading is available as an Appendix of the digital edition of the Workbook.

2 Furnished holiday lets (FHL)

Accommodation counts as a FHL if the following conditions are met:

(a) The accommodation must be **in the EEA** and available for commercial letting to the public for at least **210 days a year (the availability condition).**

(b) The accommodation must be actually let for **105 days** within the 210 days (the letting condition).

(c) The total of all lettings that exceed 31 continuous days must not exceed 155 days during the year (the pattern of occupation condition).

The advantages of having a FHL are that in some ways it is treated as if it is a trade and thus:

(a) Income qualifies as part of **relevant earnings for pension relief.**

(b) There is **no restriction for the deduction of finance costs.**

(c) Capital costs of furniture are deductible when paid (if using cash basis) or capital allowances are available (if using accruals basis) rather than using replacement furniture relief.

(d) **Rollover relief, gift relief and business asset disposal relief** are all available on disposal of the property.

The calculation of profit from an FHL is calculated in the same way as for normal property income, just with the advantages stated above. Loss relief may, however, only be set against income from the same FHL business.

Exam focus point

An explanation as to why a holiday cottage qualified as a FHL was tested in March 2020 Question 4 Pedro. The examining team stated 'most students demonstrated a good knowledge of these rules and applied them correctly to the information given in the question.'

Essential reading

See Chapter 5 of the Essential reading for more detail on the definition of a FHL.

The Essential reading is available as an Appendix of the digital edition of the Workbook.

3 Rent a room

The **first £7,500 pa** collected from a tenant renting a room in a taxpayer's main residence will be tax free.

If the rent received exceeds £7,500, the taxpayer can elect for either the assessment of:

(a) Excess rents over £7,500, but with no deduction for expenses ('alternative' basis); or

(b) Total rents received less the normal rental expenses.

Essential reading

See Chapter 5 of the Essential reading for more detail on rent a room relief including an Activity.

The Essential reading is available as an Appendix of the digital edition of the Workbook.

4 Trust income

A trust is a vehicle in which assets are legally owned by the trustees for the benefit of the beneficiaries.

There are **two types of trust for income tax purposes**:

(a) An **interest in possession trust** (a 'life interest' trust) where the income must be paid out to the beneficiary (often called the life tenant).

(b) A discretionary trust where the income is distributed at the trustees' discretion

Further detail on how these types of trust work will be covered in Chapter 12 of the Workbook. In this Chapter we consider how the income from these trusts will be taxed.

Income from discretionary trusts is received net of 45% tax. Gross it up in the income tax computation by multiplying by 100/55 and give credit for the tax already suffered when working out the final amount of tax payable. Such income is always treated as non-savings income.

If income from an interest in possession trust is paid out of the trust's non-savings income or savings income, it will be received by the beneficiary net of 20% tax and must be grossed up by multiplying by 100/80. If it is paid out of dividend income it **will be received by the beneficiary net of 7.5% tax** and must be grossed up by multiplying by 100/92.5. Each type of income is then taxed on the beneficiary under the normal rules.

> ### Exam focus point
>
> June 2010 Qu 2(iv) Poblano required an explanation of the income tax treatment of trusts. The examining team commented that 'there was the need to be specific and precise, as regards grossing up fractions and tax rates, rather than superficial and general in order to maximise the marks obtained.'

If a **minor beneficiary** receives income from a **trust set up by a parent**, then under the anti-avoidance rules the income is **taxed as the parent's income**. As we saw earlier, there is a £100 *de minimis* limit.

Activity 1: Income from trusts

Victoria received the following income in 2020/21.

	£
Building society interest	7,750
Dividends	4,500
Income from discretionary trust	8,250
Income from life interest trust	2,280

The income from the life interest trust was paid out of the trust's property business income.

Required

What income tax is repayable to Victoria?

Solution

Exam focus point

Although you need to know the rate of tax deducted from income distributions from trusts, you do not need to know how to calculate the trustees' income tax liability.

---

5 Real estate investment trusts (REITs)

Property companies may operate as **real estate investment trusts** (REITs).

REITs can **elect for their property income (and gains) to be exempt from corporation tax** and must withhold basic rate (20%) tax from distributions paid to shareholders (who cannot own more than 10% of a REIT's shares) out of these profits. These **distributions are taxed as property income, not as dividends.**

Distributions by REITs out of other income (ie not property income or gains) are taxed as dividends in the normal way.

Chapter summary

Property and trust income

UK property business

Taxation of UK property business income
- Cash basis is default calculation (unless property receipts >£150,000/business is carried on by a company/election made for accruals basis)
- Deductions
  - Incidental expenses
  - Replacement furniture relief available
- Finance cost restriction
  - Individuals only
  - Does not apply to FHL/commercial lets
  - Receive a tax reducer at 20%

Losses of a UK property business
C/f against first future profits of UK property business

Lease premiums on grant of a short lease
- On grant of a short (≤50 year) lease some of the premium is taxed on the landlord as rent in advance

	£
Premium	A
less 2% × (n–1) × A	(X)
	X

  n = no. of yrs of lease
- Trader gets deduction for amount taxed as rent spread over lease term

Furnished holiday lets
- Commercial let in EEA
- Available for 210 days pa
- Actually let for 105 days pa
- Not more than 155 days involve long term occupation (one person stays > 31 days)
- Relevant earnings for pensions
- No restriction on deduction of finance costs
- Capital costs of furniture deductible when paid (if using cash basis) or capital allowances (if accruals) rather than replacement furniture relief
- CGT reliefs (rollover, gift and business asset disposal) available

Rent a room
- Exempt if gross rents ≤£7,500.
- If gross rents >£7,500 taxed on:
  - Normal property income; or
  - Rent in excess of £7,500 (no deduction for expenses) (Alternative basis by election)

Trust income
- Income from discretionary trust is received net of 45% and is treated as non-savings income
- Income from interest in possession trusts is paid net of 20% (if paid out of trust's non-savings/savings income) and net of 7.5% (if paid out of trust's dividend income)

Real estate investment trusts
Any distribution paid by a REIT out of property income is paid net of 20% tax and is treated as property income rather than dividend income

Knowledge diagnostic

1. Taxation of UK property business income

Income from a UK property business is non-savings income.

Property business income is computed for tax years usually on a cash basis. There is a special rule about finance costs for individuals.

If a residential property is furnished, replacement of domestic items relief can be claimed.

A loss on a UK property business is carried forward to set against future profits from the UK property business.

Part of the premium received on the grant of a short lease it taxed as rent.

2. Furnished holiday lets

Special rules apply to income from furnished holiday lettings. Whilst the income is taxed as normal as property business income, the letting is treated as if it were a trade. Finance costs are not restricted, capital expenses or capital allowances are available on the furniture and the income is relevant earnings for pension purposes. However, only carry forward loss relief is available.

3. Rent a room

Up to £7,500 of gross rents received from letting a room or rooms in a main residence are tax free. If gross rents exceed £7,500, the taxpayer can elect to deduct £7,500 from the rents received instead of actual expenses.

4. Trust income

Income from trusts must be grossed up by either 100/55 (discretionary trusts) or 100/80 or 100/92.5 (interest in possession trusts).

5. REIT income

A distribution from the property income (and gains) of a REIT is grossed up by 100/80 and taxed as property income, rather than dividends. Distributions of other income are taxed as dividends in the normal way.

Further study guidance

Question practice

Now try the following from the Further question practice bank (available in the digital edition of the Workbook):

- Hamburg

Activity answers

Activity 1: Income from trusts

	Non-savings income £	Savings income £	Dividend income £	Total £
Building society interest		7,750		
Dividends			4,500	
Income from discretionary trust (× 100/55)	15,000			
Income from life interest trust (× 100/80)	2,850	–	–	
Net income	17,850	7,750	4,500	30,100
Less personal allowance	(12,500)	–	–	
Taxable income	5,350	7,750	4,500	17,600

	£
Tax on non-savings income	
£5,350 × 20%	1,070
Tax on savings income	
£1,000 × 0%	0
£6,750 (7,750 – 1,000) × 20%	1,350
Tax on dividend income	
£2,000 × 0%	0
£2,500 (4,500 – 2,000) × 7.5%	187
Income tax liability	2,607
Less: Discretionary trust tax credit	(6,750)
Life interest trust tax credit	(570)
Income tax repayable	(4,713)

6

Personal tax planning

Learning objectives

On completion of this chapter, you should be able to:

	Syllabus reference no.
Identify and advise on the taxes applicable to a given course of action and their impact	B1
Identify and understand that the alternative ways of achieving personal or business outcomes may lead to different tax consequences	B2
Advise how taxation can affect the financial decisions made by businesses (corporate and unincorporated) and individuals	B3
Assess the tax advantages and disadvantages of alternative courses of action	B4
Identify and advise on the types of investment and other expenditure that will result in a reduction in tax liabilities for an individual and/or a business	C1
Advise on legitimate tax planning measures by which the tax liabilities arising from a particular situation or course of action can be mitigated	C2
Advise on the appropriateness of such investment, expenditure or measures given a particular taxpayer's circumstances or stated objectives	C3
Advise on the mitigation of tax in the manner recommended by reference to numerical analysis and/or reasoned argument	C4
Be aware of and give advice on current issues in taxation	C6

Communicate advice, recommendations and information in the required format. For example, the use of:
  – Reports   – Memoranda
  – Letters   – Meeting notes
	D1

Present written information, in language appropriate to the purpose of the communication and the intended recipient	D2
Communicate conclusions reached, together where necessary with relevant supporting computations	D3

	Syllabus reference no.
State and explain assumptions made or limitations in the analysis provided, together with any inadequacies in the information available and/or additional information required to provide a fuller analysis	D4
Identify and explain other, non-tax, factors that should be considered	D5

Exam context

Many scenarios you will see in exam questions will contain aspects of personal tax planning. In this chapter we consider some common scenarios and look at techniques for how we might address them and how to present our answers in a clear way so as to maximise marks.

Chapter overview

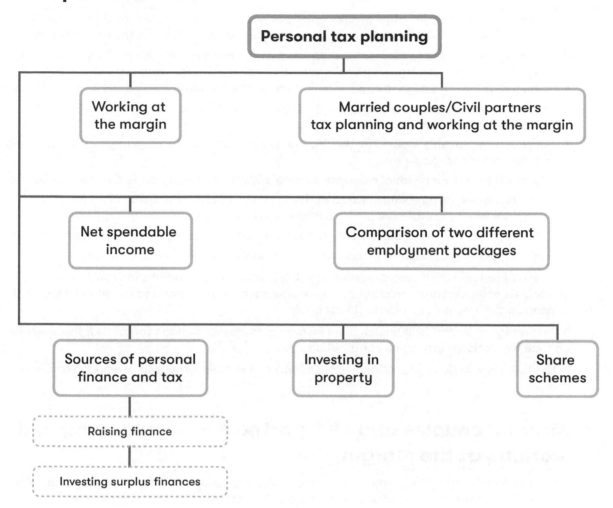

1 Working at the margin

Scenarios in your exam will often involve looking at how a course of action might change an individual's taxable income and require you to consider how this changes their tax position.

It is much quicker in this type of question to '**work at the margin**'. This means that rather than preparing two full income tax computations for the individual before and after the change, we **simply look at the change in the individual's income and calculate the difference to their tax bill**.

In order to determine the individual's marginal tax rate, and hence the rate at which their tax liability will change, we must consider:

- Their **existing taxable income** to identify whether the individual is currently a basic, higher or additional-rate taxpayer
- The **change in the individual's taxable income** and how this will change their income tax due.
  - (i) Is the new income simply taxed at the same marginal rate of tax or does it mean the individual's taxable income is pushed into a higher rate tax band?
  - (ii) Could the new income utilise previously unused savings or dividend nil rate bands?
  - (iii) Could the new income mean that the personal allowance becomes abated?

The idea of working at the margin and preparing one marginal computation rather than two full income tax computations can often be a vital **time saver** in the exam and is a **really important concept** which you will see time and time again.

If the change in income is in employment income or trade profits **don't forget** that this will also **change the national insurance contributions** due.

In the following sections you will see Activities which incorporate the idea of working at the margin.

2 Married couples and civil partners – tax planning and working at the margin

It is very common for us to see married couples/civil partnerships (CPs) in exam questions. We know that each person is taxed as a separate individual entitled to their own personal allowance and savings and dividend nil rate bands. A question may ask us to consider **how income-generating assets** (such as shares or rental properties) **should be divided between a couple in order to generate the lowest combined tax bill**.

In order to minimise a couple's overall tax liability we shall need to consider:

- Each individual's level of taxable income to **determine their marginal rate of tax**
- The **type of income** we are considering. For example, if an individual already fully utilises their savings nil rate band then this will make a difference to the additional tax if they are to receive more savings income
- Whether one member of the couple is not using their personal allowance whilst the other member is a basic rate tax payer. At this point we can consider **the transferable personal allowance.**

Consideration of **which partner should own any income-generating assets** can be useful in **minimising combined tax liabilities**.

For example, shares can be transferred between partners to provide each one with different levels of dividend income. This can be used to ensure both partners utilise their dividend nil rate band, and any extra dividends are taxed at the lowest marginal rate.

For other assets, such as rental properties, there is an automatic assumption that the property income is split 50:50 between the couple. However, an election can be made specifying the actual proportion to which each is entitled. Again, this can be used to ensure the rental income is taxed on the partner with the lower marginal rate.

Any transfer of assets between spouses/CPs will be at nil gain nil loss for capital gains purposes and exempt for IHT. (These aspects are considered later in the Workbook in the Capital taxes chapters.)

Activity 1: Minimising a married couple's tax due

Petri and Jane are a married couple with the following income during 2020/21:

	Petri	Jane
	£	£
Annual income		
Employment income	150,000	15,000
Bank interest (within ISA)	1,000	800
Dividends (within ISA)	2,200	1,800

Petri recently inherited £300,000 following the death of his father. He plans to invest £200,000 of this in UK shares earning a 4% yield per annum and the remaining £100,000 will be left on a cash deposit earning a 1% yield per annum.

A friend has suggested that Petri should alter his plans to reduce his family's income tax liability. He says Petri should gift Jane £150,000 of his inheritance and that they should each then invest two-thirds of their funds in shares with the remaining third being left on cash deposit.

Required

Calculate the income tax savings which could be achieved in a complete tax year if Petri was to follow his friend's advice and give £150,000 to Jane. In order to do this efficiently, you should just calculate the additional tax payable by Petri and Jane on the income generated by the inherited funds, rather than preparing complete income tax computations.

Solution

3 Net spendable income

Another frequently examined topic is the calculation of **net spendable income** available to an individual. This is often a **calculation for the net spendable income after a proposed course of action or comparing two alternative courses of action.**

The basic approach to follow will be to prepare a **table listing the individual's 'cash in' and 'cash out'** based on the facts in the question. A sample pro-forma is given below. Clearly, one of the important 'cash out' items will be any **tax due** from the individual – this will normally be income tax but it could also include national insurance. Usually it is easier to prepare a **separate working to calculate the tax due and reference it back into this summary table**. Keeping the tax calculation separate to the main spendable income calculation means you are **less likely to confuse which items are cash flows and which are not**. For example, a company car benefit calculation will be required to work out the income tax due for the individual but the value of the car benefit is not an actual cashflow!

An example **pro-forma** for a **net spendable income calculation** is given below and the Activity in the next section will allow you to see a calculation.

	£	£
Cash in:		
Salary	X	
Dividends/ Interest/ Rent received	X	
Other cash in per scenario	X̲	
		X
Cash out:		
Payments made per scenario	(X)	
Income tax (W1)	(X)	
NIC (W2) (if applicable)	(X̲)	
		(X̲)
Net spendable income		X̲

In a variation on this type of requirement you may be told that an individual does not have enough income to carry out a specific course of action. You will then be asked to calculate the additional cash that would be required by the individual to do this. Your approach should be to calculate net spendable income using the proforma above, including the individual's planned expenditure, which will result in a negative figure. This shortfall represents the additional cash that the individual would require to pursue their plans.

4 Comparison of two different employment packages

You may be required to advise an employee who has been offered **two different employment packages** as to which package will give the individual the **highest net spendable income or the least overall tax cost.** You will need to bring together your technical tax knowledge in terms of how the packages will be taxed and also the skill of producing comparative net spendable income/total tax cost calculations.

The following Activity illustrates how this could be tested.

Activity 2: Net spendable income of two employment packages

You should assume that today's date is 1 September 2020.

Arthur is employed by Garner Ltd currently earning a salary of £45,000 per annum. He has been offered sole use of a company car or, alternatively, a loan to enable him to purchase the same motor car himself. Under either option, Arthur will pay all fuel costs of the car himself which will amount to £60 per month.

Company car (Alternative 1)

- Garner Ltd would purchase the newly registered motor car on 1 October 2020 for £9,800, which is £500 less than the list price.

- The motor car would then immediately be made available to Arthur for his exclusive private use.

- The motor car will have CO_2 emissions of 112g/km and is petrol powered.

- Arthur will contribute £50 per month towards the private use of the motor car.

- Garner Ltd would give the motor car to Arthur after three years, when its market value is expected to be £4,000.

Loan (Alternative 2)

- Garner Ltd would provide Arthur with an interest free loan of £9,800 on 1 October 2020.

- The loan would be written off in three years' time.

- Assume Arthur would be able to negotiate the same discount from the list price of the car as Garner Ltd.

Required

Prepare calculations of Arthur's net spendable income for 2020/21 under either option.

Solution

5 Sources of personal finance and tax

5.1 Raising finance

Questions may present a scenario where we are advising an individual on how to **raise finance**. One way we could do this would be to **sell off a capital asset** (such as a rental property or shares) to realise cash. On sale of a capital asset capital gains tax may need to be paid which would reduce the after-tax cash realised for the individual. This is covered in more detail in Chapter 13 on Capital tax planning.

Rather than selling assets, we could also advise our individual to **borrow via a bank overdraft, unsecured bank loan, mortgage, credit card or hire purchase facilities**. All these methods will raise funds but will also generate interest payments.

Tax relief on these types of borrowings will be limited and is generally **only available if** the loan is a **qualifying loan** as covered in Chapter 2 on Income tax computation, for example a loan to invest in a close company or partnership. (Although note that interest relief is not available on a loan to buy shares in a close company if EIS relief is claimed for the investment).

There is also relief available **if the loan is used to purchase a rental property** as covered in Chapter 5 on property income.

5.2 Investing surplus finances

Another exam scenario might be advising a **high net worth individual** with surplus funds looking to invest them in a **tax-efficient manner**.

These could include consideration of:

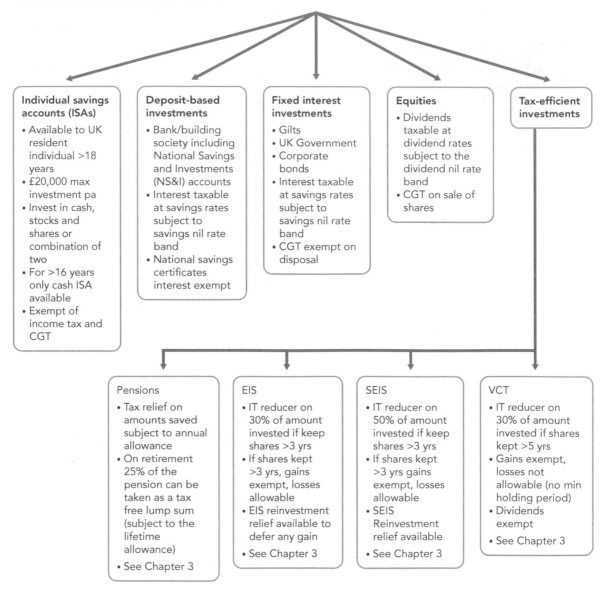

In this type of question you may be required to explain and apply the tax reliefs available on an enterprise investment scheme (EIS)/seed enterprise investment scheme (SEIS) or venture capital trusts (VCTs) investment or contributions into a pension scheme. Remember to always be very specific to the scenario.

You may also be required to:

- Advise a client about a planned sale of an EIS/SEIS or VCT investment, how the sale of the shares would be treated for tax purposes and whether the sale would trigger a claw-back of any income tax relief previously claimed (see the Activity below.)

- Compare and contrast the tax liability of an individual when they are investing in EIS/SEIS or VCT shares. You may be asked to consider two possible investments for their cash and need to understand the differing tax consequences.

To be able to answer these types of questions you will need a **strong knowledge** of the rules on tax-efficient investments as covered in Chapter 3. Your **presentation will also be important**. The examining team often state that students' answers can be poorly laid out, meaning that it is difficult to understand exactly which situation is being explained. This makes it very hard to award marks. The **use of clear headings and sub-headings** will make it easier for the marker to understand which type of scheme you are discussing in your answer. You could also consider a **tabular summary** to compare and contrast the schemes.

Activity 3: Sale of EIS shares on two different dates

Sophie expects to have taxable income in 2020/21 of £75,000 and wishes to sell her ordinary shares in Swinscoe Ltd. She subscribed for 12,000 shares in Swinscoe Ltd for £20,000 on 1 January 2019. On subscription she obtained an EIS tax reducer of £6,000.

She intends to sell all her shares for £10,000 (an arm's length price) on 1 August 2021 and will relieve her loss arising on the shares in the most tax efficient manner.

Each year Sophie realises gains on other disposals in excess of the annual exempt amount.

Required

Explain, with supporting calculations, the tax implications of selling the Swinscoe Ltd shares on 1 August 2021. Explain any advantages and disadvantages for Sophie of delaying the sale.

Solution

With regards to pension questions, scenarios might include:

- Advising a client of the **maximum pension contribution which they could make without triggering an annual allowance charge**
- Calculating a client's **income after tax and pension contributions** (perhaps after making a large pension contribution triggering an annual allowance charge)
- Some **written advice** about pensions and tax planning (see the following Activity).

Activity 4: Reduction in annual allowance

In a recent meeting with a new client, Olive, you discover the following.

Olive has regularly contributed £40,000 (gross) into her personal pension scheme in order to fully use her annual allowance. She is an additional-rate taxpayer for 2020/21 and a recent promotion means that her income levels have risen so as to reduce her annual allowance for 2020/21. This means that she has incurred an annual allowance charge.

Olive's adjusted income (for the purposes of calculating her annual allowance) was £270,000 in 2020/21 and in the previous two years it had been £145,000.

Olive makes regular capital gains in excess of her annual exempt amount each year.

Until now Olive has been investing the maximum amount each year in an individual savings account (ISA). She is now questioning whether there is any point in investing in either a cash or stocks and shares ISA as savings and dividend income are now exempt from tax up to £2,000 per tax year.

Required

Write an email to Olive which explains the reduction in her annual allowance and discusses her thoughts about ISAs.

Solution

6 Investing in property

In other questions you may be asked to give advice about starting to rent out a property. This could be a **straightforward explanation and application of the property income rules** or it could be helping someone to **decide whether or not to let their property out as a furnished holiday let (FHL)**. You could be asked to **explain the conditions to be met for the property to qualify as a FHL** and the **advantages of the property being a FHL**. This type of question would use the knowledge covered in Chapter 5 on Property income. You could also get a more complicated numerical style question looking at a **calculation of the tax saved by qualifying as a FHL**.

In this type of question you would need to:

- Compare the different incomes dependent on whether or not the property is treated as a FHL, and then
- Calculate the marginal tax on the different property incomes, and finally
- Calculate the difference in the tax due.

As we have seen above, working at the margin here rather than preparing full income tax computations would be a great time saver.

Activity 5: FHL

Quentin, a higher-rate taxpayer, currently rents out a property in South West England and anticipates the following income and expenditure during 2021/22:

	£
Rental income	20,000
Repairs and maintenance	1,000
Mortgage interest	8,000
Agent fees	3,000

Quentin also spends £1,000 per year on replacement furniture.

Quentin is currently renting the property out as a long-term rental but is considering changing his arrangements such that the property will qualify as a furnished holiday let in 2021/22.

Required

Calculate the tax Quentin will save in 2021/22 if the property meets the FHL definition rather than a long-term rental. Note that you should assume 2020/21 rates and allowances continue to apply.

Solution

7 Share schemes

Share schemes could be tested in a sub-requirement of one of your questions. These types of requirements could take several forms:

- Recommending the **most suitable form of tax-advantaged share scheme** based on the requirements of the company in the question.
- **Comparing and contrasting two (or more) tax advantaged schemes** in relation to their conditions for approval and/ or their income tax and capital gains tax consequences.
- An **explanation (possibly with supporting calculations) of the tax advantages of a particular tax-advantaged share scheme relative to a non tax-advantaged share scheme**.

- You could be asked to calculate the **net increase in wealth of an individual of selling shares acquired through a share option scheme**. An explanation as to how to handle this type of requirement is given within Skills checkpoint 2 of this Workbook.

You will need to have a thorough knowledge of the conditions relating to each type of advantaged share scheme as set out in Chapter 4 on Employment income. Another key skill will be your ability to apply the knowledge to the specifics of the scenario in answering the question. You should not be reproducing large quantities of knowledge without attempting to apply them to the scenario.

Chapter summary

```
┌─────────────────────────┐
│  Personal tax planning  │
└─────────────────────────┘
```

Working at the margin

- Working at the margin is a short-cut method of looking at how an individual's tax will change due to an action
- Remember to consider all the taxes which might be impacted

Married couples/Civil partners tax planning and working at the margin

- Consider how income generating assets should be split between spouses/civil partners to generate lowest combined tax bill
  - Determine each person's marginal rate of tax
  - Consider type of income – does it impact savings/dividend nil rate bands?
  - Can we use the transferable personal allowance?
- Shares can easily be split between partners but other jointly owned income generating assets the income is split 50/50 unless an election is made to split on actual entitlement
- For CGT purposes the assets pass between spouses at NG/NL and they are usually exempt IHT

Net spendable income

	£	£
Cash in:		
Salary	X	
Dividends/Interest/Rent received	X	
Other cash in per scenario	X	
		X
Cash out:		
Payments made per scenario	(X)	
Income tax (W1)	(X)	
NIC (W2) (if applicable)	(X)	
		(X)
Net spendable income		X

Comparison of two different employment packages

- Be able to compare two different employment packages
- You could consider which gives highest net spendable income or least overall tax cost

Sources of personal finance and tax

Raising finance
- Sale of capital asset
  - Consider CGT due
- Borrow via bank overdraft, unsecured bank loan, mortgage, credit card or hire purchase facilities
  - Tax relief on borrowings limited and only available if a qualifying loan or loan is used to purchase a rental property

Investing surplus finances
- Individual savings accounts (ISAs)
  - >18 years, max £20,000 investment pa
  - Exempt of income tax and CGT
- Deposit-based investments
  - Banks, building societies including NS&I investment accounts
  - Interest taxable at savings rates subject to savings nil rate band
- National savings certificates
  - Interest exempt
- Fixed-interest investments
  - Gilts, UK government, corporate bonds
  - Interest taxable at savings rates subject to savings nil rate band, CGT exempt on disposal
- Equities
  - Dividends taxable at dividend rate subject to dividend nil rate band, CGT on sale of shares
- Tax-efficient investments
  - Pensions – tax relief on amount saved subject to annual allowance
  - EIS – IT reducer, shares exempt if kept >3 years, EIS reinvestment relief
  - SEIS – IT reducer, shares exempt if kept >3 years, SEIS reinvestment relief
  - VCT – IT reducer, shares exempt, dividends exempt

Investing in property
- Be able to explain and apply the property income rules
- Understand when a property is a FHL and what the tax advantages are of having a FHL

Share schemes
- Be able to recommend the most suitable form of tax-advantaged share scheme
- Be able to compare two (or more) tax advantaged schemes
- Be able to explain (with supporting calculations) the tax advantages of a particular tax-advantaged share scheme
- Be able to calculate the net increase in wealth of an individual of selling shares acquired through a share option scheme

Knowledge diagnostic

1. Working at the margin

'Working at the margin' can often be a useful time saver in the exam. Rather than preparing two full tax computations and calculating the difference in the tax we look at the change in taxable income between the two alternatives and then how this changes the tax due.

2. Married couples and civil partners tax planning

Planning to minimise a couple's combined tax liability will require consideration of which member of the couple should hold income-generating assets. Consideration should be given to the existing taxable income (and components thereof) of each person so that the marginal tax rate of the income can be determined and the income allocated to the person with the lower marginal tax rate. Don't forget to consider the nil rate bands available and whether there may be any transferable personal allowance.

3. Net spendable income

In calculating an individual's net spendable income we prepare a table summarising 'cash in' and 'cash out'. Don't forget that the tax due will represent important cash outflows. Try to keep the cash flows separate from the tax calculations to avoid confusing cash and non-cash items such as taxable benefits.

4. Comparison of employment packages

When comparing two different employment packages you should 'work at the margin' to consider how the package changes the individual's taxable income in order to save time.

5. Raising finance

If an individual needs to raise funds they could consider selling a capital asset (giving capital gains tax considerations) or they could borrow. Interest payments do not usually qualify for any tax relief unless they are either qualifying loan interest payments or qualify for the property finance costs tax reducer.

6. High net worth

When advising a high net worth individual, consideration should be given to tax-efficient investments such as pension contributions or buying shares through the EIS, SEIS or VCT schemes. Make sure your technical knowledge is strong enough that you can apply it to the scenario.

A high net worth individual could also invest in a rental property and advice may be required as to how this income will be taxed or whether a property meets the conditions to qualify as a furnished holiday let.

7. Suitable schemes

Make sure you can recommend a suitable share scheme for a company. You will need to know the conditions required for the scheme to be tax advantaged, and the resulting tax. It will be important that you apply your knowledge to the scenario.

8. Presentation

Finally, your presentation in these types of questions will be vital in maximising your marks. Make sure you use headings and sub-headings to make it clear which part of the requirement you are answering.

Further study guidance

Question practice

Now try the following from the Further question practice bank (available in the digital edition of the Workbook):

- Landscape Ltd (although at present the material about close companies, needed for part (c), has not yet been covered so this part should not be attempted).

Activity answers

Activity 1: Minimising a married couple's tax due

If Petri invests the whole £300,000

Petri has taxable income of £150,000 and therefore any extra income will be taxed at the additional rate.

Dividend £200,000 × 4% = £8,000	
Tax on dividend income	
(£8,000 − £2,000) × 38.1%	
(dividend nil rate band)	2,286
Interest £100,000 × 1% = £1,000	
Tax on interest income	
£1,000 × 45% (no savings nil rate band as additional-rate taxpayer)	<u>450</u>
Total tax due	2,736

If Petri gifts Jane £150,000, and they each invest

They will each earn dividends of £4,000 (£150,000 × 2/3 × 4%)

They will each earn interest of £500 (£150,000 × 1/3 × 1%)

Petri's tax due on his £150,000 investment

Tax on dividend income	
(£4,000 − £2,000) × 38.1%	
(dividend nil rate band)	762
Tax on interest income	
£500 × 45% (no savings nil rate band as additional-rate taxpayer)	<u>225</u>
Petri's total tax due	987

Jane's tax due on her £150,000 investment

Jane has taxable income of £15,000 minus the personal allowance and therefore has plenty of the basic-rate band remaining

Tax on dividend income	
(£4,000 − £2,000) × 7.5%	
(dividend nil rate band and then basic-rate taxpayer)	150
Tax on interest income	
£500 × 0% (savings nil rate band £1,000 as basic-rate taxpayer)	<u>0</u>
Jane's total tax due	150

Tax saving through following the friend's advice

Tax due if Petri invests the whole £300,000	2,736
Tax due if each invests £150,000	
(£987 + £150)	<u>(1,137)</u>
Total tax saved by friend's advice	1,599

Note. The interest and dividends in respect of funds held in ISAs are exempt from income tax. Accordingly, they do not reduce the available savings income nil rate band or dividend nil rate band.

Activity 2: Net spendable income of two employment packages

Arthur's net spendable income

	Alternative 1 (car)	Alternative 2 (loan)
	£	£
Salary	45,000	45,000
Receipt of loan		9,800
Purchase of car		(9,800)
Payment for private use of car (£50 x 6)	(300)	
Fuel payment (£60 × 6)	(360)	(360)
Income tax (W1)(W2)	(6,698)	(6,500)
Employee's NIC (W3)	(4,260)	(4,260)
Net spendable income	33,382	33,880

Arthur should accept the loan (alternative 2) if he wishes to maximise his 2020/21 net spendable income.

Note that this does not take into account the whole three-year period of the loan/car provision and does not consider the future tax consequences of gift of the company car/write-off of the loan.

Workings

1   **Arthur's income tax due with the company car**

Car CO_2% = 14 % + (110 − 55)/5

= 25%

List price of car = £9,800 + £500

= £10,300

Car benefit = (25% × £10,300) × 6/12 − (£50 × 6)

= £1,288 − £300

= £988

Salary	45,000
Car benefit	988
Net income	45,988
Less: Personal allowance	(12,500)
Taxable income	33,488
Income tax	
£33,488 × 20%	6,698

2   **Arthur's income tax with the tax free loan**

As the interest-free loan never exceeds £10,000 it is an exempt benefit and Arthur is simply taxed on his salary less the personal allowance at 20%.

Income tax   = (£45,000 − £12,500) × 20%

= £6,500

3 **NICs**

In both situations NIC will only be due on Arthur's cash earnings of £45,000. (The car benefit is not cash earnings and the loan is not a taxable benefit.)

Class 1 employee NIC = (£45,000 − £9,500) × 12%

= £4,260

Activity 3: Sale of EIS shares on two different dates

A sale on 1 August 2021 will result in a withdrawal of EIS income tax relief as the shares will have been held for less than three years.

The IT relief withdrawn = 30% × proceeds

= 30% × £10,000

= £3,000

There will also be a capital loss on the disposal of the shares. However, when calculating the loss, the allowable cost of the shares will be reduced by the net EIS relief obtained.

	£
Proceeds	10,000
Less cost £(20,000 − (6,000 − 3,000))	(17,000)
Allowable capital loss	(7,000)

Sophie can relieve this capital loss against her general income of 2021/22 and/or 2020/21 because the shares qualified for EIS relief. This would be advantageous for Sophie as she is a higher-rate taxpayer and so will save income tax at 40% rather than capital gains tax at 20%.

Delaying the sale

If the sale was delayed until after 1 January 2022 there would be no withdrawal of the IT relief as Sophie would have held her shares for three years. This would save the £3,000 of IT relief which would now not be withdrawn.

However, the capital loss available would be reduced as the EIS relief would not have been withdrawn.

	£
Proceeds	10,000
Less cost £(20,000 − 6,000)	(14,000)
Allowable capital loss	(4,000)

Sophie would therefore have a £3,000 smaller capital loss which, as explained above, could have saved her 40% tax thus she will lose £1,200 of tax savings.

Her net tax saving is thus £1,800 (£3,000 − £1,200) by choosing to delay the sale until after 1 January 2022.

Activity 4: Reduction in annual allowance

Response as follows:

To:	Olive@business.co.uk
From:	ANAccountant@accountancybusiness.co.uk
Date:	Today
Subject:	Your pension contributions and Advice on ISAs
Dear Olive	

Further to our meeting I would like to set out an explanation of how and why your annual allowance has been reduced for 2020/21 and to provide you with some further information about ISAs to assist you in your investment choices.

Your 2020/21 Annual Allowance

While the annual allowance remains £40,000 per tax year there are rules which mean that higher earning taxpayers will have their annual allowance abated/reduced. Due to your recent promotion, this is what has happened to you during 2020/21.

The abatement of the annual allowance applies where an individual's adjusted income exceeds £240,000. Given that in the past two years your adjusted income has been £145,000 this has not impacted you. However, your 2020/21 adjusted income of £270,000 exceeds this limit and thus the reduction has taken effect.

The reduction is £1 for every £2 of income in excess of £240,000. Thus, your £270,000 adjusted income will have reduced your annual allowance by £15,000 (½ × (£270,000-£240,000)). This means that your annual allowance for 2020/21 will be £25,000.

Given your gross contribution of £40,000 exceeds this reduced annual allowance this has triggered the annual allowance charge.

ISAs

Your thoughts on ISAs are only partially correct.

The first £2,000 of dividend income is exempt from income tax each year, but any dividends in excess of this will be taxed at your marginal rate of tax which, as you're an additional-rate taxpayer, will be 38.1%. The £2,000 exemption can be referred to as the dividend nil rate band.

If you are considering investing in stocks and shares, you need to consider your current and future level of dividends. If these exceed your £2,000 nil rate band then a stocks and shares ISA, under which all dividends are exempt from income tax, is still worthwhile.

You should also remember that the disposal of investments within a stocks and shares ISA is also exempt from capital gains tax. This will be particularly relevant to you if you continue to use your annual exempt amount on other disposals.

Your comments about savings income are incorrect. As an additional rate tax payer, you are not entitled to any savings income nil rate band so all your savings income will be taxable. (The savings income nil rate band is also £1,000 for a basic rate tax payer and £500 for a higher rate tax payer not £2,000- this is the dividend nil rate band). Thus, holding your cash deposits in a cash ISA will still be beneficial to you as the income from these will be exempt.

I trust that this gives you all the information that you need. Please do not hesitate to let me know if I can be of further assistance,

Regards

A N Accountant.

Activity 5: FHL

Property income as normal long-term let

	£
Rental income	20,000
Allowable expenses:	
Repairs and maintenance	(1,000)
Agent fees	(3,000)
Replacement furniture relief	(1,000)
Property income	15,000

	£
Tax on property income	
£15,000 × 40%	6,000
Less finance cost reducer:	
£8,000 × 20%	(1,600)
Net tax on property income	4,400

Property income if FHL

	£
Rental income	20,000
Allowable expenses:	
Repairs and maintenance	(1,000)
Mortgage interest (no restriction)	(8,000)
Agent fees	(3,000)
New furniture	(1,000)
Property income	7,000
Tax on property income:	
£7,000 × 40%	2,800

Therefore, the tax saved by the property meeting the FHL conditions is £1,600 (£4,400 – £2,800).

Skills checkpoint 2
Personal tax advice

Chapter overview

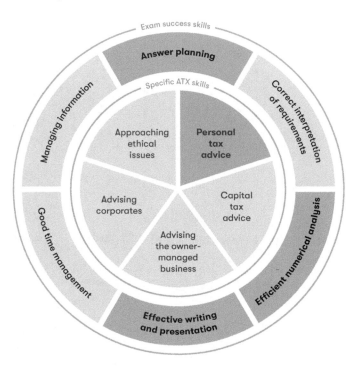

Introduction

Personal tax advice is a fundamental part of the ATX exam.

In the Personal tax planning chapter, we have considered some of the types of personal tax planning scenarios that we could see in the exam and in this skills checkpoint we consider both the exam success skills and the specific ATX skills on personal tax advice that we shall need to be successful in the exam.

It is important that we use our exam technique skills to successfully interpret the requirement and answer the question.

It is important that you refresh your memory using the **technical knowledge** presented in this Workbook before you attempt more exam standard questions.

Skills checkpoint 2: Personal tax advice

ATX Personal tax advice

The key steps in applying this skill are outlined below. They will be explained in more detail in the following sections, and illustrated by answering requirements from a past exam question.

STEP 1 Look at the mark allocation and calculate the amount of time available for the question.

STEP 2 Read the requirements and analyse them.

STEP 3 Read the scenario and highlight and/or make notes of the information that will enable you to answer the requirements.

STEP 4 Then make a plan of the points that you need to cover in your answer, including what supporting calculations you will need to do. Use key words from the requirements as headings.

STEP 5 Write up your answer using key words from the requirements as headings.

Exam success skills

The following illustration is based on a 12-mark extract from an exam question, Damiana, which appeared in the Sep/Dec 2017 sample questions.

- **Answer planning: priorities, structure and logic**. It is important in the planning stage of this question that you think about how you are going to present your answer and your calculations.
- **Efficient numerical analysis.** You will often be required to advise a client using supporting calculations. It is important that you can prepare these quickly and clearly.
- **Effective writing and presentation.** As discussed in relation to planning above, when you come to write up your answer make sure you use plenty of headings and sub-headings to clearly present your answer. It is important that your calculations are also clearly laid out using standard proformas to make it easier for markers to follow and award you marks.

Skill activity

STEP 1 Look at the mark allocation and calculate the amount of time available for the question.

Required

Explain the tax implications for Luiza if she acquires 5,000 ordinary shares in Damiana plc alternatively, (1) by means of a transfer on 1 November 2021, or (2) as a result of exercising the share options on 2 November 2024. On the assumption that she sells the shares as planned on 10 November 2024, calculate Luiza's net increase in wealth under each alternative.

(12 marks)

This is a 12-mark sub-requirement and at 1.95 minutes per mark it should take 23 minutes. On the basis of spending approximately a quarter to a third of your time on reading and planning, this time should be split approximately as follows:

- Reading the question – 3 minutes
- Planning your answer – 3 minutes
- Writing up your answer – 17 minutes

Within each of these phases, your time should be split roughly equally between the two alternatives.

STEP 2 Read the requirements and analyse them.

Required

Explain[45] the tax implications for Luiza if she acquires 5,000 ordinary shares in Damiana plc alternatively, (1)[46] by means of a transfer on 1 November 2021[47], or (2)[48] as a result of exercising the share options[49] on 2 November 2024. On the assumption that she sells the shares as planned on 10 November 2024, calculate Luiza's net increase in wealth[50] under each alternative[51].

(12 marks)

The verbs here are to 'explain' and 'calculate'.

'Explain' means to make an idea clear or show logically how a concept is developed or to give reason for a key event. The ACCA examiners have said that you should not just provide a list of points but add in some explanation of the points you're discussing.

'Calculate' means to ascertain by computation or to make an estimate of or to evaluate or perform a mathematical process. The ACCA examiners have said that you should make sure you provide description along with numerical calculations.

There are four tasks that you will need to complete to fully address this requirement. For EACH of the two alternatives you will need to explain the tax implications for Luiza of acquiring the 5,000 Damiana plc shares (Task 1 & 2) and you will then need to prepare a calculation of the net increase in wealth for EACH of the two alternatives (Task 3 & 4).

[45] Verb - refer to the ACCA definition.

[46] Sub-requirement 1.

[47] What does this mean? We will presumably find out when we read the body of the question.

[48] Sub-requirement 2.

[49] So the knowledge topic being tested here is share options - we will need to work out which type of share option we have when we read the body of the question.

[50] This will be: Proceeds from share sale, less Cost paid for shares, less Any tax, comes to Net increase in wealth X

[51] Sub-requirements 3 & 4 (One calculation for each alternative).

STEP 3 Now go back to the scenario in the question and highlight the information that will enable you to answer the requirements.

You should assume today's date is 1 September 2021.

Damiana plc:

- Is a UK-resident quoted[52] trading company

Luiza:

- Is employed as the finance director of Damiana plc, earning a gross annual salary of £165,000[53]

- Has no other source of taxable income

- Has been offered two alternative ways to acquire ordinary shares in Damiana plc

- In either case she will sell these shares on 10 November 2024 when their market value is expected to be £32.70[54] per share

- Uses her annual exempt amount[55] for capital gains tax purposes each year

Acquisition of Damiana plc shares – alternative 1:

- Damiana plc will transfer 5,000 ordinary shares (a 1%[56] holding) to Luiza on 1 November 2021 for which Luiza will pay £1 per share[57].

- The market value of these shares on 1 November 2021 is expected to be £24.50 per share.

- Damiana plc does not expect to pay a dividend in the foreseeable future.

Acquisition of Damiana plc shares – alternative 2:

- Damiana plc will grant options over 5,000 ordinary shares to Luiza on 1 November 2021 under its newly established enterprise management incentive (EMI)[58] scheme.

- The exercise price of these options will be £23.00[59] per share.

[52] Damiana plc is listed- shares are RCA for NIC purposes!

[53] Luiza is an additional rate tax payer so CGT will be at 20/28%. IT will be 45%.

[54] So Proceeds in net increase in wealth (and CGT calc) will be 5,000 shares at £32.70 = £163,500.

[55] So don't deduct in CGT calculations! (Nor is it a cashflow in wealth calculation).

[56] No BADR!

[57] This is sale at undervalue - so IT and NIC on undervalue when she gets them. Increase base cost of share from £1 cost by amount charged to IT. Then CGT on sale.

[58] Important- tells us the type of advantaged share scheme so we can know which bit of knowledge to apply.

[59] This is a discount to MV @ grant so there will be IT on exercise (and NIC as RCA). There will then be CGT on disposal. (Cost adjusted for what's charged to IT).

STEP 4 Then make a plan of the points that you need to cover in your answer, including what supporting calculations you will need to do. Use key words from the requirements as headings.

You could use a mind map similar to the one below or alternatively you could use a bullet point list or simply highlight the question.

The key is to come up with what you need to produce to fully answer the whole requirement so that you can get an idea of the level of depth you will need to cover to ensure you aim to pick up as many of the 12 marks as you can. You should consider that you will score one mark for a well-explained tax point with a half-mark for each component of a calculation that you include.

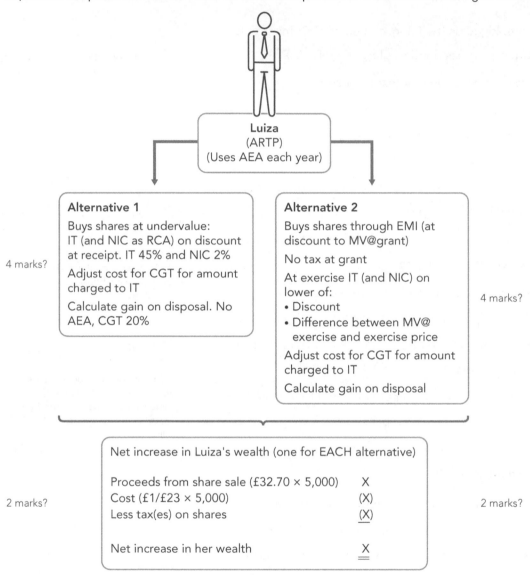

STEP 5 Write your answer using key words from the requirements as headings.

Make sure you used Alternative 1 and Alternative 2 as sub-headings to break up your answer and make it clear which part of the requirement you are answering. You must also not forget to include the net increase in wealth calculations for each alternative.

Make sure that you write in full sentences although you can be brief and make sure you have sufficient explanation/ words supporting your numbers so that the marker can understand your calculations.

Alternative 1 – transfer of shares to Luiza on 1 November 2021[60]

As Luiza is an employee of Damiana plc, she will be treated as receiving a taxable benefit equal to the amount underpaid in respect of her shares. She is an additional rate taxpayer[61], so she will incur an income tax liability of £52,875 ((£24.50 – £1) × 5,000 = £117,500 × 45%) in the tax year 2021/22. The shares are in a quoted company[62], so fall within the definition of 'readily convertible assets', therefore Luiza will also have a liability to Class 1 national insurance contributions (NICs) of £2,350 (£117,500 × 2%).

On the sale of the shares on 10 November 2024, there will be a chargeable gain of £41,000 ((£32.70 – £24.50) × 5,000) arising in the 2024/25 tax year. As Luiza will have already used her annual exempt amount[63], capital gains tax will be payable on £41,000 at the rate of 20%. Business asset disposal relief[64] will not be available as Luiza will not hold 5% of the shares in Damiana plc. The capital gains tax payable will therefore be £8,200 (£41,000 × 20%).

Luiza's net increase in wealth will be:

	£
Proceeds from share sale (£32.70 × 5,000)	163,500
Less price paid for shares (£1 × 5,000)	(5,000)
Less income tax on receipt of shares	(52,875)
Less employee's NIC on receipt of shares	(2,350)
Less CGT on sale of shares	(8,200)
Net increase in wealth	95,075

Note. You will get follow through marks for this calculation even if your numbers are wrong, so you must try to pull this summary together based on your calculations and be confident you will pick up method marks.

[60] Clear use of headings/sub-headings to break answer down.

[61] Make sure you show that you have considered which rate of tax Luiza will be paying at and show that you have correctly identified that she is an additional rate tax payer from the scenario.

[62] Note we must explain that NIC is due as the shares are RCA. And that the shares are RCA as Damiana plc is quoted.

[63] It's really important we identify specific information from our scenario and apply it in answering our questions.

[64] The Examining team say time and time again that identifying whether a relief is available or not and explaining why is a key ATX skill.

Alternative 2 – Enterprise management incentive (EMI) scheme

The value of shares in the scheme on 1 November 2021 will be £122,500 (£24.50 × 5,000), which is within the £250,000 limit.

No income tax or NICs will be payable by Luiza on the granting of the options in 2021/22.

On exercise of the options on 2 November 2024, income tax and NICs will be payable on the difference between the market value at the date of grant and the exercise price of the options, ie £7,500 ((£24.50 − £23) × 5,000). This is the amount chargeable as it is less than the difference between the market value at the date of exercise and the exercise price. The income tax and NICs payable are therefore £3,525 (£7,500 × 47%).

As before, a chargeable gain will arise on disposal of £41,000. The gain will be charged at 10% as business asset disposal relief will be available. This is because for an EMI scheme there is no requirement for the shareholder to have a minimum 5% shareholding in the company, as long as the option was granted at least two years before the date of disposal[65], and the individual has worked for the company for at least two years prior to the date of disposal. The capital gains tax payable will therefore be £4,100 (£41,000 × 10%).

[65] The relaxation of the conditions for BADR on EMI options isn't covered fully until Chapter 8 so you may not have picked this point up yet.

Luiza's net increase in wealth will be

	£
Proceeds from share sale (£32.70 × 5,000)	163,500
Less price paid for shares (£23 × 5,000)	(115,000)
Less income tax and NIC at exercise	(3,525)
Less CGT on sale of shares	(4,100)
Net increase in wealth	40,875

Examining team's comments and mark scheme

Examining team's comments

[This] part of the question concerned the acquisition of shares by an employee, either by means of a transfer, or by exercising options in an enterprise management incentive (EMI). Although few candidates scored high marks on this question part, a good number achieved a respectable score.

It appeared that many candidates ignored the last part of the requirement to calculate the taxpayer's increase in wealth under each of the alternatives, which was a shame as this should have represented relatively easy marks. It is similar to the, perhaps more familiar, requirement to calculate 'after-tax proceeds' from a transaction. In these cases, follow through marks are available as long as the candidate picks up the correct figures from their earlier calculations. The message, again, is to read the requirements of a question very carefully to ensure that what should be relatively easier marks, marks like these, are not overlooked.

Mark scheme		Marks
Alternative 1	7	
Alternative 2	7	
Max		12

Exam success skills diagnostic

Every time you complete a question, use the diagnostic below to assess how effectively you demonstrated the exam success skills in answering the question. The table has been completed below for Damiana to give you an idea of how to complete the diagnostic.

Exam success skills	Your reflections/observations
Good time management	Did you split your time evenly between alternatives 1 and 2?
Managing information	Did you pick up on all the information you needed to satisfactorily answer the requirements?
Correct interpretation of requirements	Did you explain the tax on both the alternatives and calculate the net increase in wealth for both?
Answer planning	Did you pick up the tax technical points correctly and ensure you had planned to answer each part of the requirement?
Effective writing and presentation	Did you use subheadings to show which alternative you were dealing with? Re-read your answer – does it make sense? Were your calculations clear?
Efficient numerical analysis	Did you pick up all the relevant information in the scenario, for example that Luiza was an additional rate taxpayer and that she uses annual exempt amount for capital gains tax purposes each year?
Most important action points to apply to your next question	

Summary

Success comes from technical knowledge (here on share options) and experience in how to explain the tax rules which apply in a particular scenario. It is vitally important that you can apply your knowledge to the specifics of a question.

Capital gains tax computation

Learning objectives

On completion of this chapter, you should be able to:

	Syllabus reference no.
Remember the material covered in Taxation (TX – UK) under the headings:	
'scope of taxation of capital gains'	A2(a) C1
'basic principles of computing gains and losses'	A2(a) C2
	A2(a) C3
'gains and losses on the disposal of moveable and immovable property'	
'the computation of capital gains tax'	A2(a) C5
Determine the tax implications of independent taxation and transfers between spouses	A2(b)(i)
Identify the occasions when a capital gain would arise on a partner in a partnership on the disposal of a partnership asset	A2(b)(vii)
Advise on the capital gains tax implications of transfers of property into trust	A2(c)(i)
Advise on the capital gains tax implications of property passing absolutely from a trust to a beneficiary	A2(c)(ii)
Identify connected persons for capital gains tax purposes and advise on the tax implications of transfers between connected persons	A2(d)(i)
Advise on the impact of dates of disposal	A2(d)(ii)
Evaluate the use of capital losses in the year of death	A2(d)(iii)
Extend the explanation of part disposals to include small part disposals of land	A2(e)(i)
Determine the gain on the disposal of leases and wasting assets	A2(e)(ii)

	Syllabus reference no.
Extend the explanation of the treatment of assets damaged, lost or destroyed to include capital sums received	A2(e)(iii)
Advise on the tax effect of making negligible value claims	A2(e)(iv)

Exam context

This chapter starts with a review of the capital gains tax assumed knowledge from TX – UK. This is important underpinning knowledge which may be tested in the exam and is also the starting point for the more advanced topics covered in this chapter.

You need to be able to quickly compute gains or losses and then work out a CGT liability, taking account of the losses and the annual exempt amount (AEA). Be careful where there is a mixture of residential property gains and other gains. You may need to deal with losses in the year of death.

You already know the part disposal rules but you also need to be able to deal with small part disposals of land where a gain is not immediately charged but the proceeds are deducted from cost. This technique is also used in relation to compensation for damaged assets, also dealt with in this chapter, and capital distributions from shares, dealt with in Chapter 8.

Transfers between spouses/civil partner are on a no gain, no loss basis and this can be useful for tax planning. There are also special rules for disposals between connected persons that you need to be aware of.

Partnerships may own assets and you need to be able to deal with the CGT position of individual partners.

As well as dealing with exempt chattels and wasting assets such as copyrights, you will be expected to compute gains or losses on certain transactions involving leases.

The basic concepts of assets lost, destroyed or damaged should be familiar to you from TX – UK but you need to be able to deal with more complex aspects such as where compensation proceeds are not wholly used to restore a damaged asset.

Chapter overview

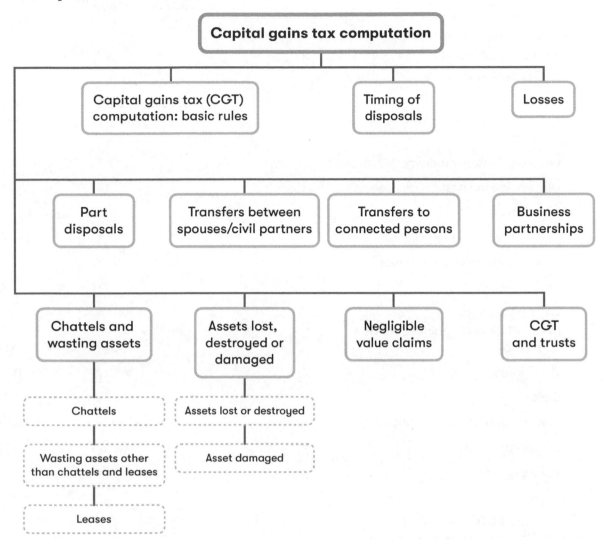

Capital gains tax computation

- Capital gains tax (CGT) computation: basic rules
- Timing of disposals
- Losses

- Part disposals
- Transfers between spouses/civil partners
- Transfers to connected persons
- Business partnerships

- Chattels and wasting assets
  - Chattels
  - Wasting assets other than chattels and leases
  - Leases
- Assets lost, destroyed or damaged
  - Assets lost or destroyed
  - Asset damaged
- Negligible value claims
- CGT and trusts

1 Capital gains tax (CGT) computation: basic rules

Three key components:

- Chargeable person
- Chargeable asset
- Chargeable disposal

	Non-residential property £	Residential property £
Proceeds (Actual proceeds/MV) (Note)	X	X
Less: Incidental costs of disposal	(X)	(X)
Cost	(X)	(X)
Enhancement expenditure	(X)	(X)
Gains before reliefs and losses	X	X
CGT reliefs	(X)	(X)
CY capital losses (Must offset vs CY gains as far as possible)	(X) (2)	(X) (1)
Trade losses	(X) (2)	(X) (1)
Gains	X	X
Less annual exempt amount (AEA)	(Bal) (2)	(12,300) (1)
B/f capital losses	(X) (2)	(X) (1)
Taxable gains	X	X
Tax @ 10%/20% (non-residential) 18%/28% (residential property)	X	X

Note. Any Structures and Buildings Allowances (SBAs) that have been claimed on a property are added to the proceeds on that property's disposal, thus increasing the chargeable gain arising. For detail on SBAs, see Chapter 14 of this Workbook.

Payment of CGT due will be by **31 January following the end of the tax year**, ie 31 January 2022 for the 2020/21 tax year.

However, Finance Act 2019 introduced **payments on account** which need to be made on disposal of a **UK residential property** on or after 6 April 2020. A return and payment on account on disposal of a UK residential property will be due **within 30 days of the completion of the disposal**. This significantly accelerates the tax payment on this type of a disposal although note that many disposals of residential property will be exempt due to private residence relief (See Chapter 8) and so this rule will mainly affect individuals with rental properties or second homes. Note that while it is the date of exchange of contract which determines which tax year a disposal falls into, the payment on account is determined based on the date of completion of the contract.

The payment on account is calculated as follows:

	£
Gain on disposal of the **UK residential property**	X
Less **current year capital losses** on **any** asset incurred up to the date of completion of the disposal	(X)

	£
Less **AEA**	(12,300)
Less **brought forward capital losses** on **any** asset	(X)
Gain to determine payment on account due	X

The individual will then have to make a **best estimate of any remaining basic rate band of tax** after income tax to determine the rate of tax (18%/28%) to apply to this gain.

At the end of the tax year the gain on the disposal of the UK residential property is still included in the main capital gains tax computation as usual. Once the CGT has been calculated the payment on account made is deducted to calculate the balance of CGT due on 31 January. This is illustrated in Activity 7 later in this chapter.

Formula provided

The tax rates (both normal and residential) and the annual exempt amount are given to you in the Tax rates and allowances available in the exam.

Exam focus point

In any question involving a disposal of a UK residential property you will either be told the taxpayer's status as higher or basic rate or given an estimate of income to allow you to calculate the estimated basic rate band remaining.

Essential reading

See Chapter 7 of the Essential reading for more detail on the computation of capital gains tax.

The Essential reading is available as an Appendix of the digital edition of the Workbook.

Activity 1: After tax proceeds on disposal

On 30 August 2020 Binni sold a freehold office building for £260,000. The building had been purchased in July 1990 for £81,000 and had been extended at a cost of £43,000 in May 2002. Binni incurred legal fees of £3,440 in connection with the disposal. Business asset disposal relief is not available on the disposal and this was Binni's only disposal in 2020/21. Binni has taxable income of £50,000 in 2020/21.

Required

Calculate Binni's after tax sales proceeds arising from this disposal.

Solution

2 Timing of disposals

A **chargeable disposal occurs on the date of the contract**, (if there is one). This may be different to date of transfer of asset.

Timing of disposals should be considered taking into account:

- **Rates of tax** in different years
- Using **losses** and **AEA**
- Availability of reliefs eg business asset disposal relief and investors' relief conditions

We look at the implications of this further in Chapter 13 Capital tax planning.

3 Capital losses

3.1 Current year capital losses

Allowable capital losses arising in a tax year are **deducted from gains arising in the same tax year** before the annual exempt amount.

3.2 Brought forward losses

Allowable losses brought forward are **deducted after the annual exempt amount.**

If there are **no gains left after deducting the annual exempt amount**, the **brought forward losses** are **carried forward** to the **next tax year.**

Activity 2: Use of current year and brought-forward losses

In 2020/21 Ted makes a gain of £25,300 on some shares he held as an investment and a gain of £10,000 on a residential property, and a capital loss of £12,000 on another asset. He also has a capital loss brought forward of £31,000.

Required

1   What is Ted's taxable gain for 2020/21 and the capital loss carried forward to 2021/22?

2   What would Ted's taxable gain be if the £31,000 loss had been a current year loss and the £12,000 loss had been a brought forward loss?

Solution

3.3 Losses in the year of death

Losses (in excess of gains) arising in the tax year in which an individual dies can be carried back three tax years on a last in, first out (LIFO) basis.

Carried back losses are set off after the annual exempt amount.

Activity 3: Losses in the year of death

Lucy died on 15 July 2020. On 1 May 2020 she made a chargeable gain of £8,500. On 17 June 2020, she made an allowable loss of £16,000. In the tax year 2019/20, Lucy had made chargeable gains of £16,700 and had taxable income of £40,000. In 2018/19, she had made chargeable gains of £21,700 and had taxable income of £10,000.

Assume that the tax rates and allowances for 2020/21 apply throughout and that none of the gains were residential property gains nor qualified for business asset disposal relief.

Required

Explain, with relevant supporting calculations, the tax relief available in respect of the allowable loss made in June 2020.

Solution

3.4 Trading losses set against chargeable gains

If a taxpayer makes a trade loss relief claim against general income, they can extend the loss relief against chargeable gains for that tax year. Details of this relief are in Chapter 15.

4 Part disposals

4.1 Basic rule

The gain is calculated as follows:

	£
Proceeds of part disposal	A
Less selling costs	(X)
	X
Less:	
Original cost $\times \dfrac{A}{A+B}$	(C)
Gain	(X)

A = MV of the part disposed of

B = MV of the remainder of the asset

Activity 4: Part disposal

Jerry bought 10 hectares of land for £10,000. He sold two hectares of land for £6,000 in the current tax year when the remaining eight hectares were worth £36,000.

Required

What is the chargeable gain from selling the two hectares and what is the cost that will be used when the remaining eight hectares are sold?

Solution

4.2 Land: small part disposals

If a **small part disposal of land** is made then the part disposal can be ignored. Instead the **proceeds are deducted from the cost** giving a reduced cost for later disposals.

Note this is a **claim** (made by the first anniversary of 31 January following the end of the tax year of disposal) and **two additional conditions** need to be met:

- **Aggregate proceeds** from sales of **all** land and buildings in the same tax year **must not exceed £20,000**; and
- **Proceeds do not exceed 20% of the market value of the land** prior to the disposal.

Activity 5: Small part disposal of land

Harvey bought 15 hectares of land for £30,000. He sells three hectares for £3,000 in the current tax year. This is his only sale of land in the current tax year although he has made other gains which have utilised his AEA. The market value of the land immediately prior to the disposal is £40,000.

Required

What is Harvey's CGT position? Assume Harvey makes any relevant claim.

Solution

5 Transfers between spouses/civil partners

Spouses and civil partners are taxed separately. Each has an individual AEA which cannot be transferred to the other spouse or civil partner.

Transfers between spouses/civil partners who are living together are on a **no gain/no loss basis.** The recipient spouse/civil partner is treated as if they acquired the asset at the transfer date for an amount equal to cost.

We look at the implications of this further in Chapter 13 Capital tax planning.

Activity 6: Transfers between spouses

Madeleine bought a Ming vase for £9,600. She subsequently transferred the vase to her husband Ultan. Ultan subsequently sold the vase in the current tax year for £24,000.

Required

What is Ultan's chargeable gain?

Solution

6 Transfers to connected persons

> **Connected persons:** Includes certain family members and business relationships

6.1 Definition

Connected persons for CGT are:

Direct relatives:

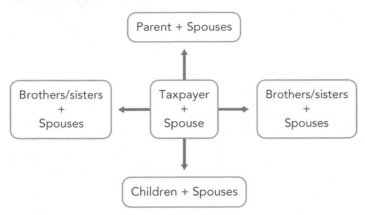

Note. Spouse also includes civil partner

Business relationships:

- A partner is connected to fellow partners and their current spouses.
- A company is connected to the persons controlling it.

6.2 Effect

The acquisition and disposal of assets between **connected persons** are deemed to take place for a consideration equal to the **market value of the asset**.

Losses from sales to a connected person can **only be relieved** against **current and future gains** on **disposals to the same connected person**.

7 Business partnerships

Where a **partnership** disposes of an asset **any gain or loss is apportioned to the partners** in their capital profit sharing ratio.

Activity 7: Comprehensive example

Maria made the following disposals during 2020/21 to unconnected persons:

(1) A residential rental property which she had bought in April 2000 for £100,000 and had incurred legal fees on acquisition of £1,200. She subsequently extended the property in 1995 at a cost of £24,000 and then sold it at auction on 15 May 2020 for £340,000. Auctioneer's fees amounted to 3% of the proceeds.

(2) Six hectares of a ten-hectare plot of land. She had acquired the land in 2007 for £250,000 and sold the six hectares on 1 September 2020 for £420,000 incurring legal fees of £3,000. The remaining four hectares were worth £200,000.

(3) A painting worth £15,000 in December 2020. She had been given it by her husband in 2010 when it was worth £12,000 and her husband had bought it in 2006 for £10,000.

(4) A necklace for £20,000 on 30 September 2020. She had inherited the necklace on the death of her grandmother in 2013 when it was worth £30,000 and her grandmother had paid £2,000 for the necklace many years before her death.

In addition, an asset was disposed of in January 2021 by a partnership in which Maria was entitled to 30% of the capital profits. The asset had been bought for £50,000 in December 2018 and disposed of for £68,000. Business asset disposal relief is not available on this disposal.

Maria had brought forward capital losses of £12,000, of which £7,000 had arisen on a disposal to her brother, and had taxable income of £42,000.

Required

What is Maria's CGT liability for 2020/21 and when will the tax be due?

Solution

---

8 Chattels and wasting assets

8.1 Chattels

Chattels are **tangible moveable property** and can be 'wasting' or 'non-wasting'.

Wasting chattels have an **expected life on disposal of 50 years or less. Non-wasting chattels** have an **expected life from date of disposal exceeding 50 years.**

Chattels disposed of for **proceeds and cost less than £6,000 are exempt from CGT,** so **no chargeable gain or allowable loss arises**. The special rules that apply when chattels have a cost and/or proceeds equal to or less than £6,000 are outside of the ATX – UK syllabus.

Otherwise, **non-wasting chattels** are **chargeable to CGT** in the normal way.

Wasting chattels are exempt from CGT, unless they are plant and machinery qualifying for **capital allowances**. If such chattels are sold for less than cost, no allowable loss arises as relief for the fall in value is given via capital allowances.

8.2 Wasting assets other than chattels and leases

Wasting assets have an **expected life on disposal of 50 years or less**. An example is a copyright.

The cost is written down on a straight line basis. So, if a taxpayer acquires such an asset with a remaining life of 40 years and disposes of it after 15 years (with 25 years remaining) only 25/40 of the cost is deducted from the disposal consideration.

8.3 Leases

There is an assignment of a lease when a lessee sells the whole of their interest. There is a **grant** of a lease when a new lease or sub-lease is created out of a freehold or existing leasehold.

There are **two types of lease transaction** that are examinable in ATX – UK:

- **Assignment** of a lease **with more than 50 years to run** (long lease)
- **Assignment** of a lease **with 50 years or less to run** (short lease)

The grant of a lease is outside the ATX – UK syllabus.

The gain or loss on the **assignment of a long lease** is computed in the **normal way.**

If the lease relates to **UK residential property,** any CGT will be payable within 30 days of the lease assignment.

On the **assignment of a short lease,** the **cost must be depreciated** using the **lease depreciation tables.** This reflects the fact that this type of lease is losing value so only the cost that relates to the period left can be deducted.

The allowable cost is given by:

$$\text{Original cost} \times \frac{X}{Y}$$

where **X is the percentage for the number of years left for the lease to run at the date of the assignment,** and **Y is the percentage for the number of years the lease had to run when first acquired.** The appropriate lease percentages will be given in the exam question where relevant.

The table only provides **percentages for exact numbers of years.** Where the **duration is not an exact number of years** the relevant percentage should be found by **adding 1/12 of the difference between the two years on either side of the actual duration** for each extra month. **Fourteen or more days count as a month.**

Activity 8: Assignment of short lease

Hugo acquired a 30-year lease on 30 September 2014 for £35,000. He sold it on 30 September 2020 for £40,000. The lease % for 24 years is 79.622 and the % for 30 years is 87.330.

Required

What is Hugo's gain?

Solution

9 Asset lost, destroyed or damaged

9.1 Asset lost or destroyed

If an asset is **lost or destroyed**, there is a **disposal of the asset** for CGT purposes and any **compensation monies** received are treated as **proceeds**. The date of disposal is the date the **compensation monies** are received and not the date the asset is lost or destroyed.

If the compensation monies are **reinvested** in a **replacement asset within 12 months**, a form of 'rollover' relief is available. The replacement asset must be of a similar function and type to the original.

If **all the insurance proceeds from an asset** are used to acquire the replacement asset, **any gain** can be **deducted from the cost** of that asset.

If **only part of the proceeds are used** to acquire the replacement asset, the **gain immediately chargeable** can be limited to the **amount not used**. The **rest of the gain** is then **deducted from the cost of the replacement asset.**

Activity 9: Asset destroyed

Lester bought a painting for £30,000 in May 2000. It was destroyed in July of the current tax year. An insurance claim was made and £45,000 was received in October of the current tax year. Lester spent £40,000 on a replacement asset one month after receiving the insurance.

Required

Compute Lester's chargeable gain and the base cost of the replacement asset.

Solution

9.2 Asset damaged

If an asset is **damaged** and **compensation monies** are received, the basic rule is that this is treated as a **part disposal** using the usual part disposal formula where:

A = compensation received

B = unrestored value of asset

Compensation monies applied in **restoring the asset**, are treated as **enhancement expenditure** on a subsequent disposal (subject to the election below).

Activity 10: Asset damaged: part disposal

James bought a holiday cottage for £40,000 in August 2001. In August of the current tax year the cottage was damaged in a fire. An insurance claim was made and £33,000 received in September of the current tax year. The cottage was valued at £45,000 after the fire.

Required

Calculate the gains arising

Solution

By **election**, however, the taxpayer can **avoid a part disposal computation**. The **compensation monies received** can instead be **deducted from the cost of the asset** if the sum is:

- **Wholly used** to restore asset
- **Partly used** to restore asset and **unused part is 'small'** (higher of 5% of capital sum and £3,000)
- **'Small' compared to value of asset** (higher of 5% of value of asset and £3,000).

If amount not used in restoring asset is not small, taxpayer can elect for amount used in restoration to be deducted from the cost; the balance will be treated as a part disposal using the restored value of the asset for B.

Essential reading

See Chapter 7 of the Essential reading for an illustration of the use of this election.

The Essential reading is available as an Appendix of the digital edition of the Workbook.

10 Negligible value claims

If a chargeable asset becomes **negligible in value** the taxpayer can **make a claim** to treat the asset as if it were **sold and then immediately reacquired** at the value stated in the claim. This gives rise to an **allowable loss**.

BPP
LEARNING
MEDIA

Essential reading

See Chapter 7 of the Essential reading for more detail on negligible value claims.

The Essential reading is available as an Appendix of the digital edition of the Workbook.

11 CGT and trusts

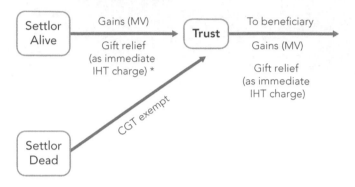

*If the gift is to a settlor-interested trust then no gift relief is available.

Essential reading

See Chapter 7 of the Essential reading for more detail on assets being transferred to and from trusts.

The Essential reading is available as an Appendix of the digital edition of the Workbook.

Chapter summary

```
                    ┌─────────────────────────────────────┐
                    │    Capital gains tax computation     │
                    └─────────────────────────────────────┘
```

Capital gains tax (CGT) computation: basic rules

- Chargeable person, disposal, asset

	Non-residential property £	Residential property £
Proceeds	X	X
Less Incidental costs of disposal	(X)	(X)
Cost	(X)	(X)
Enhancement expenditure	(X)	(X)
Gains before reliefs and losses	X	X
CGT reliefs	(X)	(X)
CY capital losses	(X) (2)	(X) (1)
Trade losses	(X) (2)	(X) (1)
Gains	X	X
Less Annual Exempt Amount (AEA)	(Bal) (2)	(12,300) (1)
B/fwd capital losses	(X) (2)	(X) (1)
Taxable gains	X	X
Tax @ 10%/20% or 18%/28%	X	X

Timing of disposals

- Rates
- Losses/AEA
- Reliefs

Losses

- Current year losses offset vs current year gains in full
- Losses b/fwd offset vs gains remaining after AEA
- Losses in year of death can be c/b three years on LIFO basis
- Trading losses can be set vs gains by extending claim for loss relief vs general income

Part disposals

- Use A/A+B × cost where A = MV part disposed of, B = MV remainder of the asset
- Small part disposal of land (elect):
  - Proceeds ≤ 20% value of land pre disposal; and
  - Proceeds all land sales in year ≤ £20,000
  - Deduct proceeds from cost of land

Transfers between spouses/civil partners

Transfers assets @ NG/NL

Transfers to connected persons

- Connected persons for CGT:
  - Direct relatives
  - Business relationships
- Proceeds deemed to be MV
- Losses can only be used vs gains on disposals to same person

Business partnerships

Apportion gain/loss using capital profit sharing ratio

Chattels and wasting assets

Chattels
- Non-wasting chattels exempt if proceeds and cost < £6,000
- Wasting chattels exempt except for P&M qualifying for capital allowances
  - No loss on sale of P&M (CAs give relief)

Wasting assets other than chattels and leases
Expected life ≤ 50 yrs cost written down on straight line basis

Leases
- Assignment of long lease (> 50 yrs) normal computation
- Assignment of short lease (≤ 50 yrs) cost depreciated using lease depreciation tables

Assets lost, destroyed or damaged

Assets lost or destroyed
- Normal computation
  - Use compensation as proceeds
  - Can rollover gain if compensation is reinvested in replacement asset within 12 months

Asset damaged
- Part disposal
  - Use compensation as proceeds
  - Use A/A+B × cost where A = compensation received, B = unrestored value of asset
- Can elect to deduct compensation from cost of asset if:
  - ≥ 95% of sum is used in restoring asset; or
  - Capital sum is < higher of 5% of asset value/£3k
- If above isn't satisfied:
  - Can elect for amount used in restoration to be deducted from cost
  - Balance treated as part disposal where A = compensation not used in restoration, B = restored value of asset

Negligible value claims

Claim to treat asset as sold and immediately reacquired @ value stated in claim to create allowable loss

CGT and trusts

- To trust:
  - Lifetime: @ MV, gift relief available (unless settlor-interested trust)
  - Death: exempt
- From trust:
  - @ MV, gift relief available

Knowledge diagnostic

1. Timing of disposal

A chargeable disposal usually occurs on the contract date. The date of disposal should be considered in relation to the use of capital losses, the annual exempt amount, the date for payment of tax and the availability of reliefs.

2. Losses in year of death

Losses (in excess of gains) arising in the tax year in which an individual dies can be carried back three tax years on a last in, first out (LIFO) basis.

3. Part disposals

On a part disposal the cost of the part disposed of is usually calculated as A/A + B where A is the MV of the part disposed of and B is the MV of the remainder of the asset. There are special rules for small part disposals of land.

4. Spouse/civil partner transfers

Transfers of assets between spouses/civil partners give rise to neither a gain nor a loss.

5. Connected persons

Disposals between connected persons are always deemed to take place for a consideration equal to market value. Any loss arising on a disposal to a connected person can be set only against a gain arising on a disposal to the same connected person.

6. Partnership disposals

On the disposal of a partnership asset, the gain or loss is apportioned to partners in their capital profit sharing ratio.

7. Chattels and wasting assets

Gains on most wasting chattels are exempt, and losses on them are not allowable. The CGT rules are modified for assets eligible for capital allowances.

Other wasting assets generally have their cost written down over time.

8. Lease disposals

An ordinary disposal computation is made on the disposal of a lease with 50 years or more to run. For leases of land with less than 50 years to run, a special table of percentages is used.

9. Insurance proceeds

The gain which would otherwise arise on the receipt of insurance proceeds may, subject to certain conditions, be deferred.

10. Negligible value claim

If a chargeable asset becomes negligible in value the taxpayer can make a claim to treat the asset as if it were sold and then immediately reacquired at the value stated in the claim thus resulting in an allowable loss.

11. CGT and trusts

Disposals of assets occur when they are transferred to and from a trust.

Further study guidance

Question practice

Now try the following from the Further question practice bank (available in the digital edition of the Workbook):

*   Sophie
*   Wendy, Henry and Dan

Further reading

There is one technical article on the ACCA website written by members of the (ATX – UK) examining team which is relevant to some of the topics covered in this chapter that you should read:

*   Trusts and Tax for (ATX – UK)

Activity answers

Activity 1: After tax proceeds on disposal

> **Tutorial note.** No SBAs would have been available on this property due to its age, so no adjustment to sales proceeds is required.

	£
Proceeds	260,000
Less selling expenses	(3,440)
Less cost	(81,000)
Less enhancement	(43,000)
Chargeable gain	132,560
Less annual exempt amount	(12,300)
Taxable gain	120,260
Tax @ 20% (taxable income ≥ basic-rate limit)	24,052
After-tax sale proceeds	
Proceeds	260,000
Less selling expenses	(3,440)
Less tax on gain	(24,052)
	232,508

Activity 2: Use of current year and brought-forward losses

1

	Property £	Other £
Gain	10,000	25,300
Current year loss (must be deducted in full)	(10,000)	(2,000)
Gain		23,300
Annual exempt amount		(12,300)
		11,000
Brought forward losses		(11,000)
Taxable gain	0	0

	£
Capital loss brought forward	31,000
Utilised in 2020/21	(11,000)
Capital loss carried forward	20,000

2

	Property £	Other £
Gain	10,000	25,300
Current year loss	(10,000)	(21,000)
		4,300
Annual exempt amount		(4,300)
Taxable gain	0	0

	£
Capital loss brought forward	12,000
Utilised in 2020/21	(0)
Capital loss carried forward	12,000

Activity 3: Losses in the year of death

The allowable loss of £(16,000) must first be offset against the chargeable gains of £8,500 in 2020/21. This will not save any capital gains tax since the gains would have been covered by the annual exempt amount (AEA).

The excess loss of £(16,000 − 8,500) = £(7,500) can be offset against the chargeable gains of the previous three years on a last in, first out basis. The losses will be set off after the AEA.

The taxable gain for 2019/20 was £(16,700 − 12,300) = £4,400. The CGT on this amount @ 20% is £880 (Lucy was a higher rate taxpayer in 2019/20). The whole of the taxable gain will be relieved and the tax will be repayable. The remaining loss of £(7,500 − 4,400) = £3,100 is carried back to 2018/19.

The taxable gain in 2018/19 was £(21,700 − 12,300) = £9,400. The loss of £3,100 can be relieved @ 10% (Lucy was a basic rate taxpayer in 2018/19) giving a tax repayment of £310.

The total tax relief in respect of the allowable loss made in June 2020 is therefore:

£(880 + 310) = £1,190.

Activity 4: Part disposal

Part disposal

	£
Proceeds	6,000
Cost (£10,000 × 6,000/(6,000 + 36,000))	(1,429)
Gain	4,571

Cost of remaining land for future CGT calculations:

= £10,000 − £1,429

= £8,571

Activity 5: Small part disposal of land

The proceeds of £3,000 is less than 20% of market value of land prior to sale (20% × 40,000 = £8,000).

No chargeable disposal occurs.

Allowable cost of land remaining

	£
Cost of 15 hectares	30,000
Less proceeds from part disposal	(3,000)
	27,000

Activity 6: Transfers between spouses

Transfer Madeleine –> Ultan: proceeds = cost

		£
ie	Cost	9,600
	Deemed proceeds	9,600

Note. No gain arises on transfer

Disposal by Ultan:

	£
Proceeds	24,000
Less cost (deemed proceeds)	(9,600)
Chargeable gain	14,400

Activity 7: Comprehensive example

	Normal rates	Res. property
	£	£
Gain on residential property (W1)		204,600
Gain on part disposal of land (W2)	247,645	
Gain on painting (W3)	5,000	
Gain on partnership asset (W5)	5,400	
Loss on necklace (W4)	–	(10,000)
	258,045	194,600
AEA (best use against gains taxable at 28%)	(0)	(12,300)
	258,045	182,300
B/f capital loss £(12,000 – 7,000) (N) (best use against gains taxable at 28%)	(0)	(5,000)
Taxable gains	258,045	177,300
Rate of tax (higher rate taxpayer)	20%	28%
CGT	51,609	49,644

Tax on the gain on the disposal of the residential property will be due within 30 days of completion of the sale, 14 June 2020. The tax due will be £52,444. [(£204,600 - £12,300 - £5,000) × 28%] The calculation of CGT for this payment on account takes into account any brought forward capital losses but only current year capital losses up to the date of disposal of the residential property. Consequently, we can include the brought forward capital losses but as the disposal of the necklace takes place after the residential property the capital loss on the necklace cannot be considered in the CGT due on the payment on account.

The remaining CGT of £48,809 (£49,644+£51,609-£52,444) will be due by 31 January 2022.

Note. The loss of £7,000 on the disposal to Maria's brother can only be set against gains on disposals to him.

Workings

1 **Rental property (residential property)**

	£
Proceeds (340,000 × 97%)	329,800
Cost	(101,200)
Enhancement	(24,000)
Gain	204,600

2 **Part disposal**

	£
Proceeds (420,000 – 3,000)	417,000
Cost £250,000 × 420,000/(420,000 + 200,000)	(169,355)
Chargeable gain	247,645

3 **Painting**

	£
Proceeds	15,000
Less cost (deemed cost to her husband due to NGNL transfer)	(10,000)
Chargeable gain	5,000

4 **Necklace**

	£
Proceeds	20,000
Less cost (probate value)	(30,000)
Allowable loss	(10,000)

5 **Partnership asset**

	£
Proceeds	68,000
Less cost (probate value)	(50,000)
Chargeable gain	18,000
Maria's share of chargeable gain 30% of £18,000	5,400

Activity 8: Assignment of short lease

		£
Proceeds		40,000
Cost	£35,000 × 79.622/87.330	(31,911)
Chargeable gain		8,089

Activity 9: Asset destroyed

	£
Proceeds	45,000
Cost	(30,000)
	15,000
Taxable now (compensation monies not reinvested 45,000 – 40,000)	(5,000)
Deferred gain	10,000

Base cost of new asset = £40,000 – £10,000 = £30,000

Activity 10: Asset damaged: part disposal

	£
Proceeds	33,000
Less cost £40,000 × (33,000/(33,000 + 45,000))	(16,923)
Chargeable gain	16,077

8

Shares and securities, CGT reliefs

Learning objectives

On completion of this chapter, you should be able to:

	Syllabus reference no.
Remember the material already covered in Taxation (TX – UK) under the headings:	
'gains and losses on the disposal of movable and immovable property'	A2(a) C3
'gains and losses on the disposal of shares and securities'	A2(a) C4
'the computation of capital gains tax'	A2(a) C5
'the use of exemptions and reliefs in deferring and minimising tax liabilities arising on the disposal of capital assets'	A2(a) C6
Extend the explanation of the treatment of rights issues to include the small part disposal rules applicable to rights issues	A2(f)(i)
Define a qualifying corporate bond (QCB), and understand what makes a corporate bond non-qualifying. Understand the capital gains tax (CGT) implications of the disposal of QCBs in exchange for cash or shares	A2(f)(ii)
Apply the rules relating to reorganisations, reconstructions and amalgamations and advise on the most tax efficient options available in given circumstances	A2(f)(iii)
Understand and apply enterprise investment scheme (EIS) reinvestment relief	A2(g)(i)
Understand and apply seed enterprise investment scheme (SEIS) reinvestment relief	A2(g)(ii)
Advise on the availability of business asset disposal relief in relation to associated disposals	A2(g)(iii)
Understand and apply the relief that is available on the transfer of an unincorporated business to a limited company	A2(g)(iv)

	Syllabus reference no.
Understand the capital gains tax implications of the variation of wills	A2(g)(v)

Exam context

You need to revise the identification rules for individuals and the computation of gains on disposals that were covered in TX – UK. You will also be expected to deal with additional complexities on the rules for rights issues, takeovers and reorganisations.

The ATX – UK examining team have stressed that CGT reliefs are a vital element of capital taxes planning.

First you need to refresh your knowledge of the conditions for the reliefs studied in TX – UK: private residence relief (PRR), business asset disposal relief, investors' relief, gift relief and replacement of business assets (rollover) relief.

Then you need to add knowledge of four new reliefs: incorporation relief, enterprise investment scheme (EIS) reinvestment relief, seed enterprise investment scheme (SEIS) reinvestment relief and variation of wills.

For all these reliefs you need to be able to spot where they apply and use them in the most tax-efficient manner.

Chapter overview

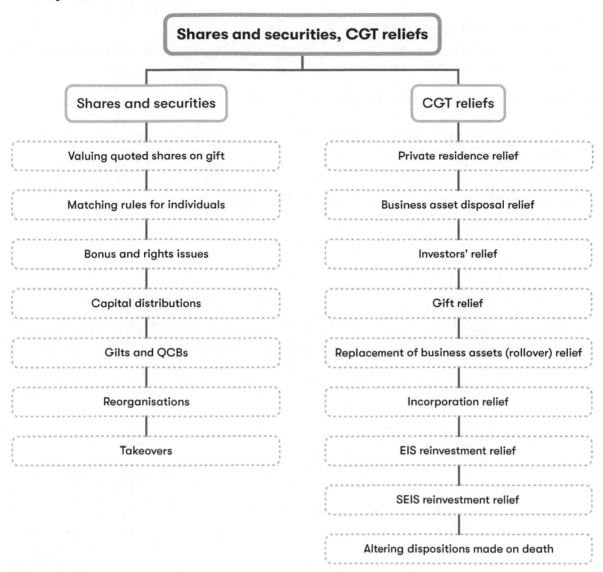

Shares and securities, CGT reliefs

Shares and securities
- Valuing quoted shares on gift
- Matching rules for individuals
- Bonus and rights issues
- Capital distributions
- Gilts and QCBs
- Reorganisations
- Takeovers

CGT reliefs
- Private residence relief
- Business asset disposal relief
- Investors' relief
- Gift relief
- Replacement of business assets (rollover) relief
- Incorporation relief
- EIS reinvestment relief
- SEIS reinvestment relief
- Altering dispositions made on death

BPP
LEARNING
MEDIA

1 Shares and securities

1.1 Valuing quoted shares on gift

Quoted shares disposed of by way of a **gift** (including **sales at undervalue**) are **valued at the mid-price** based on the quoted price on the disposal day.

Activity 1: Valuation of quoted shares on gift

Byron transferred 1,000 shares in Ares plc, a quoted company, to his son. The prices on the day of disposal were 200p–204p.

Required

Calculate the deemed proceeds to be used in the gain calculation.

Solution

1.2 Matching rules for individuals

Disposals are **matched with acquisitions** in the following order:

- Acquisitions on **same day**
- Acquisitions in **next 30 days**, if more than one acquisition on a 'first in, first out' (FIFO) basis
- **Share pool**

The **share pool aggregates all purchases** except for those made on the same day as the disposal or within the following 30 days.

Activity 2: Disposal of shares

Mel had the following transactions in the shares of Gibbon plc:

1 September 1994	Bought 3,000 shares for £8,000
1 May 2002	Bought 1,500 shares for £7,500
10 August 2020	Sold 4,000 shares for £32,000

| 20 August 2020 | Bought 500 shares for £2,800 |

Required

Calculate Mel's chargeable gain.

Solution

1.3 Bonus and rights issues

1.3.1 Bonus issues

Bonus issue shares are **issued in proportion** to the **original shareholding**. The **original shareholding is increased by the bonus issue shares.**

Since **bonus shares are free shares**, issued at no cost, there is **no need to adjust the original cost.**

1.3.2 Rights issue: shares taken up

Right issue shares are **issued in proportion** to the **original shareholding.** The **original shareholding** is **increased by the rights issue shares.**

The **rights issue shares** are **paid for** and this results in an **adjustment to the original cost.**

 Essential reading

See Chapter 8 of the Essential reading, for an illustration of a disposal of shares following a rights issue.

The Essential reading is available as an Appendix of the digital edition of the Workbook.

1.3.3 Rights issues: rights sold nil paid

If a shareholder **does not take up the rights to the rights issue shares** but **sells those rights to a third party,** without making any payment to the company, a **part disposal occurs** because this is a treated as a capital distribution.

$$\frac{A}{A + B}$$

Where:

A = proceeds from sale of rights

B = market value of the shares retained

If however the proceeds **are less than the higher of £3,000 and 5% of the value of the shareholding at the time of the issue, no gain arises**. Instead the **proceeds are deducted from original cost. This treatment will automatically apply** unless the shareholder elects to for a part disposal (eg to use available annual exempt amount).

Activity 3: Sale of rights nil paid

Henry bought 7,000 £1 shares in Tristan Ltd for £7,000 (ie at par) on 1 February 2000. The company made a 1:2 rights issue. Henry did not take up his rights, instead he sold them to a third-party for £4,000. The market value of the shares retained were worth £50,000.

Required

Calculate Henry's chargeable gain.

Solution

1.4 Capital distributions

Capital distributions, for example, during the **liquidation of a company, are treated in the same way as the sale of rights nil paid.**

Essential reading

See Chapter 8 of the Essential reading for an illustration of the capital distribution on liquidation

The Essential reading is available as an Appendix of the digital edition of the Workbook.

1.5 Gilts and qualifying corporate bonds (QCBs)

Gilt-edged securities (UK Government and Government guaranteed securities as shown on the Treasury list) **(gilts)** and **qualifying corporate bonds (QCBs)** are **exempt assets** for **individuals**. Therefore, **no chargeable gain nor allowable loss** will arise on **disposal**.

A **QCB** is a **security** (eg loan stock) which:

- Is a **normal commercial loan;**
- Is expressed in **sterling;**
- Is **acquired after 13.3.84;** and
- Has **no provisions for conversion to or redemption in other currencies.**

1.6 Reorganisations

> **Reorganisation:** Where new shares or a mixture of new shares and securities are issued by a company in exchange for the original shareholding.

If the **new shares and securities are quoted**, then the **cost of the original shareholding** is **apportioned** by reference to the **market values of the new shares and/or securities** on the **first day of quotation** after the reorganisation.

Illustration 1: Reorganisation

An original quoted shareholding of 3,000 shares is held in a share pool with a cost of £13,250. There is a reorganisation whereby each ordinary share is exchanged for two 'A' ordinary shares (quoted at £2 each) and one preference share (quoted at £1 each).

Required

How will the original cost be apportioned?

Solution

Share pool

	New holding	MV £	Cost £
'A' Ords 2 new shares	6,000	12,000	10,600
Prefs 1 new shares	3,000	3,000	2,650
Total		15,000	13,250

12/15 × £13,250 = cost of ordinary shares

3/15 × £13,250 = cost of preference shares

1.7 Takeovers

> **Takeovers:** When **control of a company passes** to another company, by the **acquisition of shares.**

1.7.1 Takeover for cash only

If the **takeover offer** is for cash only, there is a **normal disposal** of the original shareholding and a **gain or loss** arises.

1.7.2 Takeover for shares and/or securities

If the **takeover offer** is 'paper for paper' (ie **new shares or a mixture of new shares and securities are issued by the acquiring company** in exchange for **the original shareholding**), no gain or loss arises. The **cost of original shareholding holding** is apportioned in the **same way as for a reorganisation.**

Paper for paper transactions are only treated as not giving rise to any immediate CGT liability if the transactions are entered into for *bona fide* **commercial reasons** and **not for tax avoidance.** The **acquiring company** must obtain **clearance from HMRC** to ensure the above condition has been met.

1.7.3 Takeover for cash and shares and/or securities

If there is a **cash element** on the takeover there is a **disposal for CGT purposes.** The **cost** of the **original shareholding** needs to be **apportioned** between the **cash and new shares and/or securities** received.

The **cash element** is treated as the **proceeds of a part disposal** and **A/A + B rule** applied to cost, where:

A = cash element

B = value of non-cash element(s), ie market value at date of takeover.

If cash element is **less than the higher of 5% of the value of the total holding post- takeover and £3,000 then no disposal has taken place.** Instead the cash is deducted from the cost of the non-cash element(s) for future disposals. This **treatment will automatically apply** unless the shareholder elects to for a part disposal.

> ### Exam focus point
>
> Takeovers with a cash element of consideration were tested in March 2020 Question 1 Corey. The examining team stated 'it appeared that a large number of candidates were not prepared for this question, as answers were generally poorer than on recent occasions when this has been examined, with the majority of students not apportioning the cost, or calculating a gain on the cash element.'

Essential reading

See Chapter 8 of the Essential reading for an illustration of a takeover involving shares and cash.

The Essential reading is available as an Appendix of the digital edition of the Workbook.

1.7.4 Takeover where securities are QCBs

If **QCBs are given in exchange for the original shareholding** and a **gain arises** using **market value of the QCBs at takeover**, this **gain is deferred** until the **QCBs are sold.**

Thus, on **disposal of the QCB** there is **no gain or loss on the QCB itself**, the **deferred gain** from the original share sale will **become chargeable.**

In Chapter 13 Capital tax planning, Activity 4 shows calculations on a takeover with mixed consideration including QCBs.

 Essential reading

See Chapter 8 of the Essential reading for details of the interaction of takeovers with business asset disposal and investors' relief

The Essential reading is available as an Appendix of the digital edition of the Workbook.

 Exam focus point

Takeover with corporate bonds were tested in June 2011 Question 4 Capstan. The examining team commented that 'there was often confusion as to the treatment of the sale of the corporate bonds. Many candidates who knew that corporate bonds are exempt from capital gains tax went on to calculate a gain on the sale and include it in the taxable capital gains for the year. Also, many candidates were not able to identify the gain on the original shares that was frozen at the time of the paper for paper exchange and then charged when the corporate bonds were sold.'

2 Capital gains tax reliefs

2.1 Private residence relief (PRR)

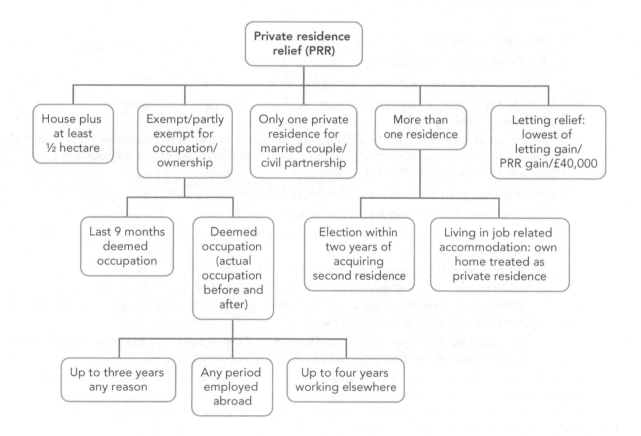

Essential reading

See Chapter 8 of the Essential reading for more details of private residence relief. If you studied Taxation prior to Finance Act 2020 you should note that the relief is now renamed private residence relief rather than principal private residence relief and that the rules as to when letting relief is available have changed so that it is now only available where the owner is in shared occupancy with the tenant. Where the whole property is let out letting relief is no longer available. See the Essential reading for further detail.

The Essential reading is available as an Appendix of the digital edition of the Workbook.

2.2 Business asset disposal relief (formerly Entrepreneurs' relief)

PER alert

One of the competencies you require to fulfil Performance objective 17 Tax planning and advice of the PER is to assess the tax implications of proposed activities or plans of an individual or entity with reference to relevant and up to date legislation. You can apply the knowledge you obtain from this section of the text to help to demonstrate this competence.

2.2.1 Disposals qualifying for relief

An individual can claim business asset disposal relief on the following disposals:

- Qualifying businesses (whole or part):
  - Sole trader
  - Partnership interest
  - Furnished holiday lettings

    Relief is only available in respect of gains on business assets (investments do not qualify).

    The whole or part of the business must be disposed of as going concern (unless it has ceased, see below).

- The disposal of shares in a trading company which is the individual's personal company and of which the individual is also an officer (eg director) or employee of the company (no restriction for investments held by company).

  A personal company is one where the individual:
  - Holds at least 5% of the ordinary share capital; and
  - Can exercise at least 5% of the voting rights in the company by virtue of that holding of shares; and
  - Either or both of the following conditions are met:
    ○ Is entitled, by virtue of that holding of shares, to at least 5% of the profits available for distribution to equity holders and, on a winding up would be beneficially entitled to at least 5% of the assets so available; or
    ○ Would be beneficially entitled to at least 5% of the proceeds in the event of a disposal of the whole of the ordinary share capital of the company.

The business/shares must have been owned throughout a period of two years before disposal. On a disposal of shares, this period can include ownership of a business which has been incorporated as a going concern by a transfer of all assets (ignoring cash) in exchange, wholly or partly, for those shares.

If the business has ceased, it must have been owned throughout a period of two years before cessation and disposal must be within three years after cessation – this can cover the disposal of individual assets.

2.2.2 Restriction on goodwill

The **general rule** is that **goodwill is not eligible for business asset disposal relief** if it is **disposed of by an individual to a close company** where **the individual and close company are related**. Close companies are covered in more detail in Chapter 21 and an individual is related to a company they are a shareholder of the company. Thus, this restriction will apply in the relatively common situation where a sole trader incorporates their business.

The **restriction is relaxed** so that **goodwill does still qualify for business asset disposal relief** if the individual holds <5% of the shares or holds ≥5% and sells all their shares to another company within 28 days. This is designed to cover the situation where **an individual might choose to incorporate their business to facilitate its sale.**

2.2.3 Enterprise management incentive (EMI) shares

Shares acquired **via enterprise management incentive (EMI) share options** have some **special rules:**

- There is **no requirement to own 5% of the shares** in the company.
- The **ownership period** is calculated **from the date of grant**. There is no ownership period for the shares themselves.

2.2.4 Associated disposals

Business asset disposal relief is also available where an **individual disposes of** either:

- **Whole or part of partnership business;** or
- **Shares in a qualifying company**

and **at the same time disposes of** a **separate asset** that had been **used in the partnership where they are partner** or **in the company's trade.**

If **market value rent** is received for the asset **no business asset disposal relief is available.** If rent is below market value, **business asset disposal relief** is **proportionately withdrawn.**

2.2.5 Operation of the relief

Disposal of assets qualifying for business asset disposal relief are treated as a **single chargeable gain (net off gains and losses).**

This **chargeable gain** is taxed at **10%.**

If the **individual has disposals of assets not qualifying for business asset disposal relief in the tax year:**

- **Set off losses and the annual exempt amount** against gains **not qualifying for business asset disposal relief first.**
- **Deduct gains qualifying for business asset disposal relief from amount of basic rate band** available before gains not qualifying for business asset disposal relief.

The relief covers the **first £1 million of chargeable gains.** This is a **lifetime limit** so can apply to successive disposals.

A **claim for the relief** must be made by **first anniversary of 31 January following tax year of disposal.** For a **2020/21 disposal**, the taxpayer must claim by **31 January 2023**.

Formula provided

The lifetime limit and 10% rate of tax are given in the Tax rates and allowances available in the exam.

Exam focus point

The lifetime limit for business asset disposal relief was reduced from £10 million to £1 million on 11 March 2020. However, for Advanced Taxation (ATX-UK), the ACCA will only expect you to know the £1 million limit.

Activity 4: Business asset disposal relief with associated disposal

Becca and Gerald had carried on trade in partnership since 2010, sharing capital profits equally. On 10 August 2020, they sold the partnership to Wilson, an unconnected sole trader. Gains and losses arose on chargeable partnership assets were as follows:

	£
Offices	35,600
Warehouse	(15,000)
Investments	41,600

In addition, on 10 August 2020, Gerald sold Wilson a shop which Gerald had let out to the partnership at 20% of market rent. The gain on the shop was £9,000.

Gerald has taxable income of £21,000 in 2020/21. He has no other chargeable assets. He has not previously made a claim for business asset disposal relief (BADR).

Required

Calculate Gerald's CGT liability for 2020/21.

Solution

2.3 Investors' relief

Investors' relief is a similar relief to business asset disposal relief. It applies to gains on qualifying shares which must satisfy the following conditions:

(a) **New ordinary shares** in an **unlisted trading company** (or unlisted holding company of a trading group) which have been **subscribed for** by the **individual making the disposal**.

(b) **Issued by the company on or after 17 March 2016 and held continuously** by that individual usually for **at least three years** from **the later of 6 April 2016 and the date of the issue of the shares** until **the date of disposal**.

There is **no minimum shareholding** requirement.

The individual normally must not be an officer or employee of the company (nor any connected company). There are limited exceptions for unremunerated officers and employees who subsequently join the company.

The **rate of tax** on investors' relief gains **is 10%**. There is a **£10 million lifetime limit of gains on which investors' relief can be claimed.**

 ### Formula provided

The lifetime limit and 10% rate of tax are given to you in the Tax rates and allowances available in the exam.

2.4 Gift relief

2.4.1 Gift relief for disposals of business assets

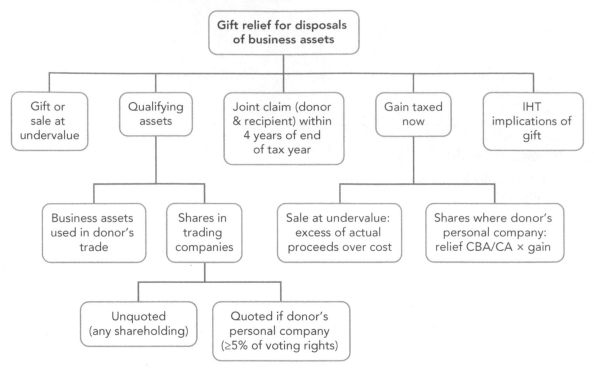

Essential reading

See Chapter 8 of the Essential reading for more details of gift relief for disposals of business assets.

The Essential reading is available as an Appendix of the digital edition of the Workbook.

2.4.2 Gift relief for disposals of agricultural property

Gift relief can be claimed on the **gift** or **sale at undervalue** where the **asset gifted is agricultural property** which would attract **inheritance tax (IHT) agricultural property relief** (APR) (see Chapter 11).

There are **no restrictions** for **periods of non-agricultural use** or for **partial agricultural use.**

2.4.3 Gifts where there is an immediate charge to inheritance tax (IHT)

Gift relief can be claimed on the **gift** or **sale at undervalue** of **any assets** which are **subject to an immediate IHT charge** (see Chapter 11).

Transfers subject to an immediate IHT charge include most gifts to trusts. A transfer will be regarded as chargeable to IHT even if it falls within the nil rate band or is covered by the IHT annual exemption. The **trustees** must be **UK resident** for gift relief to be available.

Gifts to **settlor interested trusts,** however, **do not qualify for gift relief**. These are trusts from which the settlor, or their spouse/civil partner or minor child (who is neither married nor in a civil partnership) can benefit.

The claim is made by the settlor alone within **four years** after the end of the tax year of the transfer (by **5 April 2025** for a disposal in **2020/21**).

2.4.4 Interaction of IHT and gift relief

If gift relief is claimed on a **transfer of business assets or agricultural property,** and that **transfer is (or later becomes) chargeable to IHT,** then when **the recipient disposes of the assets, their gain is reduced by the IHT finally payable** (but not so as to create a loss).

2.4.5 Anti-avoidance rules

The general rule is that **gift relief is not available if the** recipient **is not UK resident** at the time of the disposal to them. However, gift relief is available if the asset is UK residential property (see Chapter 9).

If the recipient **ceases to be UK resident** within **six years from the end of the tax year of the disposal to them**, the gain held over under gift relief will be assessed on the **recipient** immediately before they become non-UK resident.

> ### Assessment focus point
>
> Gift relief is normally used whenever a business or business asset is gifted, but you should look out for the restriction for a non-resident donee. You should also consider whether retaining the asset until death so as to obtain the tax-free uplift to probate value would be advantageous.

2.5 Replacement of business assets (rollover) relief

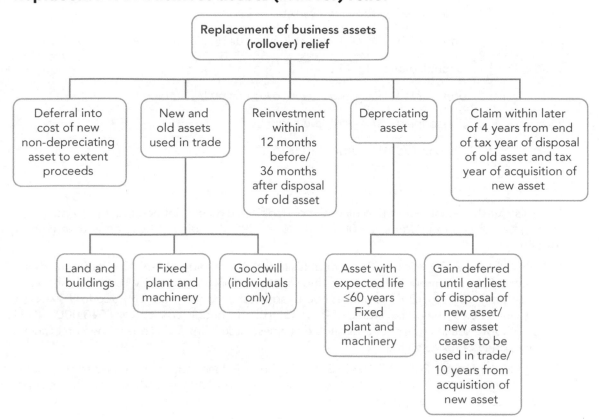

Essential reading

See Chapter 8 of the Essential reading for more details of rollover relief.

The Essential reading is available as an Appendix of the digital edition of the Workbook.

Activity 5: Comprehensive example

Mick disposed of the following assets during the tax year 2020/21:

(1) On 19 May 2020, Mick sold a freehold warehouse for £522,000. The warehouse was purchased on 6 August 2003 for £258,000, and was extended at a cost of £99,000 during April 2005. In January 2009, the floor of the warehouse was damaged by flooding and had to be replaced at a cost of £63,000. The warehouse was sold because it was surplus to the

business's requirements as a result of Mick purchasing a newly built warehouse in December 2019 for £500,000. Both warehouses have always been used for business purposes in a wholesale business run by Mick as a sole trader.

(2) On 24 September 2020, Mick sold 700,000 £1 ordinary shares in Rolling Ltd, an unquoted trading company, for £3,675,000. Rolling Ltd has 10,000,000 shares in issue. He had originally purchased 500,000 shares in Rolling Ltd on 2 June 2007 for £960,000. On 1 December 2012, Rolling Ltd made a 3-for-2 bonus issue. Mick has been a director of Rolling Ltd since 1 January 2007.

(3) On 30 June 2020, Mick sold a house for £308,000. The house had been purchased on 1 January 2003 for £93,000. On 10 June 2009, Mick had incurred legal fees of £5,000 in relation to a boundary dispute with his neighbour. Throughout the 210 months of ownership the house had been occupied by Mick as follows:

Months	
30	Occupied – 20% of house let to a tenant
22	Unoccupied – Travelling overseas
24	Unoccupied – Required to work overseas by his employer
106	Occupied solely by Mick
12	Unoccupied – Required to work overseas by his employer
13	Unoccupied – Travelling overseas
3	Unoccupied – Lived with sister
210	

Mick also let the house out during all of the periods when he did not occupy it personally. Throughout the period 1 January 2003 to 30 June 2020 Mick did not have any other main residence.

(4) On 24 June 2020, Mick made a gift of his entire 12% holding of 12,000 £1 ordinary shares in Reward Ltd, an unquoted trading company, to his son. The market value of the shares on that date was £98,400. The shares had been purchased on 15 March 2006 for £39,000. On 24 June 2020, the market value of Reward Ltd's chargeable assets was £540,000, of which £460,000 was in respect of chargeable business assets. Mick has never been an officer or employee of Reward Ltd.

(5) On 19 September 2020, Mick sold 2,000 £1 shares in Line Ltd, an unquoted trading company for £10,000. Mick had subscribed for these shares on 10 August 2017 at par. Mick has never been an officer or employee of Line Ltd.

Mick has capital losses brought forward of £25,000. He has never claimed either business asset disposal relief or investors' relief on any disposals prior to 2020/21.

Required

Calculate Mick's CGT liability for 2020/21 assuming all beneficial claims are made.

Solution

2.6 Incorporation relief

2.6.1 Introduction

Incorporation involves the **disposal of assets** by **an unincorporated business** (sole trader, partnership) to **a company.**

Incorporation results in **chargeable gains** (or **allowable losses**) on the **disposal of chargeable assets** which are taxable. **Incorporation relief** allows the **net gains** to be **deferred into the base cost of any shares received as consideration from the company.**

If a **structure/building on which SBAs have been claimed is transferred as part of the incorporation, SBAs claimed to date are not added to the proceeds of the gains calculation at the date of incorporation** (as they would be in the case of a normal disposal of such a structure/building). **Instead the company is treated as having always owned the asset. SBAs are claimed by the company following the incorporation** and, on a subsequent disposal of the structure/building by the company, **all the SBAs claimed to date** (by both the sole trader/partnership and the company) **are added to the proceeds in the gains calculation** ie there will be a higher chargeable gain on a future disposal.

Incorporation relief is **automatically** available. However, individuals can **elect** that incorporation relief should **not** apply (eg if the net gains would be covered by the annual exempt amount). The election must be made **within two years of 31 January following the end of the tax year** in which incorporation occurs (ie by 31 January 2024 for incorporation in 2020/21). A taxpayer may elect to disapply incorporation relief, for example if business asset disposal relief could be claimed on the incorporation disposal but not on a subsequent disposal of the shares received such as where the company is not the individual's personal company. If the shares do qualify for business asset disposal relief, remember that the ownership of the unincorporated business is included as part of the ownership period for the shares so that a disposal within two years of incorporation may still attract relief.

2.6.2 Conditions for incorporation relief

In order for incorporation relief to apply, **all the following conditions** need to be satisfied:

- **All** assets (except cash) transferred to company
- Transfer as a **going concern**
- Consideration **wholly or partly in shares**

2.6.3 The amount of the relief

$$\text{Gain deferred} = \text{Gain} \times \frac{\text{MV of shares received}}{\text{MV of total consideration}}$$

Business asset disposal relief may be available on remaining gain if conditions satisfied. We look at the implications of this further in Chapter 13.

Activity 6: Incorporation relief

Brian transfers his lawnmower business (started in 1994) in September 2020 to a newly formed company in exchange for £650,000 ordinary £1 shares (to be issued at par) and £150,000 cash. Brian will be the only shareholder in the company. The following gains arose at the date of transfer:

	£
Freehold building (acquired in 2000)	75,000
Goodwill	95,000
Leasehold building	52,500
Plant and machinery (all assets worth <£6,000)	60,000

Brian intends to keep his shares for the foreseeable future.

Required

Calculate Brian's CGT liability for 2020/21 assuming that he is a higher rate taxpayer, does not have any other chargeable assets and has not made any claims for business asset disposal relief. Show the base cost of the shares.

Solution

2.7 EIS reinvestment relief

2.7.1 Deferral of gain on disposal of asset

If an individual disposes of **any chargeable asset** and **invests in Enterprise Investment Scheme (EIS) shares** the **gain on the asset** can be deferred. The **EIS shares** must be **issued** between **one year before** and **three years after** the disposal of the asset.

Maximum deferral is the **lower** of:

- **Amount subscribedfor the EIS shares**; and
- **Amount specified in claim.**

The **claim** can be for the **maximum amount** or a **lower amount** if desired (eg to use the AEA).

A claim for relief must be made within five years from 31 January following the end of the tax year in which the EIS shares were issued ie by 31 January 2027 if the shares are issued in 2020/21.

Activity 7: EIS reinvestment relief

Alan disposed of a painting for £300,000 in November 2020, giving a chargeable gain of £60,000. This is his only disposal in 2020/21.

He subscribed £70,000 in a company which qualified under the EIS rules in September 2020.

Required

What will be the deferred gain, assuming Alan makes the most tax-efficient claim?

Solution

2.7.2 Deferred gain becoming chargeable

The **deferred gain** will become **chargeable** on any of the following events:

- **EIS shares disposed of by investor** (except to spouse/civil partner)
- **EIS shares disposed of by investor's spouse/civil partner** (if acquired from investor)
- **Investor becomes non-UK resident** within **three years of share issue**
- **Investor's spouse/civil partner becomes non-UK resident** within **three years of share issue** (if acquired from investor)
- **EIS shares cease to be eligible for relief** (eg company ceases to be qualifying company)

The **deferred gain becomes chargeable in the year of the event**, not the year when the original gain was made (if different).

If the deferred gain would have been eligible for business asset disposal relief, a claim can be made for business asset disposal relief to apply when it comes back into charge. This claim must be made by the first anniversary of 31 January following the tax year in which the deferred gain comes back into charge.

2.8 SEIS reinvestment relief

2.8.1 Exemption of gain on disposal of asset

Seed enterprise investment scheme (SEIS) reinvestment relief is available if an **individual disposes of any chargeable asset** and **subscribes for qualifying SEIS shares** in the **same year**.

Maximum deferral is the **lower** of:

- **50% of the gain matched with the amount invested in SEIS shares**; and
- **Amount specified in the claim**.

The **claim** can be for the **maximum amount** or a **lower amount** if desired (eg to use the AEA).

A claim for relief must be made within five years from 31 January following the end of the tax year in which the EIS shares were issued ie by 31 January 2027 if the shares are issued in 2020/21.

If a **claim has been made, for income tax purposes,** for **all or some of the SEIS shares to be treated as issued in the previous tax year** then, **if a claim for SEIS reinvestment relief is made,** it must **also apply to gains made in that previous tax year**.

Note that, in contrast to EIS reinvestment relief, **SEIS reinvestment relief exempts the gain,** rather than just deferring it.

2.8.2 Withdrawal of relief

SEIS reinvestment relief is **withdrawn or reduced** if the SEIS shares are **disposed of within three years of acquisition**.

If **shares are not disposed of at arm's length** (eg gifted, sold to a connected person) **all of the SEIS income tax relief** and **all of the CGT SEIS reinvestment relief** will be **withdrawn** in respect of **those shares**. The withdrawal is effected by a **chargeable gain** being treated as arising **in the tax year in which the shares were issued** equal to the amount of SEIS reinvestment relief attributable to those shares.

If the **shares are disposed of at arm's length** (eg sold to an unconnected third party) the **amount of SEIS income tax relief withdrawn** is **restricted to a maximum of 50% of the consideration received** and the **same proportion of CGT SEIS reinvestment relief** will **also be withdrawn**. Again this will be **effected** by a **chargeable gain** being treated as arising **in the tax year in which the shares were issued**.

Activity 8: SEIS reinvestment relief

Ciaran disposed of a statue realising a chargeable gain of £65,000 during 2020/21. He subscribed £70,000 for shares in Octopus Ltd (a qualifying SEIS company) in the same tax year. His income tax liability for 2020/21 was sufficient to obtain full income tax relief.

Ciaran sold the shares in Octopus Ltd on 6 September 2022 for £55,000 in an arm's length transaction.

Required

1   Compute the maximum amount of SEIS reinvestment relief Ciaran could obtain in 2020/21.

2   Explain how much SEIS reinvestment relief would be withdrawn on the disposal of the shares in 2022/23.

Solution

2.9 Altering dispositions made on death

If the terms of a **disposition made on death** (eg a will) are **changed within two years**, by a **variation** or a **disclaimer**, the change will **not be a disposal for the original beneficiary** for CGT purposes.

The assets are treated as being **acquired by the new beneficiary** at **probate value** (ie at death) and not at their value when the change is made.

We look at the implications of this further in Chapter 13.

Essential reading

See Chapter 8 of the Essential reading for more detail on altering dispositions made on death.

The Essential reading is available as an Appendix of the digital edition of the Workbook.

Chapter summary

Shares and securities, CGT reliefs

Shares and securities

Valuing quoted shares on gift

Lower price plus one-half of the difference between the two prices

Matching rules for individuals

- Same day
- Next 30 days (FIFO)
- Share pool

Bonus and rights issues

- Bonus issue: treat as acquired on same date as underlying shares
- Rights issue: as for bonus issue except add cost of rights
- Sale of rights nil paid:
  - Treat as part disposal where A = proceeds from sale of rights and B = market value of the shares retained
  - If proceeds < the higher of £3,000 or 5% of value of the shareholding at the time of sale, no gain arises, proceeds deducted from cost (automatic but can elect to use part disposal instead)

Capital distributions

Treat as for sale of rights nil paid

Gilts and QCBs

Exempt

Reorganisations

Original cost of quoted shares apportioned by reference to the MVs of new shares and/or securities on first day of quotation after reorganisation

Takeovers

- Cash only:
  - Normal disposal
- Shares and securities only (paper for paper):
  - No disposal
  - Apportion original cost as for reorganisation
- Cash and shares and/or securities:
  - Part disposal for cash element where A = cash element and B = MV of non-cash element(s) at takeover
  - If proceeds < higher of £3,000 or 5% of value of shareholding at time of sale, no gain arises, proceeds deducted from cost (automatic but can elect to use part disposal instead)
- Securities are QCBs
  - Gain arises using proceeds as MV at takeover, gain deferred until disposal of QCB
- Shareholder can elect to disapply reorganisation/takeover treatment
  - Use if existing shares qualify for BADR/IR but new shares/securities won't qualify

CGT reliefs

Private residence relief

- Gain × period of occupation/period of ownership
- Occupation = actual + deemed occupation
  - Last 9 months of ownership always treated as deemed occupation (provided some actual occupation beforehand)
  - If preceded and followed by actual occupation include:
    (1) Up to three years for any reason
    (2) Any period when employed overseas
    (3) Up to four years if required to live elsewhere due to work (includes self-employment)
- Part occupation – PRR withdrawn proportionately if not occupied for residence purposes
- If more than one residence:
  - Elect which to be used as private residence
  - If live in job-related accommodation, can treat own residence as private residence
- Letting relief (only with shared occupation): lowest of letting gain, PRR gain, £40,000

Business asset disposal relief

- 10% tax rate
- First £1m of qualifying gains (lifetime limit)
- Qualifying gains are disposals of:
  - Sole trader business
  - Partnership interest
  - Furnished holiday letting (FHL)
  - Shares in trading company where individual has 5% shareholding and is officer/employee of company

CGT reliefs continued

Business asset disposal relief continued

- Goodwill: restriction if disposal to close company by related party
- Conditions satisfied for ≥ two years prior to disposal/ cessation
- EMI shares: no ownership requirement, two years runs from grant
- Available on associated disposals ie partner/ shareholder sells one of the above and at the same time sells asset that has been used in partnership/company's trade

Investors' relief

- 10% tax rate
- First £10m of qualifying gains (lifetime limit)
- New ordinary shares in unquoted trading company subscribed for by taxpayer on or after 17 March 2016 and held for ≥ three years
- No minimum shareholding
- Normally taxpayer not officer/employee of company

Gift relief

- Disposal @ MV
- Joint claim by donor/donee unless to trust
- Donee usually must be UK resident
- Qualifying assets
  - Business asset
  - Unquoted trading company shares
  - Quoted shares in personal trading co (≥ 5% shareholding)
  - Gifts immediately chargeable to IHT (to and from trusts)
- Gain on gift of shares eligible for relief = MV CBA/ MV CA where CBA = chargeable business assets, CA = chargeable assets
- Sale at undervalue
  - Excess of actual proceeds over cost taxed immediately

Replacement of business assets (rollover) relief

- Old and new asset must be used in taxpayer's trade
- Claim: by later of four years from the end of the tax year(s) of disposal of the old asset/ new asset acquired
- Qualifying assets
  - Land and buildings
  - Fixed plant and machinery
  - Goodwill
- Timing of replacement
  - 12 months before → 36 months after
- Any proceeds not reinvested = taxable immediately
- Depreciating assets
  - Short (< 60 yr) lease, fixed P&M
  - Gain 'held' over (deferred) until earliest of new asset sale, new asset not used in trade, new asset acquisition + 10 years
  - Can elect to transfer gain to non-depreciating asset before deferred gain crystallises

Incorporation relief

- Gain deferred = MV of shares received/MV total consideration
- All assets (except cash) must be transferred
- Transfer of going concern
- Deferred gain reduces base cost of shares
- Automatic (can elect to disapply)
- BADR may be claimed for gain left in charge

EIS reinvestment relief

- Gain on any chargeable asset
- Invest in EIS shares
- Maximum deferral lower of:
  - Amount subscribed for the EIS shares
  - Amount specified in claim
- Freeze gain until:
  - Shares sold
  - Shares cease to be eligible for relief
  - Individual becomes UK non-resident within three years of issue of shares
- Deferred gain will qualify for BADR when crystallises if original gain qualified for BADR
- Same reinvestment period as for replacement of business asset relief

SEIS reinvestment relief

- Gain on any chargeable asset
- Invest in SEIS shares in the same tax year or previous tax year if c/b claim made for IT
- Maximum exemption lower of:
  - 50% of the gain matched with the amount invested in SEIS shares
  - Amount specified in the claim
- Relief withdrawn or reduced if shares sold within three years

Altering dispositions made on death

- Variation or disclaimer of distribution of assets within two years of death
- Original beneficiary: no disposal of assets
- New beneficiary: take assets at probate value
- For variation: need to state alteration applies for CGT

Knowledge diagnostic

1. Shares and securities

- There are special rules for matching shares sold with shares purchased. Disposals are matched first with shares acquired on the same day, then within the following 30 days and finally with the share pool.
- On an alteration of share capital or a takeover, the general principle is only to tax gains immediately if cash is paid to the investors.
- Gilts and QCBs held by individuals are exempt from CGT.
- If a reorganisation involves the acquisition of QCBs, a gain to the date of the takeover is computed but is 'frozen' until the disposal of the QCB.

2. Private residence relief (PRR)

There is an exemption for gains on private residences, but the exemption may be restricted because of periods of non-occupation or because of business use.

There is also a relief for letting out a private residence if the gain arising during the letting would not be covered by the main relief up to a maximum of £40,000. There must be shared occupation with the owner while the property is let to qualify for letting relief.

3. Business asset disposal relief and investors' relief

Business asset disposal relief (BADR) applies on the disposal of a business and certain trading company shares. The rate of tax on gains qualifying for BADR is 10%.

Investors' relief applies on disposals of qualifying shares in unlisted trading companies of which the investor is not an officer or employee. The rate of tax on gains qualifying for investors' relief is 10%.

4. Deferral reliefs

Gift relief is available on both outright gifts and sales at an undervalue of business assets and agricultural land. Gift relief is also available on gifts which are immediately chargeable to inheritance tax.

When business assets falling within certain classes are sold and other such assets are bought, it is possible to defer gains on the assets sold by claiming rollover relief. If an amount less than the proceeds of the old asset is invested in the new assets, a gain equal to the difference will be chargeable up to a maximum of the actual gain.

When an individual transfers their unincorporated business to a company, the gain arising will be deducted from the cost of the shares received, unless the individual elects otherwise.

Gains can be deferred if an individual invests in shares in an EIS company and can be partially exempted if an individual invests in shares in a SEIS company.

5. Variations

A variation can be used to vary a will after death and can have CGT consequences.

Further study guidance

Question practice

Now try the following from the Further question practice bank (available in the digital edition of the Workbook):

- John and Matilda
- Briony

Activity answers

Activity 1: Valuation of quoted shares on gift
Value at 200 + ½ (204 − 200) = 202
Value of transfer
1,000 × 202p = £2,020

Activity 2: Disposal of shares
Match with acquisition 20 August 2020

	£
Proceeds (32,000 / 4,000) × 500)	4,000
Cost	(2,800)
Gain	1,200

Match with share pool

	£
Proceeds (32,000 / 4,000) × 3,500)	28,000
Cost	(12,056)
Gain	15,944

Share pool

	No.	Cost £
1 September 1994	3,000	8,000
1 May 2002	1,500	7,500
	4,500	15,500
Disposal	(3,500)	(12,056)
	1,000	3,444

Total gains = £1,200 + £15,944 = £17,144

Activity 3: Sale of rights nil paid
Treat as part disposal.

	£
Proceeds	4,000
$\text{Cost} \dfrac{4,000}{4,000 + 50,000} \times 7,000$	(518)
	3,482

This is not a small part disposal as proceeds are greater than the higher of £3,000 and 5% × £50,000.

Activity 4: Business asset disposal relief with associated disposal

	£	£
Net gain on partnership business assets		
(35,600 − 15,000) × 1/2	10,300	
Gain on business element of associated disposal		
9,000 × (100 − 20) = 80%	7,200	
	17,500	
CGT @ 10% (BADR)		1,750
Gain on non business partnership asset		
41,600 × 1/2	20,800	
Gain on non business element of associated disposal		
9,000 × 20%	1,800	
	22,600	
Less annual exempt amount	(12,300)	
Taxable gain	10,300	
CGT		
(37,500 − 21,000 − 17,500) = No BR band remaining, therefore: 10,300 @ 20%		2,060
Total CGT 2020/21		3,810

Activity 5: Comprehensive example

Mick – chargeable gains 2020/21

	Gains on residential property	Gains not qualifying for BADR	Gains qualifying for BADR	Gains qualifying for investors' relief
	£	£	£	£
Warehouse (W1)		22,000		
Rolling shares (W2)		2,137,400	1,000,000	
House (W3)	19,000			
Reward Ltd shares (W6)		8,800		
Line Ltd shares (W7)				8,000
Chargeable gains	19,000	2,168,200	1,000,000	8,000
Less annual exempt amount	(12,300)	(0)	(0)	(0)
	6,700	2,168,200	1,000,000	8,000
Less brought-forward capital losses	(6,700)	(18,300)	(0)	(0)
Taxable gains	0	2,149,900	1,000,000	8,000

	Gains on residential property	Gains not qualifying for BADR	Gains qualifying for BADR	Gains qualifying for investors' relief
	£	£	£	£
Rate of tax	20%		10%	10%
CGT	429,980		100,000	800
Total CGT liability				530,780

Workings

1 Freehold warehouse

	£	£
Disposal proceeds		522,000
Less: Cost	258,000	
Enhancement expenditure – extension	99,000	
Enhancement expenditure – floor	0	
		(357,000)
Chargeable gain		165,000
Rollover relief		(143,000)
Taxable now		22,000
Proceeds	522,000	
Reinvested	(500,000)	
Proceeds not reinvested are taxable now	22,000	

Note. The cost of replacing the warehouse floor is revenue expenditure as the floor is a subsidiary part of the property.

The base cost of the replacement factory is £357,000 (500,000 – 143,000).

BADR is not available on the gain as this is a disposal of an asset, not all or part of a sole trader business.

2 Shares in Rolling Ltd

	£
Disposal proceeds	3,675,000
Less cost (W)	(537,600)
Chargeable gain	3,137,400

As Mick is an employee with >5% holding in Rolling Ltd which is a trading company and he has held his shares for more than two years, the gain will be eligible for BADR thus the first £1 million is taxed at 10%.

3 Share pool

	Number	Cost £
Purchase June 2007	500,000	960,000

	Number	Cost £
Bonus issue December 2012 500,000 × 3/2	750,000	0
	1,250,000	960,000
Disposal September 2020 960,000 × 700,000/1,250,000	(700,000)	(537,600)
Balance carried forward	550,000	422,400

4 House

	£
Proceeds	308,000
Less cost	(93,000)
Less enhancement expenditure (defending title to property)	(5,000)
Gain	210,000
Less Private residence exemption (W4)	(185,000)
Letting exemption (W5)	(6,000)
Gain after exemptions	19,000

5 Private residence exemption

	Exempt months	Chargeable months	Total months
Actual occupation – 20% let	24	6	30
Deemed occupation – up to three years any reason	22		22
Deemed occupation – any time employed overseas	24		24
Actual occupation	106		106
Working overseas (no deemed occupation as no actual occupation after)		12	12
Unoccupied – travelling overseas (13 - 6)		7	7
Last 9 months – always treated as period of occupation	9	–	9
Totals	185	25	210

Private residence exemption £210,000 × 185/210 = £185,000

Note. In calculating the private residence exemption, any periods of absence while working overseas, a maximum of four years' absence while working elsewhere in the UK, and a maximum of three years' absence for any reason, are treated as deemed occupation, usually provided that they are preceded and followed by a period of actual occupation. The second period working overseas is therefore not a period of deemed occupation as it was not followed by a period of actual occupation.

6 **Letting exemption**

Lowest of:

(i)	Gain in letting period £210,000 × 6/210 (must have shared occupation with owner)	£6,000
(ii)	Gain exempt under PRR (W2)	£185,000
(iii)	Maximum exemption	£40,000
	Therefore, letting exemption is	£6,000

7 **Reward Ltd shares**

	£
Deemed proceeds	98,400
Less cost	(39,000)
Gain before hold over relief	59,400
Gift relief (59,400 × 460,000/540,000)	(50,600)
Taxable now	8,800

Hold-over relief is restricted to £50,600 (£59,400 × 460,000/540,000), being the proportion of chargeable business assets to chargeable assets. BADR is not available, as Mick is not an officer or employee of the company. Investors' relief is not available as the shares were acquired before 17 March 2016 (and were not subscribed for).

8 **Line Ltd shares**

	£
Proceeds	10,000
Less cost	(2,000)
Gain	8,000

Investors' relief is available on these shares as they were subscribed for by Mick on or after 17 March 2016, have been owned for at least three years and Mick is not an officer or employee of the company.

Activity 6: Incorporation relief

	Gains qualifying for BADR	Gains not qualifying for BADR
	£	£
Gains on chargeable assets:		
Building	75,000	
Goodwill (no BADR as >5% of shares)		95,000
Leasehold	52,500	–
	127,500	95,000
Less incorporation relief (650,000/800,000) × 127,500/95,000	(103,594)	(77,188)

	Gains qualifying for BADR	Gains not qualifying for BADR
	£	£
Taxable now	23,906	17,812
AEA	–	(12,300)
Taxable gain	23,906	5,512
CGT %	10%	20%
CGT	2,391	1,102

	£
MV of shares acquired	650,000
Less incorporation relief	
(103,594 + 77,188)	(180,782)
Base cost of shares	469,218

Activity 7: EIS reinvestment relief

A claim can be made to defer £47,700.

	£
Gain before relief	60,000
Less EIS reinvestment relief	(47,700)
Gain	12,300
Less AEA	(12,300)
Taxable gain	–

Activity 8: SEIS reinvestment relief

1   SEIS income tax relief would be 50% × £70,000 = £35,000.

As Ciaran invested 100% of the chargeable gain in the shares he can claim a maximum of 50% of the gain.

50% × £65,000 = £32,500

2   Sale of shares within three years at arm's length

Income tax relief withdrawn is:

50% × £55,000 = £27,500

This is 27,500/35,000 = 78.57% of original income tax relief

Therefore, reinvestment relief is reduced by this same proportion, ie 78.57% × £32,500 = £25,536

This amount will be treated as a gain arising in the year the SEIS shares were issued.

9

Overseas personal taxation

Learning objectives

On completion of this chapter, you should be able to:

	Syllabus reference no.
Remember the material covered in Taxation (TX – UK) under the headings 'The scope of income tax' and 'The scope of capital gains tax'	A1(a) B1 A2(a) C1
Explain and apply the concepts of residence, domicile and deemed domicile and advise on the relevance to income tax	A1(b)(i)
Advise on the availability of the remittance basis to UK resident individuals	A1(b)(ii)
Advise on the tax position of individuals coming to and leaving the UK	A1(b)(iii)
Determine the income tax treatment of overseas income	A1(b)(iv)
Understand the relevance of the OECD model double tax treaty to given situations	A1(b)(v)
Calculate and advise on the double taxation relief available to individuals	A1(b)(vi)
Identify the concepts of residence, domicile and deemed domicile and determine their relevance to capital gains tax	A2(b)(ii)
Advise on the availability of the remittance basis to non-UK domiciled individuals	A2(b)(iii)
Determine the UK taxation of foreign gains, including double taxation relief	A2(b)(iv)
Conclude on the capital gains tax position of individuals coming to and leaving the UK	A2(b)(v)
Advise on the UK taxation of gains on the disposal of UK land and buildings owned by non-residents	A2(b)(vi)

Exam context

The topics in this chapter are mostly new to you as they were not examinable in TX – UK. The exception is the test of residence which determines whether an individual is UK resident or not. However, in ATX – UK you will also be required to deal with tax years which are split into resident and non-resident parts.

You may be asked to state the rules which determine whether a person is domiciled or deemed domiciled in the UK. This is an area of tax law which has recently changed and so is highly examinable.

You need to be able to explain how the rules on residence, domicile and deemed domicile affect an individual's liability to UK tax. This includes the remittance basis charge for long-term residents who are not UK domiciled nor deemed domiciled.

Do not be caught out by the overseas aspects of CGT. The most useful exclusion is that individuals who are non-UK resident are not taxable on their UK gains, even on assets situated in the UK. A significant exception is the disposal of UK land, both residential and non-residential. There are also rules to stop individuals avoiding CGT by becoming temporarily non-UK resident.

Double taxation relief is an important aspect where an individual receives overseas income or makes overseas gains which have been taxed in the source country. You are expected to know about double taxation agreements, in outline, and to use unilateral double taxation relief for both income and gains.

Chapter overview

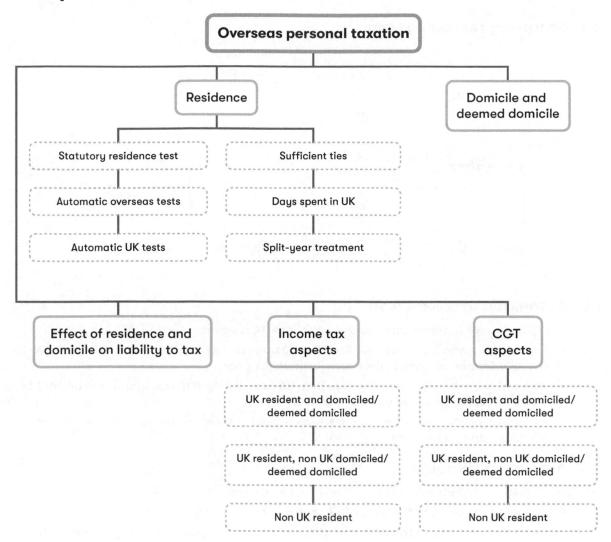

Overseas personal taxation

- Residence
  - Statutory residence test
  - Automatic overseas tests
  - Automatic UK tests
  - Sufficient ties
  - Days spent in UK
  - Split-year treatment
- Domicile and deemed domicile

- Effect of residence and domicile on liability to tax

- Income tax aspects
  - UK resident and domiciled/deemed domiciled
  - UK resident, non UK domiciled/deemed domiciled
  - Non UK resident

- CGT aspects
  - UK resident and domiciled/deemed domiciled
  - UK resident, non UK domiciled/deemed domiciled
  - Non UK resident

1 Residence

1.1 Statutory residence tests

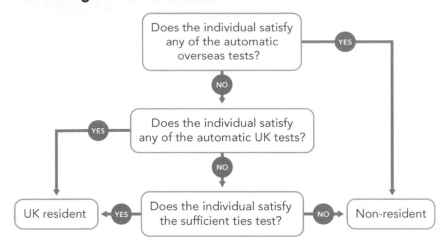

1.2 Automatic overseas tests

The following will **automatically** be treated as **not UK resident:**

- An individual who is in the UK for **less than 16 days** during a tax year and who has been **UK resident for one or more of the previous three tax years**
- An individual who is in the UK for **less than 46 days** during a tax year and who has **not been resident during the previous three tax years**
- An individual who **works full time overseas** subject to them **not being in the UK for more than 90 days during a tax year**

1.3 Automatic UK tests

The following will **automatically** be treated as **UK resident:**

- An individual who is **in the UK for 183 days or more** during a tax year
- An individual who is **in the UK for 30 days in the tax year** and whose **only home** is in the UK
- An individual who carries out **full-time work in the UK during a 365-day period,** some of which falls within the tax year

1.4 Sufficient ties tests

If an individual's residence **cannot be determined by any of the automatic tests** their status will be determined by the **number of ties they have with the UK**. There are **five ties:**

- Having **close family** (spouse/civil partner or minor child) in the UK
- Having a **house in the UK** which is **available for at least 91 days** in the tax year and is **made use of** during the tax year
- Doing **substantive work in the UK,** where 40 days or more is viewed as substantive
- Being in the UK for **more than 90 days** during **either of the two previous tax years**
- **Spending more time in the UK** than in **any other country** in the tax year (only if **individual who was UK resident in any of the previous three tax years**).

The **following table** shows the **number of ties needed to be UK resident** by reference to the **number of days in the UK:**

Days in UK	Previously resident	Not previously resident
Less than 16	Automatically not resident	Automatically not resident
16 to 45	Resident if 4 UK ties (or more)	Automatically not resident
46 to 90	Resident if 3 UK ties (or more)	Resident if 4 UK ties
91 to 120	Resident if 2 UK ties (or more)	Resident if 3 UK ties (or more)
121 to 182	Resident if 1 UK tie (or more)	Resident if 2 UK ties (or more)
183 or more	Automatically resident	Automatically resident

 Formula provided

This table is given to you in the Tax rates and allowances available in the exam.

1.5 Days spent in the UK

A **day in the UK** is **any day** in which an individual is **present in the UK at midnight.**

 Activity 1: Residence

1. Abbey has been resident in Canada for many years. In the current tax year she came to the UK on holiday on three occasions, amounting to 40 days in total.

   Required

   Will Abbey be treated as UK resident in the current tax year?

2. Zoe has always lived in the UK and her only home is also in the UK. However, she is only present in that home for 30 days in the current tax year.

   Required

   Will Zoe be treated as UK resident in the current tax year?

3. Oliver (a widower) has a home in the UK as well as one in Sweden. He was UK resident (spending at least 10 months of every year in the UK) until one year ago when he moved permanently to Sweden. In the current tax year he spends 100 days in the UK visiting family and friends. The remainder of the year was spent in Sweden. His brother and sister-in-law are his only family members living in the UK.

   Required

   Will Oliver be treated as UK resident in the current tax year?

Solution

Exam focus point

The determination of an individual's residence status was tested in Corey in the March 2020 ATX exam. The Examiner said that in this type of question students should note the following:

- Unless given in the scenario, or excluded in the scenario, you should start with the process of determining someone's resident status by considering the automatic overseas and UK residence tests. Many students overlooked these.

- When considering the number of UK ties someone has, knowledge must be precise. Clearly most students made use of the information in the tax tables, but didn't fully understand it. The tables say that someone who is in the UK for 91 - 120 days, who has been previously resident, needs only two ties to be UK resident in the current tax year. However, this omits the information that it relates only to the previous three tax years, when, in this case the individual has been non-resident.

- When discussing the number of ties and individual satisfies, a good approach is to consider each in turn, and state whether or not it applies. This will ensure you maximise your mark in this type of question.

- The requirement asked for a conclusion. This is usually worth one mark, and just requires the student to conclude sensibly from what they have written, but a minority of candidates did not do this.

1.6 Split-year treatment

An individual can **split the tax year** into a **UK part (taxable)** and an **overseas part (not taxable)** if they are **UK resident**, using the tests above for that year, in a **number of scenarios**.

The **split year treatment** applies to **individuals leaving the UK** where:

- The **individual leaves the UK** to begin **full time work overseas**
- The **individual's partner** (spouse, civil partner or someone with whom the individual lives) **leaves the UK to begin full time work overseas** and the **individual leaves the UK in order to continue to live with them**
- The **individual leaves the UK** to **live abroad, sells their UK house**, spends a **minimal amount of time in the UK** and **establishes ties with the overseas country**

The **split-year treatment** applies to **individuals coming to the UK** where:

- The individual **comes to the UK, acquires a home in the UK** and the individual **does not have sufficient ties to the UK** in order to be UK resident prior to obtaining the UK home
- The **individual comes to the UK** to **work full time** for a period of **at least a year** and the individual **does not have sufficient ties to the UK in order to be UK resident before coming to the UK**
- The **individual returns to the UK** following a period where **the individual or partner has worked full time overseas**

Essential reading

See Chapter 9 of the Essential reading for illustrations of split-year treatment.

The Essential reading is available as an Appendix of the digital edition of the Workbook.

2 Domicile and deemed domicile

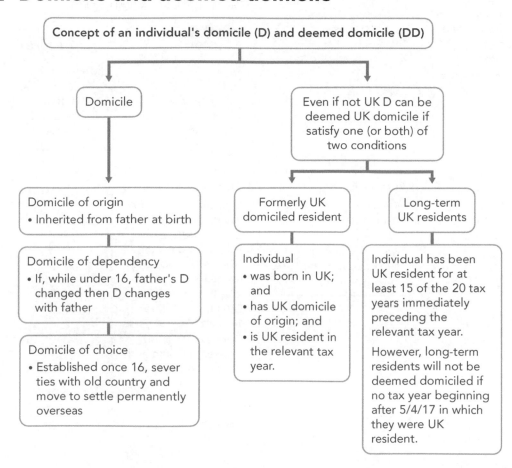

Concept of an individual's domicile (D) and deemed domicile (DD)

Domicile

Even if not UK D can be deemed UK domicile if satisfy one (or both) of two conditions

Domicile of origin
- Inherited from father at birth

Domicile of dependency
- If, while under 16, father's D changed then D changes with father

Domicile of choice
- Established once 16, sever ties with old country and move to settle permanently overseas

Formerly UK domiciled resident

Individual
- was born in UK; and
- has UK domicile of origin; and
- is UK resident in the relevant tax year.

Long-term UK residents

Individual has been UK resident for at least 15 of the 20 tax years immediately preceding the relevant tax year.

However, long-term residents will not be deemed domiciled if no tax year beginning after 5/4/17 in which they were UK resident.

Essential reading

See Chapter 9 of the Essential reading for illustrations of deemed domicile.

The Essential reading is available as an Appendix of the digital edition of the Workbook.

3 Effect of residence and domicile on liability to tax

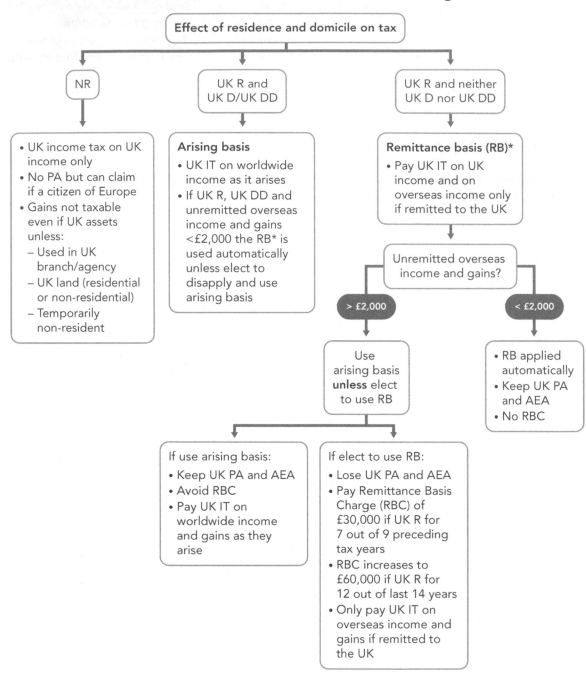

Effect of residence and domicile on tax

NR
- UK income tax on UK income only
- No PA but can claim if a citizen of Europe
- Gains not taxable even if UK assets unless:
  - Used in UK branch/agency
  - UK land (residential or non-residential)
  - Temporarily non-resident

UK R and UK D/UK DD

Arising basis
- UK IT on worldwide income as it arises
- If UK R, UK DD and unremitted overseas income and gains <£2,000 the RB* is used automatically unless elect to disapply and use arising basis

UK R and neither UK D nor UK DD

Remittance basis (RB)*
- Pay UK IT on UK income and on overseas income only if remitted to the UK

Unremitted overseas income and gains?

> £2,000

Use arising basis **unless** elect to use RB

< £2,000
- RB applied automatically
- Keep UK PA and AEA
- No RBC

If use arising basis:
- Keep UK PA and AEA
- Avoid RBC
- Pay UK IT on worldwide income and gains as they arise

If elect to use RB:
- Lose UK PA and AEA
- Pay Remittance Basis Charge (RBC) of £30,000 if UK R for 7 out of 9 preceding tax years
- RBC increases to £60,000 if UK R for 12 out of last 14 years
- Only pay UK IT on overseas income and gains if remitted to the UK

Formula provided

The remittance basis charge is given to you in the Tax rates and allowances available to you in the exam.

Essential reading

See Chapter 9 of the Essential reading for more detail on the remittance basis.

The Essential reading is available as an Appendix of the digital edition of the Workbook.

4 Income tax aspects

4.1 UK resident and UK domiciled/deemed domiciled individuals

Individuals who are UK resident and UK domiciled or UK deemed domiciled are taxed on UK income and overseas income on an arising basis.

The **overseas income** is put into the **appropriate column** of the income tax computation depending on **its source** ie **property business income** or **pension income** in **non-savings column**, **interest income** in the **savings income column** and **dividends** in **dividend income column**.

> ### Exam focus point
>
> In Corey in the March 2020 exam an individual who had been non-resident became UK resident and students were asked to state how becoming UK resident would affect their liability to UK income tax. Many students did not score full marks due to a lack of precision. Simply stating 'he would be liable to UK income tax' is not enough. Students needed to make clear this applies to overseas income, as well as UK income.
>
> In Emma, Question 2 in the December 2019 exam students were asked to explain how an individual's overseas rental income would be taxed in the UK based on their residence and domicile. The examining team said 'many students decided the individual was not UK domiciled but did not realise they would actually be deemed UK domicile. It is vital students have an in-depth understanding of the detail of the ATX-UK tax rules; a superficial understanding of the rules is not enough to score well in this exam.'

4.2 UK resident but non-UK domiciled/deemed domiciled individuals

4.2.1 Remittance basis

Individuals who are **UK resident but neither UK domiciled nor UK deemed domiciled** are taxable on **UK income** on an **arising basis**.

If they are using the **remittance basis** for **overseas income**, they will put **all remitted overseas income into the non-savings income column** (it loses its source nature and all becomes non-savings income). Therefore, the **benefits** of the **savings income nil rate band and dividend nil rate band** are **lost**.

An individual who **makes a claim for the remittance basis** (ie automatic remittance basis does not apply) is **not entitled** to a **personal allowance**.

4.2.2 Remittance basis charge (RBC)

Individuals are liable to the RBC in a tax year if they:

- **Claim the remittance basis for the tax year;** and
- Are **aged 18 or over in the tax year,** and
- Have been **UK resident** for **at least seven of the nine tax years immediately preceding that tax year.**

The **amount of the RBC** in a tax year depends on the **length of time the individual has been resident in the UK**:

- An individual who has been resident for **12 of the 14 tax years** immediately preceding that tax year has a **RBC of £60,000.**
- An individual who has been resident for **seven of the nine tax years** immediately preceding that tax year (but not yet 12 of the last 14 tax years) has a **RBC of £30,000.**

4.2.3 Claiming the remittance basis

As the **remittance basis needs to be claimed** each tax year those eligible **will need to decide whether to claim or not.**

Activity 2: Remittance basis claim

Claire has been resident for the last nine years but is not UK domiciled and was born overseas. In 2020/21 Claire has the following income:

	£
UK trading income	10,000
Overseas income	80,000

She remits £15,000 of her overseas income to the UK.

Required

Determine whether or not Claire should claim to use the remittance basis in 2020/21.

Solution

4.3 Non-UK resident individuals

Non-UK resident individuals are **liable to income tax** on **UK income** only.

In general, **non-UK resident individuals** are **not entitled** to a **personal allowance**.

Essential reading

See Chapter 9 of the Essential reading for more detail on individuals not resident in the UK.

The Essential reading is available as an Appendix of the digital edition of the Workbook.

5 Capital gains tax (CGT) aspects

5.1 UK resident and UK domiciled/deemed domiciled individuals

In general, **individuals** who are **UK resident and either UK domiciled or deemed domiciled in a tax year** are **taxable** on disposals of **UK and overseas assets** in that tax year on an **arising basis**. This means that **gains are chargeable** and **losses are allowable** on all disposals.

5.2 UK resident and non-UK domiciled/deemed domiciled individuals

Individuals who are **resident in the UK but neither domiciled nor deemed domiciled in the UK in a tax year are taxable on disposals of UK assets** on an **arising basis. They are taxable on disposals of overseas assets** on a **remittance basis** if they make a **claim for the remittance basis** or it **applies automatically** because their unremitted income and gains are less than £2,000 in the tax year.

Otherwise they are taxable on disposals of overseas assets on an arising basis.

Individuals who claim the remittance basis are not entitled to the annual exempt amount.

Essential reading

See Chapter 9 of the Essential reading for more detail on losses for UK resident and non-UK domiciled/deemed domiciled individuals.

The Essential reading is available as an Appendix of the digital edition of the Workbook.

5.3 Non-UK resident individuals

5.3.1 General rule

A **non-UK resident individual** who makes a disposal of a **UK asset** is generally **not chargeable to CGT** so does not have **chargeable gains** and **does not make allowable losses.**

However, in the following **three circumstances, gains/losses** will be **chargeable/allowable:**

- Trade operated through a UK branch or agency
- UK land
- Individuals who are temporarily non-UK resident

These are explained in further detail below.

5.3.2 Trade operated through a UK branch or agency

CGT applies where:

- A non-UK resident individual **carries on a trade in the UK** through **a branch or agency**; and
- There is a disposal of **a UK asset**, which has been:
    - Used in or for the **purposes of the trade**; or
    - Used or held or acquired **for the purpose of the branch or agency.**

5.3.3 UK land

CGT applies if there is a disposal of **UK residential land** (which includes any buildings built on the land) **on or after 6 April 2015** by a **non-UK resident individual.**

CGT applies if there is a disposal of **UK non-residential land on or after 6 April 2019** by a **non-UK resident individual.** To calculate the gain or loss, such land is treated as **disposed of and reacquired at market value at 5 April 2019** (and thus the base cost for the future disposal will be the market value as at 5 April 2019).

However, the individual **can make an election for the normal basis of calculation to apply** using original cost eg to create an allowable loss.

Exam focus point

In the **ATX – UK exam**:

- UK land disposed of by a non-UK resident individual will **always have been acquired after 5 April 2015**; and
- Land will either be **wholly residential** or **wholly non-residential** throughout the period of ownership.

The rules also apply to indirect holdings of land eg through a company, but these are **not examinable** in ATX – UK.

An individual who has UK land gains is entitled to **the annual exempt amount.**

Losses on UK land incurred by non-resident individuals can only be set against **gains on UK land in the same tax year, later tax years** or if **carried back on death.**

The **rate of CGT** on such gains **depends on** the total of the **individual's taxable UK income and gains. Residential land gains** are taxable **at 18%/28%** and **non-residential gains** are taxable **at 10%/20%.**

CGT payable on **UK residential** land disposals is **due within 30 days** of the disposal, as for UK resident individuals.

Activity 3: Disposals by non-UK resident

Assume it is December 2020.

Xander has never been UK resident.

He inherited three UK assets from his mother on her death in August 2015 as follows:

	Probate value	Market value at 6.4.19	Net sale proceeds if sold now
	£	£	£
House	420,000	485,000	490,300
Shop	150,000	168,000	175,000
Quoted shares	90,000	87,000	85,000

Xander will have UK taxable income of £25,000 in the tax year 2020/21.

Required

Calculate Xander's CGT liability if he sells all three assets in December 2020, and state the relevant payment dates.

Solution

Essential reading

See Chapter 9 of the Essential reading for more detail on reliefs for disposals by non-UK resident individuals.

The Essential reading is available as an Appendix of the digital edition of the Workbook.

5.3.4 Individuals who are temporarily non-UK resident

If a **UK resident individual** becomes non-UK resident for **less than five years** (starting with the date of departure and ending on the day before the date of return) they remain **subject to CGT** in respect of **assets acquired before leaving the UK** (unless those assets are otherwise chargeable on disposals during the non-resident period as branch/agency assets or as UK land).

The **individual must have been UK resident** for at least **four of the seven previous tax years before the tax year** in which they **become non-UK resident**.

Gains/losses made during the **tax year of departure** are **dealt with in that tax year** under normal rules.

Gains/losses made in the non-UK resident period will be **chargeable/allowable** in the **tax year of return** (either a full tax year or the UK part of a split tax year).

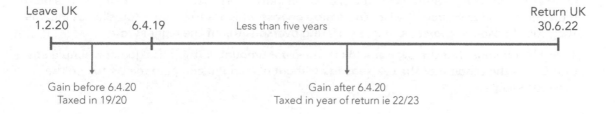

Exam focus point

The temporary non-residence rules were tested in Corey in the March 2020 exam and the examiner said it was disappointing to see how few students recognised that Corey would have been regarded as temporary non-resident for CGT purposes. The Examiner went on to say that this topic is frequently tested, and often not flagged, leaving it as a test of students' knowledge and skill to be able to identify when it applies. The key is question practice

Essential reading

See Chapter 9 of the Essential reading for an illustration of gains chargeable on an individual who is temporarily non-UK resident.

The Essential reading is available as an Appendix of the digital edition of the Workbook.

6 Double taxation relief (DTR)

6.1 Introduction

As we have seen, **UK tax** can apply to the **worldwide income/gains** of **UK resident individuals** and the **UK income/gains** of **non-UK resident individuals.**

When other countries adopt the **same approach** it is clear that **some income/gains may be taxed twice:**

- In the **country where they arise**
- In the **country where the individual resides**

Double taxation relief (DTR) as a result of **international agreements** may avoid the problem, or at least diminish its impact.

Essential reading

See Chapter 9 of the Essential reading for detail on double taxation agreements.

The Essential reading is available as an Appendix of the digital edition of the Workbook.

6.2 Unilateral relief for income tax

If no relief is available under a double taxation agreement, UK legislation provides for unilateral relief.

DTR is always given on a source-by-source basis, as the lower of:

- **UK income tax** on the **gross overseas income**; and
- **Overseas tax** on the **same income.**

The **UK tax** is the **difference between**:

- UK tax before DTR on **all income including overseas income**; and
- UK tax on all income **except overseas income.**

Overseas income is treated as the **top slice** of an individual's income and, where there is **more than one overseas source**, the **individual may choose which is to be their top slice of income.** They will choose the **overseas source suffering overseas tax at the highest rate.**

It may be **obvious that the overseas tax is the lower amount.** In this case **you can simply state that DTR is the amount of the overseas tax** without needing to compute the UK tax on the overseas source.

Activity 4: DTR

Neil has earned income of £39,050 for 2020/21. In addition, he has overseas income, the **gross** amount taxable in 2020/21 being:

Overseas loan stock interest £6,000 (including overseas tax £920)

Overseas property income £6,500 (including overseas tax £3,250)

Neil is resident and domiciled in the UK.

Required

Calculate his UK income tax liability, assuming that unilateral double taxation relief applies.

Solution

6.3 Unilateral relief for CGT

If no relief is available under a double taxation agreement, UK legislation provides for unilateral relief.

DTR is the **lower** of:

*   **UK CGT** on **overseas asset** (set losses, AEA and basic rate band against UK gain(s) first to maximise UK tax on overseas gain); and
*   **Overseas tax** on the **same asset**.

Chapter summary

Overseas personal taxation

Residence

Statutory residence test
See section *Statutory residence test* in the additional revision content

Automatic overseas tests
- Previously UK resident, <16 UK days
- Not previously UK resident, <46 UK days
- Full-time overseas work, not in UK >90 days

Automatic UK tests
- ≥183 UK days
- ≥30 UK days & UK (only) home used
- Full-time UK work

Sufficient ties
- Table in Rates and allowances
- UK ties
  - Close family
  - Available accommodation
  - Substantive work
  - > 90 UK days in either of two previous tax years
  - In UK more than any other country (only if previously UK resident)

Days spent in UK
Present at midnight

Split-year treatment
- UK part (taxable), non-UK part (not taxable)
- Includes
  - Leaving UK for full-time work overseas
  - Coming to UK and acquiring UK home
  - Coming to UK for full-time work ≥ 1 yr
  - Returning to UK after full time work

Domicile and deemed domicile

See section *Domicile and deemed domicile* in the additional revision content

Effect of residence and domicile on liability to tax

See section *Effect of residence and domicile on liability* to tax in the additional revision content

Income tax aspects

UK resident and domiciled/ deemed domiciled

- UK and overseas income on arising basis
- Overseas income keeps original source

UK resident, non-UK domiciled/ deemed domiciled

- UK income on arising basis
- Overseas income may be remittance basis
- RB automatic if unremitted income and gains < £2,000, otherwise needs claim
- Remitted income = non-savings income
- No PA if remittance basis claim
- RBC if remittance basis claim and UK resident ≥ 7/9 previous tax years
- Remittance basis claim decision each tax year

Non UK-resident

- UK income only
- Generally, no PA

CGT aspects

UK resident and domiciled/ deemed domiciled

UK and overseas gains/losses on arising basis

UK resident, non-UK domiciled/ deemed domiciled

- UK gains/losses on arising basis
- Overseas gains may be remittance basis, losses allowable (election if remittance basis claim)
- No AEA if remittance basis claim
- RBC as for income tax

Non UK-resident

- Generally, not chargeable to CGT even on UK assets
- Exceptions
  - UK branch/agency
  - UK land (residential since 6.4.15, non-residential since 6.4.19)
  - Temporarily non-UK resident up to five years, non-resident gains/losses on pre-departure assets taxable/ allowable on return

Additional revision content

Statutory residence test

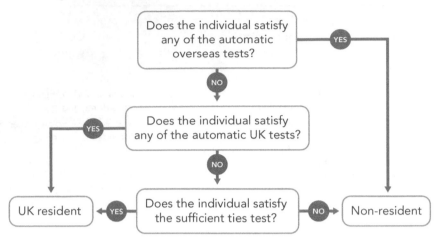

Domicile and deemed domicile

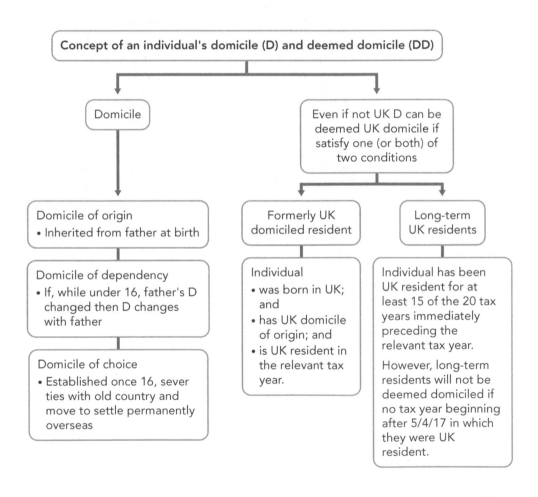

Effect of residence and domicile on liability to tax

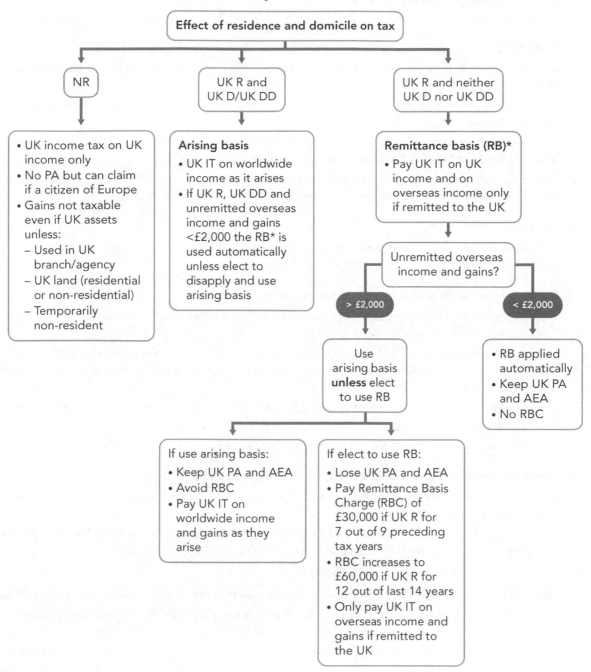

Effect of residence and domicile on tax

NR
- UK income tax on UK income only
- No PA but can claim if a citizen of Europe
- Gains not taxable even if UK assets unless:
  - Used in UK branch/agency
  - UK land (residential or non-residential)
  - Temporarily non-resident

UK R and UK D/UK DD

Arising basis
- UK IT on worldwide income as it arises
- If UK R, UK DD and unremitted overseas income and gains <£2,000 the RB* is used automatically unless elect to disapply and use arising basis

UK R and neither UK D nor UK DD

Remittance basis (RB)*
- Pay UK IT on UK income and on overseas income only if remitted to the UK

Unremitted overseas income and gains?

> £2,000

< £2,000

Use arising basis **unless** elect to use RB

- RB applied automatically
- Keep UK PA and AEA
- No RBC

If use arising basis:
- Keep UK PA and AEA
- Avoid RBC
- Pay UK IT on worldwide income and gains as they arise

If elect to use RB:
- Lose UK PA and AEA
- Pay Remittance Basis Charge (RBC) of £30,000 if UK R for 7 out of 9 preceding tax years
- RBC increases to £60,000 if UK R for 12 out of last 14 years
- Only pay UK IT on overseas income and gains if remitted to the UK

Knowledge diagnostic

1. Residence

An individual will automatically not be UK resident if they meet any of the automatic overseas tests.

An individual, who does not meet any of the automatic overseas tests, will automatically be UK resident if they meet any of the automatic UK tests.

An individual who has not met any of the automatic overseas tests nor any of the automatic UK tests will be UK resident if they meet the sufficient ties test.

In general, an individual is either resident or non-resident for the whole of a tax year. However, in certain circumstances, the tax year may be split into UK and overseas parts.

2. Domicile

An individual may be UK domiciled under general law or deemed UK domiciled as a formerly UK domiciled resident or as a long-term UK resident.

3. Impact of residence and domicile – income tax aspects

A UK resident who is UK domiciled or deemed domiciled is liable to UK income tax on UK and overseas income as it arises.

An UK resident individual who is neither UK domiciled nor UK deemed domiciled is liable to UK income tax on income arising in the UK and may be entitled to be taxed on overseas income on the remittance basis.

An individual who claims the remittance basis and is a long-term UK resident is required to pay the Remittance Basis Charge (RBC) on unremitted income and gains.

A non-UK resident is liable to UK income tax only on income arising in the UK.

4. Impact of residence and domicile – capital gains tax aspects

A UK resident who is UK domiciled or deemed domiciled is liable to UK capital gains tax (CGT) on UK and overseas gains as they arise.

A UK resident individual who is neither UK domiciled nor deemed domiciled is liable to UK CGT on UK gains and may be entitled to be taxed on overseas gains on the remittance basis.

A non-UK resident is generally not liable to CGT.

From 6 April 2015, disposals of UK residential property by non-UK residents are subject to CGT.

From 6 April 2019, disposals of UK non-residential property by non-UK residents are subject to CGT. Only the gain or loss accruing since 6 April 2019 is chargeable/allowable.

PRR may be available on disposals of UK residential properties by non-UK resident individuals but is restricted for tax years where the individual is neither UK tax resident nor satisfies a 'day count test'.

Individuals who are temporarily non-UK resident are subject to CGT if they make disposals during the non-UK resident period of assets acquired before they became non-UK resident.

5. Double taxation relief

Double taxation relief may be available to reduce the burden of taxation. It is generally given by reducing the UK tax charged by the lower of UK and overseas tax.

Further study guidance

Question practice

Now try the following from the Further question practice bank (available in the digital edition of the Workbook):

*   Maria, Felix and Susan
*   Robert

Further reading

There is one technical article on the ACCA website written by members of the ATX – UK examining team which is relevant to some of the topics covered in this chapter that you should read:

*   International aspects of personal taxation for Advanced Taxation (ATX – UK)

Activity answers

Activity 1: Residence

1 No, Abbey will not be treated as UK resident under the second automatic overseas test. She was not resident in any of the three previous years and spends less than 46 days in the UK in the current tax year.

2 Yes, Zoe meets the second automatic UK test, so will be treated as UK resident in the current tax year.

3 Yes, Oliver will be treated as UK resident in the current tax year. He has been resident in the UK for one of the previous three years so would only need two ties to be resident, as he has been in the UK for 91 to 120 days.

He has an accommodation tie and has spent more than 90 days in the UK in one of the previous two tax years (no family tie, no country tie, no UK work tie).

Activity 2: Remittance basis claim

Claim to use remittance basis

	Non-saving income
	£
UK trading income	10,000
Overseas income (remitted)	15,000
Taxable income (no personal allowance)	25,000
IT liability	£
25,000 × 20%	5,000
Annual tax charge on unremitted income	30,000
Income tax liability if remittance basis claimed	35,000

No claim to use remittance basis (tax on arising basis on worldwide income)

	Non-saving income
	£
UK trading income	10,000
Overseas income	80,000
Net income	90,000
Less PA	(12,500)
Taxable income	77,500
IT liability	£
37,500 × 20%	7,500
40,000 × 40%	16,000
77,500	23,500

Therefore, Claire should not claim the remittance basis.

Activity 3: Disposals by non-UK resident

	Residential gain	Non-residential gain
	£	£
House £(490,300 – 420,000)	70,300	
Shop £(175,000 – 168,000)		7,000
Shares – not chargeable to CGT so no allowable loss	–	0
Chargeable gains	70,300	7,000
Less AEA (best use)	(12,300)	–
Taxable gains	58,000	7,000

CGT:	
£12,500 (37,500 – 25,000) @ 18%	2,250
£45,500 (58,000 – 12,500) @ 28%	12,740
£7,000 @ 20%	1,400
CGT liability	16,390

The CGT on the residential property of £14,990 (£2,250 + £12,740) is due within 30 days of the disposal. The remaining CGT of £1,400 is due on the usual payment date for 2020/21 (31/1/22).

Activity 4: DTR

	Non-savings income	Savings income
	£	£
Employment income	39,050	
Property income	6,500	
Interest	–	6,000
	45,550	6,000
Less PA	(12,500)	–
	33,050	6,000

IT:		
NSI 33,050 × 20%		6,610
SI 500 × 0% (higher rate taxpayer)		0
	3,950 × 20%	790
	37,500	
	1,550 × 40%	620
		8,020
Less DTR (W1)		(2,630)
Income tax liability		5,390

Workings

1   **Exclude property income first as it suffers highest rate of overseas tax.**

	Non-savings income	Savings income
	£	£
Employment income	39,050	
Interest	–	6,000
Net income	39,050	6,000
Less PA	(12,500)	–
Taxable income	26,550	6,000

IT: 26,550 × 20%	5,310
1,000 × 0% (now basic rate taxpayer)	0
5,000 × 20%	1,000
	6,310

2   **DTR lower of:**

	£
(i) Overseas tax	3,250
(ii) UK tax (8,020 − 6,310)	1,710
∴ £1,710	

3   **Now exclude loan stock interest.**

	Non-savings income
	£
Employment income/net income	39,050
Less PA	(12,500)
Taxable income	26,550

IT: 26,550 × 20%	5,310

4   **DTR lower of:**

	£
(i) Overseas tax	920
(ii) UK tax (6,310 − 5,310)	1,000
∴ £920	

Total DTR = 1,710 + 920 = £2,630

10

Personal tax administration

Learning objectives

On completion of this chapter, you should be able to:

	Syllabus reference no.
Remember the material covered in Taxation (TX – UK) under the headings:	
'The systems for self-assessment and the making of returns'	A6(b) A3
'The time limits for submission of information, claims and payment of tax including payments on account'	A6(b) A4
'The procedures relating to compliance checks, appeals and disputes'	A6(b) A5
'Penalties for non-compliance'	A6(b) A6
Advise on the increased penalties which apply in relation to offshore matters	A6(b)(i)

Exam context

In any tax advice question, you must consider the administrative requirements and time limits. You must know the taxpayer's responsibilities for making returns and paying tax, and the rules that HMRC can use to enforce compliance.

This chapter is mainly a revision of material studied in TX – UK. The new topic is the increased penalties which apply in relation to offshore matters.

Chapter overview

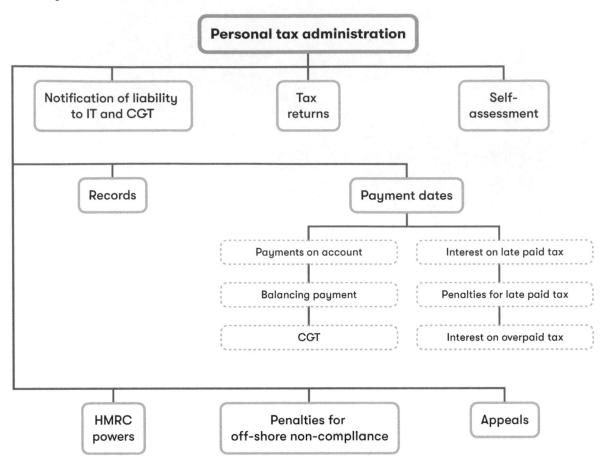

1 Notification of liability to income tax and capital gains tax (CGT)

1.1 Duty to notify

The taxpayer has a **duty to notify liability to income tax and/or CGT** to HM Revenue & Customs (HMRC) by **5 October following end of tax year**, unless they have received a notice from HMRC to file a return.

A taxpayer who has **no chargeable gains** and who is **not liable to higher rate tax** does not have to give notice of chargeability if all their income:

- Is taken into account under **PAYE**;
- Is from a source of income **not subject to tax under a self-assessment**;
- Has had (or is treated as having had) **income tax deducted at source**; or
- Is **savings income and/or dividend income falling within the savings income nil rate band and the dividend nil rate band**.

1.2 Penalties for failure to notify liability

A **common penalty regime** applies for failure to notify chargeability to, or liability to register for income tax, national insurance contributions (NICs), CGT, corporation tax and VAT. Penalties are **behaviour related**, increasing for more serious failures, and are based on the **'potential lost revenue' (PLR)**:

- Up to **30% of PLR** if non-deliberate failure to notify
- Up to **70% of PLR** if deliberate failure to notify, increased to **100% if also concealment**

Penalties can be reduced if **taxpayer makes disclosure** and are **more generous** if **disclosure is unprompted** (can be **reduced to 0%** for a **non-deliberate failure if unprompted disclosure within 12 months**).

Essential reading

See Chapter 10 of the Essential reading for more details on penalties for failure to notify.

The Essential reading is available as an Appendix of the digital edition of the Workbook.

2 Tax returns

2.1 Filing dates

HMRC usually issues a **notice to the taxpayer requiring them to file a tax return**.

Paper returns must usually be filed by **31 October following the end of the tax year**.

Electronically delivered returns must usually be filed by **31 January following the end of the tax year**.

PER alert

One of the competencies you require to fulfil Performance Objective 16 Tax compliance and verification of the PER is to explain tax filing and payment requirements and the consequences of non-compliance to clients. You can apply the knowledge you obtain from this section of the Workbook to help demonstrate this competence.

Essential reading

See Chapter 10 for more details on the filing dates for tax returns.

The Essential reading is available as an Appendix of the digital edition of the Workbook.

2.2 Penalties for late filing

The **penalty date** for **filing a late return** is the **day after the filing date**.

Penalties for filing on or after penalty date are as follows:

0–3 months	£100
3–6 months	Further penalty: £10 per day (maximum 90 days)
6–12 months	Further penalty: greater of 5% of tax liability and £300
12 months +	Further penalty: greater of % of tax liability (conduct based) and £300

Essential reading

See Chapter 10 of the Essential reading for more details on penalties for late filing where the failure continues after the end of the 12-month period.

The Essential reading is available as an Appendix of the digital edition of the Workbook.

2.3 Penalties for errors

A **common penalty regime** applies to **incorrect self-assessment tax returns, self-assessment corporation tax returns** and **misdeclarations on a value added tax (VAT) return**.

Penalties are **behaviour related** and are **based on the PLR** as a **result of the error**. For example, if there is an **understatement of tax**, this **understatement** will be **the PLR**. Penalties can be **reduced** if taxpayer makes **disclosure** and are **more generous** if disclosure is **unprompted**.

The maximum and minimum amount of penalties are as follows:

Taxpayer behaviour	Maximum penalty	Minimum penalty – unprompted disclosure	Minimum penalty – prompted disclosure
Deliberate and concealed	100%	30%	50%
Deliberate but not concealed	70%	20%	35%
Careless	30%	0%	15%

Formula provided

The penalty percentages will be given to you in the Tax Rates and Allowances available in the exam.

Activity 1: Penalty for error

Alexander is a sole trader. He files his tax return for the tax year 2020/21 on 10 January 2022. The return shows his trading income to be £60,000. In fact, due to carelessness, his trading income should have been stated to be £68,000. Alexander has no other income.

Required

Compute the maximum penalty that could be charged by HMRC on Alexander for his error.

Solution

3 Self-assessment

A **self-assessment** is a **calculation of the amount of taxable income and gains** after **deducting reliefs and allowances**, and a **calculation of income tax and CGT payable** after taking into account **tax deducted at source.**

If the taxpayer is filing a **paper return, they may make the tax calculation on their return or ask HMRC to do so on their behalf.** In either case, this is treated as a 'self-assessment' by the taxpayer.

If the taxpayer wishes HMRC to make the calculation for Year 1, a paper return must be filed:

- **On or before 31 October in Year 2, or**
- **If the notice to file the tax return is issued after 31 July in Year 2, within three months of the notice**

If the taxpayer is filing an **electronic return, the calculation of tax liability is made automatically when the return is made online.**

Essential reading

See Chapter 10 of the Essential reading for more details on amending self-assessments.

The Essential reading is available as an Appendix of the digital edition of the Workbook.

4 Records

All taxpayers must retain all records required to enable them to make and deliver a correct tax return.

Records must usually be retained until the later of:

- **Five years after the 31 January following the tax year** where the **taxpayer is in business** (as a sole trader or partner or letting property). Note that this applies to all of the records, not only the business records;
- **One year after the 31 January following the tax year otherwise.**

The **maximum penalty** for each **failure to keep and retain records** is **£3,000 per tax year.**

5 Payment dates

5.1 Payments on account

Income tax and Class 4 NICs are payable by **two equal payments on account** by **31 January (during the tax year)** and **31 July (following the end of the tax year)**. Each **payment on account** is equal to **50%** of the **previous tax year's income tax and Class 4 NIC liability** (the 'relevant amount').

Exam focus point

Due to the Coronavirus outbreak and its impact on individuals and businesses, the government permitted taxpayers to defer certain tax payments, including the payment on account of income tax and NIC for the tax year 2019/20 that was due on 31 July 2020, and any VAT payments that fell due between 30 March and 30 June 2020. The ACCA examining team have advised that, where relevant, you should assume the taxpayer has NOT chosen to defer these payments.

Activity 2: Payments on account

Sue is a self-employed writer who paid tax for 2019/20 as follows:

	£
Total amount of income tax charged	9,200
This included tax deducted on company loan stock	1,200
She also paid Class 4 NIC	1,900

Required

Compute the payments on account for income tax and Class 4 NIC for 2020/21 and state by what dates are they due.

Solution

Essential reading

See Chapter 10 of the Essential reading for more details on the circumstances where payments on account are not required and on claims to reduce payments on account.

The Essential reading is available as an Appendix of the digital edition of the Workbook.

5.2 Balancing payment

Any **balancing payment** is payable by **31 January following the end of the tax year** (which will also **include all the Class 2 NICs**).

5.3 CGT

CGT is payable by **31 January following the end of the tax year.** However, for disposals of **residential property** a **payment on account** must be made **within 30 days of completion of the disposal** (as covered in Chapter 7).

5.4 Interest on late paid tax

Interest is chargeable on **late payment of payments on account** and **balancing payments** from **due date** until **day before actual payment date.**

5.5 Penalties for late paid tax

Where the **balancing payment and/or CGT is paid late,** the **penalty date is 30 days after the due date.**

The **following penalties** apply:

On or before penalty date	0%
Not more than 5 months after penalty date	5% of unpaid tax
Between 5 months and 11 months after penalty date	10% of unpaid tax
More than 11 months after penalty date	15% of unpaid tax

5.6 Interest on overpaid tax

Interest on overpaid tax (repayment supplement) is **payable** from the **original date of payment** until the **day before the repayment of tax** is made.

Repayment supplement paid to individuals is tax free.

6 HMRC powers

6.1 Compliance checks

HMRC must give **notice of a compliance check** into a return **by the first anniversary** of the **actual filing date** if the **return is filed on or before the filing date**.

If the **return is filed after the filing date**, HMRC must **give notice** by the **quarter day following the first anniversary of the actual filing date**. The quarter days are 31 January, 30 April, 31 July and 31 October.

Essential reading

See Chapter 10 of the Essential reading for more details of HMRC powers in relation to determinations, discovery assessments and dishonest conduct of tax agents.

The Essential reading is available as an Appendix of the digital edition of the Workbook.

7 Penalties for offshore non-compliance

> **Offshore matter:** Relates to **income arising from a source in a territory outside the UK, assets situated or held in a territory outside the UK**; and **activities carried on wholly or mainly in a territory outside the UK.**

There may be **increased penalties** for **offshore non-compliance**. The **rates** are linked to **how much information** the **particular offshore territory shares with HMRC** so that the more difficult it is for HMRC to obtain information, the higher the penalty.

There is an **additional penalty** where there is a **relevant offshore asset move** intended to **prevent or delay HMRC from discovering a potential loss of revenue**.

Penalties may also be imposed on **those** who **enable offshore non-compliance.**

8 Appeals

Appeals must first be made to HMRC.

The **taxpayer may be offered**, or may **ask for**, an **'internal review'**, which will be **made by** an **objective HMRC review officer** not previously connected with the case.

If there is no internal review, or the taxpayer is unhappy with the result of an internal review, the case may be heard by the Tax tribunal.

Essential reading

See Chapter 10 of the Essential reading for more details of appeals.

The Essential reading is available as an Appendix of the digital edition of the Workbook.

Chapter summary

Personal tax administration

Notification of liability to IT and CGT

- By 5 October following end of tax year
- Penalty based on PLR:
  - 30% non-deliberate
  - 70% deliberate
  - 100% deliberate and concealed
- Penalties reduced if disclosure (to 0% for non-deliberate failure if unprompted disclosure)

Tax returns

- By 31 October following end of tax year for paper return
- By 31 January following end of tax year for electronically submitted returns
- Penalties for late filing:
  - 0 to 3 mths: £100
  - 3 to 6 mth: Further penalty: £10 per day (maximum 90 days)
  - 6 to 12 mths: Further penalty: greater of 5% of tax liability and £300
  - ≥12 mths: greater of % of tax liability (conduct based) and £300
- Penalties for errors
  - See Tax Rates and Allowances available in exam

Self-assessment

- Taxable income/gains and tax after deductions at source
- Paper return: can ask HMRC to do assessment on taxpayer's behalf
- Electronic return: automatic
- Amendment by taxpayer: within 12 months after filing date
- Amendment by HMRC: within 9 months of actual filing date

Records

- All records that are required to make and deliver correct tax return
- Retain until:
- 5 years after 31 January following end of tax year if in business
- 1 year after 31 January following end of tax year otherwise
- Penalty for failure: £3,000 per tax year

Payment dates

Payments on account

- Payments on account:
  - 31 January during tax year
  - 31 July following end of tax year
  - Each 50% of previous year's IT and Class 4 NIC liability ('relevant amount')
  - Not required if the relevant amount is <£1,000
  - Can claim to reduce payments on account

Balancing payment

31 January following end of tax year (includes Class 2 NIC)

CGT

31 January after end of tax year (or 30 days from completion for payment on account on UK residential property)

Interest on late paid tax

- On late payment of payments on account and balancing payments
- From due date until day before actual payment date

Penalties for late paid tax

- For balancing payment/CGT:
  - Within 30 days (penalty date): 0%
  - Within 5 mths of penalty date: 5%
  - Within 5 to 11 mths of penalty date: 10%
  - More than 11 mths of penalty date: 15%

Interest on overpaid tax

From original date of payment until day before repayment of tax made

HMRC powers

- Compliance check notice by HMRC:
  - By first anniversary of actual filing date if return filed on or before filing date
  - By quarter day following first anniversary of the actual filing date if filed after filing date
- Determination: of amounts liable to tax
- Discovery assessment: to recover tax lost, eg if careless/deliberate understatement
- Dishonest conduct of tax agents: HMRC may issue penalty up to £50k

Penalties for off-shore non-compliance

- Increased penalties for offshore non-compliance
- Additional penalty for off-shore asset move to avoid HMRC discovery
- Penalties imposed on enablers of offshore non-compliance

Appeals

- To HMRC
- Internal review may be offered
- Otherwise, cases heard by Tax Tribunal

BPP LEARNING MEDIA

Knowledge diagnostic

1. Taxpayer obligations

Individuals must notify their chargeability to income tax or CGT by 5 October following the end of the tax year. A common penalty regime applies to late notification of chargeability.

Tax returns must usually be filed by 31 October (paper) or 31 January (electronic) following the end of the tax year.

Two payments on account and a final balancing payment of income tax and Class 4 NICs are due. Class 2 NICs and CGT are payable at the same time as the balancing payment. Interest is payable on late paid tax.

2. Penalties

A penalty can be charged for late filing of a tax return based on how late the return is and how much tax is payable.

There is a common penalty regime for errors in tax returns, including income tax, NICs, corporation tax and VAT. Penalties range from 30% to 100% of the Potential Lost Revenue. Penalties may be reduced.

A penalty is chargeable where a balancing payment and/or CGT is paid after the due date and is based on the amount of the unpaid tax.

There may be increased penalties for off-shore non-compliance and an additional penalty where there is a relevant offshore asset move intended to prevent or delay HMRC from discovering a potential loss of revenue. Penalties may also be imposed on those who enable offshore non-compliance.

3. Compliance checks and disputes

A compliance check into a return can be started by HMRC within a limited period.

Disputes between taxpayers and HMRC can be dealt with by an HMRC internal review or by a Tribunal hearing.

Further study guidance

Question practice

Now try the following from the Further question practice bank (available in the digital edition of the Workbook):

- Mark, Sarah and Meredith

Activity answers

Activity 1: Penalty for error

Potential lost revenue (PLR) as a result of Alexander's error is: £(68,000 – 60,000) = £8,000 × [40% (income tax) + 2% (Class 4 NICs] = £3,360.

Alexander's error is careless, so the maximum penalty for the error is: £3,360 × 30% = £1,008.

Activity 2: Payments on account

		£
Income tax:		
Total income tax charged for 2019/20		9,200
Less tax deducted at source on loan stock for 2019/20		(1,200)
		8,000
Class 4 NIC		1,900
'Relevant amount'		9,900
Payments on account for 2020/21:		
31 January 2021	£9,900 × 50%	4,950
31 July 2021	£9,900 × 50%	4,950

11

Inheritance tax computation

Learning objectives

On completion of this chapter, you should be able to:

	Syllabus reference no.
Remember the material covered in Taxation (TX – UK) under the heading: 'scope of inheritance tax, basic principles of computing transfers of value, the liabilities arising on chargeable lifetime transfers and on the death of an individual, the use of exemptions in deferring and minimising inheritance tax liabilities'	A3(a) D1 D2 D3
Identify excluded property	A3(b)(ii)
Advise on the principles of valuation including the related property rules	A3(c)(i)
Advise on the availability of business property relief (BPR) and agricultural property relief (APR)	A3(c)(ii)
Identify exempt transfers	A3(c)(iii)
Advise on the tax implications of chargeable lifetime transfers	A3(d)(i)
Advise on the tax implications of transfers within seven years of death	A3(d)(ii)
Advise on the tax liability arising on a death estate	A3(d)(iii)
Understand and apply the tapered withdrawal of the residence nil rate band where the net value of the estate exceeds £2 million	A3(d)(iv)
Advise on the relief for the fall in value of lifetime gifts	A3(d)(v)
Advise on the operation of quick succession relief	A3(d)(vi)
Advise on the reduced rate of inheritance tax payable when a proportion of a person's estate is bequeathed to charity	A3(d)(ix)
Advise on the use of reliefs and exemptions to minimise inheritance tax liabilities	A3(f)(i)

Exam context

In the ATX – UK exam, you will be expected to deal with basic inheritance tax (IHT) transfers and the death estate but also the more advanced technical rules covered in this chapter.

Sections 1 to 7 of this chapter are mainly revision of the basic principles of IHT covered in TX – UK. These cover the meaning of transfer of value, chargeable transfer and potentially exempt transfer, the diminution in value principle, the seven year accumulation principle taking into account changes in the level of the nil rate band, the tax implications of lifetime transfers and computation of the relevant liabilities, and the computation of tax liability on a death estate. It is important that you have a good understanding of these topics before you move onto the more advanced aspects in the remainder of the chapter.

Sections 8 to 12 cover new topics which are: the relief for fall in value of lifetime gifts, valuation rules (including overseas property), Business Property Relief and Agricultural Property Relief, additional aspects relating to the death estate, and Quick Succession Relief. One or more of these topics may well be tested in ATX – UK questions so make sure you know when and how the rules apply.

You will be expected to use your knowledge of IHT to advise clients about minimising inheritance tax liabilities. We will develop this aspect further in Chapter 13 Capital tax planning.

Chapter overview

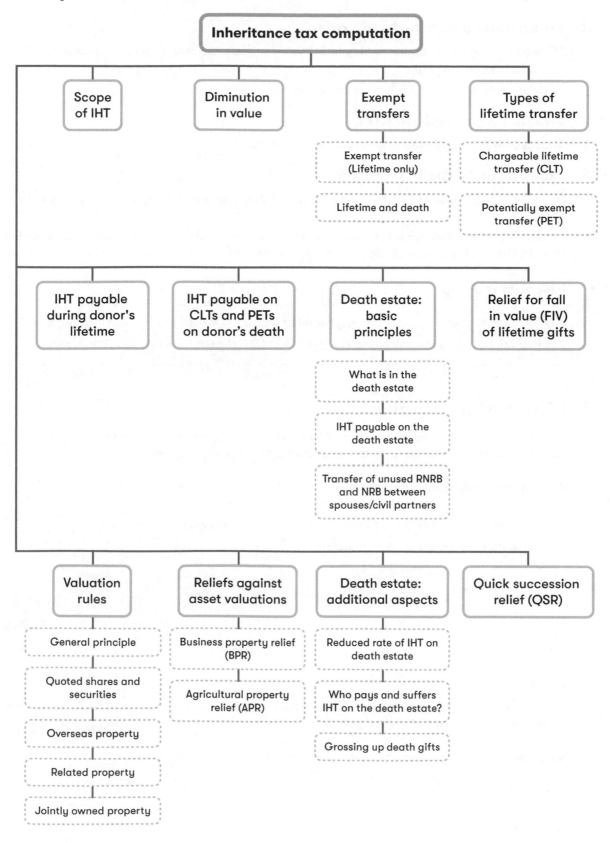

Inheritance tax computation

- Scope of IHT
- Diminution in value
- Exempt transfers
  - Exempt transfer (Lifetime only)
  - Lifetime and death
- Types of lifetime transfer
  - Chargeable lifetime transfer (CLT)
  - Potentially exempt transfer (PET)

- IHT payable during donor's lifetime
- IHT payable on CLTs and PETs on donor's death
- Death estate: basic principles
  - What is in the death estate
  - IHT payable on the death estate
  - Transfer of unused RNRB and NRB between spouses/civil partners
- Relief for fall in value (FIV) of lifetime gifts

- Valuation rules
  - General principle
  - Quoted shares and securities
  - Overseas property
  - Related property
  - Jointly owned property
- Reliefs against asset valuations
  - Business property relief (BPR)
  - Agricultural property relief (APR)
- Death estate: additional aspects
  - Reduced rate of IHT on death estate
  - Who pays and suffers IHT on the death estate?
  - Grossing up death gifts
- Quick succession relief (QSR)

1 Scope of inheritance tax (IHT)

1.1 When does a charge to IHT arise?

IHT is a **tax** on **gifts** or **'transfers of value'**. There are **two main chargeable occasions:**

- **Lifetime transfers;** and
- **Death estate,** ie gifts made on death (eg in will).

1.2 Who is chargeable to IHT?

Chargeable persons include **individuals** and **trustees.**

1.3 Exceptions to the IHT charge

There are **some transfers** which are **specifically stated in legislation to be excepted from the IHT charge.**

The **most important example** is **transfers of excluded property** which is **overseas assets owned by individuals who are not UK domiciled nor deemed domiciled** (see Chapter 12).

Essential reading

See Chapter 11 of the Essential reading for more details on exceptions to the IHT charge.

The Essential reading is available as an Appendix of the digital edition of the Workbook.

2 Diminution in value

The **value of the asset transferred for IHT** is always measured as the **diminution in value of the donor's wealth** ('loss to donor'), **not the amount gained by the donee.**

Activity 1: Diminution in value

Jonny owns 75% of an unquoted investment company. He gives 30% to his son.

Shareholdings on this date were valued at:

	£
75%	370,000
45%	200,000
30%	105,000

Required

Calculate the value transferred for IHT purposes and calculate the value to be used for proceeds in the capital gains tax (CGT) computation.

Solution

The **diminution in value principle** also means that **transfers must be grossed up if the donor pays the lifetime IHT** (see the section below called 'IHT payable during donor's lifetime').

We look at **more valuation rules** in the section below called 'Valuation rules'.

3 Exempt transfers

3.1 Exempt transfers (lifetime only)

The **following transfers** are **exempt** if **made during the donor's lifetime:**

- **Small gifts**
- **Normal expenditure out of income**
- Gifts in **consideration of marriage/civil partnership**
- Gifts **covered by annual exemption(s)**

Essential reading

See Chapter 11 of the Essential reading for more detail on these exempt transfers.

The Essential reading is available as an Appendix of the digital edition of the Workbook.

3.2 Spouse/civil partner exemption (lifetime and death)

Gifts **between spouses** or **partners in a civil partnership** are **exempt transfers.**

If the **donor spouse/civil partner is UK domiciled or deemed domiciled** (see Chapter 12) **but the donee spouse/civil partner is not UK domiciled nor deemed domiciled, the spouse exemption is limited to a cumulative total equal to the amount of the nil rate band at the date of the transfer** ie £325,000 for 2020/21.

3.3 Other exempt transfers (lifetime and death)

Transfers to UK charities are exempt transfers.

Gifts to a qualifying political party **are exempt transfers.** A political party qualifies if, **at the general election** preceding the transfer of value, either:

- At least **two members** were **elected** to the **House of Commons**; or
- **One member was elected** and **the party polled at least 150,000 votes.**

Gifts for national purposes are exempt transfers. Eligible recipients include museums and art galleries.

4 Types of lifetime transfers

4.1 Chargeable lifetime transfers (CLTs)

CLTs are gifts to a trust. They are **chargeable at the time of the gift** so that **lifetime IHT may be payable.**

If the **donor dies within seven years** of making a CLT, additional IHT may **become payable on death.**

> **Exam focus point**
>
> Where CLTs and PETS are made in the same year the CLTs should be made first to use any available exemptions. If used up against the PETs an exemption will be wasted if the PET never becomes chargeable.

4.2 Potentially exempt transfers

Any other gifts, ie **gifts to individuals** other than spouses/civil partners, **are PETs.**

A **PET is treated** as **exempt during donor's lifetime** so **no lifetime IHT is payable.**

If **the donor dies seven years or more after the PET is made,** the **PET is an exempt transfer** so **no IHT is payable on it** and **it does not enter into the cumulative total of transfers.**

If **the donor dies within seven years after PET is made,** the **PET becomes a chargeable transfer and IHT may be payable on it.**

5 IHT payable during donor's lifetime (Lifetime tax)

Follow this procedure:

(a) Prepare a **timeline** and **mark on CLTs** and **PETs**

(b) Value each **gift** remembering the **diminution in value** principle

(c) Deduct **valuation reliefs** (Business Property Relief and Agricultural Property Relief – see the section called 'Reliefs against asset valuation' below)

(d) Deduct **exemptions** (see 'Exempt transfers' section above). Remember that annual exemptions are allocated against gifts in date order

(e) For each **CLT,** deduct **available nil rate band (NRB)** which is the **NRB at the time of the gift** less any CLTs in the seven years before that gift.

(f) Tax the **excess over the NRB** at **20/80** (ie 25% or ¼) **if the donor pays the IHT** (net transfer) or **20% if trustees pay the IHT** (gross transfer). If the question is silent, assume the donor pays the IHT

(g) Calculate the **gross value of gift** (**'gross chargeable transfer'**) for cumulation. This is the **transfer of value plus the IHT if the donor pays** and **just the transfer of value if the trustees pay**

A proforma for this calculation can be found in the additional revision content after the chapter summary for this chapter.

Formula provided

NRBs will be given to you in the Tax rates and allowances available in the exam.

Essential reading

See Chapter 11 of the Essential reading for an illustration of the computation of lifetime IHT.

The Essential reading is available as an Appendix of the digital edition of the Workbook.

6 IHT payable on CLTs and PETs on donor's death (death tax on lifetime gifts)

IHT is charged on CLTs and PETs made within seven years of the donor's death. This **IHT is payable by the donee.**

Follow this procedure:

(a) Use the **timeline** prepared for working out lifetime IHT. Mark **seven years** before the **donor's death.**

(b) **Delete all PETs more than seven years before death.** These are now exempt transfers.

(c) Start with the **earliest gift within seven years of death.**

(d) **IHT charged** on the **value of the gift after reliefs and exemptions.**

(e) Deduct **available nil rate band (NRB)** which is the **NRB at the time of deathless any previous chargeable transfers in the seven years before that gift.** Previous chargeable transfers are (1) CLTs and (2) PETs that have become chargeable.

(f) Tax **excess over available NRB** at **40%.**

(g) **Deduct** any **taper relief.**

The **following table,** showing the percentage reduction depending on the period between date of gift (PET/CLT) and death, should be used to calculate the taper relief:

Period	Percentage reduction
0–3	0%
3–4	20%
4–5	40%
5–6	60%
6–7	80%

(h) **Deduct any IHT paid in donor's lifetime** (CLTs only).

A proforma showing this calculation can be found in the additional revision content after the chapter summary for this chapter.

Formula provided

The table above will be given to you in the Tax rates and allowances available in the exam.

Essential reading

See Chapter 11 of the Essential reading for illustrations of the computation of IHT on lifetime transfers on the death of the donor.

The Essential reading is available as an Appendix of the digital edition of the Workbook.

7 Death estate: basic principles

7.1 What is in the death estate?

Set out below is the layout of a **standard death estate computation**:

X DECEASED

DATE OF DEATH...

	£	£
Freehold land (eg main residence)	X	
Less mortgages and accrued interest	(X)	
		X
Business/agricultural property	X	
Less BPR/APR (see the section called 'Relief against asset valuation' below)	(X)	
		X
Shares and securities		X
Insurance policy proceeds		X
Leasehold land		X
Cars		X
Personal chattels		X
Debts due to deceased		X
Cash (including accrued bank deposit interest)		X
		X
Less: Debts owed by deceased	X	
Funeral expenses	X	(X)
		X
Less: Exempt transfers (see the section above called 'Exempt transfers')		(X)
		X
Gifts with reservation (see Chapter 12)		X
Chargeable estate		X

Essential reading

See Chapter 11 of the Essential reading for more detail about debts and funeral expenses in the death estate.

The Essential reading is available as an Appendix of the digital edition of the Workbook.

7.2 IHT payable on the death estate

7.2.1 Residence nil rate band (RNRB)

The **RNRB is available in calculating the IHT due on an individual's death estate** only if:

- The **individual dies on or after 6 April 2017**; and
- The **individual owned a home (main residence)** in **which they lived which forms part of their death estate**; and
- The **main residence passes to the individual's direct descendent(s)**. A direct descendant includes **children and grandchildren**. It does not include nieces, nephews or siblings.

The **available RNRB** is the **lower** of:

- **£175,000 for 2020/21** plus **any transferred RNRB from a spouse/civil partner** (see later in this section); and
- The **value of the main residence** passing to direct descendent(s). Note this is **after deducting any repayment or interest-only mortgage secured on the property.**

The **RNRB is tapered** if an **individual's net estate exceeds £2 million**. The **net estate** is calculated as the **value of all assets less liabilities** but is **before the deduction of any exemptions** such as the **spouse or charity exemptions** and **any reliefs** such as **agricultural property relief (APR)** or **business property relief (BPR)**. The **RNRB is tapered by £1 for every £2 the net estate exceeds £2 million**. Consequently, once the net estate exceeds £2.35 million, the **RNRB will have been tapered to nil.**

The **RNRB is deducted from the total value of the death estate,** rather than directly from the value of the main residence in the death estate, and is **deducted before the NRB.**

Exam focus point

ACCA have stated that **a question will make it clear if the RNRB is available**. Thus if there is no mention of a main residence do not consider a RNRB.

There are other aspects to the RNRB. Neither of the following are examinable in ATX – UK:

- **Protection of the RNRB** where an individual downsizes to a less valuable property or where a property is disposed of; and
- Nominating which property should qualify where there is more than one main residence.

Formula provided

The residence nil rate band, nil rate bands and tax rates are given to you in the Tax rates and allowances available in the exam.

Activity 2: Tapering RNRB

Pietr died on 31 August 2020 leaving a main residence worth £600,000, on which there was secured a repayment mortgage of £520,000, and cash and other assets worth £2,100,000. Debts and funeral expenses amounted to £25,000. Pietr left cash and jewellery worth £500,000 to his wife and the remainder of his estate to his son.

Required

What is the available RNRB for use in calculating the IHT due on Pietr's death estate?

Solution

7.2.2 Nil rate band (NRB)

Once **any RNRB has been deducted**, any **available nil rate band (NRB) is then deducted**.

The **available NRB is £325,000** for deaths in 2020/21 **less chargeable transfers in the seven years before death**. The **available NRB is deducted** from the **value of the death estate**.

7.2.3 Computing IHT on the death estate

Follow this procedure:

*   **Compute** the **value of the chargeable death estate**.
*   **Deduct** the **available RNRB**.
*   **Deduct** the **available NRB**.
*   **Charge the excess remaining** at **40%** (but see later section for 'grossing up death gifts'). **This IHT is payable by the personal representatives** (PRs) of the deceased.

 Essential reading

See Chapter 11 of the Essential reading for an illustration of the computation of IHT payable on the death estate.

The Essential reading is available as an Appendix of the digital edition of the Workbook.

A proforma of the death estate and the IHT on the death estate can be found in the additional revision content after the chapter summary at the end of this chapter.

7.3 Transfer of unused RNRB and NRB between spouses/civil partners

7.3.1 General principle

If a **spouse/civil partner dies without fully using their NRB and/or RNRB**, a claim can be made to **transfer the unused amount(s)** to the **other spouse/civil partner** on **death of the survivor** to **enhance the survivor's nil bands on death**.

Claims are usually **made by the survivor's PRs** within **two years of the end of the month of the survivor's death**.

7.3.2 NRB

The **enhanced NRB** is available to be used **against lifetime transfers** and **the death estate**.

If the **NRB has increased since the death of the first spouse/civil partner, uprate the unused NRB proportionately.**

7.3.3 RNRB

Provided the **surviving spouse/civil partner dies on or after 6 April 2017** leaving their **main residence** to **direct descendant(s)**, the **enhanced RNRB** can be used against the **death estate.**

If the **RNRB has increased since the death of the first spouse/civil partner, uprate the unused RNRB proportionately.**

If the **first spouse/civil partner died prior to 6 April 2017** they are **deemed to have had a RNRB**, all of which will be available for transfer to the surviving spouse (ie £175,000 if the survivor dies in 2020/21).

Activity 3: Transfer of RNRB and NRB

George died on 1 June 2007 leaving an estate valued at £400,000. He left £300,000 of his estate, including his main residence, to his wife Mildred and the balance to his son.

Required

Assuming Mildred dies on 1 September 2020, what nil rate band(s) will be available to her? Assume that she leaves her estate, including the main residence, to her son.

Solution

Activity 4: Comprehensive example

James died on 22 January 2021. He had made the following gifts during his lifetime:

(1) On 9 October 2013, a cash gift of £235,000 to a trust. No lifetime IHT was payable in respect of this gift.

(2) On 14 May 2017, a cash gift of £420,000 to his daughter.

(3) On 2 August 2019, a gift of a property valued at £260,000 to his son. By the time of James' death on 22 January 2021, the property had increased in value to £310,000.

On 22 January 2021, James' estate consisted of the following assets:

(1) A main residence valued at £710,000. This had an outstanding repayment mortgage of £94,300.

(2) A portfolio of ordinary shares valued at £192,600

(3) A motor car valued at £21,900.

James owed £9,400 in respect of credit card debts and had also verbally promised to pay the £4,600 medical costs of a friend. The cost of James' funeral amounted to £5,800.

Under the terms of his will, James left his entire estate to his children.

The nil rate band of James' wife was 40% utilised when she died 10 years ago.

Required

Calculate the IHT which will be payable as a result of James' death, and state who will be responsible for paying the IHT.

Solution

---

8 Relief for fall in value (FIV) of lifetime gifts (fall in value relief)

If an **asset is gifted during lifetime** and **either:**

- Before the donor's death, the asset is **sold in an arm's length transaction to an unconnected person for an amount lower than original value; or**

- The **market value (MV) of the asset at the death of the donor is lower than the original value**

then the **donee can make a claim** that the **death IHT on the lifetime gift is based on the lower value.**

However, when **calculating the available NRB on other gifts (including the death estate)** the **original value** has to be used.

Activity 5: Fall in value of lifetime gift

Mark made a gift of some property to his daughter for £230,000 on 1 March 2016. He then gave a cash gift to his son of £210,000 on 2 October 2019. Mark's only other lifetime transfer was a gift to a trust on 14 August 2012, which resulted in a gross chargeable transfer of £105,000.

Mark died on 21 August 2020. At his death, the value of the property given to his daughter had fallen to £200,000.

Required

Calculate the IHT liabilities on these gifts arising on Mark's death.

Solution

9 Valuation rules

9.1 General principle

The **IHT value** of **any property** is the **open market value** at the **time of the transfer.**

9.2 Quoted shares and securities

Quoted shares and securities are **valued** at the **lower of:**

- '¼ up': the **lower (bid) of the two closing prices + ¼ of the difference between this and the higher (offer) price;** or
- **Average** of **highest** and **lowest marked bargains.**

These rules are different to the rules used for CGT purposes which are simply to use the **lower of the two prices shown plus one-half of the difference between the two prices** (see Chapter 8).

An **adjustment is needed** for any **ex-dividend or ex-interest quotations** for **shares or securities in the death estate.** The next dividend or the net interest payment needs to be **included in the death estate.** No adjustment is needed for gifts of shares and securities during lifetime.

Essential reading

See Chapter 11 of the Essential reading for an illustration of the valuation of quoted shares and details of valuations of unquoted shares and securities, unit trusts, and life policies.

The Essential reading is available as an Appendix of the digital edition of the Workbook.

9.3 Overseas property

Overseas property is **converted into sterling** at the **exchange rate** (the 'buy' or 'sell' rate) that gives the **lowest sterling valuation.**

On death, **additional administrative expenses** in relation to **administering the overseas property** are **deductible from the total estate** up to a **maximum of 5%** of the **value of the overseas property.**

Capital taxes paid overseas may **give rise to double taxation relief** (see Chapter 12).

9.4 Related property

KEY TERM

> **Related property:** Property is **related** if it is **owned by:**
> - **Donor's spouse/civil partner;** or
> - **Charity, charitable trust, political party or national heritage body**, where the property was given on an **exempt transfer** by **either spouse/civil partner** and **owned by the body within the last five years.**

The **related property rules** exist to **reduce the IHT saving** which could be obtained by **making a transfer piecemeal, partly via an exempt transfer.**

Where **an individual transfers property** where there is also **related property**, the **effect of the rules** is to **consider the individual's share in the whole of the property** when valuing the transfer.

The **valuation used** is the **higher of:**
- The value using the **normal rules** (ie ignoring the related property); and
- The **related share** (ie including the related property).

Activity 6: Related property

Mike holds 55% of the shares in a family investment company. His wife holds 25%. The balance of the share capital is held by other members of Mike's family.

Mike wants to gift his entire shareholding to a friend.

The following share values have been agreed at the date of the gift.

80%	£400,000
60%	£270,000
55%	£240,000
45%	£135,000
35%	£90,000
20%	£50,000
10%	£20,000

Required

Calculate the value of the shares to be transferred to his friend that will be used in the IHT computation.

Solution

9.5 Jointly owned property

Property may be **jointly owned** as **tenants in common** (passes on death under will or intestacy) or as **joint tenants** (passes on death automatically to the other joint tenant(s)).

In **either case**, the **deceased's interest in the property** is **part of death estate**.

If the **other owner** is the **spouse/civil partner of the deceased**, the **related property rules apply**.

10 Reliefs against asset valuation

10.1 Business property relief (BPR)

10.1.1 General principles

When **relevant business property is transferred** in **lifetime** or **on death**, BPR may be **given against the value of the asset**. Remember that it is **deducted before exemptions**.

10.1.2 Relevant business property and rates of relief

Relevant business property and the **rates of relief** are as follows:

Sole proprietor's business or **partnership share**	100%
Shares in an **unquoted trading company**	100%
Securities in an **unquoted company** which (either alone or with other securities or unquoted shares) **gave the donor control** immediately before the transfer	100%
Shares or securities in a **quoted company** which (either alone or with other securities or unquoted shares) **gave the donor control** immediately before the transfer	50%

Land, buildings, plant and machinery owned by donor and used either in a partnership in which donor is a partner or a company which the donor controls	50%

When **determining whether control applies**, include **related property**.

Shares or securities do not qualify as relevant business property if the company is an **investment company** or a **company dealing in shares and securities** or **land and buildings**.

10.1.3 Minimum period of ownership

The **donor** must usually have **owned the property** for **two years** preceding the transfer.

Alternatively, together with a **replacement property**, the donor must have **owned the property** for **at least two years** out of the **last five years**.

10.1.4 Excepted assets

> **Excepted assets:** An asset that:
> - Has **not been used wholly or mainly in the business in the last two years**; and
> - Is **not required for future use in the business**.

BPR is not available on excepted assets.

Examples include:
- **Large cash balances**
- **Investments**
- **Private use assets**

10.1.5 Additional conditions for lifetime gifts

When **calculating the death IHT due on a lifetime gift, BPR is usually only available if the donee still owns the property as relevant business property** at the **date of the donor's death** (or the **donee's death if earlier**).

These **conditions are also fulfilled** if the **donee disposed of the original property** but **reinvested all of the disposal proceeds** in **replacement property** within **three years** of the disposal.

Activity 7: Business property relief

Henry gifted 3,200 shares in Henry Ltd to his daughter. This represented 16% of the company's share capital which he had held for the last 5 years and was worth £100,000.

The company's net assets at that date were:

	£
Freehold	400,000
Plant and machinery	80,000
Goodwill	150,000
Investments	170,000
Net current assets	200,000
	1,000,000

Required

1 Show the IHT valuation of the shares gifted.

2 What would happen to the valuation if Henry died within seven years of the gift and his daughter no longer held the shares?

Solution

Essential reading

See Chapter 11 of the Essential reading for more details about business property relief.

The Essential reading is available as an Appendix of the digital edition of the Workbook.

10.2 Agricultural property relief (APR)

10.2.1 General principles

When **agricultural property is transferred** in **lifetime** or **on death**, **APR** may be **given against the agricultural value of the asset.** Remember that it is **deducted before exemptions.**

10.2.2 Agricultural property and rate of relief

Agricultural property must be **situated in the European Economic Area (EEA),** which includes the UK.

The **rate of relief** is **100%.**

APR is given before BPR. If the **non-agricultural part of the value of the property** meets the **relevant business property conditions, BPR** will be **available** on that **value.**

10.2.3 Minimum period of ownership/occupation

The **agricultural property** must usually have been:

- **Owned and occupied for agricultural purposes** by the **donor** for **at least two years immediately before the transfer** (ie the donor farms the land); or
- **Owned by donor** for at least **seven years immediately before the transfer** and **used for agricultural purposes throughout that time by either the donor or a tenant** (ie the property is or has been let out).

10.2.4 Shares/securities in farming companies

APR will also be given where the **donor transfers shares or securities, part of the value** of which are **attributed to the agricultural value of agricultural property** forming part of the company's assets.

The **donor must have control** (taking into account **related property**) **of the company** immediately before the transfer.

APR is given as if the **company's interest in the agricultural property** was **owned directly** by the **controlling shareholder.**

10.2.5 Additional conditions for lifetime gifts

When **calculating the death IHT due on a lifetime gift, APR is usually only available if the donee still owns the property as agricultural property** at the **date of the donor's death** (or the **donee's death if earlier**).

These **conditions are also fulfilled** if the **donee disposed of the original property** but **reinvested all of the disposal proceeds** in **replacement property** within **three years** of the disposal.

Activity 8: Agricultural property relief

On Edna's death, her estate included the following assets:

(1) A farm that she owned for eight years. The farm was let to a tenant throughout this period. The farm was valued at £180,000 and the agricultural value was £95,000.

(2) Shares in an unlisted farming company, which she controlled, which were valued at £175,000. The company owns land which it farmed for four years prior to Edna's death. The agricultural value is 20% of the company's net assets at the date of her death. Edna had owned the shares for five years.

Required

Calculate the value of these assets to be included in the estate.

Solution

Essential reading

See Chapter 12 of the Essential reading for more details about agricultural property relief.

The Essential reading is available as an Appendix of the digital edition of the Workbook.

Activity 9: Comprehensive example (2)

Drew made the following gifts during his life:

(1) 20 March 2012: Cash gift to his daughter of £40,000.

(2) 3 June 2015: A gift to his nephew of half of his 10% shareholding in Grandstand Ltd, an unquoted investment company. Drew's wife, Mary, has a 20% holding and they have both owned these shares for many years.

The value of the shareholdings have been agreed as follows:

5%	£100,000
10%	£230,000
25%	£750,000
30%	£1,050,000

(3) 14 October 2015: A 4% shareholding in Davies plc to his son. It is a quoted trading company which he has owned for five years. The 4% holding represents 170,000 shares.

The closing prices were £2.00–£2.10 and marked bargains for the day were £1.98 and £2.06.

(4) 9 June 2016: A gift of £200 to each of his five grandchildren

(5) 23 November 2016: Gift to a trust of £335,000.

Drew died on 13 September 2020.

Required

Calculate the IHT payable on the gifts as a result of his death, assuming all non-cash gifts are still held by the donees at that date (assume trustees pay any lifetime IHT).

Solution

11 Death estate: additional aspects

11.1 Reduced rate of IHT on death estate

11.1.1 Overview of death estate computation

As seen earlier, the **death estate** comprises **assets less of liabilities of the deceased**. From this any **exempt legacies are deducted** to come down to the **chargeable estate**. The **available RNRB and NRB are then deducted** and the **balance is usually taxed at 40%**. However, if a **large gift to charity has been made**, a **36% rate of IHT may apply**.

11.1.2 Reduced rate of IHT

The **estate is taxed at 36%** if **at least 10% of an individual's net estate has been left to a charity** (ignoring the deduction available in respect of legacies to charities).

The **net estate** is the **assets owned reduced by liabilities, exemptions, reliefs and the available NRB** but with **no deduction** for the **charitable donation** nor any **RNRB**.

This **reduced rate** is **given in addition to the exemption** available to **charitable legacies**.

 ## Activity 10: Reduced rate of IHT

Fiona died, leaving an estate valued at £1.4 million (this was before deducting any exempt transfers).

In her will she wished to leave £200,000 to the RSPCA, with the balance, including her main residence worth £600,000, going to her son.

Fiona has made no lifetime gifts. She is a divorcee.

Required

Calculate the IHT payable on her estate.

Solution

11.2 Who pays and suffers IHT on the death estate?

	Paid by	Usually suffered by
UK assets	PRs	Residuary beneficiary
Overseas assets	PRs	Beneficiary of asset
Gift with reservation (see Chapter 12)	Donee of asset	Donee of asset

Activity 11: Who pays and suffers IHT on death estate?

James died on 13 November 2020.

On this date he owned the following assets:

	£
UK main residence	168,000
Shares	10,000
Villa in Spain	40,000
Cash	30,000

Funeral expenses totalled £1,000.

James' lifetime gifts were as follows:

15 January 2011	Gift to son, cash on occasion of his marriage	£144,000
10 June 2016	Gift to his daughter, cash	£307,000

Required

What is the IHT on the lifetime transfers and the chargeable estate, assuming that the villa is left to his daughter and everything else is left to his son? Show clearly who pays and who suffers the IHT.

Solution

11.3 Grossing up death gifts

Specific gifts of UK assets on death must be **grossed up** if the **residue of the estate** is left to an exempt recipient.

Essential reading

See Chapter 12 of the Essential reading for an illustration of grossing up death gifts.

The Essential reading is available as an Appendix of the digital edition of the Workbook.

12 Quick succession relief (QSR)

KEY TERM

> **Quick succession relief:** Given if an **asset/estate is charged to IHT twice** in a period of **five years.**

The **rate of relief** is as follows:

Period between transfers	Percentage of first amount of IHT credited
0–1 years	100%
>1–2 years	80%
>2–3 years	60%
>3–4 years	40%
>4–5 years	20%

The **amount of the relief** is **calculated** as follows:

Percentage as determined above $\times \dfrac{\text{Net value of gift/legacy}}{\text{Gross value of gift/legacy}} \times$ IHT paid on original transfer

Activity 12: Quick succession relief

Kyle transferred shares to Lara on his death on 4 March 2016. The chargeable (ie gross) value of the transfer was £48,531 including IHT of £8,420 paid by Kyle's estate.

On 8 May 2020 Lara died, leaving a chargeable estate valued at £330,000. She had made no lifetime transfers.

Required

Show the IHT liability on Lara's estate.

Solution

Chapter summary

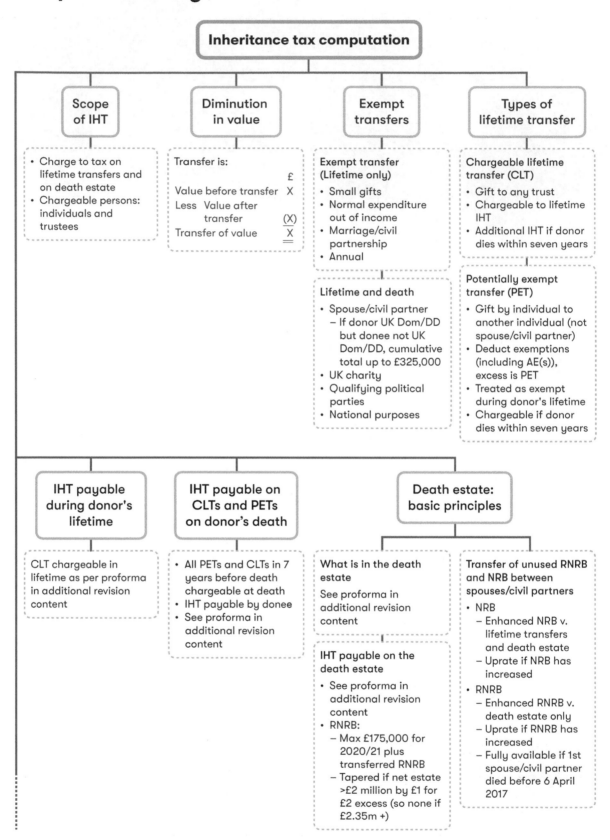

Inheritance tax computation

Scope of IHT

- Charge to tax on lifetime transfers and on death estate
- Chargeable persons: individuals and trustees

Diminution in value

Transfer is:

	£
Value before transfer	X
Less Value after transfer	(X)
Transfer of value	X

Exempt transfers

Exempt transfer (Lifetime only)
- Small gifts
- Normal expenditure out of income
- Marriage/civil partnership
- Annual

Lifetime and death
- Spouse/civil partner
  - If donor UK Dom/DD but donee not UK Dom/DD, cumulative total up to £325,000
- UK charity
- Qualifying political parties
- National purposes

Types of lifetime transfer

Chargeable lifetime transfer (CLT)
- Gift to any trust
- Chargeable to lifetime IHT
- Additional IHT if donor dies within seven years

Potentially exempt transfer (PET)
- Gift by individual to another individual (not spouse/civil partner)
- Deduct exemptions (including AE(s)), excess is PET
- Treated as exempt during donor's lifetime
- Chargeable if donor dies within seven years

IHT payable during donor's lifetime

CLT chargeable in lifetime as per proforma in additional revision content

IHT payable on CLTs and PETs on donor's death

- All PETs and CLTs in 7 years before death chargeable at death
- IHT payable by donee
- See proforma in additional revision content

Death estate: basic principles

What is in the death estate

See proforma in additional revision content

IHT payable on the death estate
- See proforma in additional revision content
- RNRB:
  - Max £175,000 for 2020/21 plus transferred RNRB
  - Tapered if net estate >£2 million by £1 for £2 excess (so none if £2.35m +)

Transfer of unused RNRB and NRB between spouses/civil partners
- NRB
  - Enhanced NRB v. lifetime transfers and death estate
  - Uprate if NRB has increased
- RNRB
  - Enhanced RNRB v. death estate only
  - Uprate if RNRB has increased
  - Fully available if 1st spouse/civil partner died before 6 April 2017

Relief for fall in value (FIV) of lifetime gifts

- Value of lifetime gift has fallen
- IHT on death calculated using value @ death
- Reduced value cannot be used for cumulation purposes

Valuation rules

General principle

MV at time of transfer

Quoted shares and securities

- Lower of:
  - ¼ up; or
  - Average of highest and lowest marked bargains

Overseas property

- Convert to £ to give lowest value
- Extra admin expenses up to 5% of asset deducted from total estate
- DTR

Related property

- Property owned by:
  - Spouse/civil partner
  - Charity, charitable trust, political party or national heritage body
- Value transfer as proportion of related property holding, if higher than unrelated value

Jointly owned property

Normally divided 50:50

Reliefs against asset valuations

Business property relief (BPR)

- Reduces transfer value (before AE(s) if lifetime transfer)
- Usually 100% relief
- Minimum period of ownership
  - 2 yrs if purchased
  - 2 out of 5 yrs if replacing
- Excepted assets: no BPR
- Death tax on lifetime gifts
  - Donee must retain as business property until donor's death
- No BPR if under contract for sale at date of transfer

Agricultural property relief (APR)

- Reduces transfer value (before AE(s) if lifetime transfer)
- 100% against agricultural value of EEA property
- Minimum period of ownership
  - 2 yrs ownership if owner occupied
  - 7 yrs ownership if tenanted
- Also applies to shares/ securities in farming companies
- BPR may also apply if owner occupied
- Death tax on lifetime gifts
  - Donee must retain as agricultural property until donor's death
- No APR if under contract for sale at date of transfer

Death estate: additional aspects

Reduced rate of IHT on death estate
- ≥ 10% of net estate left to charity
- 36% rate applies to estate

Who pays and suffers IHT on the death estate?
- Pay:
  - PRs: on UK and overseas other than GWROB
  - GWROB: donee
- Suffer
  - UK assets: residuary beneficiary
  - Overseas assets: beneficiary of asset
  - GWROB: donee

Grossing up death gifts
- Specific gift of UK asset, residue exempt
- IHT on legacy payable out of residue so gross up using 40/60 on excess

Quick succession relief (QSR)

- Percentage as determined below × $\dfrac{\text{Original net transfer}}{\text{Original gross transfer}}$ × Tax paid on earlier transfer
- Rate of relief

Period between transfers	Percentage of first tax charge credited
0–1 years	100%
>1–2 years	80%
>2–3 years	60%
>3–4 years	40%
>4–5 years	20%

Additional revision content – IHT computation proformas

Lifetime tax on a CLT

	£	£
Value before		X
Less: Value after		(X)
Transfer of value		X
Less: BPR/APR		(X)
		X
Less: Exemptions		(X)
CLT (gross/net)		X
Less:		
NRB at date of gift	X	
Less CLTs in seven years before gift	(X)	
Available NRB		(X)
Excess		X
IHT on excess @ 20% (trust pays) or 20/80 (donor pays)		X

	Trust pays (gross)	CLT
Gross CLT	Donor pays (net)	CLT + IHT

CLTs and PETs on death

	£	£
CLT (gross)/PET		X
Less		
NRB at date of **death**	X	
Chargeable transfers (CLTs/PETs now chargeable) in seven years before **gift**	(X)	
Available NRB		(X)
Excess		X
IHT on excess @ 40%		X
Less taper relief (in Tax Rates and Allowances) if death between 3–7 yrs		(X)
Lifetime IHT (CLT only)		(X)
IHT payable (no refunds if negative)		X

Death estate

X deceased

Date of death...

	£	£
Freehold land (eg main residence)	X	
Less: Mortgages and accrued interest	(X)	
		X
Business/agricultural property	X	
Less: BPR/APR	(X)	
		X
Other assets, eg quoted shares, cash		X
		X
Less: Debts owed by deceased	X	
Funeral expenses	X	(X)
		X
Less: Exempt transfers eg spouse/civil partner, charity		(X)
		X
Gifts with reservation		X
Chargeable estate		X

IHT on death estate (Chapter 11)

	£	£
Chargeable estate		X
Less: RNRB (max £175k + transferred from spouse/civil partner)		(X)
NRB at date of death + transferred from spouse/civil partner	X	
Less: chargeable transfers (CLTs/PETs now chargeable) in seven years before death	(X)	
Available NRB		(X)
Excess		X
IHT on excess @ 40% (payable by PRs, suffered by beneficiaries)		X

Knowledge diagnostic

1. IHT computation - basics

IHT applies to transfers to trusts, and transfers to individuals within the seven years before death and transfers on death.

If excluded property (overseas assets owned by individual who is not UK domiciled or deemed domiciled) is given away, there are no IHT consequences.

IHT is charged on what a donor loses. If the donor pays the IHT on a lifetime gift they lose both the asset given away and the money with which they paid the IHT due on it so grossing up is required.

Exemptions may apply to make transfers or parts of transfers non-chargeable. Some exemptions only apply on lifetime transfers (annual, normal expenditure out of income, marriage/civil partnership), whilst some apply on both life and death transfers (eg spouses/civil partners, charities, political parties).

2. Lifetime IHT

Lifetime IHT may be payable on chargeable lifetime transfers (CLTs) but potentially exempt transfers (PETs) are treated as exempt during the donor's lifetime. The available nil rate band (NRB) is after CLTs made in the seven years before this CLT.

3. Death tax on lifetime gifts

IHT may be payable if a donor dies within seven years of making a CLT or a PET. The available NRB is after chargeable transfers made in the seven years before this transfer. Taper relief applies if the gift is at least three years but less than seven years before the donor's death.

4. Death tax on the death estate

When someone dies, we must bring together all their assets to find the value of their death estate and then charge IHT on it (to the extent that it is not exempt), taking account of the available residence nil rate band (RNRB) and the available NRB after transfers made in the seven years before death.

5. Transfer of RNRB/NRB from spouse/civil partner

If one spouse/civil partner does not use up their whole RNRB and/or NRB on death, the excesses may be transferred to the surviving spouse/civil partner.

6. Fall in value relief

If an asset falls in value between a lifetime gift and death, fall in value relief reduces the IHT payable on death.

7. Valuing quoted shares

Quoted shares are valued for IHT at the lower of '¼ up' and average of highest and lowest marked bargain.

8. Overseas assets

Additional administrative expenses are deductible (up to 5% of the value of overseas property) in relation to administering such property on death.

9. Related property

Related property must be valued as a proportion of the value of the whole of the related property if this produces a higher value than the stand-alone value.

10. BPR

Business property relief (BPR) can reduce the values of assets by 100% or 50%.

11. APR

Agricultural property relief (APR) usually reduces a transfer of agricultural property by 100% of agricultural value.

12. Reduced rate for charitable giving

The rate of IHT on a death estate is reduced to 36% if at least 10% of the estate is left to charity.

13. IHT administration

The PRs pay IHT on the death estate (other than on gifts with reservation) but it is suffered by beneficiaries. Gross up specific gifts of UK assets on death if the residue of the estate is left to an exempt recipient.

14. QSR

Quick succession relief applies where there are two charges to IHT within five years.

Further study guidance

Question practice

Now try the following from the Further question practice bank (available in the digital edition of the Workbook):

- Rodin

Further reading

There is one technical article on the ACCA website written by members of the ATX – UK examining team which is relevant to some of the topics covered in this chapter that you should read:

- Inheritance tax and capital gains tax for Advanced Taxation (ATX – UK)

Activity answers

Activity 1: Diminution in value

	£
Before transfer (75%)	370,000
After transfer (45%)	(200,000)
IHT value	170,000

MV for CGT = gift of 30% holding = £105,000

Activity 2: Tapering RNRB

Pietr's net estate (before reliefs and exemptions) is:

	£
Main residence (600,000 − 520,000)	80,000
Cash and other assets	2,100,000
Less debts and funeral expenses	(25,000)
Chargeable estate	2,155,000

As this exceeds £2 million the RNRB will be tapered:

	£
RNRB	175,000
Less ½ (2,155,000 − 2,000,000)	(77,500)
Tapered RNRB	97,500

Pietr's available RNRB will be the lower of:

	£
Available RNRB	97,500
Value of the main residence passing to direct descendants	80,000

Thus, the RNRB available to offset against Pietr's death estate will be £80,000.

Note. Note that as Pietr's wife is still alive there is no need to consider any transfer of unused RNRB or NRB.

Activity 3: Transfer of RNRB and NRB

	£
1 June 2007 George's estate	400,000
Less exempt transfer to Mildred	(300,000)
Chargeable estate	100,000
Nil band on death estate 2007/08	300,000
Less used against estate	(100,000)

	£
Unused nil band for transfer to Mildred on her death	200,000

Thus, the proportion of unused NRB to be passed to Mildred is 2/3

Note that as George's death is prior to 6 April 2017, the RNRB would not have been available.

On Mildred's death in September 2020

As Mildred died after 6 April 2017 owning a main residence left to a direct descendant the RNRB will be available. On George's death no RNRB would have been used as it was not available so Mildred will be entitled to an additional 100% RNRB.

	£
RNRB available (including 100% from George) (200% × £175,000)	350,000
RNB available (including 67% from George) (167% × £325,000)	542,750

Note. Note that whilst the £542,750 NRB will be available to Mildred on both death IHT on transfers within seven years of death and on the death IHT on the death estate the RNRB of £350,000 is **only** available on calculation of the death IHT on Mildred's death estate. The RNRB which is then claimed would also depend on the value of the main residence being left to the son. Assuming the main residence was worth more than £350,000 the full RNRB of £350,000 could be deducted.

Activity 4: Comprehensive example

Lifetime transfers within seven years of death

14 May 2017

	£
Gift	420,000
Less: Annual exemption (AE) 2017/18	(3,000)
AE 2016/17 b/f	(3,000)
Potentially exempt transfer	414,000
Less: Available nil band rate (NRB)(W)	(291,000)
Excess	123,000
£123,000 @ 40%	49,200
Taper (3–4 yrs) 20%	(9,840)
	39,360

Payable by James's daughter

2 August 2019

	£
PET	260,000
Less: AE 2019/20	(3,000)
AE 2018/19 b/f	(3,000)

		£
		254,000
IHT £254,000 @ 40%		101,600

(no NRB available, no taper relief as death within three years)

Payable by James's son

Death estate

	£	£
Main residence	710,000	
Less outstanding repayment mortgage	(94,300)	
Net value of main residence		615,700
Shares		192,600
Car		21,900
Gross estate		830,200
Less credit card debt (not gratuitous promise)	9,400	
Less funeral expenses	5,800	
		(15,200)
Chargeable estate		815,000
Less available RNRB £175,000 × 2 (lower than £615,700)		
(including 100% unused RNRB from wife)		(350,000)
No available NRB		
Excess		465,000
IHT liability £465,000 @ 40%		186,000

Payable by James's PRs

Working

Available NRB

	£	£
NRB at date of death including spouse's unused NRB: 160% × £325,000		520,000
Gift 9 October 2012	235,000	
Less: AE 2013/14	(3,000)	
Less: AE 2012/13 b/f	(3,000)	(229,000)
NRB available		291,000

Activity 5: Fall in value of lifetime gift

Death IHT

	£
CLT 14.8.12 – no additional IHT since >7 years before death	
PET 1.3.16 Gift	230,000
AE 2015/16	(3,000)
2014/15 b/f	(3,000)
Original PET	224,000
Less fall in value (230,000 – 200,000)	(30,000)
Revised PET	194,000

No IHT payable since covered by remaining NRB of 325,000 – 105,000 = 220,000

	£	£
PET 2.10.19 Gift		210,000
AE 2019/20		(3,000)
2018/19 b/f		(3,000)
PET		204,000
NRB at date of death	325,000	
Less chargeable transfer <7 years (original value)	(224,000)	
Available NRB		(101,000)
		103,000
Death IHT @ 40%		41,200
No taper relief since <3 years		

Activity 6: Related property

Related property valuation:

$$\frac{55\%}{55\% + 25\%} \times £400,000 = £275,000$$

Unrelated valuation = £240,000.

Therefore the £275,000 valuation will be used in the IHT computation.

Activity 7: Business property relief

1

	£
Value of shares	100,000
Less BPR (exclude excepted assets)	
£100,000 × (1,000k - 170k)/1,000k = £83,000	
× 100%	(83,000)

	£
	17,000

2 If Henry died and his daughter no longer held the shares, BPR would not be available. Value of shares would therefore be £100,000.

Activity 8: Agricultural property relief

Edna

	£
(a) Value of farm	180,000
Less APR (100% × £95,000)	(95,000)
	85,000

   No BPR because the farm is an investment

	£
(b) Shares in farming company	175,000
Less: APR 100% (20% × £175,000)	(35,000)
BPR 100% (80% × £175,000)	(140,000)
	–

Activity 9: Comprehensive example (2)

Life IHT
23 November 2016 – CLT

	£	£
Gift		335,000
AE: 2016/17		(3,000)
2015/16 (used by June 15 PET)		0
Gross chargeable transfer		332,000
Nil rate band (NRB) at date of transfer	325,000	
Less chargeable transfers in previous seven years	0	
Available NRB		(325,000)
		7,000
IHT @ 20%		1,400

Death IHT:
20 March 2012 – PET
More than seven years before death – Exempt
3 June 2015 – PET

	£
Value before: 10/30 × 1,050,000	
(The related property valuations are clearly higher)	350,000

			£
Value after: 5/25 × 750,000			(150,000)
Diminution in value			200,000
Less AE 2015/16			(3,000)
2014/15 b/f			(3,000)
			194,000

Within available NRB at death (£325,000) so no death IHT

14 October 2015 – PET

Valuation rules

		£	£
Lower of:			
2.00 + 1/4 (2.10 – 2.00) = £2.025			
½ (1.98 + 2.06) = 2.02			
170,000 × 2.02			343,400
No BPR (quoted with no control)			
NRB at death		325,000	
Less chargeable transfers in previous seven years		(194,000)	
Available NRB			(131,000)
Excess			212,400
IHT @ 40%			84,960
Less taper relief four to five years, 40%			(33,984)
IHT payable			50,976

9 June 2016

All gifts covered by small gift exemption.

23 November 2016 – CLT

		£	£
Gross chargeable transfer			332,000
NRB at death		325,000	
Less chargeable transfers in previous seven years (194,000 + 343,400)		(537,400)	
			0
Excess			332,000
IHT @ 40%			132,800
Less taper relief three to four years, 20%			(26,560)
Less lifetime IHT			(1,400)
IHT payable			104,840

Activity 10: Reduced rate of IHT

Fiona's net estate is £1,075,000 (£1,400,000 – £325,000).

Therefore, the reduced rate is available as the charitable donation is more than 10% × £1,075,000 = £107,500.

The IHT liability on the estate will be:

36% × (1,400,000 – 200,000 – 175,000 – 325,000) = £252,000.

Activity 11: Who pays and suffers IHT on death estate?

Death IHT

PET 15 January 2011 – outside seven years – exempt

PET 10 June 2016

	£	£
Gift to daughter		307,000
AE – 2016/17		(3,000)
AE – 2015/16 b/f		(3,000)
Gross chargeable transfer		301,000
NRB at death	325,000	
Chargeable transfers in previous seven years	–	
Available NRB		(325,000)
		Nil

No IHT payable as covered by NRB

Death estate

	£
UK main residence	168,000
Shares	10,000
Cash	30,000
Less funeral expenses	(1,000)
UK assets	207,000
Overseas assets: villa in Spain	40,000
Chargeable estate	247,000

IHT on estate

40% × (247,000 – 168,000 – (325,000 – 301,000)) = £22,000

Average rate (22,000/ 247,000) × 100% = 8.907%

IHT on UK assets

	£
207,000 × 8.907%	18,437

– Paid by PRs

– Suffered by residuary beneficiary (son)

IHT on overseas assets

	£
40,000 × 8.907%	3,563

- Paid by PRs
- Suffered by beneficiary (daughter)

Activity 12: Quick succession relief

Lara

Chargeable estate £330,000

	£
IHT (330,000 − 325,000) × 40%	2,000
Less QSR (4 to 5 years)	
$8,420 \times \dfrac{40,111}{48,531} \times 20\%$	(1,392)
IHT payable on estate	608

12 Inheritance tax: further aspects

Learning objectives

On completion of this chapter, you should be able to:

	Syllabus reference no.
Remember the material covered in Taxation (TX – UK) under the heading: 'payment of inheritance tax'	A3(a) D4
Explain the concepts of domicile and deemed domicile and understand the application of these concepts to inheritance tax (IHT)	A3(b)(i)
Identify excluded property	A3(b)(ii)
Identify and advise on the tax implications of the location of assets	A3(b)(iii)
Identify and advise on gifts with reservation of benefit	A3(b)(iv)
Advise on the operation of double tax relief for IHT	A3(d)(vii)
Advise on the IHT effects and advantages of the variation of wills	A3(d)(viii)
Define a trust	A3(e)(i)
Distinguish between different types of trust	A3(e)(ii)
Advise on the IHT implications of transfers of property into trust	A3(e)(iii)
Advise on inheritance tax implications of property passing absolutely from a trust to a beneficiary	A3(e)(iv)
Identify the occasions on which IHT is payable by trustees	A3(e)(v)
Identify the occasions on which IHT may be paid by instalments	A3(g)(i)
Advise on the due dates, interest and penalties for IHT purposes	A3(g)(ii)

Exam context

The topics in this chapter are mostly new to you at ATX – UK. The exception is the basic rules on payment of inheritance tax (IHT) but you will also be expected to advise on the occasions where IHT may be paid in instalments and on interest and penalties.

You have already met the concepts of domicile and deemed domicile in relation to income tax and capital gains tax. There are similar, but slightly different, rules relating to IHT. The location of assets is also an important aspect since the rules for overseas assets are beneficial to individuals who are not UK domiciled nor deemed domiciled.

The anti-avoidance rule for gifts with reservation is designed to ensure that individuals are taxed on what they have effectively given away entirely. You need to be able to identify when this situation arises and the IHT consequences.

The CGT rules for variations were discussed in Chapter 8. You also need to be able to deal with the IHT aspects.

Trusts are useful in tax planning. The trustees retain control over assets until they deem a beneficiary to be sufficiently capable of looking after them. Be aware of the IHT implications for trusts.

Chapter overview

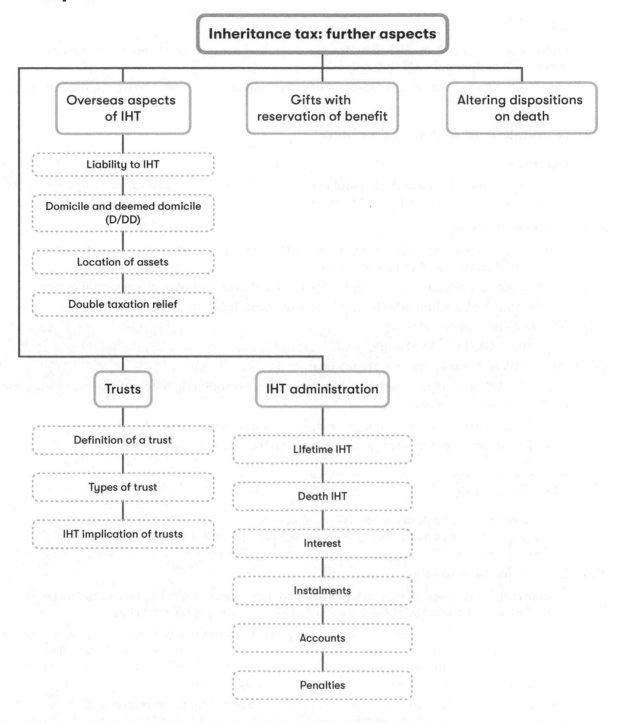

BPP LEARNING MEDIA

1 Overseas aspects of IHT

1.1 Liability to IHT

Individuals who are **UK domiciled or deemed domiciled** are taxed on **transfers of worldwide assets (ie whether in the UK or overseas).**

Individuals who are not **UK domiciled nor deemed domiciled** are taxed on **transfers of UK assets only.**

1.2 Domicile and deemed domicile

1.2.1 Domicile

The rules on **domicile under the general law apply to IHT** as for income tax and capital gains tax (see Chapter 9 Overseas personal taxation).

1.2.2 Deemed domicile

A person is also **deemed to be domiciled in the UK** for IHT purposes at the time a transfer is made if they satisfy **any one of three** conditions:

- They were **domiciled in the UK within the three years immediately preceding that time.**
- The individual is a **formerly UK domiciled individual.** This is an individual who:
  - Was born in the UK; and
  - Has a **UK domicile of origin**; and
  - Is **UK resident in the relevant tax year**; and
  - Was **UK resident in at least 1 of the 2 tax years immediately before the relevant tax year.**
- The individual is **UK resident:**
  - For **at least 15 of the 20 tax years immediately preceding the relevant tax year**; and
  - For **at least 1 of the 4 tax years ending with the relevant tax year.**

> ### Exam focus point
>
> The **rules on deemed domicile for IHT** are **similar** to those covered earlier for income tax and capital gains tax **but not quite the same. Make sure you know the differences!**

1.2.3 Election for UK domicile

An **individual** who is **not UK domiciled or deemed domiciled** can elect to be **treated as UK domiciled for the purposes of IHT** if their **spouse/civil partner is UK domiciled.**

This may be **beneficial** where the **spouse exemption is restricted** (see Chapter 11 Inheritance tax computation). However, the election also has the effect of **bringing the non UK domiciled individual's assets situated outside the UK within the charge to IHT.** It is therefore important to consider **both these aspects** before the election is made.

The election can be made while the **UK domiciled spouse or civil partner is alive** (lifetime election) or it can be made **in the two years following the death of the UK domiciled spouse/civil partner (death election).**

UK domicile is treated as **taking effect on a date specified in the election within seven years before the date of the election** (for a lifetime election) or **within seven years before the UK domiciled spouse/civil partner's death** (for a death election).

The election is **irrevocable** but will **lapse if the individual is non-UK resident for four consecutive years.**

1.3 Excluded property

Overseas assets of an individual who is **not UK domiciled nor deemed domiciled** are **excluded property** and so are **ignored for IHT purposes.**

1.4 Location of assets

The following **location rules determine whether assets are situated in the UK or overseas:**

- **Land and buildings** are located in the country where they are **physically located.**
- A **debt** is in the country of residence of the **debtor.**
- **Life policies** are in the country where **proceeds are payable.**
- **Registered shares and securities** are in the country where they are **registered.**
- **Bearer securities** are where the **certificate of title is located.**
- **Bank accounts** are at the **branch where the account is kept.**
- An **interest in a partnership** is where the **business is carried on.**
- **Goodwill** is where the **business is carried on.**
- **Tangible property** (eg a chattel) is at its **physical location.**

1.5 Double taxation relief

Where a **transfer is made of** an **overseas asset**, both **UK IHT and overseas capital tax** may be **payable** on **that asset.**

DTR is available against the **UK IHT** for the **overseas tax paid.**

Relief may be given under a **double taxation agreement**, but if not then the **unilateral DTR is given as follows.**

DTR is the **lower of:**

- **Overseas tax paid**
- **UK IHT** attributable to the **overseas asset**

If the overseas asset is part of the death estate, UK IHT is found by applying following fraction to the value of the asset:

$$\frac{\text{UK IHT (after QSR)}}{\text{Value of chargeable estate}}$$

Activity 1: DTR

Susan died leaving a chargeable estate of £360,000. This included a villa in Spain worth £40,000 in respect of which Spanish death duties of £10,000 were paid. Susan made no gifts during her lifetime. She is UK domiciled and left her estate to her niece.

Required

Calculate the IHT payable as a result of Susan's death.

Solution

2 Gifts with reservation of benefit

2.1 Definition

Gift with reservation of benefit: A **gift** where a **transfer of an asset** is **made by an individual** but some **reservation of benefit** is **retained by that individual.**

Examples include **gifting a house** but **continuing to live in it without paying a market rent** and **gifting assets to a trust** of which the **individual is a beneficiary.**

The gift with reservation rules will not be applied:

- If **full consideration** (eg market rent) is given for any **right of occupation or enjoyment retained or assumed by the donor**
- If the **circumstances of the donor change** in a way that was **unforeseen at the time of the original gift** and the **benefit provided by the donee to the donor** only represents **reasonable provision** for the **care and maintenance of the donor, being an elderly or infirm relative.** This exception only applies to **interests in land.**

Exam focus point

Gifts with reservation of benefit were tested in December 2011 Question 2 Mirtoon. The examining team commented that 'the vast majority of candidates knew all about gifts with reservation and answered this part of the question well'.

2.2 IHT implications of gift when made

Where a **gift with reservation is made,** it is **treated in the same way as any other gift at the time it is made,** so is a **potentially exempt transfer** (if the gift is to an individual such as a son or daughter) or a **chargeable lifetime transfer** (if the gift is to a trust).

2.3 Reservation existing on death

The **asset is deemed to be included** in the donor's estate at **its value at the death of the donor.** If the **asset was the donor's main residence** when it was gifted, it will therefore be entitled to the **residential nil rate band. The lifetime gift will be ignored.**

Alternatively, it **may** be **treated as a lifetime transfer** but **ignored in the death estate.**

HM Revenue & Customs (HMRC) will treat it in whichever way produces the **higher total tax liability** (ie taking account of the effect of these two alternatives on all other gifts).

We look at the implications of this further in Chapter 13 Capital tax planning.

Activity 2: Gift with reservation of benefit

Margherita gave her main residence to her daughter on 10 August 2018 when it was valued at £500,000. Margherita always used her annual exemption in April each year but made no other transfers for IHT. She divorced from her husband many years ago.

Margherita continued to live in the house rent free until her death on 17 September 2020. The house was then worth £525,000. Margherita's net death estate amounted to £120,000 which she left to her daughter.

Required

Calculate the IHT payable as a result of Margherita's death.

Solution

2.4 Reservation released within seven years before death

Rather than the original gift being taxed as a lifetime transfer, the gift may instead be taxed on the basis of it being a **PET at the time the reservation ceased**, the IHT being based on **its value at the time of the release. Annual exemptions are not usable** on this **deemed PET** when reservation ceases.

Again, **HMRC will treat the gift as taxable** in whichever way produces the higher total tax liability.

3 Altering dispositions on death

Within two years of a death the terms of a will can be changed in writing, either by a variation of the terms of the will made by the persons who benefit or would benefit under the dispositions, or by a disclaimer, with the change being effective for IHT purposes.

The **variation or disclaimer will not be treated as a transfer of value.**

Inheritance tax will be calculated as if the terms contained in the variation replaced those in the will.

If a **legacy is disclaimed**, it will **pass under the terms of the will** (or possibly under the intestacy rules) to some other person and tax will apply **as if the will originally directed the legacy to that new recipient.**

There is a similar provision for CGT. **This was covered in Chapter 8 Shares and securities, CGT reliefs.**

If the beneficiaries making the variation wish the relevant terms of the will to be treated as **replaced by the terms of the variation, it is necessary to state this in the variation.** The statement can apply for inheritance tax or capital gains tax or both.

Where a disclaimer is made, the relevant terms in the will are *automatically* treated as replaced by the terms of the disclaimer for both IHT and CGT purposes, regardless of whether this is stated in the disclaimer or not.

We look at the implications of this further in Chapter 13.

4 Trusts

4.1 Definition of a trust

> **Trust:** A **legal arrangement** under which a **person**, the **settlor**, **transfers property to other person(s)**, the **trustee or trustees**, who **are required to deal with the trust property on behalf of certain specified persons**, the **beneficiaries**. It is the **legal separation** of **ownership** and **benefit**.

4.2 Types of trust

4.2.1 Introduction

Trusts fall into **two main types:**

- Those where an **interest in possession** exists
- Those with no interest in possession – generally referred to as **discretionary trusts**

4.2.2 Interest in possession trusts

The person(s) having the **interest in possession** has the **immediate right to any income as it arises**.

The person(s) having the interest in possession is often referred to as the **life tenant** if the interest in possession exists for the duration of their life.

The **person to whom the property will pass on the death of the life tenant** is often referred to as the **remainderman** and is said to have a **reversionary interest** in the trust property (usually **excluded property** for IHT).

Illustration 1: Interest in possession

Alfie dies and leaves his house to an interest in possession trust so that his wife, Carole can live there during her life and then the house passes to his son, Bren.

Required

How will Carole and Bren be referred to?

Solution

Carole = life tenant

Bren = remainderman

4.2.3 Discretionary trusts

Nobody has an entitlement to any income of the trust. Income will be paid out to **beneficiaries** at the **discretion** of the trustees.

There **does not have to be a specific remainderman** with a **vested (ie certain) interest**. The **trustees could also have discretion over the distribution of the capital when the trust ends.**

BPP
LEARNING
MEDIA

4.3 IHT implications of trusts

For ATX – UK exam purposes the **IHT treatment of both types of trust** is the same and is set out below:

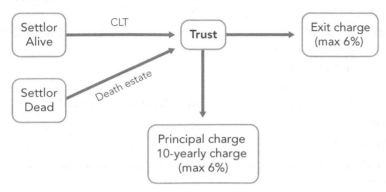

 Essential reading

See Chapter 12 of the Essential reading for more detail on the IHT implications of trusts.

The Essential reading is available as an Appendix of the digital edition of the Workbook.

5 IHT administration

5.1 Lifetime IHT

If a **chargeable lifetime transfer (CLT)** is made between **6 April and 30 September, IHT is due 30 April following,** otherwise IHT is due six months from end of month of transfer.

5.2 Death IHT

IHT on **lifetime gifts** is due **six months from end of month of death**.

IHT on the **death estate** is due **six months from end of month of death** or on **delivery of account** if earlier.

5.3 Interest

Interest on lifetime IHT runs from **the due date to the day before payment.**

Interest on death IHT runs from **six months after the end of the month when death occurred to the day before payment.**

Interest (not taxable) is paid on repayments of tax from the date of payment to the day before repayment.

5.4 IHT Instalments

IHT may be paid in **ten equal annual instalments** on **certain assets** which are:
* **Transferred on death,** or
* **Chargeable lifetime transfers (CLTs)** where donee pays the tax
* **Potentially exempt transfers** where the **donee has kept the property** (usually until the donor's death)

The **instalment option applies to:**

- Land
- **All shares where donor had control**
- **Unquoted shares** if:
  - The **tax on them together with that on other instalment property** represents **at least 20% of the total liability** on the estate on a death, or
  - **Tax cannot be paid without undue hardship,** or
  - **Value is >£20,000** and the **nominal value of the shares is at least 10% of all the shares in the company,** or, if the shares are ordinary shares, **at least 10% of the ordinary shares**
- **Business or an interest in a business**

The **first instalment** is due for payment:

- On **death transfers and liabilities arising as a result of death, six months after the end of the month in which death occurred**
- On **CLTs,** on the **normal due date of payment**

If the **property is sold, all outstanding IHT must then be paid.**

Essential reading

See Chapter 12 of the Essential reading for more detail on IHT administration.

The Essential reading is available as an Appendix of the digital edition of the Workbook.

Chapter summary

```
┌─────────────────────────────────────┐
│   Inheritance tax: further aspects   │
└─────────────────────────────────────┘
```

Overseas aspects of IHT

Liability to IHT
- UK D/DD: on worldwide assets
- Non-UK D/DD:
  - On UK situated assets only
  - Overseas assets excluded property

Domicile and deemed domicile (D/DD)
- Domicile – permanent home
- UK deemed domicile for IHT:
  - <3 yrs since becoming non-UK domiciled
  - Formerly UK domiciled
  - UK resident 15 of 20 tax yrs preceeding this year and for at least 1 of 4 tax yrs ending this tax yr
- Election for UK domicile if non-UK D/DD individual and spouse/civil partner UK D
  - Spouse/civil partner exemption no longer restricted
  - But worldwide assets now in charge to IHT

Location of assets
- Land and buildings: Physical location
- Debtor: Residence of debtor
- Life policies: Where payable
- Registered shares and securities: Country of registration
- Bearer securities: Location of certificate
- Bank accounts: Branch location
- Tangible property: Physical location
- Goodwill: Where business conducted

Double taxation relief
- Lower of:
  - Overseas tax paid
  - UK IHT attributable to the overseas asset (use average rate after QSR)

Gifts with reservation of benefit

- Transfer of an asset but some reservation of benefit retained eg
  - Gifting a house but continuing to live in it
  - Gifting assets to trust of which beneficiary
- Not reservation if:
  - Full consideration given for use of asset
  - Reason for reservation = care/maintenance of elderly or infirm relative
- Treated as any other gift at the time made
- If benefit retained to death charge higher of IHT on:
  - Asset as part of death estate (RNRB available if main residence when given)
  - Original lifetime transfer
- If benefit released in lifetime charge higher of IHT on:
  - PET when reservation ceased (no AEs)
  - Original lifetime transfer

Altering dispositions on death

- Variation or disclaimer of distribution of assets within two years of death
  - Old beneficiary does not make disposal
  - New beneficiary takes as if given to them directly
- For variation: need to state alteration applies for IHT

Trusts

Definition of a trust
Legal separation of ownership and benefit of property

Types of trust
- Interest in possession trust
  - Income to life tenant for life
  - On death of life tenant, assets pass to remainderman
- Discretionary trust
  - No-one has entitlement to income or capital
  - Trustees have discretion over distribution

IHT implication of trusts

IHT administration

Lifetime IHT
Due 6 mths from end of mth of transfer or following 30 April if made between 6 April – 30 September

Death IHT
- Lifetime gifts: 6 mths from end of month of death
- Death estate: 6 mths from end of month of death or delivery of account if earlier

Interest
- Lifetime IHT: from due date to date before payment
- Death IHT: from 6m from end of month of death to day before payment

Instalments
- Available on:
  - Transfer on death
  - CLT if donee pays tax
  - PET if donee has kept property
- Ten equal annual instalments usually starting on due date
- Applies to:
  - Land and buildings
  - All shares where donor had control
  - Most unquoted shares
  - Business or an interest in a business
- If property sold, all outstanding IHT must be paid immediately

Accounts
- On death within 12 mths of death
- On CLT within 12 mths of gift

Penalties
- Late delivery of account
  - 0 to 6 mths: lower of £100 and IHT on account
  - 6 to 12 mths: further penalty lower of £100 and IHT on account
  - ≥12 mths: £3,000 if IHT payable on account
- Penalties for error: as for IT
- Penalties for late payment: as for IT

Knowledge diagnostic

1. Overseas aspects of IHT

A UK-domiciled or deemed-domiciled individual is subject to IHT on transfers of all assets, wherever situated.

An election may be made for a non- UK domiciled individual who is, or was, the spouse or civil partner of a UK UK-domiciled individual, to be treated as UK domiciled for IHT purposes.

Overseas assets of individuals not UK domiciled nor deemed domiciled are not subject to IHT.

2. Gift with reservation of benefit

The gifts with reservation of benefit rules prevent IHT being avoided by enabling HMRC the option of taxing the gift when it was made or either when the reservation was released or on the donor's death.

3. Variations/Disclaimers

A variation or disclaimer can be used to vary a will after death. This can have IHT and CGT consequences.

4. IHT and trusts

A trust separates ownership (trustees) and benefit (beneficiaries) of assets.

There is a CLT when a trust is set up. The trust suffers the IHT principal charge once every ten years and the exit charge when property leaves the trust.

5. IHT administration

IHT is administered by HMRC Inheritance Tax. The due date for payment depends on the type of event giving rise to the charge to tax.

The liability to pay IHT depends on the type of transfer and whether it was made on death. In certain circumstances, IHT may be paid by instalments over 10 years.

Further study guidance

Question practice

Now try the following from the Further question practice bank (available in the digital edition of the Workbook):

- Rhys

Further reading

There is one technical article on the ACCA website written by members of the ATX – UK examining team which is relevant to some of the topics covered in this chapter that you should read:

- Trusts and tax

Activity answers

Activity 1: DTR

	£	£
Chargeable estate		360,000
IHT payable		
(360,000 – 325,000) × 40%		14,000
Less DTR lower of		
Overseas tax	10,000	
UK IHT		
$\dfrac{14,000}{360,000} \times 40,000$	1,556	(1,556)
		12,444

Note. That no RNRB needs to be considered as Susan did not leave a main residence to a direct descendant.

Activity 2: Gift with reservation of benefit

The gift of the house is a potentially exempt transfer when it is made so is treated as exempt during Margherita's lifetime.

On her death the following computations need to be made:

Computation 1: include house in death estate, ignore lifetime gift

	£
House (valued at death)	525,000
Other assets	120,000
Chargeable estate	645,000
Less: Residence nil rate band	(175,000)
Nil rate band	(325,000)
Amount chargeable at 40%	145,000
IHT payable	58,000

Computation 2: charge lifetime gift of house, ignore in death estate

Lifetime gift

	£
House (valued at gift)	500,000
Less: Nil rate band	(325,000)
Amount chargeable at 40%	175,000
IHT payable (no taper relief within 3 years of death)	70,000

The residence nil rate band is not available on life gifts.

Death estate

	£
Other assets	120,000
IHT payable at 40% (nil rate band used against lifetime gift)	48,000
Total IHT £(70,000 + 48,000)	118,000

HMRC will use Computation 2 as this gives the higher total tax liability.

13

Capital tax planning

Learning objectives

On completion of this chapter, you should be able to:

	Syllabus reference no.
Identify and advise on the taxes applicable to a given course of action and their impact.	B1
Identify and understand that the alternative ways of achieving personal or business outcomes may lead to different tax consequences.	B2
Calculate the receipts from a transaction, net of tax and compare the results of alternative scenarios and advise on the most tax efficient course of action.	B2(a)
Assess the tax advantages and disadvantages of alternative courses of action.	B4
Understand the statutory obligations imposed in a given situation, including any time limits for action and advise on the implications of non-compliance.	B5
Advise on legitimate tax planning measures, by which the tax liabilities arising from a particular situation or course of action can be mitigated.	C2
Advise on the mitigation of tax in the manner recommended by reference to numerical analysis and/or reasoned argument.	C4
Communicate advice, recommendations and information in the required format: for example the use of Reports, Letters, Memoranda and Meeting notes.	D1
Present written information, in language appropriate to the purpose of the communication and the intended recipient.	D2
Communicate conclusions reached, together, where necessary with relevant supporting computations.	D3
State and explain assumptions made or limitations in the analysis provided; together with any inadequacies in the information available and/or additional information required to provide a fuller analysis.	D4

	Syllabus reference no.
Identify and explain other, non-tax, factors that should be considered.	D5

Exam context

A key aspect of ATX – UK, which differs from TX – UK, is that you will be expected to use the technical knowledge that you have gained in the previous chapters in this section to give capital tax advice to clients.

In Sections 1 to 8 of this chapter we look at some scenarios that may arise in ATX questions and show the techniques you can use to prepare your answer.

In Section 9 we provide an overview of CGT and IHT and in Sections 10 and 11 we give summaries of CGT reliefs and IHT reliefs respectively. You will find these especially useful in the revision phase of your studies.

Chapter overview

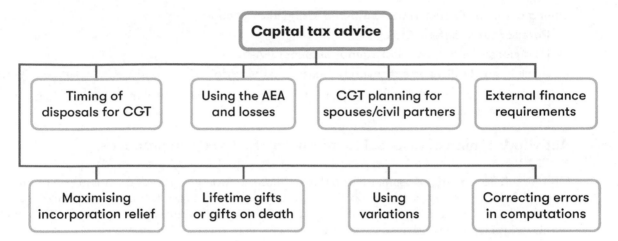

1 Timing of disposals for CGT

Timing of disposals should be considered taking into account:

- **Rates of tax** in different tax years
- Using **losses** and the **annual exempt amount** (AEA)
- Availability of **reliefs** eg satisfying business asset disposal relief and investors' relief conditions.

You are told the assumed date at the start of each question and it's vital that you take this into account in considering the facts.

Activity 1: Timing of disposal to maximise after-tax sale proceeds

On 1 March 2019 Yvette subscribed for 6,000 £1 shares at par in Wye Ltd, a trading company. This was a 15% shareholding giving proportionate voting rights, rights on distributions and to assets on winding up. She became a director of Wye Ltd on 25 May 2019, earning a salary of £15,000 each month payable at the end of each month.

Wye Ltd has become very successful and Yvette has received three offers for her shares:

Offer 1

Contract date: 31 March 2021 at £115 per share

Offer 2

Contract date: 30 April 2021 at £110 per share

Offer 3

Contract date: 31 May 2021 at £105 per share

In each case, Yvette will immediately resign as a director of Wye Ltd such that she will no longer be employed by the company following the disposal of her shares. After the sale of her shares Yvette will take an extended career break for at least 18 months to consider new projects so she will have no other income during this period.

Yvette's only other disposal will be of a residential property in June 2021 realising gain of £12,300. She has not made any CGT claims previously.

Required

Advise Yvette which of the three offers will give her the maximum after-tax sale proceeds. Assume that the tax rates and allowances in 2020/21 also apply in 2021/22.

Solution

2 Using the annual exempt amount (AEA) and losses

Every individual has an **AEA** which is **£12,300 in 2020/21**. They may also make (capital or trading) losses in the current tax year or have brought-forward capital losses. You may be asked **how the AEA and available losses can be used** by **selling a number of quoted shares**.

There are **two steps** to follow:

Step 1: **Compute** the **gain** on **each share.**

Step 2: **Divide the total of the AEA and the available losses by the gain per share to give the number of shares to be sold,** if necessary, **rounding down** the number of shares.

Activity 2: Using the AEA and losses

Thyme has a holding of 10,000 £1 ordinary shares in Herb plc, a quoted trading company, which she had purchased in 2010 for £2.20 per share. The current market value of the shares is £6.40 per share.

Thyme will not make any other disposals in the tax year 2020/21 and has therefore not utilised her annual exempt amount. She has a capital loss brought forward from 2019/20 of £(1,200).

Required

Compute the number of shares that Thyme can sell in the tax year 2020/21 without incurring a charge to capital gains tax.

Solution

3 CGT planning for spouses/civil partners

Since **transfers between spouses/civil partners are on a no-gain no-loss basis,** it may be **beneficial to transfer the whole or part of an asset to the spouse/civil partner** with an **unused AEA and/or losses** or with **taxable income below the basic rate limit.**

The donee spouse/civil partner can then make a disposal to a third party, either alone (if the whole asset is transferred) or jointly with the donor spouse/civil partner (if only part of the asset is transferred).

Activity 3: Inter-spouse transfer

Arabella inherited a house on the death of her mother in June 2017 when it was valued at £480,000. The house has been unoccupied since then. Arabella will sell the house in December 2020 for £525,000. She has decided to give one-third of the proceeds (£175,000) to her husband, Dominic. Neither Arabella nor Dominic have any other chargeable assets. In the tax year 2020/21, Arabella has taxable income of £80,000 and Dominic has taxable income of £20,000.

Required

Calculate the capital gains tax saving which would be achieved if Arabella were to give Dominic a one-third interest in house prior to its sale (as opposed to cash of £175,000 following the sale).

Solution

It is **very important** that the **donee spouse/civil partner does not have any arrangement to pay back their net proceeds of sale to the donor spouse/civil partner.** If such an arrangement is in place, **HM Revenue & Customs** may contend that the **no gain no loss disposal was not valid** and treat the **donor spouse as making the entire disposal.**

4 Calculating external finance requirements

A **common exam question** involves **an individual who is planning a new business** which will be **partly financed by the disposal of assets** or **an inheritance** and **partly by external finance.** You will be asked to compute **how much external finance will be required.**

There are **three steps** to follow:

Step 1 **Compute** the **CGT liability** on the disposal of the assets or the **IHT liability** on the inheritance.

Step 2 **Compute** the **post-tax proceeds/inheritance** (ie proceeds less CGT or assets less IHT).

Step 3 **Compute** the **external finance required** (ie total finance less post-tax proceeds).

 ## Illustration 1: External finance requirement with IHT

Jaiden intends to start a new business and will need to raise total finance of £1,200,000 to do so. This business will be partly financed by an inheritance which Jaiden will receive following the recent death of his grandmother, Karen and partly by external finance.

Karen died on 1 November 2020. Jaiden inherited the whole of Karen's estate, which was valued at £900,000. The estate consisted of her main residence (valued at £400,000), together with furniture, cash and quoted shares. Karen had not made any gifts during her life.

Karen had been married to Joe for many years. He died on 10 January 2015. Joe left his estate to Karen. On 1 May 2014, Joe had given gave £160,000 to Jaiden. This was the only lifetime gift that Joe had made.

Required

Calculate how much external finance Jaiden will need to raise.

Solution

Step 1 *Compute the IHT liability*

		£
Karen's estate		900,000
Less Residence nil rate band		
	Karen	(175,000)
	Joe transferred to Karen	(175,000)
Less Nil rate band		
	Karen	(325,000)
	J transferred to K £(325,000 – (160,000 – 3,000 AE 14/15 – 3,000 AE 13/14 b/f))	(171,000)
Excess		54,000
IHT @ 40%		21,600

Step 2 *Compute the post-tax inheritance*

	£
Karen's estate	900,000
Less IHT on estate	(21,600)
Post-tax inheritance	878,400

Step 3 *Compute the external finance required*

	£
Total cost of project	1,200,000
Less post-tax inheritance	(878,400)

	£
External finance required	<u>321,600</u>

Note. The external finance requirement may be higher if Joe incurs any costs disposing of Karen's estate (for example, estate agent's fees and conveyancing costs on selling the home).

Activity 4: External finance requirement with CGT

Amanda plans to start up a new business and will need to raise total finance of £310,000 to do so.

She is planning to sell 34,080 shares in Granada plc for £83,496 and £20,000 6% Granada plc non-convertible loan stock for £23,920 to raise some of the funds, with the balance being obtained via a bank loan on 1 February 2021.

The shares and loan stock were acquired as follows:

(1)   Amanda was given 11,360 Forte plc shares by her uncle on 1 May 2016. At that time they were worth £70,432.

(2)   On 1 September 2018 Forte plc was taken over by Granada plc. Amanda received 34,080 shares in Granada, £8,000 in cash and £20,000 6% Granada non-convertible loan stock (a qualifying corporate bond) in exchange for the shares in Forte plc.

The shares and loan stock were worth £78,344 and £22,720 respectively on 1 September 2018.

Amanda has taxable income of £60,000 in 2020/21 and will make no other chargeable disposals in the tax year. Business asset disposal relief does not apply on any of the disposals.

Required

Calculate how much external finance Amanda will need to raise.

Solution

5 Maximising incorporation relief

Incorporation relief applies **automatically** and to the **fullest extent possible**. Therefore it **cannot be restricted** to **utilise losses brought forward** and the **AEA**.

However, **it is possible to manipulate the amount of non-share consideration received** (whether in cash, loan stock, or left on loan account) **so that the gain remaining chargeable is equal to losses plus the AEA.**

You may find it **easier to work backwards from the amount that you want to leave chargeable.**

Illustration 2: Maximising incorporation relief

Antonio transferred his business (market value £120,000) to a company on 16 August 2020, realising a gain of £90,000. He had capital losses brought forward of £6,000 and will not otherwise use his AEA in 2020/21.

Required

Advise Antonio how much of the consideration he should take as shares and how much he should leave on loan account.

Solution

Work backwards to calculate the incorporation relief required to defer sufficient gains to utilise AEA and losses:

	£
AEA	12,300
Losses	6,000
Gain covered by AEA/losses	18,300
Less total gain	(90,000)
Incorporation relief required	71,700

Once the incorporation relief figure is obtained, calculate the share consideration required:

Total consideration × (Deferred gain/Gain)

£120,000 × (71,700/90,000) = £95,600

Antonio should therefore take shares worth £95,600 and leave the balance of £24,400 (£120,000 – £95,600) on loan account.

6 Lifetime gifts or gifts on death?

This is **another common exam scenario**. Your client has an **asset** and is thinking of either making a **gift of it in their lifetime** or waiting to **gift it on their death**. You need to think about both the **capital gains tax issues** and the **inheritance tax issues**.

The following relate to a **gift of an asset to an individual other than to a spouse/civil partner,** eg a gift to a son or daughter.

On a lifetime gift, unless the asset is **exempt** (eg motor car, small value chattels), the **donor** will make a **disposal at market value**. You need to consider whether **gift relief applies** (only if **business assets** or **transfer to a trust**) and the **effect of the relief** (it **defers the gain** by **reducing the cost** for the **donee**). If there is **no gift relief** such that the donor may have a **CGT liability**, you need to think about whether the donor has any **losses** and/or **AEA** available and their **rate of tax**.

The **disposal of an asset on death** is **exempt** for **CGT** and the **beneficiary** takes the asset at **probate value**.

On a lifetime gift for inheritance tax, the **annual exemption** for the **current tax year** and **previous tax year** may be **available**. Otherwise the transfer will be a **potentially exempt transfer.** Consider whether the **gift with reservation of benefit** rules would apply, for example on a gift of a house in which the donor continues to live without paying a market rent. **The transfer may attract business property relief (BPR) and/or agricultural property relief (APR)** – but remember that **the donee** must usually **still own the property as BPR or APR property (as appropriate)** at the **donor's death.** You need to consider **if the donor is likely to survive seven years from making the transfer** and **the effects if they do not,** including **taper relief.**

For IHT in respect of a gift on death, there will be a **chargeable transfer.** You should also consider **BPR** and **APR,** the available **nil rate band** and whether the **residence nil rate band** will apply (this will also apply to **gift with reservation of benefit properties**).

Also think about **non-tax issues.** The donor will still need **somewhere to live** and **sufficient income to cover their day to day living needs!**

These are **just some of the issues** that might arise – remember that you need to **apply your technical knowledge** to the **precise facts of the scenario** in the question.

Activity 5: Lifetime gifts or gifts on death?

Stephen owns the following assets:

	£
Main residence	800,000
Cash	220,000
Motor car	18,000
Investment (10%) in Aardvark Ltd, a trading company, which holds approximately 15% of its total balance sheet and its chargeable assets as investments and cost Stephen £100,000 in 2010	400,000
Other chattels	39,000
Total	1,477,000

Stephen has made no lifetime gifts, is 65 years of age and in good health. Stephen has a healthy pension from his previous employment which is more than sufficient for his day-to-day living needs and is therefore interested in passing down all of the above assets in the most tax-efficient manner to various members of his family. Stephen is a higher-rate taxpayer. He has heard that it might be tax efficient for him to give away his main residence but continue to live there and pay a market rent which would be a way of passing cash to members of his family.

Stephen's wife, Sarah, died in a road traffic accident in 2011 and the half-share in the main residence passed to Stephen at that time. Sarah had made no lifetime gifts before her death and had no other assets at the date of her death.

Required

Discuss the relative advantages and disadvantages of Stephen giving the above assets in either life or on death to his family. Assume current rates and allowances continue to apply.

Solution

7 Using variations

You may be asked to advise on whether it would be better to make a **lifetime gift of assets acquired by inheritance** or to **make a variation of the disposition on death**. You need to think about both the **capital gains tax issues** and the **inheritance tax issues**.

The following relate to a **gift other than to a spouse/civil partner,** eg a gift to a son or daughter.

If a valid **variation of a will** is made **within two years of death**, there will be **no CGT disposal** of the **varied assets** by the **individual making the variation.** Instead, **the new beneficiary** will take **the assets** at **probate value.** You need to consider whether **the new beneficiary** will **dispose of the assets in the foreseeable future** and **their CGT liability position** in that event.

For **IHT purposes,** there will be **no transfer of value by the individual making the variation** and the **new beneficiary** will be treated **as if the assets had passed directly to them.**

Again, these are **just some of the issues** that might arise – remember that you need to **apply your technical knowledge** to the **precise facts of the scenario** in the question.

Activity 6: Lifetime gift or variation?

The following is an extract from an email from your manager concerning Clive and his daughter Imogen, both of whom are clients of your firm

To:	XXX
From:	Manager
Date:	XXXX
Subject:	Clive and Imogen

Clive and Imogen are coming to see me tomorrow. Clive's father, Trevor, died in May 2019 and in his will he left some quoted shares, then worth £15,000, to Clive. The shares form 0.01% of the shares in issue.

The shares are now worth £28,000. Clive has mentioned giving the shares to Imogen by way of a lifetime gift. Imogen may sell the shares a few months after the gift when she hopes they will have further increased in value.

I think that it might be a better idea for Clive to vary his father's will to pass the shares to Imogen.

Please prepare some notes for my meeting about the capital gains tax and inheritance tax implications of both a lifetime gift and a variation.

From the client files you ascertain the following additional information:

Clive is in poor health. He is a widower, but his wife used all of her nil rate band when she died.

He has assets worth about £500,000 which he will leave to Imogen in his will.

He has not made any previous transfers of value for inheritance tax nor any disposals for capital gains tax.

He is a higher-rate taxpayer.

Required

Prepare the notes for the meeting as requested by your manager

Solution

7.1 Using variations to obtain the reduced rate of IHT

A **variation of a will** may be made **to increase the amount given to charity,** so that the **estate** then **qualifies for the reduced rate.**

Although the **gross value of the remaining estate is then lower for the other beneficiaries of the will,** the **reduced rate of IHT on this lower amount** may **outweigh the cost of the increased gift to charity** and **increase the net assets passing to other beneficiaries.**

 ### Illustration 3: Using a variation to obtain the reduced rate of IHT

Barry died on 1 July 2020 leaving a gross chargeable estate valued at £860,000. In his will, he left a donation of £60,000 to charity and the rest of his estate to his son, Trig. Barry's available nil rate band at his death was £170,000.

Required

1   Explain why the reduced rate of IHT is not available on Barry's estate under his will and compute the amount that Trig will receive under the will.

2   Suggest a variation of Barry's will which will enable to reduced rate to be used and calculate the amount that Trig would receive under the varied will.

Solution

1   Barry's net estate for the purposes of working out whether the reduced rate applies is £(860,000 − 170,000) = £690,000. Therefore at least 10% × £690,000 = £69,000 must be left to charity for the reduced rate of IHT to apply to the death estate.

   The reduced rate is not available because Barry's charitable donation is less than £69,000. The inheritance tax on Barry's death estate is therefore £(860,000 − 60,000 − 170,000) = £630,000 × 40% = £252,000. Trig will receive net assets of £(860,000 − 60,000 − 252,000) = £548,000.

2   A variation could be used to increase the charitable donation by £9,000 to £69,000. This would reduce the inheritance tax liability to £(860,000 − 69,000 − 170,000) × 36% = £223,560. This is a saving of £252,000 − £223,560 = £28,440 which is greater than the additional charitable donation. Trig will receive net assets of £(860,000 − 69,000 − 223,560) = £567,440.

7.2   Using a variation to avoid limit on spouse/civil partner exemption

Where **assets have been received by a UK domiciled/deemed domiciled individual as an inheritance** and they want to **pass those assets** to their **non-UK domiciled spouse/civil partner,** a **variation** can be used to **redirect the assets** so they **pass directly from the deceased to the spouse/civil partner. This** avoids the limitation on the spouse/civil partner exemption where a **donor spouse is UK domiciled/deemed domiciled** but the **donee spouse is not.**

An alternative method would be for the **non-UK domiciled/deemed domiciled spouse to elect to be treated as UK domiciled to avoid the limitation.** However, this means that **their worldwide assets** will be **subject to IHT.**

Activity 7: Using a variation to avoid limit on spouse exemption

Tarak has always been UK resident and domiciled. He created a discretionary trust in September 2016 with a cash gift of £350,000.

Tarak's wife, Miri, moved to the UK in January 2015. Tarak and Miri were married in June 2016. Miri is UK resident but she remains domiciled in the country of Atlantis where she has substantial assets. Tarak gave Miri quoted shares worth £250,000 in July 2018.

Tarak's father died on 1 September 2019 and left his entire estate to Tarak. The estate included a holiday cottage valued at £180,000. Tarak wants to give this cottage to Miri in May 2021.

Required

1   Explain the extent to which Tarak's proposed gift of the cottage to Miri could result in an inheritance tax (IHT) liability. Ignore any annual exemptions.

2   Identify TWO ways in which how this potential liability might be avoided.

3   Advise Tarak which of these two ways is likely to prove the more tax efficient.

Solution

8 Correcting errors in computations

Another **common exam question** asks you to look at a **computation of tax made by an inexperienced colleague**, advise on the **errors made** and prepare a **correct computation**. This is a **good test** of your **technical knowledge**. We recommend a **three-step approach** to such questions.

Step 1 First, have a **look at the computation** and **identify any obvious mistakes. Common errors** in **capital taxes computations** include **incorrect use of exemptions and reliefs,** using the **wrong rates of tax,** and not **cumulating previous transfers for IHT. Some errors cannot be immediately spotted** and **some of the computation may be correct** so **just looking at the computation won't be sufficient.**

Step 2 **Take the information from the question** and do **your own tax computation,** taking into account the issues you have identified in Step 1.

Step 3 **Compare your computation** with the **incorrect computation** and identify the errors.

Activity 8: Correcting errors in IHT computation

Tonya died on 10 August 2020. She used her annual exemption in April each year and made a number of other lifetime transfers. Tonya never married.

A colleague of yours, who has not very much experience of inheritance tax (IHT), has prepared the following computation of the IHT implications of Tonya's death on her lifetime transfers.

7 May 2011

Chargeable lifetime transfer of £350,000 – exempt transfer as more than seven years before death.

14 October 2014

Gift to nephew Simon

	£
Share in partnership manufacturing garden furniture	170,000
Land used by partnership in its trade	60,000
	230,000
Less business property relief @100%	(230,000)
Potentially exempt transfer	0

Within available nil rate band at date of death (£325,000)

I have checked that at Tonya's death Simon was a partner in the partnership and the land was used by the partnership in its trade so BPR is still available on this gift.

17 May 2020

Gift of main residence to niece Orla

		£
Main residence		550,000
Less:	Residence nil rate band (lower of £550,000 and £175,000)	(175,000)
	Available nil rate band	(325,000)
Excess		50,000
IHT @ 40%		20,000

Required

Identify and explain the errors in the computation prepared by your colleague and calculate the correct amount of IHT due.

Solution

9 Overview of capital gains tax and inheritance tax

	CGT	IHT
Arises on	• Sales • Gifts or sales at an undervalue • Lifetime transactions only	• Gifts or sales at an undervalue • On death or within seven years of death
Relevant value	Market value of the gift	Diminution in value of donor's estate
Relevance of residence, ordinary residence and domicile	Liability to CGT: • On all assets if UK resident • On some UK assets if not UK resident If resident but not UK domiciled/deemed domiciled:	If non-UK domiciled: • Overseas assets are not subject to UK IHT Residency is relevant when considering deemed UK domicile

	CGT	IHT
	• Gains on overseas assets can be taxed on remittance basis (may require payment of £30,000/£60,000 remittance basis charge)	
Transfer to spouse or civil partner	No gain, no loss	Exempt (but restricted to £325k if donee is not UK domiciled/deemed domiciled)
The importance of timing	Need to consider the tax year of disposal which will determine: • Rate of tax payable by the vendor/donor • Availability of AEA/losses • Relief conditions	Need to consider: • The availability of the annual exemption • The use of the nil rate band in the previous seven years • The availability of taper relief • No IHT if survive gift for seven years
Exemptions	Various assets are exempt, including: • Wasting chattels • Low value non-wasting chattels • Main residence • AEA	All assets are subject to IHT with one important exception: • Overseas assets owned by an overseas domiciled individual Certain gifts exempt including: • Small gifts, marriage gifts • Gifts out of income • Annual exemption
Reliefs available in respect of business assets	Rollover relief • Requires proceeds to be invested in replacement business assets Gift holdover relief Business asset disposal relief Investors' relief	Business property relief
Other reliefs	Gift holdover relief for agricultural property Enterprise investment scheme/ Seed EIS: • Requires proceeds to be invested in unquoted trading company shares	Agricultural property relief
Other matters to consider	• Double tax relief • Due dates	• Residence nil rate band • Quick succession relief • Double tax relief • Due dates • Who is responsible for paying any tax due and who suffers it

10 CGT reliefs summary

	Business asset disposal relief (BADR)			Investors' relief (IR)	Gift relief (GR)	
Scenario in question	Individual selling shares	Selling a sole trader or partnership business	Ceasing to trade and selling the assets	Individual selling shares	Gift or sell an asset at less than MV	Gift shares
Conditions	≥5% ordinary share capital in trading company and director or employee, for 2 years	Own the business for two years	Sell assets within three years of ceasing to trade and was trading for two years before cessation	Subscribed for new ordinary shares in trading company on or after 17 March 2016, owned for three years. Not usually director or employee.	Business assets used in trade, OR Unquoted shares, OR Quoted shares if own ≥5% of the company. Joint election needs to be made (unless to trust) Donee needs to be UK resident.	
Rules	Gains taxed at 10% AEA and losses taken off non-BADR gains £1 million lifetime limit			Gains taxed at 10% AEA and losses taken off non-IR gains £10 million lifetime limit	Gain calculated using MV Donor is taxed on the gain which is equal to the actual proceeds less cost. If this is negative then no gain is taxed. Gain which is taxed could be eligible for BADR/IR. Deferred gain is deducted from the MV to get to the base cost.	Gain calculated using MV. Gain deferred is equal to the gain × CBA/CA. Gain which is taxed could be eligible for BADR/IR. Deferred gain is deducted from the MV to get to the base cost.

	Rollover + holdover relief	EIS reinvestment	SEIS reinvestment	Incorporation relief	Private residence relief (PRR)
Scenario in question	Company or an individual who buys an asset and sells another asset	Individual sells an asset and reinvests in EIS shares	Individual sells an asset and reinvests in SEIS shares	Individual is selling business to a company (incorporating)	Individual sells main residence
Conditions	Both assets need to be land and buildings or FIXED plant and machinery or goodwill. Amounts need to be invested between 12 months before the disposal to 36 months after.	Reinvest gain between 12 months before to 36 months after the disposal	Reinvest gain within the same tax year	Must transfer all assets (except cash) to company. The business must be transferred as a going concern. The consideration must be wholly or partly in shares.	House has to be private residence
Rules	Donor is taxed on the gain equal to the net proceeds (after disposal costs) not reinvested. Deferred gain is deducted from the cost of the new asset to get the base cost. If the new asset is FIXED plant and machinery then the deferred gain is not deducted	Max gain deferred is lower of gain and amount subscribed in EIS shares. Could choose a lower amount to utilise capital losses and AEA. The deferred gain is usually taxed when the shares are sold.	Only 50% of the gain which has been reinvested can be exempted. If shares are sold within three years then the exempt gain is taxed.	The gain which can be deferred is equal to the gain x (MV of shares / MV of total consideration). The deferred gain is deducted from the MV (base cost) of the shares.	Proportion of gain which is exempt is the proportion of the ownership for which there has been actual or deemed occupation. If the property has been let with shared owner occupation then letting relief is also available.

	Rollover + holdover relief	EIS reinvestment	SEIS reinvestment	Incorporation relief	Private residence relief (PRR)
	from the cost but instead deferred until earliest of three dates.				

11 IHT reliefs summary

	Agricultural property relief (APR)	Business property relief (BPR)
Scenario in question	Gifting agricultural property to someone	Gifting business assets to someone or Gifting shares to someone
Conditions	If donor is farmer then need to own it for two years. If donor rents out the farm then need to own it for seven years.	Relevant business property Ownership – two years Not on excepted assets (eg investments)
Rules	100% relief for the agricultural value. Could get BPR on the remainder. Use AE after APR and BPR. Would still be available if donor dies within seven years if the asset is still owned by the donee as agricultural property.	100% or 50% relief depending on the asset. Use AE after you give BPR. Would still be available if donor dies within seven years if the asset is still owned by the donee as business property

	Fall in value	Taper relief	Quick succession relief (QSR)
Scenario in question	Individual gifts an asset which drops in value between gift and the death of the donor	Donor dies between three and seven years after a gift has been made	Two people die within five years of each other
Conditions	None	None	Asset needs to have been passed down from the first deceased to the second deceased
Rules	Reduction in the value of the asset is deducted before the NRB within the death tax calculation	Once the death tax on a lifetime gift has been calculated a percentage of it need not be paid due to taper relief	Apply the relief after the tax has been calculated in the death tax pro-forma

Chapter summary

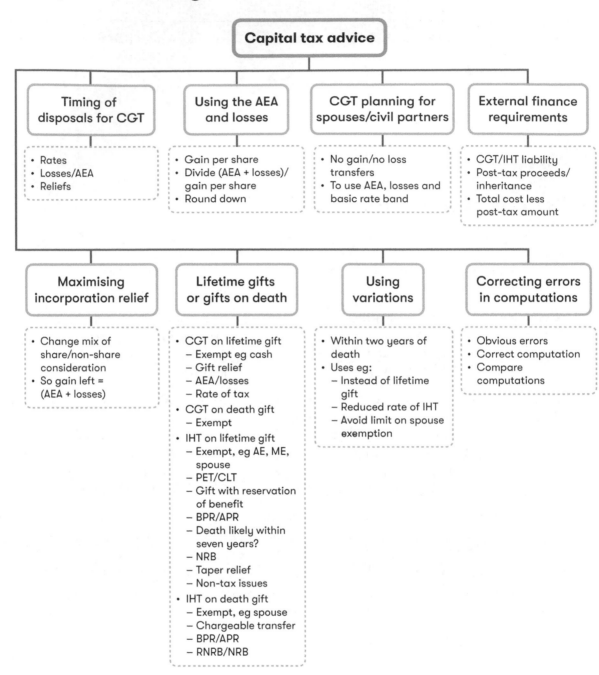

Capital tax advice

Timing of disposals for CGT
- Rates
- Losses/AEA
- Reliefs

Using the AEA and losses
- Gain per share
- Divide (AEA + losses)/ gain per share
- Round down

CGT planning for spouses/civil partners
- No gain/no loss transfers
- To use AEA, losses and basic rate band

External finance requirements
- CGT/IHT liability
- Post-tax proceeds/ inheritance
- Total cost less post-tax amount

Maximising incorporation relief
- Change mix of share/non-share consideration
- So gain left = (AEA + losses)

Lifetime gifts or gifts on death
- CGT on lifetime gift
  - Exempt eg cash
  - Gift relief
  - AEA/losses
  - Rate of tax
- CGT on death gift
  - Exempt
- IHT on lifetime gift
  - Exempt, eg AE, ME, spouse
  - PET/CLT
  - Gift with reservation of benefit
  - BPR/APR
  - Death likely within seven years?
  - NRB
  - Taper relief
  - Non-tax issues
- IHT on death gift
  - Exempt, eg spouse
  - Chargeable transfer
  - BPR/APR
  - RNRB/NRB

Using variations
- Within two years of death
- Uses eg:
  - Instead of lifetime gift
  - Reduced rate of IHT
  - Avoid limit on spouse exemption

Correcting errors in computations
- Obvious errors
- Correct computation
- Compare computations

Knowledge diagnostic

1. Timing

Timing of disposals for CGT involve thinking about rates of tax, use of the AEA and losses, and conditions for reliefs.

2. Using the AEA and losses

The AEA and available losses can be used by selling a number of quoted shares calculated by considering the gain per share.

3. Planning for spouses/civil partners

It may be beneficial to transfer the whole or part of an asset to a spouse/civil partner before disposal to use their AEA, losses and basic rate band.

4. External finance requirements

External finance required is the difference between the total cost of the project and post-tax proceeds (CGT) or post-tax inheritance (IHT).

5. Maximising incorporation relief

Incorporation relief can be maximised by manipulating the amount of non-share consideration received so that the gain remaining chargeable is equal to losses plus the AEA.

6. Lifetime gifts or gifts on death?

If a client is thinking of either making a gift of assets in their lifetime or wait to gift assets on their death, you need to consider both IHT and CGT aspects.

7. Using variations

Variations can be used to reorganise gifts made on death to obtain CGT and IHT advantages.

8. Correcting errors in computations

If you are asked to correct errors in a tax computation, first identify any obvious errors and then prepare a correct computation and compare with the incorrect one.

Further study guidance

Question practice

Now try the following from the Further question practice bank (available in the digital edition of the Workbook):

- Hubert
- Stuart and Rebecca

Activity answers

Activity 1: Timing of disposal to maximise after-tax sale proceeds

Offer 1

	£
Proceeds 6,000 × £115	690,000
Less cost	(6,000)
Gain	684,000
Less AEA 20/21	(12,300)
Taxable gain	671,700

No BADR as not officer for two years before disposal

Additional rate taxpayer in 2020/21 so all gain taxed at 20%

CGT	134,340
Net proceeds £(690,000 − 134,340)	555,660

Offer 2

	£
Proceeds 6,000 × £110	660,000
Less cost	(6,000)
Gain	654,000
Less AEA 2021/22 (use against residential property)	(0)
Taxable gain	654,000

No BADR as not officer for two years before disposal

Basic-rate taxpayer − BRB left is £37,500 − (15,000 − 12,500) = 35,000

CGT

35,000 at 10%	3,500
619,000 at 20%	123,800
Total	127,300
Net proceeds £(660,000 − 127,300)	532,700

Offer 3

	£
Proceeds 6,000 × £105	630,000
Less cost	(6,000)
Gain	624,000
Less AEA 2021/22 (use against residential property)	(0)
Taxable gain	624,000

BADR as all conditions satisfied for two years before disposal

CGT at 10%	62,400
Net proceeds £(630,000 − 62,400)	567,600

Therefore Offer 3 gives the maximum after-tax sale proceeds.

Activity 2: Using the AEA and losses

The gain per share is £(6.40 – 2.20) = £4.20.

Thyme can make a gain of up to £(12,300 + 1,200) = £13,500 without incurring a charge to capital gains tax.

She can therefore sell (13,500/4.20) = 3,214 shares (rounded **down**).

Check: 3,214 × £4.20 = £13,499.

Activity 3: Inter-spouse transfer

Arabella's CGT liability would be £((525,000 – 480,000) – 12,300) × 28% = £9,156.

If she gave one-third of the house to Dominic (no gain, no loss), on sale she would have two-thirds of the gain and he would have one-third.

Arabella's CGT liability would be £(((525,000 – 480,000) × 2/3) – 12,300) × 28% = £4,956.

Dominic's CGT liability would be £(((525,000 – 480,000) × 1/3) – 12,300) × 18% = £486.

The CGT saving would be £(9,156 – 4,956 – 486) = £3,714.

This could also be calculated as tax saved by using Dominic's AEA (£12,300 × 28% = 3,444) and tax saved by using Dominic's basic rate band £(2,700 × (28 –18)% = 270).

Activity 4: External finance requirement with CGT

Step 1 *Compute the CGT liability*

On 1 September 2018

Cash element creates part disposal at takeover. Shares and loan stock do not. However, the gain on the acquisition of the loan stock is calculated up to the date of the takeover.

	MV at takeover	Cost
	£	£
Cash	8,000	5,166
Shares	78,344	50,594
Loan stock	22,720	14,672
	109,064	70,432

Frozen gain on Granada plc loan stock (QCB)

	£
MV at takeover	22,720
Cost	(14,672)
Frozen gain	8,048

On 1 February 2021

Gain on sale of Granada plc shares

	£
Proceeds	83,496
Cost (see above)	(50,594)
	32,902

On sale of Granada plc loan stock

No gain arises on sale of loan stock because it is a QCB.

However, the frozen gain on takeover will now become chargeable.

	£
Gains (32,902 + 8,048)	40,950
AEA	(12,300)
	28,650
CGT payable @ 20% (taxable income ≥ basic rate limit)	5,730

Step 2 *Compute the post-tax proceeds*

	£
Sale proceeds of shares	83,496
Sale proceeds of loan stock	23,920
Less CGT on sales	(5,730)
Post-tax proceeds	101,686

Step 3 *Compute the external finance required*

	£
Total cost of project	310,000
Less post-tax proceeds of sale	(101,686)
External finance required	208,314

Activity 5: Lifetime gifts or gifts on death?

Because when Sarah died she had not made any lifetime gifts, 100% of the nil band will be available to offset against the inheritance tax liability when Stephen dies (effectively doubling the nil band from £325,000 to £650,000 using current rates). Sarah would also not have used any residence nil rate band (RNRB) as her death was prior to its introduction and so, if the main residence is left on Stephen's death to direct descendants, then there will be a £350,000 RNRB available to offset against the death estate in the death tax calculation.

Main residence

The main residence is the most significant asset in Stephen's estate. If it were gifted in lifetime the capital gains tax (CGT) liability would be nil, as the entire gain would be covered by the private residence exemption. The value transferred will be a potentially exempt transfer for inheritance tax (IHT) purposes and would not be subject to IHT unless Stephen died within the next seven years.

However, Stephen would still need somewhere to live so it is unlikely to be practical to gift the main residence in lifetime. Gifting the main residence in lifetime while continuing to live in the residence would be ineffective for IHT purposes as it would be a gift with reservation of benefit, unless a market rental is paid.

Ordinarily, this means that giving the main residence away but continuing to live in it is not particularly good IHT planning, but as Stephen appears to have a significant amount of cash which he wants to pass to family members anyway, he could gift the house in lifetime and use the cash balance to pay the rent, which would then mean that the gift with reservation of benefit rules would not apply and there would be no IHT liability as long as he lived for another seven years. However, the rent paid by Stephen would be liable to income tax on the recipient.

If the main residence is gifted through the death estate, there will be an automatic CGT uplift to market value, and the residence will be included in the death estate at its market value at that time. As mentioned above, an additional £350,000 RNRB would become available to reduce the IHT on the death estate provided Stephen left the main residence to direct descendants, ie children/grandchildren. Thus, it is recommended that Stephen retain the residence until his death in order to access the additional RNRB which would not be available on a lifetime transfer which is not a gift with reservation of benefit. This would save £140,000 (2 × £175,000 × 40%).

Cash

The cash is not a chargeable asset for capital gains tax purposes so can be given in lifetime without any CGT effect. A lifetime gift of cash would be a potentially exempt transfer for IHT purposes and would therefore be completely exempt from IHT if Stephen survived the gift by at least seven years. Additionally, the cash can be given in small amounts to maximise the benefit of the annual exemption. It is recommended that the cash is given in lifetime to minimise the overall IHT liability (although this is subject to the point above, regarding the gift of the house in lifetime).

Motor car

The motor car is not a chargeable asset for CGT purposes, so again can be given in lifetime without any CGT effect. The gift would again be a potentially exempt transfer for IHT purposes and, subject to the practical difficulties that may arise if Stephen does not actually have a car, a gift in lifetime would be most effective.

Aardvark shares

The disposal of the shares in Aardvark Ltd in lifetime would be a market value disposal for capital gains tax purposes and a potentially exempt transfer for IHT purposes. A gain of £300,000 (400,000 – 100,000) will arise if Stephen gives the shares away in lifetime, but, because this is an unquoted trading company, gift relief will be available to defer part of the gain. The part of the gain that relates to the investment activities in Aardvark Ltd cannot be deferred under the gift relief provisions. This means a gain of £45,000 (W1) will arise and, assuming a full annual exempt amount is available, a CGT liability of £6,540 will arise for Stephen.

If Stephen is a director or employee of Aardvark Ltd, the capital gain of £45,000 may qualify for business asset disposal relief. If business asset disposal relief is available, the CGT liability would be £3,270 (W2).

If the potentially exempt transfer becomes chargeable for IHT purposes (because Stephen dies within seven years) business property relief (BPR) is potentially available, but again this relief is restricted to the business (not investment) activities so 15% of the potentially exempt transfer will be subject to IHT on death. This is, however, subject to the condition that the recipient still owns the shares when the potentially exempt transfer becomes chargeable.

If the shares are gifted through the death estate, there is an automatic capital gains tax uplift to market value (which removes the CGT liability of £6,540 above) but the shares will be included in the death estate at their current market value, although BPR will again be available to restrict the amount chargeable with the 15% of the company value that relates to investments.

If the shares are given through the death estate, this is a significantly better result for CGT purposes (as the gift relief option is merely a deferral, rather than an exemption from CGT). It means that the recipient of the shares could sell them immediately without triggering any CGT liability.

Chattels

Chattels are generally not subject to capital gains tax on a disposal in lifetime, so these assets could be given away without any CGT liability arising. Such a gift would be a potentially exempt transfer but could be covered by the use of lifetime exemption such as the annual exemption or, possibly, the marriage exemption if appropriate.

Workings

1 CGT

	£
Proceeds	400,000
Cost	(100,000)
	300,000
Less gift relief (85%)	(255,000)
	45,000
Less annual exempt amount	(12,300)
	32,700 @ 20% = 6,540

2 CGT with BADR

Gain £32,700 × 10% = £3,270

Activity 6: Lifetime gift or variation?

Notes for meeting

Lifetime gift

IHT

Clive will make a transfer of value of £28,000 on the gift to Imogen. Business property relief is not available as Clive does not have a controlling interest.

The annual exemptions for 2020/21 and 2019/20 will be available. The balance of £(28,000 – 6,000) = £22,000 will be a potentially exempt transfer (PET).

If Clive dies within seven years of the gift the PET will become chargeable. It will be within Clive's nil rate band and so there will be no IHT to pay on it (and so taper relief is not relevant). However, it will use up this amount of his nil rate band available to set against his death estate so increasing the tax by £22,000 × 40% = £8,800.

CGT

If Clive gives the shares to Imogen, he will make a chargeable gain of £(28,000 – 15,000) = £13,000.

Gift relief cannot be claimed because quoted company shares, where the company is not the transferor's personal company, are not business assets and there is no immediate charge to IHT.

Clive's annual exempt amount of £12,300 is available so the taxable gain will be £(13,000 – 12,300) = £700. Clive will therefore have a CGT liability of £700 × 20% = £140 in 2020/21.

Imogen will receive the shares at market value of £28,000. If the shares further increase in value she will have a gain. However, she may be able to use her annual exempt amount and/or losses to cover some of this gain.

Variation

IHT

There will be no transfer of value by Clive on the variation. Imogen will be treated as receiving the shares under Trevor's will. There will be no change in the IHT liability on Trevor's estate.

CGT

Imogen will receive the shares at probate value. If the shares further increase in value she will have a gain of £13,000 plus the gain she would have made if the shares had been passed to her by way of lifetime gift. Again, she may be able to use her annual exempt amount and/or losses to cover some of this gain.

Activity 7: Using a variation to avoid limit on spouse exemption

1   Tarak is UK domiciled but Miri is non-UK domiciled (and cannot be deemed domiciled given her residence profile) so the IHT spouse exemption on gifts by Tarak to Miri is limited to a maximum of £325,000. Since Tarak made a transfer of £250,000 to Miri in July 2018, only £75,000 of this limit remains.

Therefore Tarak's gift of the cottage worth £180,000 to Miri would be a potentially exempt transfer of £(180,000 − 75,000) = £105,000, which would give rise to an inheritance tax liability if Tarak were to die within seven years of the gift since he has used his nil rate band in the seven years before this gift on the CLT made in September 2016.

2   The potential liability could be avoided in either of the following ways:

(1)   The terms of Tarak's father's will could be altered by a deed of variation, so the cottage is left directly to Miri. This would avoid the need for Tarak to make a potentially exempt transfer to Miri.

(2)   Miri could elect to be treated as UK domiciled for the purposes of IHT. This would mean that all gifts from Tarak would be exempt under the spouse exemption with no upper limit.

3   The downside of Miri electing to be treated as UK domiciled would be that any non-UK assets owned by Miri would cease to be outside the scope of UK IHT. Since Miri has substantial assets in Atlantis, this means that the use of the variation is likely to prove the more tax-efficient option.

Activity 8: Correcting errors in IHT computation

7 May 2011

Chargeable lifetime transfer of £350,000 – this transfer is not exempt (only potentially exempt transfers become exempt if the donor survives seven years) and will cumulate with transfers in the next seven years (ie the transfer on 14 October 2014, but not the transfer on 17 May 2020).

14 October 2014

Gift to nephew Simon

The land used by the partnership only attracts BPR at the rate of 50%.

	£	£
Share in partnership manufacturing garden furniture	170,000	
Less: BPR @ 100%	(170,000)	
		0
Land used by partnership in its trade	60,000	
Less: BPR @ 50%	(30,000)	
		30,000
Potentially exempt transfer		30,000
IHT @ 40% (nil rate band used by CLT)		12,000
Less: taper relief (5 to 6 years) @ 60%		(7,200)
IHT payable by Simon		4,800

17 May 2020

Gift of main residence to niece Orla

The residence nil rate band only applies if the main residence is part of the death estate.

BPP LEARNING MEDIA

	£
Main residence	550,000
Less: Available nil rate band £(325,000 – 30,000)	(295,000)
Excess	255,000
IHT @ 40% (no taper relief as within three years of death)	102,000

Skills checkpoint 3
Capital tax advice

Chapter overview

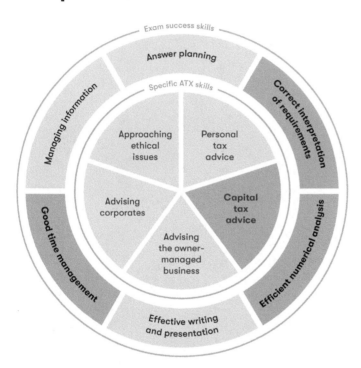

Introduction

The ATX exam could require you to deal with capital taxes: capital gains tax (CGT) and/or inheritance tax (IHT).

In a Section A question, you may be presented with a complex personal tax scenario of which capital taxes are a part.

Capital taxes may also appear in a Section B question in a slightly more structured way. The question extract we will be looking at in this Skills checkpoint is a good example of the Section B style.

Both Section A and Section B questions may involve considering more than one tax (typically CGT and IHT) for one transaction. For example on a lifetime gift there may be a CGT disposal and an IHT transfer of value. You must make sure you deal with each tax separately.

Exemptions and reliefs are particularly important when advising a client on capital tax issues and it is vital that you get clear in your mind which exemption or reliefs apply to each tax. You will not impress the examining team if you discuss IHT Business Property Relief in the context of CGT! The question in this Skills Checkpoint is a good introduction to how to deal with this style of question as it involves the lifetime gift of a farm and its subsequent disposal by the donee which has both CGT and IHT consequences.

In this Skills Checkpoint we will focus on three general exam success skills and the specific ATX – UK skill on capital tax advice. Once you are familiar with these skills, you can then use them to tackle further capital taxes advice questions. Do make sure that you refresh your memory using the technical knowledge presented in this Workbook before you attempt more exam standard questions.

Skills checkpoint 3: Capital tax advice

ATX capital tax advice

The key steps in applying this skill are outlined below. They will be explained in more detail in the following sections, and illustrated by answering requirements from a past exam question.

STEP 1   Work out how many minutes you have to answer the question.

STEP 2   Read the requirements and analyse them.

STEP 3   Read the scenario and highlight and/or make notes of the information that will enable you to answer the requirements, making sure you identify the different taxes involved.

STEP 4   Prepare an answer plan.

STEP 5   Write your answer. Use sub-headings for each tax to show which you are writing about.

Exam success skills

The following illustration is based on a 14-mark extract from an exam question, Adam, which appeared in the Sep/Dec 2017 sample questions. These three exam success skills are particularly important:

- **Correct interpretation of requirements.** You must make sure that you deal with all relevant taxes in your answer. This is particularly important in giving capital tax advice as there will often be both CGT and IHT implications of a single transaction. You also have two taxpayers in this question so it is important to make sure you are clear which of them you are focused on in each part.

- **Good time management.** ATX – UK questions are usually divided into parts and sometimes sub-parts. You must make sure that you only spend about 1.95 minutes per mark. This is particularly relevant where the parts or sub-parts are of very different lengths as in this question. You also need to think about the balance of taxes in your answer: sometimes you can deal with one tax in a few sentences but the other requires a longer explanation.

- **Effective numerical analysis.** You will often be required to advise a client using supporting calculations. It is important that you can prepare these quickly and clearly. You need to decide whether you need to show calculations in separate workings (more than one line needed) or as part of your narrative answer (a few figures which can be shown in one line).

Skill activity

STEP 1   Work out how many minutes you have to answer the question.

It is worth spending approximately a quarter to a third of your time on reading and planning and the rest of the time writing up your answer.

For 3 marks in part (a) you have about 6 minutes so spend a minute reading the question, a minute jotting down three points you need to make (one for each mark) and then the remaining 4 minutes writing them up.

For 11 marks in part (b) you have about 21 minutes. This time should be split approximately as follows:

- Reading the question – 3 minutes
- Planning your answer – 3 minutes
- Writing your answer – 15 minutes

Required

(a) Explain the capital gains tax and inheritance tax implications for Sabrina of the planned gift of Eastwick Farm to Adam on 1 January 2022, and the reasons why the financial adviser has determined that neither tax may be payable by her as a consequence of his gift.

Note. Detailed calculations are NOT required for this part.

3 marks

Required

(b) Explain, with supporting calculations, Adam's potential capital gains tax liability on a future sale of Eastwick Farm and the inheritance tax implications for him of being gifted the farm by Sabrina on 1 January 2022 if, as he intends, he leases the farm to a tenant farmer, and Sabrina dies before 1 January 2029.

11 marks

STEP 2   Read the requirements and analyse them.

Required

(a) Explain[66] the capital gains tax and inheritance tax implications for Sabrina[67] of the planned gift of Eastwick Farm to Adam on 1 January 2022, and the reasons why the financial adviser has determined that neither tax may be payable[68] by her as a consequence of his gift.

Note. Detailed calculations are NOT required[69] for this part.

3 marks

[66] Verb - refer to the ACCA definition.

[67] Focus on Sabrina's tax position in this part.

[68] Taxes are usually not payable because of exemptions or reliefs.

[69] Really important to follow this note!

Required

(b) Explain[70], with supporting calculations[71], Adam's potential capital gains tax liability[72] on a future sale of Eastwick Farm and the inheritance tax implications for him of being gifted the farm by Sabrina on 1 January 2022 if, as he intends, he leases the farm to a tenant farmer, and Sabrina dies before 1 January 2029[73].

11 marks

[70] Verb - refer to the ACCA definition.

[71] Good idea to do the calculations first and then build your explanation around them. Refer to the verb 'Calculate' in the ACCA definition.

[72] Links to part (a) but from Adam's point of view, and also his disposal.

[73] Dates given in a question are very important.

In ACCA exams, the verb 'Explain' means to make an idea clear or show logically how a concept is developed or to give reason for a key event. The examining team has said that you should not just provide a list of points but add in some explanation of the points you're discussing.

In ACCA exams, the verb 'Calculate' means to ascertain by computation or to make an estimate of or to evaluate or perform a mathematical process. Because these are supporting calculations, they need to be integrated with the 'Explain' element of your answer. Just providing calculations will not be sufficient to gain a reasonable mark for this question, even if they are correct.

STEP 3 Read the scenario and highlight and/or make notes of the information that will enable you to answer the requirements, making sure you identify the different taxes involved.

You should assume that today's date is 1 December 2021.

Sabrina:

- Is UK resident and domiciled

- Has made one previous lifetime gift of £350,000 into a discretionary trust[74] for her grandchildren on 1 September 2021

- Inherited Eastwick Farm[75] from her husband, Sam, on his death on 1 July 2020

- Has managed the farm[76] since this date

Sam:

- Owned and farmed Eastwick Farm for many years prior to his death on 1 July 2020

- Had made lifetime gifts which used the whole of his nil rate band[77] for inheritance tax purposes

Sabrina – proposal to gift Eastwick Farm to Adam:

- Sabrina plans to retire from running the farm on 31 December 2021.

- She has been informed by a financial adviser[78] that she could gift the farm to Adam when she retires without paying any capital gains tax or inheritance tax.

- She has decided to gift the farm to Adam on 1 January 2022.

[74] IHT chargeable lifetime transfer, will use up AEs and NRB.

[75] IHT agricultural property relief (APR). Think about ownership period.

[76] IHT business property relief (BPR). Think about ownership period.

[77] So no transfer of NRB to spouse possible.

[78] Hint here that this person knows what they are talking about so likely to be right!

Eastwick Farm – valuation of land and buildings:

	1 July 2020	1 January 2022 (estimated)
	£	£
Agricultural value	385,000	396,000
Market value	502,000	544,000

Note. The agricultural value is used for IHT APR

Adam:

- Is UK resident and domiciled

- Is an additional-rate taxpayer[79]

- Uses his annual exempt amount[80] for capital gains tax purposes each year

- Is in full-time employment[81] and will lease Eastwick Farm to a tenant farmer[82]

[79] Important for rate of tax for CGT.

[80] Common simplification so don't waste time deducting it in your answer.

[81] Not running farm as business so no CGT BADR available.

STEP 4 Prepare an answer plan.

You need to note the technical details you need in order to answer both requirements fully. This will enable you to get an idea of the level of depth you will need to cover to ensure you aim to pick up as many of the 14 marks as you can.

[82] Donee needs to own asset as agricultural property at death of donor.

You will usually score one mark for a well explained tax point with an additional half a mark for each component of a calculation that you include.

In a capital tax advice question it is important to deal with CGT and IHT separately and you should use sub-headings to make sure that you are answering in relation to each tax. You don't necessarily need to spend the same amount of time on each tax – the relative balance of the taxes should become apparent as you plan your answer.

Here we have produced a bullet-point list under the relevant sub-headings, but you could use a spider diagram if you prefer.

(a) **CGT**
- Gain on gift
- Gift relief – why available and effect for Sabrina

IHT
- Potentially exempt transfer – why and effect for Sabrina

(b) **CGT**
- Gift relief – effect for Adam on disposal (compute gain)
- Rate of tax on gain – no business asset disposal relief (compute tax)

IHT
- Agricultural property relief (APR) – is it available? (compute amount)
- Business property relief (BPR) – is it available? (compute amount)
- Potentially exempt transfer – additional rules for APR/BPR and effect of death within seven years (compute tax)

You will see that in part (b), you should be spending more time on the IHT aspects than the CGT aspects, say about two-thirds to three-quarters of the 21 minutes available.

Remember that there are usually more marks available than the maximum number stated in the question so you don't have to make all the points in order to attain a good mark for the question.

STEP 5 Write your answer. Use sub-headings for each tax to show which you are writing about.

(a) Implications for Sabrina of the gift of Eastwick Farm to Adam on 1 January 2022[83]

[83] Useful heading to keep referring back to when writing your answer.

Capital gains tax (CGT)

On the gift of the farm to Adam, chargeable gains will arise[84] on the chargeable assets gifted. These will be computed by reference to the market values of the assets at the date of the transfer, ie 1 January 2022. Their base costs will be their market values at the date of Sam's death, ie 1 July 2020.

[84] Don't be afraid to state basic principles briefly before considering more difficult points such as availability of reliefs.

However, gift relief will be available[85] as this is the gift of a business, and the financial adviser has assumed that this will be claimed. As no proceeds will have been received from Adam, the whole of the gain can be deferred, such that Sabrina will have no liability to CGT.[86]

[85] Clearly state (1) what relief is relevant, (2) why it applies, (3) how it works in this particular situation.

[86] Important to link back to requirement about financial adviser's reasons.

Inheritance tax (IHT)

The gift will be a potentially exempt transfer as it is a gift to an individual, so Sabrina will have no liability to IHT[87].

[87] Again, link back to financial adviser's reasons.

(b) **Implications for Adam of the gift of Eastwick Farm on 1 January 2022**

CGT

The claim for gift relief[88] is a joint claim by both the donor and donee, so Adam will have to agree to this.

[88] You might have dealt with the claim in part (a) and should have been given credit for it.

If the claim is made, the chargeable gains on the gift of the farm of £42,000 (£544,000 – £502,000)[89] will be deferred.

[89] Supporting calculation. Does not need to be in separate working if just a few figures.

Adam's base cost in each of the assets will be their market value less the chargeable gain on the gift.

Accordingly, if a claim for gift relief is made, Adam's chargeable gain on the future disposal will be greater.

If Adam leases the farm to a tenant farmer, business asset disposal relief will not be available[90] on any subsequent disposal, as the farm will be an investment for Adam; he will not be carrying on a business. As Adam will be an additional rate taxpayer, the gift relief claim will generate an additional CGT liability of £8,400[91] (£42,000 × 20%).

IHT

The gift of the farm by Sabrina on 1 January 2022 will qualify for agricultural property relief (APR) at the rate of 100% on the agricultural value[92] on 1 January 2022 of £396,000. Sabrina has been managing the farm since her husband's death and although she has owned the farm herself for less than two years, as she inherited it from her husband on his death, his period of ownership can be added to hers, such that the two-year holding period is satisfied.

The excess of the market value over the agricultural value on 1 January 2022 of £148,000 (£544,000 – £396,000) is eligible for business property relief (BPR)[93] at the rate of 100%, because Sabrina, as owner, has been farming the land herself, and, as above for APR, the two-year ownership requirement is satisfied.

In the case of Sabrina's death before 1 January 2029, ie within seven years of making the transfer, it is important that Adam still owns the farm at the date of her death.[94] This is because, provided the farm still constitutes agricultural property, ie it is used for agricultural purposes by the tenant to which it is let, APR will be available on the agricultural value.

[90] Also important to identify when relief is not available.

[91] Make sure you satisfy the requirement to calculate the additional CGT liability.

[92] State what relief is available, why and how it works.

[93] Again, state what, why and how.

[94] Important additional condition for APR.

BPP LEARNING MEDIA

However, as Adam is not intending to farm it himself, no BPR will be available on Sabrina's death.[95] Accordingly, the £148,000 excess of the market value over the agricultural value of the farm will be liable to inheritance tax at the rate of 40%. Sabrina's annual exemptions for 2021/22 and 2020/21 and her Nil Rate Band have been used on the earlier transfer into the discretionary trust.

[95] Also vital to identify when relief is not available.

Adam will therefore have a maximum potential inheritance tax liability of £59,200 (£148,000 × 40%)[96].

[96] Essential supporting calculation.

will be available to reduce this amount if Sabrina survives until at least 1 January 2025 (three years after making the gift).

Any inheritance tax payable by Adam will be deductible[98] when computing the chargeable gain arising on a subsequent disposal of the farm (but cannot be used to create an allowable loss).

[98] Technical point not vital to getting good marks.

Examining team's comments and mark scheme

Examining team's comments

This question was focused on the proposed gift of a farm and required comprehensive consideration of the reliefs available for both capital gains tax – gift relief and business asset disposal relief – and inheritance tax – agricultural property relief (APR) and business property relief (BPR).

Many candidates scored around half marks – good, but could probably have been better if exam skills used effectively – by demonstrating knowledge of the basic principles of capital gains tax and inheritance tax, including the use of exemptions and the recognition of the relevant tax rates to be applied. However, recognition of the reliefs available, and their application, was disappointing.

An ability to identify and apply appropriate reliefs for both capital gains tax and inheritance tax is an important skill in ATX–UK (a very important point), and candidates are again encouraged to practise more past exam questions, particularly those involving both capital taxes, in order to improve on this (use BPP's Practice and Revision Kit which has numerous past exam questions involving capital taxes).

Additionally, when a scenario involves a number of transactions, to be carried out at different times, by different people, it is important to provide this information – who is making the gift/sale, and when – to accompany calculations and provide appropriate context.

Candidates who do this are able to score much higher marks, by demonstrating understanding of the tax implications in context, than those candidates who just provide calculations without any accompanying details.

Mark scheme   Marks

(a) Capital gains tax   2

     Inheritance tax – potentially exempt transfer   1

Max   3

(b) Gift relief claim/CGT payable   3½

     APR/BPR on original gift   4½

     APR/BPR as a result of Sabrina's death within seven years   2

     Potential IHT payable   2½

     IHT deductible on subsequent sale   1

Max   11

Total Marks   14

Note. Look at the split of marks for part b; only 3½ for CGT but 10 for IHT!

Exam success skills diagnostic

Every time you complete a question, use the diagnostic below to assess how effectively you demonstrated the exam success skills in answering the question. The table has been completed below for Adam to give you an idea of what questions could be asked to complete the diagnostic.

Exam success skills	Your reflections/observations
Good time management	Did you spend too long on part (a)? Only three marks were available! Did you spend an appropriate amount of time discussing IHT in part (b)? It is not always necessary to balance your answer between the taxes.
Managing information	Did you pick up on all the information you needed to satisfactorily answer the requirements? For example, did you spot that Sabrina inherited the farm from her spouse so she was entitled to treat his ownership as hers for both APR and BPR?
Correct interpretation of requirements	Did you follow the note in part (a) **not** to provide supporting calculations? But **did** you provide them in part (b)? And did you calculate Adam's CGT liability, not just his gain? Did you make sure to focus on Sabrina in part (a) and Adam in part (b)? Or was your answer muddled up between them?
Answer planning	Did you deal with both CGT and IHT in both parts (a) and (b)? Did you make sure you dealt with them separately and didn't write about reliefs for one tax applying to the other?
Effective writing and presentation	Did you use subheadings to show which tax you were dealing with? Were your calculations clear? Or were the figures jumbled up?
Efficient numerical analysis	Did you pick up all the relevant information in the scenario? For example, did you take into account that Adam was an additional rate taxpayer and that he uses annual exempt amount

Exam success skills	Your reflections/observations
	for capital gains tax purposes each year?

Most important action points to apply to your next question

Summary

In this Skills checkpoint, we have seen that the specific ATX – UK skill on capital tax advice may involve dealing with transactions which with both CGT and IHT, as in the case of Sabrina's gift of her farm to Adam. Exemptions and reliefs are very important: remember the what, why, how approach. You may also need to think about why an exemption or relief does not apply in a particular situation.

We also focused on three exam success skills. Correct interpretation of the requirements involved remembering to consider both CGT and IHT and which taxpayer was relevant for each part. Time management was particularly important in this question as the parts were unequal in length. Efficient numerical analysis involved producing in-line calculations embedded in your narrative explanations.

Using these skills will help you to become a successful student so make sure you use them when you attempt further capital tax advice questions.

Sole traders

Learning objectives

On completion of this chapter, you should be able to:

	Syllabus reference no.
Remember the contents of Taxation (TX – UK) under the headings:	
'Income from self-employment'	A1(a)B3
'National insurance contributions for... self-employed persons'	A1(a)B6
Advise on a change of accounting date	A1(d)(i)
Advise on the allocation of the annual investment allowance between related businesses	A1(d)(iii)

Exam context

At least one of your exam questions will centre around a sole trader and it is thus vital that you are confident as to how a sole trader is taxed. Much of what is covered in this chapter is assumed knowledge from Taxation (TX – UK) but this should not make it feel less important in your studies. The Examining Team frequently state that it is assumed knowledge that is letting students down in their exam. Understanding the mechanics of tax for a sole trader will give you the 'core' marks that you need to be successful in your exam.

Rather than being asked to calculate taxable trade profits you are more likely to be asked about the effect on after tax income of a business action such as taking on an additional contract or employee. This will involve calculating the incremental profits, deducting tax payable, and taking any other costs (and their possible tax savings) into account. This will normally include VAT considerations. To be able to do this you need a full understanding of the rules for calculating taxable trade profits and allocating them to tax years.

If you are asked to calculate the tax cost of a business strategy you should always take into account capital allowances. This could apply when considering a particular contact, or when comparing the costs of different assets, or it could be in a buy or lease context.

Chapter overview

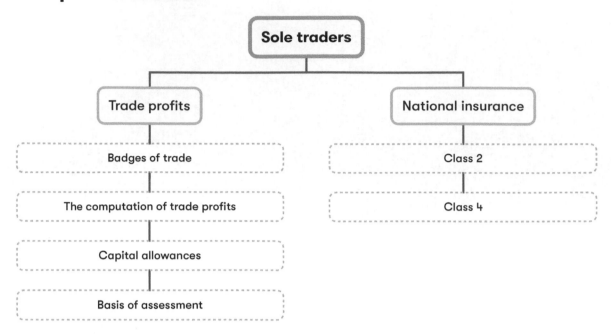

1 Trade profits

1.1 Badges of trade

Where an individual **buys and sells item(s)** a decision will need to be made as to whether this constitutes a sole trade business.

If a trade is carried on then the profits of the trade will need to be taxed as **trade profits** whereas if there is **no trade** consideration will need to be given as to whether there is a **capital gain** on a one off sale of an asset.

In determining whether a trade is being carried on consideration must be given as to whether the **'badges of trade'** are being exhibited.

The badges of trade are:

- **Subject matter**
- **Frequency of transactions**
- **Existence of similar trading transactions of interests**
- **Length of ownership**
- **The organisation of the activity as a trade**
- **Supplementary work and marketing**
- **Profit motive**
- **The way in which the asset sold was acquired**
- **Method of finance**
- **The taxpayer's intentions**

The decision as to whether a trade is being carried on is not straightforward and has been the basis for many **tax cases**. In your exam you should aim to consider and **apply the badges of trade to the scenario** in the question and then make a **conclusion** based on the **majority** of the badges.

Essential reading

The badges of trade are assumed knowledge from Taxation (TX – UK). See Chapter 14 of the Essential reading for more detail on the badges of trade.

The Essential reading is available as an Appendix of the digital edition of the Workbook.

1.2 The computation of trade profits

1.2.1 Adjustment to profits

As seen in Taxation (TX – UK), the taxable trading profits are not the same as the accounting profits of the business.

Profits before tax from the statement of profit or loss need **adjusting to follow the tax legislation.**

The standard process of adjusting the accounting profit to give the taxable trading profits is given below:

	£
Net profit before tax per accounts	X
Add back:	
Items charged in the accounts but not deductible for trading profits purposes	X
Income taxable under trading profits which has not been included in the accounts	X
Deduct:	
Items included in the accounts but not taxable under trading profits	(X)

		£
Expenditure which is deductible under trading profits but has not been charged in the accounts		(X)
Capital allowances		(X)
Adjusted profits for accounting period (AP)		X

Essential reading

See Chapter 14 of the Essential reading for more detail on the adjustment to profit.

The Essential reading is available as an Appendix of the digital edition of the Workbook.

Illustration 1: Adjustment to profit

Jack is a sole trader, carrying on a trade making garden furniture. His profit and loss account for the year ended 30 June 2020 shows the following:

	Note	£	£
Gross profit for year	(1)		142,000
Add: Interest receivable			2,000
			144,000
Less: Wages and NICs	(2)	52,360	
Rent and rates		32,450	
Repairs and renewals	(3)	1,350	
Miscellaneous expenses	(4)	600	
Jack's income tax		12,200	
Bad debts	(5)	800	
Legal/professional expenses	(6)	650	
Depreciation		1,000	
Charitable donations	(7)	60	
Transport costs		1,600	
Interest	(8)	1,000	
Lighting and heating		2,310	
Sundry expenses	(9)	3,110	(109,490)
Net profit			34,510

Notes.

1 Sales include £1,000 reimbursed by Jack for stock taken for personal use representing cost price. The selling price of the stock would have been £1,400.

2 Included in wages are Jack's drawings of £60 per week, his class 2 NICs of £159, and wages of £12,000 for his wife's part-time employment in the business (wages which would have been paid to any employee doing the same work would be £10,000).

Repairs and renewals are:

	£
Decoration of showroom	300
New heating system	1,000
Boiler maintenance fee	50
	1,350

Miscellaneous expenses are:

	£
Political donation	100
Gifts to customers of 20 table lanterns with Jack's logo	200
Jack's private medical insurance premium	300
	600

Bad debts are:

	£	£
Trade debt written off		400
Loan to employee written off		200
General provision for bad debts	400	
Less opening provision	(200)	2000
		800

Legal and professional expenses are:

	£
Fees relating to acquisition of a new machine	100
Fees for a speeding fine	50
Accountancy fees	500
	650

3   Two charitable donations made: one of £40 to a local charity and one of £20 to Oxfam.

4   Interest consists of £800 bank overdraft interest and £400 interest on overdue tax.

Sundry expenses are:

	£
Entertaining customers	400
Staff party	250
Subscription to trade association	340
Speeding fine for Jack while on a delivery	120
Other expenses (all allowable)	1,000
	3,110

Required

Prepare a statement of taxable trading income (before capital allowances).

Solution

Jack

Taxable trading income (before capital allowances)
Y/e 30 June 2020

		£
Net profit per accounts		34,510
Add: Disallowable expenditure		
	Drawings £60 × 52	3,120
	Jack's NIC	159
	Excess wages to wife	2,000
	New heating system	1,000
	Political donation	100
	Private medical insurance for Jack	300
	Jack's income tax	12,200
	Non-trade debt written off	200
	Increase in general bad debt provision	200
	Fees on acquisition of machine (capital asset)	100
	Fees relating to speeding offence	50
	Depreciation	1,000
	Oxfam donation	20
	Interest on overdue tax	400
	Jack's speeding fine	120
	Entertaining customers	400
		55,879
Trading income not shown in accounts		
Goods for own consumption (£1,400 – £1,000)		400
		56,279
Less: Non-trading income		
	Interest receivable	(2,000)
Taxable trading income (before capital allowances)		54,279

1.2.2 The cash basis

Usually businesses prepare accounts using **generally accepted accounting principles** for tax purposes. In particular, this means that income and expenses are dealt with on an **accruals basis**.

Certain **small businesses** may **elect** to use **cash accounting** (known as **'the cash basis'**) rather than the accruals basis for the purposes of calculating their taxable trading income.

The scheme is available to sole traders and partnerships if their **receipts in the tax year do not exceed £150,000.**

Formula provided

The £150,000 cash basis limit will be given to you in the Tax rates and allowances available in the exam.

When using the **cash basis taxable trading profits are calculated** as:

- **Cash receipts**, less
- **Deductible business expenses actually paid in the period**

Certain expenses can be calculated and deducted on **a flat rate basis** rather than deducting the actual amount incurred. In Advanced Taxation (ATX – UK) you should assume that **where a business elects to use the cash basis that they will use fixed rate expenses rather than deducting actual expenses.** The expenses to which this applies are:

- Expenditure on **motor cars**; and
- **Business premises partly used as the trader's home.**

The **fixed rate mileage expense is claimed for business miles.** There will be a deduction of **45p per mile** for the **first 10,000 business miles**, then **25p per mile thereafter.**

For **business premises being partly used as the trader's home** there is a deduction based on **how many people use the business premises each month as a private home:**

Number of relevant occupants	Non-business use amount
1	£350
2	£500
3 or more	£650

Formula provided

The fixed rate mileage expenses are the same as for employment income and are given in the Rates and Allowances available in the exam. If the business premise rates are required they will be given in your exam question. Be careful when using these amounts – they are not the deductible expense but the disallowable amount.

If the cash basis produces a **trading loss** the only relief available is to **carry forward the loss against future trading profits.** The **other usual loss reliefs** available to a sole trader using the accruals basis of accounting are **not available.**

Exam focus point

The detailed cash basis rules are quite complex. These more complex aspects are not examinable in Advanced Taxation (ATX – UK). In any exam question involving an unincorporated business, it should be assumed that the cash basis is not relevant unless it is specifically mentioned.

Essential reading

See Chapter 14 of the Essential reading for an illustration of the cash basis.

The Essential reading is available as an Appendix of the digital edition of the Workbook.

1.3 Capital allowances

1.3.1 The capital allowances computation

In part of the adjustment to profit calculation, capital allowances will need to be calculated. **Capital allowances** are the **tax equivalent to depreciation** and, once calculated, can be **deducted from the tax adjusted profit to obtain the taxable profits** of a business (sole trader, partnership or company). The detail of the capital allowance computation is assumed knowledge from Taxation (TX – UK) and a reminder of the computation is summarised here.

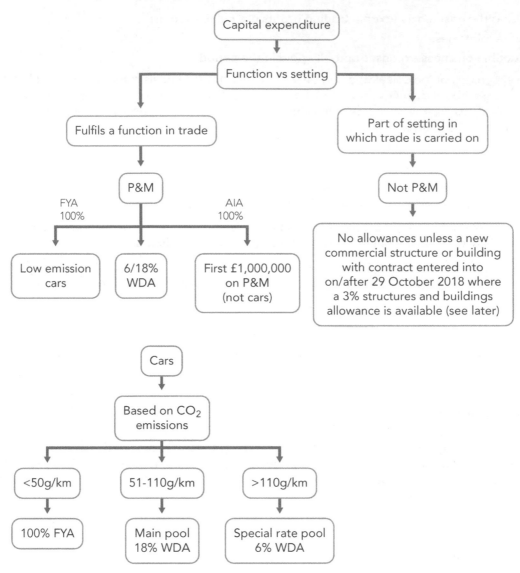

Continue to depool if private use by sole trader/partner.

The following format is recommended for use in the exams, for each accounting period.

	AIA	FYA	Main pool	Special rate pool	Short life assets	Private used asset (40%)	Allowances
	£		£	£	£	£	£
TWDV b/fwd			X	X		X	
Additions	X	X	X	X	X		
Disposal (proceeds limited to cost)			(X)			(X)	

	AIA	FYA	Main pool	Special rate pool	Short life assets	Private used asset (40%)	Allowances
	£	£	£	£	£	£	£
			—	—	—	—	
AIA	(X)						X
Tfr to MP/SRP			X	X			X
			X	X	X	X	
FYA 100%		(X)					X
		—					
WDA 18%/6%			(X)	(X)	(X)	(X)	
						× 60%	X
			—	—	—	—	—
TWDV cfwd			X	X	X	X	X

Essential reading

See Chapter 14 of the Essential reading for more detailed revision of capital allowances.

The Essential reading is available as an Appendix of the digital edition of the Workbook.

Exam focus point

The limit of the annual investment allowance changed on 1 January 2021, meaning that computing the AIA available has more complex rules than are contained within this Workbook. The ACCA have stated that questions will not be set which require the knowledge of what the more complex rules are, and you will be tested on an AIA of £1 million irrespective of the accounting period of the business.

1.3.2 Cessation of trade

A common scenario which we see in the Advanced Taxation (ATX – UK) exam is a **business being sold** and thus **ceasing to trade**. This has **specific capital allowance consequences** which you must be able to explain and apply in exam questions.

In the **final period of account** (sole traders and partnerships) or **accounting period** (company):

- **Add in any additions** as usual
- **Deduct any disposals (limited to cost).** Even if assets aren't sold there is a deemed disposal of assets at market value at the date trade ceases
- Give **no FYAs, AIA or WDAs**
- Instead, bring all pools down to **nil with balancing adjustments**.

If, however, the trade passes from **one connected person to another** then both parties can make a 'succession election' which avoids the balancing adjustments and results in the plant and machinery transferring at **tax written down value**. (For the transferor, trade still ceases and so no allowances are available to the transferor in the final period). If **no succession election is made**, the transferor is deemed to **sell their plant and machinery for market value even if no proceeds are paid and there will be balancing adjustments** as outlined above.

An individual is **connected** with their **spouse, their, or their spouse's brothers, sisters, ancestors and lineal descendants, with their spouses, with business partners and their spouses and relatives, and with a company they control** (either alone or in conjunction with persons connected to them). '**Spouses**' include **civil partners.**

Activity 1: Cessation of trade

Mezan ceased to trade on 31 December 2020 after several years in business. His last period of account was the nine-month period to 31 December 2020. On 1 April 2020 the TWDV values of plant and machinery are as follows:

	£
Main pool	12,000
SR pool (integral features)	18,000

The following transactions took place during the period ended 31 December 2020:

15.4.20	Purchased a van	5,000
31.8.20	Purchased motor car, CO_2 emissions 112 g/km	22,000
2.9.120	Sold a van (original cost £18,000)	(9,800)

Mezan kept the car for himself when the market value was £17,500. He scrapped the integral features for no consideration and he sold the other assets for £10,000.

Required

Calculate Mezan's capital allowances for the period ended 31 December 2020.

Solution

1.3.3 Allocation of annual investment allowance between related businesses

Related businesses are entitled to a **single AIA** between the businesses. The businesses may allocate the AIA between them as they think fit.

> **Related businesses:** Businesses are **related** if they are **carried on or controlled by the same individual or partnership** and either:
> - The businesses are **engaged in the same activity**; or
> - The businesses **share the same premises**.
>
> A business is controlled by a person in a tax year if it **is controlled by the person at the end of the chargeable period for that business ending in that tax year**.

The **nature of expenditure** by one business may be relevant when deciding how to **allocate the AIA** between businesses. For example, it is more efficient to set the AIA against special rate pool expenditure because of the lower rate of subsequent writing down allowances on the special rate pool (6% pa) as opposed to the main pool (18% pa).

There are **similar** (but separate) **rules** relating to **companies under common control and companies in a group.** We will deal with these rules when we look at companies later in this workbook.

Activity 2: Capital allowance

Obama incurs the following transactions in the year ended 31 March 2021.

		£
1.5.20	Plant & machinery	200,000
1.7.20	Plant & machinery	120,000
1.8.20	Integral feature	1,010,000
1.9.20	Car (CO_2 emission 100g/km)	24,000
Disposals		
1.10.20	Sold short-life asset for	10,000

Tax written-down values on 1.4.20 were as follows:

	£
Main pool	180,000
Short-life asset (bought June 2018)	15,000
Van (20% private use)	10,000

Required

Calculate the capital allowances available for the year ended 31 March 2021.

Solution

1.3.4 Structures and buildings allowance

A structures and buildings allowance (SBA) is available for qualifying expenditure on new commercial structures and buildings for contracts entered into on/after 29 October 2018. For the purpose of the ATX-UK exam, all expenditure will have been incurred on or after 6 April 2020 (or 1 April 2020 for companies).

Qualifying expenditure is expenditure on the construction of the building or structure itself (or the acquisition cost if bought from a developer), but not the cost of land, nor the cost of planning permission, fees and stamp taxes.

Where an existing building is renovated or converted, this expenditure may qualify (even if the underlying property was constructed prior to 29 October 2018).

Commercial structures and buildings include:

- Offices
- Retail and wholesale premises
- Factories
- Warehouses
- Walls
- Bridges
- Tunnels

Residential property or any part of a building which functions as a dwelling does not qualify for SBAs.

Exam focus point

You should assume that for any question involving the purchase (as opposed to a new construction) of a building, the SBA is not available unless stated otherwise.

The allowance is given at 3% **straight line**, over a 33 1/3 year period.

Each building or structure is treated separately, and enhancement expenditure is treated separately to the underlying building.

For SBAs to be claimed, the relevant asset must be in qualifying use, for example used in a trade or property letting business. If the asset is used partly in a trade and part rented out then the SBA must be apportioned. The part relating to trade use is deductible in determining trade profits and the part relating to rental is deductible in determining the property income to be taxed.

The allowance is pro-rated for accounting periods which are not 12 months in length, or where the structure or building is **brought into use or sold during the period**. This is in contrast to plant and machinery allowances which are given in full in the period of acquisition (with no WDA at all in the period of disposal).

There is no balancing adjustment on sale of an SBA asset; however, an adjustment is made to the chargeable gain or capital loss arising, by adding the SBA claimed to the seller's disposal proceeds. This may be referred to as a 'sales adjustment'.

The new purchaser takes over the remaining allowances (based on the original cost) over the remainder of the 33 1/3 year period. The seller time apportions relief up to the date of the disposal.

If the SBA asset is sold as part of an incorporation then the sole trader/ partnership does not make the sales adjustment as explained above (unless incorporation relief is disclaimed). Instead, the company claims SBAs on the original eligible cost and, on the future disposal of the SBA asset by the company, all the SBAs claimed to date (by both the company and sole trader/ partnership) are added to the company's disposal proceeds ie there will be a higher chargeable gain for the company on a future disposal. (See the earlier chapter covering CGT reliefs).

If the SBA asset is sold either to a connected person or within a 75% corporate capital gains group there is also no sales adjustment. As with incorporation above, the "transferee" continues to claim SBAs on the original eligible cost and, on a subsequent disposal of the asset, adds all the SBAs of both the transferor and the transferee to its disposal proceeds in its gains calculation.

Formula provided

The 3% SBA rate is stated in the Tax rates and allowances provided to you in the exam.

Activity 3: SBAs

Dumpling Ltd purchased a newly-constructed office building from a developer for £2,050,000 on 1 July 2020 and brought it into use immediately. The purchase price of £2,050,000 includes £50,000 relating to solicitor's fees and other acquisition costs.

Dumpling Ltd prepares accounts to December each year.

Required

What are the maximum SBAs available to Dumpling Ltd in the year ended 31 December 2020?

Solution

Activity 4: Sale of a structure or building with SBA

Dumpling Ltd continued to use the office building for its trade until 30 June 2023, when it was sold to Suet plc for £2,500,000 (excluding land). Suet immediately started using the office for trading purposes.

Suet plc prepares its accounts to March each year.

Required

What are the tax consequences to Dumpling Ltd in the year ended 31 December 2023 and for Suet plc in the year to 31 March 2024?

Solution

1.4 Basis of assessment

The adjustment to profit and calculation of capital allowances all occur for the **period for which the sole trader prepares their accounts**. It is only at the end of the process that we consider **how to fit the periods of account into tax years**. This is done by applying the **basis period rules** which were covered in Taxation (TX – UK).

The basis period rules are summarised in the sections below with some Activities to help recap this knowledge.

Exam focus point

One of the common reasons which the Examining Team give as to why students struggle in Advanced Taxation is poor assumed knowledge from Taxation (TX – UK). In particular, the basis period rules are often noted as topics which need to be improved.

Essential reading

See Chapter 14 of the Essential reading for more detailed revision of basis period rules and further activities for you to work through to ensure you understand the rules fully.

The Essential reading is available as an Appendix of the digital edition of the Workbook.

The topic regarding change of accounting date is a topic which is new at Advanced Taxation (ATX – UK).

1.4.1 Continuing to trade – current year basis

The profits taxed in a **tax year** (6 April – 5 April) are the profits of the **accounting period ending in that tax year.**

Activity 5: Current year basis

A sole trader prepares accounts to the year ended 30 June 2020.

Required

Which tax year will the profits of the year ended 30 June 2020 be taxed in?

Solution

1.4.2 A new business – opening year rules

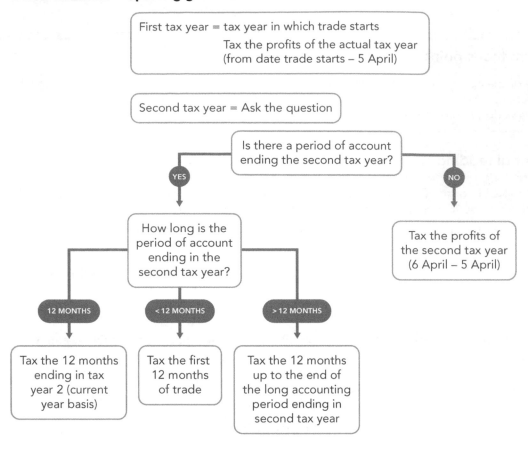

First tax year = tax year in which trade starts

Tax the profits of the actual tax year
(from date trade starts – 5 April)

Second tax year = Ask the question

Is there a period of account ending the second tax year?

YES

NO

How long is the period of account ending in the second tax year?

Tax the profits of the second tax year (6 April – 5 April)

12 MONTHS

< 12 MONTHS

> 12 MONTHS

Tax the 12 months ending in tax year 2 (current year basis)

Tax the first 12 months of trade

Tax the 12 months up to the end of the long accounting period ending in second tax year

Third and subsequent tax years:

Keep asking 'Is there an accounting period ending in this tax year?'– once you have a 12 month accounting period ending in the tax year you are in the current year basis and will stay in it year on year until you either cease to trade or have a change of accounting date (see next below).

Activity 6: Opening year rules (1)

Linda starts trading on 1 January 2019. She decides on a 30 June year end and her results are:

	£
6m to 30.6.19	18,000
y/e 30.6.20	48,000

Required

1 What are the assessments for the first three tax years?

2 What are the overlap profits?

Solution

Activity 7: Opening year rules (2)

Agnetha begins trading on 1 December 2019 and draws up her first accounts to 31 May 2021, her chosen year end. She makes £36,000 of profit in this period.

Required

1 What are her first three years' assessments?

2 What are her overlap profits?

Solution

1.4.3 Cessation of trade – closing year rules

The **final tax year** will be the tax year which includes the **date on which trade ceased**.

In our final tax year, we tax:	£
Any **profits not yet taxed**	X
Less overlap profits	(X)
Trade profits	X

The best way to work out **'any profits not yet taxed'** is to go back to the **penultimate tax year**. In the penultimate tax year use the **current year basis period** rules to work out what was taxed and the profits not yet taxed can then be identified.

Activity 8: Closing year rules

Albert, who has been trading for some years making up his accounts to 31 December, ceases to trade on 30 April 2020 with profits as follows:

	£
Year to 31.12.19	22,000
4 months to 30.4.20	12,000

The overlap profits arising in the opening years of his trade were £3,500.

Required

What are the assessments for 2019/20 and 2020/21?

Solution

1.4.4 Change of accounting date

Once a sole trader has a **12-month accounting period ending in a tax year** they will fall into using the current year basis period rules. They will continue to use these rules until they either **cease to trade or choose to change their accounting date such that they produce a non 12-month set of accounts.**

Where there is a non 12-month set of accounts **special rules** exist to work out what trading profits will be taxed in the 'year of change'. These rules were not covered in your Taxation (TX – UK) paper and are new at Advanced Taxation (ATX – UK).

Essential reading

The basics are covered here and for further practise you should see the Essential reading for this chapter.

The Essential reading is available as an Appendix of the digital edition of the Workbook.

The following **steps** must be followed to establish which trade profits are taxed where there has been a change of accounting date:

(a) Establish the **'year of change'** (YOC). This is **the first tax year where the current year basis isn't possible.** (ie the first tax year where we can't tax 12 months of profits).

(b) For all tax years **before the YOC** we will use the **current year basis period** rules to establish the tax year in which the profits are taxed. (This will be using the current year basis with the 12 months to the **original year end date**.)

(c) For all tax years **after the year of change** we will use the **current year basis period** rules again. This time, however, we will be using the current year basis with the 12 months to **the new year end date**.

(d) We are left to consider the **YOC**. Here we will be left with a time period of profits which have not yet been taxed in the year before or after the YOC. We will refer to this **period of untaxed profit as a 'gap'**. Dependent on the **length of the 'gap'** we have different rules as to what we tax in the YOC. These rules have the effect that we will always be taxing a 12-month period as the trader will have traded throughout the whole 12-month tax year so 12 months of profit should be taxed:

- If the **'gap' is >12 months** – we **tax the 'gap'** but then **deduct an appropriate amount of overlap profits from commencement of trade to bring the gap down to 12 months**, if possible. (So, for example, if the 'gap' is 15 months we would deduct three months of overlap, assuming we had three months overlap available).

- If the **'gap' is <12 months** – we **tax the 'gap'** but in order to tax twelve months overall **we tax the twelve-month period to the end of the 'gap'**. This effectively ends up **creating some further overlap profits** at the end of the final period to the original year end date. These further overlap profits are combined with overlap profits from commencement of trade and can be used on a future change of accounting date or on cessation of trade.

A change in accounting date and these basis period rules occur **automatically** if the trader changes their accounting date in their **first three tax years**. However, in **other cases, the following conditions** must be met for the change in basis period to be able to occur:

- The trader must **notify HMRC of the change by 31 January, following the tax year in which the change is made** (by 31 January 2022 for a change made during 2020/21).

- The **period of account** resulting from the change must **not exceed 18 months**.

- There must have been **no previous change of accounting date in the last five tax years** (unless the second change is made for **genuine commercial reasons**).

Activity 9: Change of accounting date (1)

Bee makes up accounts to 31 August until changing her accounting date to 31 May. Her results are as follows:

	£
Y/e 31.8.19	20,000
9 months to 31.5.20	15,000
Y/e 31.5.21	30,000

	£
Y/e 31.5.22	40,000

Required

What are Bee's assessments for 2019/20, 2020/21, 2021/22 and 2022/23?

Solution

Activity 10: Change of accounting date (2)

Zoe makes up accounts to 30 June until changing to 31 December. Her results are as follows:

	£
Y/e 30.6.19	25,000
Y/e 30.6.20	30,000
6 months to 31.12.20	15,000
Y/e 31.12.21	35,000

Zoe has nine months of overlap profits totalling £21,000.

Required

What are Zoe's assessments for 2019/20, 2020/21 and 2021/22?

Solution

2 National insurance

The self-employed (sole traders and partners) pay NICs in two ways: Class 2 and Class 4 NIC.

2.1 Class 2

Class 2 NICs are paid at a **flat rate of £3.05 per week** (2020/21) provided **taxable trade profits exceed the small profits threshold of £6,475** (2020/21).

Class 2 NICs are **paid** over by the individual through self-assessment **by 31 January following the tax year** Therefore, for 2020/21, Class 2 NICs are due by 31 January 2022.

2.2 Class 4

In addition to Class 2 NICs the self-employed individual must also pay **Class 4 NIC** if their **taxable trade profits exceed the lower NIC limit of £9,500** for 2020/21. Class 4 NIC will be **due at 9% of trade profits in excess of £9,500** up to the upper limit of £50,000 for 2020/21. **If trade profits exceed £50,000 Class 4 NIC will be due at 2% on the excess.**

If the trader has **trade losses** in a tax year then **no NICs** will be due.

Formula provided

The rates and limits for Class 2 and 4 NICs will be given to you in the Tax Rates and Allowances available in the exam.

Essential reading

See Chapter 14 of the Essential reading for more detail on how losses are treated for Class 4 NIC purposes.

The Essential reading is available as an Appendix of the digital edition of the Workbook.

Class 4 NICs are **paid** by the self-employed individual through **self-assessment** and are thus due through **payments on account on 31 January and 31 July with a balancing payment on 31 January following the tax year**. If payments are made late interest will be charged.

Chapter summary

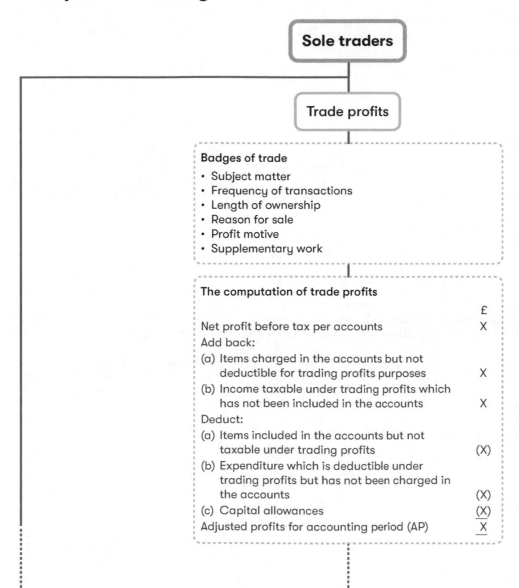

Sole traders

Trade profits

Badges of trade
- Subject matter
- Frequency of transactions
- Length of ownership
- Reason for sale
- Profit motive
- Supplementary work

The computation of trade profits

	£
Net profit before tax per accounts	X
Add back:	
(a) Items charged in the accounts but not deductible for trading profits purposes	X
(b) Income taxable under trading profits which has not been included in the accounts	X
Deduct:	
(a) Items included in the accounts but not taxable under trading profits	(X)
(b) Expenditure which is deductible under trading profits but has not been charged in the accounts	(X)
(c) Capital allowances	(X)
Adjusted profits for accounting period (AP)	X

Capital allowances

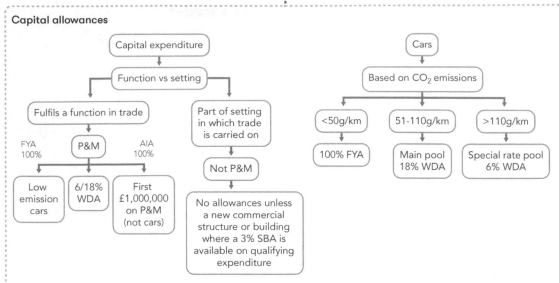

- Continue to depool if private use by sole trader/partner
- The following format is recommended for use in the exams, for each accounting period.

	AIA	FYA	Main pool	Special rate pool	Short life assets	Private used asset (40%)	Allowances
	£	£	£	£	£	£	£
TWDV b/fwd			X	X		X	
Additions	X	X	X	X	X		
Disposal (proceeds limited to cost)			(X)			(X)	
AIA	(X)		—	—	—	—	X
Tfr to MP/SRP			X	X			X
			X	X	X	X	
FYA 100%		(X)					X
		=					
WDA 18%/6%			(X)	(X)	(X)	(X) × 60%	X
TWDV cfwd			X	X	X	X	X

- Cessation of trade
  - Add additions and deduct disposals (limited to cost)
  - No FYA, AIA or WDAs
  - Bring all pools to zero with balancing adjustments
- Related businesses are entitled to a single AIA

Trade profits continued

Basis of assessment

- Continuing to trade
  - Use current year basis – tax 12 month accounting period ending in the tax year
- Opening year rules
  - First tax year = tax year in which trade starts: Tax the profits of the actual tax year (from date trade starts – 5 April)
  - Second year = ask the question:

- Third and subsequent tax years:
  Keep asking 'Is there an accounting period ending in this tax year?'– once you have a 12 month accounting period ending in the tax year you are in the current year basis and will stay in it year on year until you either cease to trade or have a change of accounting date (see next below).
- Closing year rules
  - In our final tax year, we tax:

	£
Any profits not yet taxed	X
Less overlap profits	(X)
Trade profits	X

- Change of accounting date
  - Establish 'year of change' (YOC) (ie first year where CYB isn't possible)
  - For all tax years before YOC use CYB to original y/e date
  - For all tax years after YOC use CYB to new y/e date
  - In YOC the 'gap' is taxed
  - If gap > 12 mths – assess all profits of gap - get relief for any overlap profits to reduce gap to 12 mths
  - If gap < 12 mths – assess all profits of gap and some months from previous year – creates overlap profits to make up 12 mths

National insurance

Class 2

- Flat rate £3.05 per week
- Provided taxable trade profits exceed small profits threshold of £6,475
- Paid through self-assessment by 31 January following the tax year

Class 4

- 9% of profits between £9,500 and £50,000
- 2% of profits above £50,000
- Paid through self-assessment with payments on account due 31 January and 31 July and a balancing payment 31 January following the tax year

Knowledge diagnostic

1. Badges of trade

The badges of trade can be used to decide whether or not a trade exists.

2. Adjustment to profit

The accounts profits need to be adjusted in order to establish the taxable trade profits.

An individual who is carrying on a trade may elect for the profits of the trade to be calculated on the cash basis (instead of in accordance with generally accepted accounting principles) in certain circumstances.

Fixed rate expenses can be used in relation to expenditure on motor cars and business premises partly used as the trader's home.

3. Capital allowances

Capital allowances are available on plant and machinery.

Statutory rules generally exclude specified items from treatment as plant, rather than include specified items as plant.

With capital allowances computations, the main thing is to get the layout right. Having done that, you will find that the figures tend to drop into place.

Businesses are entitled to an annual investment allowance (AIA) of £1,000,000 for a 12-month period of account. Related businesses share one allowance between them.

A first-year allowance (FYA) at the rate of 100% is available on new low emission cars. FYAs are never pro-rated in short periods of account.

Most expenditure on plant and machinery qualifies for a WDA at 18% every 12 months.

The special rate pool contains expenditure on thermal insulation, long life assets, features integral to a building, solar panels, and cars with CO_2 emissions over 110g/km. The AIA can be used against such expenditure. The WDA is 6% for a 12-month period.

An asset which is used privately by a trader is dealt with in a single asset pool (column) and the capital allowances are restricted.

Motor cars are generally dealt with in the special rate pool (cars emitting over 110g/km) or the main pool, unless there is private use by the trader.

Short life asset elections can bring forward the allowances due on an asset.

Capital allowances are available on assets acquired by hire purchase or long lease.

Balancing adjustments usually apply when a business ceases.

If a business is transferred to a connected person, the written down value of plant and machinery can be transferred thus avoiding a balancing charge.

A 3% pa structures and buildings allowance is available for qualifying expenditure on new commercial structures and buildings where contracts are entered into on/after 29 October 2018. Qualifying expenditure is on the construction cost (or acquisition cost if bought from a developer), but not the cost of the land, nor the cost of planning permission, fees and stamp taxes. The SBA is only available once the structure/building is brought into use and must be time apportioned if brought into use/ sold in the accounting period.

When a structure or building is sold the seller and buyer must both time apportion their SBAs. The buyer takes on the seller's original qualifying expenditure to continue their 3% SBA. The seller must add the SBAs claimed to date to the building's disposal proceeds in its gain calculation.

4. Basis periods

Basis periods are used to link periods of account to tax years.

In opening and closing years, special rules are applied so that a new trader can start to be taxed quickly, and a retiring trader need not be taxed long after their retirement.

On a change of accounting date, special rules apply for fixing basis periods.

5. National insurance

The self-employed pay Class 2 and Class 4 NICs. Class 4 NICs are based on the level of the individual's taxable profits. Class 2 NICs are paid at a weekly flat rate.

Further study guidance

Question practice

Now try the following from the Further question practice bank (available in the digital edition of the Workbook):

- Helen
- Sheila

Activity answers

Activity 1: Cessation of trade

	Main pool	SRP	Allowances
	£	£	£
9 m/e 31.12.20			
TWDV b/fwd	12,000	18,000	
Addition – van	5,000		
– car		22,000	
Disposal – van	(9,800)		
Cessation – disposal proceeds / MV of car	(10,000)	(17,500)	
	(2,800)	22,500	
Balancing allowance	–	(22,500)	22,500
Balancing charge	2,800	–	(2,800)
	Nil	Nil	19,700

Activity 2: Capital allowance

	AIA	Main pool	SRP	SLA	Private use (80%)	Allowances
	£	£	£	£	£	£
Y/e 31.3.21						
TWDV b/f		180,000		15,000	10,000	
Purchase 1.5.20		200,000				
Purchase 1.7.20		120,000				
Purchase 1.8.20	1,010,000					
Purchase 1.9.20		24,000				
Disposals 1.10.20				(10,000)		
		524,000		5,000		
AIA*	(1,000,000)					1,000,000
To SR pool			10,000			
					(1,800)	
WDA 18%		(94,320)			× 80%	95,760
WDA 6%			(600)			600
BA				(5,000)		5,000
				–	–	1,101,360
TWDV c/f		429,680	9,400	–	8,200	

*AIA allocated to additions qualifying for 6% rate of WDA in priority to those qualifying for the 18% rate of WDA

Activity 3: SBAs

£2,000,000 × 3% × 6/12 = £30,000

The cost of acquisition excludes acquisition fees. The SBA must be time-apportioned in the year of acquisition.

Activity 4: Sale of a structure or building with SBA

Dumpling Ltd will be able to claim an SBA for 6 months in is year ended 31 December 2023 so £30,000 (£2,000,000 × 3% × 6/12).

In its gain calculation on the sale of the building, the SBAs claimed to date of £180,000 (£2,000,000 × 3% × 3 years) will need to be added to Dumpling Ltd's disposal proceeds of £2,500,000.

Suet plc will be able to claim SBAs of £45,000 (£2,000,000 × 3% × 9/12) in its year ended 31 March 2024.

Note there is no uplift to the cost qualifying for SBAs for any increase in value over Dumpling Ltd's ownership of the building.

Activity 5: Current year basis

The profits of the year ended 30 June 2020 are taxed in 2020/21

(30 June 2020 falls in the tax year 2020/21).

Activity 6: Opening year rules (1)

1   As follows:

		£
2018/19	Actual	
	1.1.19–5.4.19 3/6 × 18,000	9,000
2019/20	Short AP ending in 19/20	
	Therefore 1st 12 months	
	1.1.19–31.12.19	
	18,000 + 6/12 × 48,000	42,000
2020/21	CYB y/e 30.6.20	48,000

2   As follows:

	£
Overlap profits	
1.1.19 – 5.4.19 3/6 × £18,000	9,000
1.7.19 – 31.12.19 6/12 × £48,000	24,000
	33,000

Activity 7: Opening year rules (2)

1 As follows:

			£
2019/20	1.12.19–5.4.20		
	4/18 × 36,000		8,000
2020/21	No AP ending in 20/21		
	Actual basis		
	6.4.20–5.4.21 12/18 × 36,000		24,000
2021/22	Long AP ending in 21/22		
	Therefore 12 months to 31.5.21		
	12/18 × 36,000		24,000

2 As follows:

		£
Overlap profits		
	1.6.20–5.4.21 10/18 × 36,000	20,000

Activity 8: Closing year rules

Final year 2020/21

2019/20	y/e 31.12.19	22,000
2020/21	4 months to 30.4.20	12,000
	Less overlap relief	(3,500)
		8,500

Activity 9: Change of accounting date (1)

Year of change 2020/21.

		£
2019/20	y/e 31.8.19	20,000
2020/21	Gap 9 months to 31.5.20	
	Therefore 12 months to 31.5.20	
	(3/12 × 20,000) + 15,000	20,000
2021/22	y/e 31.5.21	30,000
2022/23	y/e 31.5.22	40,000

Creates overlap profits

        1.6.19–31.8.19 (3/12 × 20,000)   5,000

Activity 10: Change of accounting date (2)

Year of change 2020/21.

		£
2019/20	y/e 30.6.19	25,000
2020/21	Gap 18 months to 31.12.20 (£30,000 + £15,000)	45,000
	Less 6/9 × 21,000	(14,000)
		31,000
2021/22	y/e 31.12.21	35,000

15

Sole trader losses and partnerships

Learning objectives

On completion of this chapter, you should be able to:

	Syllabus reference no.
Remember the material already covered in Taxation (TX – UK) under the heading: 'income from self-employment'	A1(a)B3
Advise on the relief available for trading losses following the transfer of a business to a company	A1(d)(ii)
Establish the relief for capital losses on shares in unquoted trading companies	A2(f)(iv)

Exam context

There are various ways in which a trader can obtain relief for trading losses. You are likely to have to advise on the most beneficial way of obtaining relief. To be able to do this correctly it is vital that you understand the basic loss relief options available to the individual and that you read the scenario carefully to establish whether the taxpayer has any particular requirements, such as to obtain relief as soon as possible. The planning aspects as to the most beneficial use of the losses is covered in Chapter 18 Owner-managed business tax planning.

A question involving any aspect of unincorporated businesses may deal with a partnership rather than a sole trader. The principles are exactly the same, whether you are considering incremental income, possible claims for capital allowances or loss reliefs. Just remember that profits are apportioned to partners in the profit sharing ratio for the period of account after allocating interest on capital and/or salaries.

Chapter overview

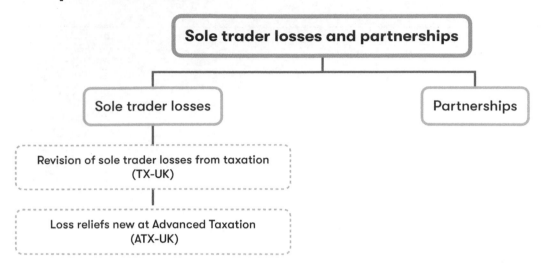

1 Sole trader losses

The basic rules regarding when a sole trader incurs a **trade loss** and how that trade loss can be utilised to save tax are assumed knowledge from your Taxation (TX – UK) studies. We revise them briefly here with some Activities to help you test your knowledge.

1.1 Revision of sole trader losses from Taxation (TX – UK)

1.1.1 Ongoing trade losses revision

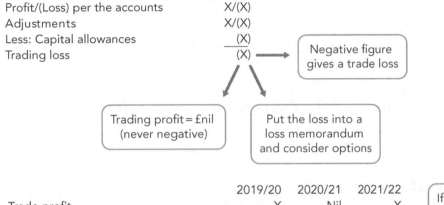

	2019/20	2020/21	2021/22
Trade profit	X	Nil	X
Less trade loss b/f			(X)
Interest income	X	X	X
Dividend income	X	X	X
Property income	X	X	X
Total income	X	X	X
Less qualifying interest	(X)	(X)	(X)
Net income (before losses)	X	X	X
Less current year &/or prior year trade loss	(X)	(X)	
Net income	X	X	X
Less PA	(X)	(X)	(X)
Taxable income	X	X	X

If no other claims are made, or for any trade loss left after any claims, the balance is **carried forward** and offset against the **first available future trade profits of the same trade:**
- offset as much as possible
- offset as soon as possible

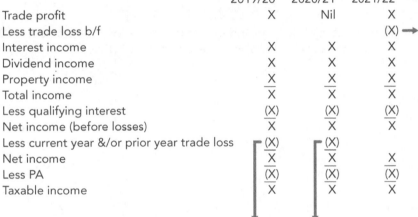

The trade loss can be offset against the **current year and/or prior year general income**:
- These are separate claims (31.1.23 for 2020/21 loss)
- If a claim is made offset as much loss as possible (can't restrict to preserve the PA)

Once a claim has been made against general income of the current or prior year the claim can be extended to **convert the remaining trade loss into a capital loss of that same** year.
This claim can only be made in a year where claim against general income has **first** been a made. The maximum trade loss left to be converted into a capital loss is the lower of:
- the trade loss left after the claim against general income; and
- current years gains less current year capital losses less brought forward capital losses

(See Essential reading for more detail.)

Cap on income tax relief:
If the loss relief is claimed against general income the maximum loss that can be relieved is the higher of:
- £50,000, and
- 25% × individual's adjusted total income

Adjusted total income = total income − gross personal pension contributions

The cap does not restrict the loss that can be claimed against profits of the same trade for the preceding tax year. Any remaining loss can be carried forwards against future profits from the same trade.

Planning for how to best utilise the trade losses will be covered in Chapter 18 Owner-managed business tax planning.

Exam focus point

In Question 4 Rosa of the December 2019 exam students were asked to identify and explain reliefs available for a trading loss and to calculate the maximum tax saving as a result of these reliefs. The examining team said 'some students wrote very generally about loss reliefs, without applying their knowledge to the facts of the question, which lost them marks. A significant number seemed unaware of the technical rules on the restriction of income tax reliefs against total income and were unable to factor these in to their calculations. A thorough understanding of the technical rules from all areas of the syllabus is a requirement to do well in this exam.'

Essential reading

See Chapter 15 of the Essential reading for more revision of the basic trade loss reliefs.

The Essential reading is available as an Appendix of the digital edition of the Workbook.

Activity 1: Ongoing trade loss relief

Poppy commenced trading on 1 October 2006 making up her accounts to 30 September 2007 and annually thereafter. Her recent results and projected results are:

Year ended	£
30.9.19	20,000
30.9.20	(140,000)
30.9.21	8,000
30.9.22	4,000

She has received property income as follows:

	£
2019/20	80,000
2020/21	120,000
2021/22	70,000
2022/23	60,000

Required

Compute Poppy's net income for 2019/20 to 2022/23, assuming maximum trade loss relief against general income claims are made.

Solution

Activity 2: Converting trade loss to capital loss

Mr Cubitt has general income of £15,000 for 2020/21. He also has net capital gains of £29,000 for 2020/21 all arising from assets not qualifying for business asset disposal relief. In the year ended 31 December 2020 he incurred a trading loss of £40,000. He also has capital losses brought forward of £13,000 at 6 April 2020.

Required

Assuming Mr Cubitt relieves his trading loss in the current year, show his taxable income and chargeable gains for 2020/21.

Solution

1.1.2 Opening year trade losses revision

In addition to the loss reliefs available to the ongoing sole trader, an additional loss relief is available for **trade losses incurred in the first four tax years** of a trade. The trade loss can be **carried back to the three preceding tax years to be offset against general income on a first in, first out (FIFO) basis**.

This special opening year loss relief is available through a **claim** which must be made by the 31 January 2023 for a trade loss incurred in 2020/21. If a claim is made **as much loss as possible must be offset**. The taxpayer cannot choose to relieve the loss against just one or two of the preceding three years nor to relieve only part of the loss.

The relief is also **capped** at the higher of £50,000 and 25% of adjusted total income as revised above.

When calculating trade losses in opening year of a trade, the **trade loss must not be double counted**. If basis periods overlap, a loss in the overlap period is allocated to the earlier tax year only.

Activity 3: Opening year trade loss relief

Micky commenced trading on 1 September 2019. Results are as follows:

		£
31.8.20	Loss	(36,000)
31.8.21	Profit	20,000
31.8.22	Profit	26,000
31.8.23	Profit	32,000

Required

How could the loss be relieved?

Solution

1.1.3 Closing year trade losses revision

The **terminal loss** is calculated as the trade loss incurred in the **last 12 months of trade increased by any overlap profits**. It is calculated by reference to each tax year falling in the final 12-month period. If the results for either of the tax years produces a profit, the profit is ignored in the terminal loss relief calculation.

In your exam either a **tabular or time-line calculation** of the terminal loss can be helpful and both are revised in the Illustration below.

A claim under **terminal loss relief** is due by 31 January 2025 for a trade loss incurred in 2020/21.

In addition to the loss reliefs available to the ongoing sole trader, an additional loss relief is available when a trader **ceases to trade during a tax year**. A **terminal loss relief claim** allows the sole trader to offset their terminal loss against their **trading profits of the tax year of cessation and then to carry it back against the trading profits of the three preceding years, on a last in, first out (LIFO) basis**.

Illustration 1: Terminal loss relief

A business which commenced on 1 May 2007 making up accounts to 30 September each year ceased trading on 30 June 2021. The most recent results were:

Year 30 September 2018	£8,000 profit
Year 30 September 2019	£10,000 profit
Year 30 September 2020	£4,000 profit
Period to 30 June 2021	£27,000 loss

There were overlap profits brought forward of £2,000.

Required

Show how the loss will be relieved under terminal loss relief.

Solution

First, let's calculate the terminal loss using both the tabular and time-line calculations.

	£
Unrelieved trading loss from 6 April to date of cessation	
6.4.21 – 30.6.21	
3/9 × 27,000	9,000
Overlap profits	2,000
Unrelieved trading loss (if any) arising from a date 12m before cessation to 5 April	
1.7.20 – 5.4.21	
3/12 × 4,000 + 6/9 × (27,000)	17,000
Terminal loss	28,000

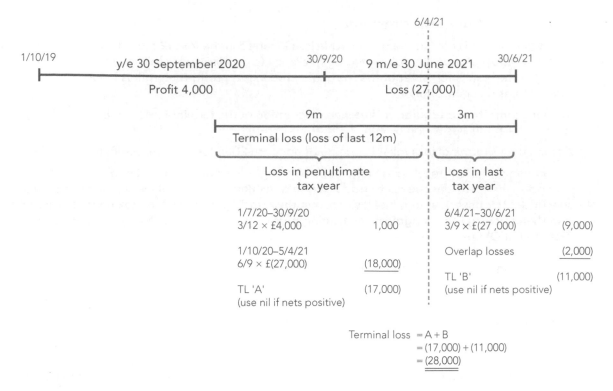

The terminal loss is thus £28,000 and it can be offset against trade profits of the final tax year (2021/22) and then carried back against trade profits of the preceding three years on a LIFO basis.

	2018/19	2019/20	2020/21	2021/22
	£	£	£	£
Trading income	8,000	10,000	4,000	–
Terminal loss relief	(3) (8,000)	(2) (10,000)	(1) (4,000)	

As always, a loss memorandum should be used to track use of the loss.

		£
Terminal loss available		28,000
Terminal loss relief		
20/21	(1)	(4,000)
19/20	(2)	(10,000)
18/19	(3)	(8,000)
Loss remaining		6,000

Exam focus point

Terminal loss relief was tested in June 2015 Question 1(b) Jodie. The examining team commented that 'many candidates were able to calculate the terminal loss reasonably accurately and to calculate the tax saving at the margin without preparing detailed income tax computations.'

1.2 Loss reliefs – new at Advanced Taxation (ATX – UK)

1.2.1 Incorporation relief

The sole trader will **cease to trade** as their business **transfers to the company** and so consideration will need to be given as to how any unused trade losses can be used.

The usual current year and/or prior year offset against general income claims are, of course, still available to the trader as is a terminal loss claim. However, given there will be no further profits of the same trade a carried forward relief will not be available.

Provided **certain conditions are met**, the sole trader can **carry forward their trade loss to offset against the first available income from the company**. This involves offsetting the trade loss against any **salary, dividends or interest they receive from the company**. The offset is against the first income that the trader receives from the company but if multiple sources of income from the company are received the loss can be offset against the income in the most tax-efficient manner.

In order for this relief to be available the consideration for the transfer of the business must be **wholly or mainly (at least 80%) in shares** which must be **retained** by the vendor throughout the tax year in which the loss is relieved.

The scenario of incorporation will be covered in further detail in Chapter 18 Owner-managed business tax planning.

A scenario which you could potentially see in your exam would be a sole trader choosing to incorporate their business so as to trade through a company. This has lots of different tax consequences and so makes for a good exam question.

1.2.2 Losses on unquoted shares

Capital losses on shares in unquoted trading companies (originally subscribed for) can be offset against general income of the taxpayer for the year in which the loss arose and/or the preceding year.

A claim for relief is only available if the shares satisfy the conditions for the **EIS/SEIS** scheme (see earlier in the Workbook) although income tax relief does not have to have been claimed. The deadline for the claim is 31 January 2023 for a loss incurred in 2020/21.

This loss relief is also **capped** as described in the essential reading to this chapter.

2 Partnerships

Rather than testing a sole trader scenario in an exam question, you may see a scenario involving a partnership. These questions allow you to be tested on all the usual aspects we would see in a sole trader question with the added complication of dealing with a partnership and so are an ideal question to test your understanding. All your knowledge of how partnerships are taxed is assumed knowledge from Taxation (TX – UK).

The process for determining the profits on which partners are taxed is summarised in the diagram below.

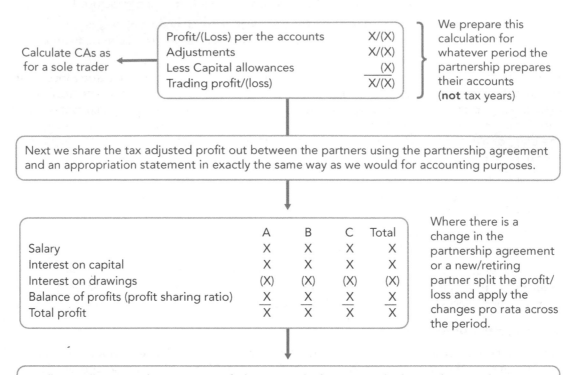

Start with the profit per the partnership accounts and adjust as for a normal sole trader. (Any 'salary' of a partner should be added back as an appropriation of profit here and will be taken into account in the appropriation of profit process below.)

Calculate CAs as for a sole trader ←

Profit/(Loss) per the accounts	X/(X)
Adjustments	X/(X)
Less Capital allowances	(X)
Trading profit/(loss)	X/(X)

We prepare this calculation for whatever period the partnership prepares their accounts (**not** tax years)

Next we share the tax adjusted profit out between the partners using the partnership agreement and an appropriation statement in exactly the same way as we would for accounting purposes.

	A	B	C	Total
Salary	X	X	X	X
Interest on capital	X	X	X	X
Interest on drawings	(X)	(X)	(X)	(X)
Balance of profits (profit sharing ratio)	X	X	X	X
Total profit	X	X	X	X

Where there is a change in the partnership agreement or a new/retiring partner split the profit/ loss and apply the changes pro rata across the period.

Finally, we allocate each partner's profit/loss using the basis period rules applying to that partner.

- Ongoing partner – use current year basis period rules
- New partner – use opening year basis period rules
- Retiring partner – use closing year basis period rules

If there is a trade loss overall then each partner can choose how to use their share of the loss separately according to their own personal tax position.

A **limited liability partnership** limits the partners' liability for debts of the partnership. It is taxed in virtually the same way as for unlimited liability partnerships as described above.

Exam focus point

Partners are effectively taxed in the same way as sole traders with just one difference. Before you tax the partner you need to take each set of accounts (as adjusted for tax purposes) and divide the trade profit (or loss) between each partner. Then carry on as normal for a sole trader – each partner is treated as a sole trader in respect of their trade profits for each period of account.

Essential reading

See Chapter 15 of the Essential reading for more revision of how partnerships are taxed with Activities for you to try.

The Essential reading is available as an Appendix of the digital edition of the Workbook.

Chapter summary

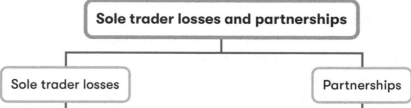

Sole trader losses and partnerships

Sole trader losses

Partnerships

Sole trader losses

Revision of sole trader losses from taxation (TX-UK)

- Where there's a trade loss the taxable trading profits are £nil and the loss is recorded in a loss memorandum where we track how the loss is used
- For any loss left after other claims, it is automatically carried forward vs first available trade profits of the same trade:
  - Offset as much as possible, as soon as possible
- Trading loss relief against general income:
  - Offset vs CY and/or PY general income
  - All or nothing claim (due 31/1 + 1 yr after end of tax year of loss)
- Trading loss relieved against gains:
  - Extension claim available after a CY and/or PY claim against general income
  - Converts remaining trade loss into a capital loss of CY and/or PY
  - Must have made a claim vs general income in that year first
  - Trade loss converted is lower of (1) trade loss left after general income claim and (2) current year gains less current year capital losses less brought forward capital losses
- Where loss claim is against general income: Maximum deductions = higher of (1) £50k and (2) 25% x adjusted total income:
  - This cap applies to CY and/or PY claim vs general income, opening year loss relief and unquoted share loss relief
- Opening year loss relief:
  - Trade loss in first four tax years
  - Carry-back against general income of 3 preceding years on a FIFO basis
  - All or nothing claim (due 31/1 + 1 yr after end of tax year of loss)
- Terminal loss relief:
  - Terminal loss = loss of last 12 m + overlap profits
  - Set TL against trade profits of final tax year and 3 preceding tax years on a LIFO basis
  - All or nothing claim (due 31/1 + 1 yr after end of tax year of loss)
- Trade losses can be used in the same way for Class 4 NIC but only offset against trade profits when calculating Class 4 trade profits.

Loss reliefs new at Advanced Taxation (ATX-UK)

- Incorporation relief:
  - Carry forward trade loss to offset against future income from company incorporated into
  - Need > 80% of consideration in shares which are retained through tax year of claim
- Losses on unquoted shares:
  - Capital losses on EIS/SEIS shares subscribed for can be offset vs general income of CY and/or PY

Partnerships

- Allocating profits between partners:
  - Split using partnership agreement and appropriation statement as for accounting purposes
  - Watch for a change in the agreement - time apportion profits
  - Each partner taxed separately on their share of the profits
- Change in membership of partnership:
  - Time apportion appropriation for date of change
  - Use opening year rules for new partner
  - Use closing year rules for retiring partner
- If a trade loss each partner can choose how to use their share of the loss based on their tax position.
- A limited liability partnership is taxed in virtually the same way as a normal partnership.

Knowledge diagnostic

1. Ongoing business trade loss reliefs

Sole trader trading losses may be relieved against future profits of the same trade, against general income and against capital gains.

A trading loss carried forward must be set against the first available profits of the same trade.

Where a loss relief claim is made, trading losses can be set against general income (and also gains if a further claim is made) in the current tax year and/or general income (and also gains if a further claim is made) in the preceding tax year.

2. Losses on incorporation

If a business is transferred to a company, a loss of the unincorporated business can be set against income received from the company.

3. Opening year losses

In opening years, a special relief involving the carry back of losses against general income is available. Losses arising in the first four tax years of a trade may be set against general income in the three years preceding the loss-making year, relieving the earliest year first.

4. Closing year losses

On the cessation of trade, a loss arising in the last 12 months of trading may be set against trading profits of the tax year of cessation and the previous three years, relieving the last year first.

5. Other loss points

Capital losses arising on certain unquoted shares can be set against general income of the year of the loss and/or against general income of the preceding year.

Loss relief cannot be claimed against general income unless the loss-making business is conducted on a commercial basis.

An individual taxpayer can only deduct the greater of £50,000 and 25% of adjusted total income when making a claim for loss relief against general income.

6. Partnerships

A partnership is simply treated as a source of profits and losses for trades being carried on by the individual partners. Divide profits or losses between the partners according to the profit-sharing ratio in the period of account concerned. If any of the partners are entitled to a salary or interest on capital, apportion this first, not forgetting to pro-rate in periods of less than 12 months.

The commencement and cessation rules apply to partners individually when they join or leave.

Partners are entitled to the same loss reliefs as sole traders and make independent loss relief claims.

Further study guidance

Question practice

Now try the following from the Further question practice bank (available in the digital edition of the Workbook):

- Arrol and Louisa
- ABC Partnership

Activity answers

Activity 1: Ongoing trade loss relief

	2019/20	2020/21	2021/22	2022/23
	£	£	£	£
Trading income	20,000	–	8,000	4,000
Carry forward relief			(3) (8,000)	(4) (4,000)
Property income	80,000	120,000	70,000	60,000
Relief against general income	(1) (70,000)	(2) (50,000)	–	–
Net income	30,000	70,000	70,000	60,000

Loss memorandum

Y/e 30.9.20 (2020/21)		140,000	
General income PY			(20,000 +
19/20		(1) (70,000)	50,000*)
CY			
20/21		(2) (50,000)	
		20,000	
Carry forward			
21/22		(3) (8,000)	
22/23		(4) (4,000)	
		8,000	

Note. *The amount offset against trading income is unrestricted (£20,000) but the amount used against property income is restricted to the higher of £50,000 or 25% of £100,000, ie £50,000.

Activity 2: Converting trade loss to capital loss

	£
General income 2020/21	15,000
Loss relief against general income	(1) (15,000)
Taxable income	–
Gains	29,000
Loss relief against gains (W1)	(2) (16,000)
	13,000
AEA	(12,300)
	700
B/f capital losses	(700)
Taxable gains	–

Maximum offset lower of:

(1) Loss remaining 40,000 – 15,000 =	25,000
(2) Gains less capital losses b/fwd	
29,000 – 13,000	16,000

Loss memorandum

Y/e 31.12.20	40,000
Relief against general income	(1) (15,000)
Relief against gains	(2) (16,000)
Trade loss left	9,000

Capital loss c/fwd 13,000 – 700 = £12,300

Activity 3: Opening year trade loss relief

	£
Trading income 2019/20–2023/24	
2019/20 1.9.19–5.4.20	–
2020/21 y/e 31.8.20	–
2021/22 y/e 31.8.21	20,000
2022/23 y/e 31.8.22	26,000
2023/24 y/e 31.8.23	32,000

	£
Loss of 2019/20	
2019/20 7/12 × 36,000 =	21,000

Relief against general income (+ gains) in 2019/20 +/or 2018/19

Early years loss relief 2016/17 + 2017/18 + 2018/19

C/fwd to 2021/22 (as no trade profits to offset against in 2020/21)

	£
Loss of 2020/21	
2020/21 y/e 31.8.20	36,000
Less relieved in 19/20	(21,000)
	15,000

Relief against general income (+ gains) in 2020/21 +/or 2019/20

Early years relief in 2017/18 + 2018/19 + 2019/20

Carried forward to 21/22, 22/23 etc.

16 Corporation tax for single companies

Learning objectives

On completion of this chapter, you should be able to:

	Syllabus reference no.
Remember the material already covered at Taxation (TX – UK) under the headings:	
'The scope of corporation tax'	A4(a) E1
'Taxable total profits'	A4(a) E2
'The comprehensive computation of the corporation tax liability'	A4(a) E4
'The use of exemptions and reliefs in deferring and minimising corporation tax liabilities'	A4(a) E6
Identify qualifying research and development expenditure, both capital and revenue, and determine the reliefs available by reference to the size of the individual company/group	A4(c)(i)
Recognise the alternative tax treatments of intangible assets and conclude on the best treatment for a given company	A4(c) (iii)
Remember the material already covered in Taxation (TX – UK) under the heading 'chargeable gains for companies'	A4(a) E3
Determine the application of the substantial shareholdings exemption	A4(f)(i)
Remember the material already covered in Taxation (TX – UK) under the headings:	
'Systems for self-assessment and making of returns'	A6(b) A3
'Time limits for the submission of information, claims and payment of tax'	A6(b) A4
'Procedures relating to compliance checks, appeals and disputes'	A6(b) A5
'Penalties for non-compliance'	A6(b) A6

Exam context

Although you are unlikely simply to be asked to calculate the corporation tax payable for an accounting period, you may have to be able to work out tax savings or additional tax costs when giving advice about using losses, new projects, etc. You may be asked to comment on how certain types of income would be included in the taxable total profits computation where there are special rules, such as for loan relationships, intangible fixed assets and research and development expenditure. You may well also be asked to compute chargeable gains or losses for a company as part of a tax planning question so you must know the rules in this part of the chapter very well. You must know the rules regarding administration as the company's obligations could form a part of any question.

Chapter overview

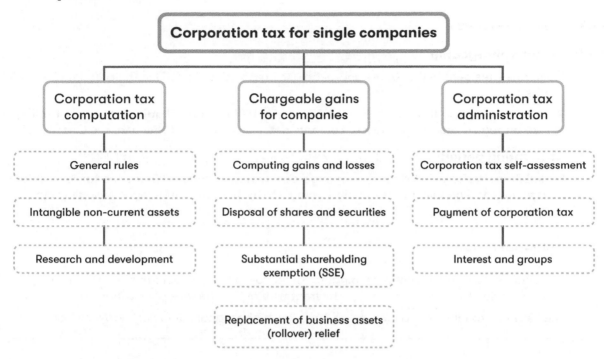

Corporation tax for single companies

Corporation tax computation
- General rules
- Intangible non-current assets
- Research and development

Chargeable gains for companies
- Computing gains and losses
- Disposal of shares and securities
- Substantial shareholding exemption (SSE)
- Replacement of business assets (rollover) relief

Corporation tax administration
- Corporation tax self-assessment
- Payment of corporation tax
- Interest and groups

BPP LEARNING MEDIA

1 Corporation tax computation

1.1 General rules

1.1.1 Persons chargeable

Companies **resident in the UK** are chargeable to corporation tax (CT) in the UK on their **worldwide profits.**

Non-resident companies are liable to UK CT on any **UK income and gains if they are trading in the UK through a branch or agency.** For more detail on company residence, see Chapter 22.

1.1.2 Accounting periods

CT liabilities are calculated for a company's **accounting periods,** whereas the **tax** is calculated by reference to **financial years** (running from 1.4 to 31.3). Accounting periods usually coincide with a company's period of account, but there are some exceptions.

Essential reading

See Chapter 16 of the Essential reading, for the detailed rules on determining accounting periods for corporation tax purposes, and for the treatment of long periods of account.

The Essential reading is available as an Appendix of the digital edition of the Workbook.

1.1.3 Pro-forma corporation tax computation

> ## PER alert
>
> One of the competencies you require to fulfil Performance Objective 15 Tax computations and assessments of the PER is to prepare or contribute to the computation or assessment of tax computations for single companies, groups or other entities. You can apply the knowledge you obtain from this section of the text to help to demonstrate this competence.

A Ltd: Corporation tax computation for the X months to:

	£	£
Adjusted profits	X	
Less capital allowances	(X)	
Trading profit		X
Investment income		X
Overseas income		X
Miscellaneous income		X
UK rental income		X
Chargeable gains (deduct capital losses b/f)		X
Total profits		X
Less losses relieved by deduction from total profits		(X)
Less qualifying charitable donations (paid basis):		(X)
Taxable total profits (TTP)		X
Corporation Tax: 19% × TTP		X

Essential reading

See Chapter 16 of the Essential reading, for a recap of the assumed knowledge from Taxation-UK in relation to the calculation of figures within each heading of the above pro-forma.

The Essential reading is available as an Appendix of the digital edition of the Workbook.

1.1.4 Rates of corporation tax

Formula provided

The **rate of corporation tax** has been **19%** since Financial Year 17 (y/e 31 March 18). It is given in the Tax rates and allowances available to you in the exam.

1.1.5 Dividends and augmented profits

Dividends received by a company are usually exempt and are not included in TTP.

> ## Exam focus point
>
> The examining team has stated that dividends which are taxable in the hands of the recipient company are **not examinable** in the Advanced Taxation (ATX – UK) exam.

Augmented profits is the figure used to determine whether or not a company is required **to pay its corporation tax via quarterly instalments** (see later in this chapter). **Augmented profits = taxable total profits plus non-group dividends received.**

1.1.6 Loan relationships

KEY TERM

> **Loan relationships:** Income and expenses recorded in the accounts in relation to **money debts** (where a company has either borrowed or lent money) are referred to as **loan relationship debits and credits**.

The accounts figures are generally taxable (income) and deductible (expenses) on an **accruals basis,** and will be classified as either trading, or non-trading:

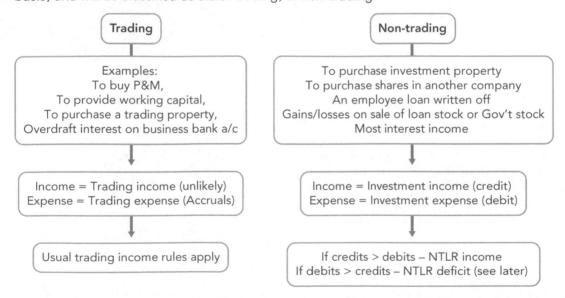

Incidental costs of loan finance (debits) will also be deductible under the loan relationship rules. This includes costs directly related to varying the terms of the loan relationship and abortive loan relationship costs (ie where the loan relationship is not actually taken out).

Activity 1: Single company corporation tax example

Lucky Ltd was incorporated on 20 July 2020 and commenced trading on 1 December 2020. The following information is available for the five-month period 1 December 2020 to 30 April 2021:

(1) The operating profit for the five-month period ended 30 April 2021 is £1,432,600. Advertising expenditure of £4,700 (incurred during September 2020), depreciation of £14,700, and amortisation on a lease of £9,000 have been deducted in arriving at this figure.

The amortisation relates to a premium which was paid on 1 December 2020 to acquire a leasehold warehouse on a 12-year lease. The amount of premium assessed on the landlord as income was £46,800. The warehouse was used for business purposes by Lucky Ltd throughout the period ended 30 April 2021.

(2) Lucky Ltd purchased the following assets during the period 20 July 2020 to 30 April 2021:

		£
19 August 2020	Computer	31,500
22 January 2021	Integral features	206,000
31 January 2021	Office equipment	264,500
17 March 2021	Motor car	12,800

The integral features of £206,000 are in respect of expenditure on electrical systems, a ventilation system and lifts which are integral to a freehold office building owned by Lucky Ltd.

The motor car has a CO_2 emission rate of 49 grams per kilometre.

(3) Lucky Ltd made a loan to another company for non-trading purposes on 1 February 2021. Loan interest income of £700 was accrued at 30 April 2021.

Required

Calculate Lucky Ltd's corporation tax liability for the five-month period ended 30 April 2021.

Solution

1.2 Intangible non-current assets

1.2.1 Introduction to the intangible non-current assets regime

Intangible non-current assets are defined for taxation purposes in the same way as for accounting purposes. Examples include:

(a) **Intellectual property** (eg patents, copyrights)

(b) **Goodwill**

(c) **Marketing-related intangible assets** (eg registered trademarks, internet domain names)

(d) **Customer-related intangible assets** (eg customer lists, customer relationships)

There are two potential tax treatments, dependent on the type of intangible asset.

1.2.2 Tax treatment of most intangibles held for trading purposes

Amounts shown as **expenses in the statement of profit or loss are allowed for tax purposes** (and any **income from the intangible is taxable trade income**). For example, royalty payments debited to the statement of profit or loss on an accruals basis are allowed for tax purposes. This treatment includes accounting amortisation and adjustments (accounting profits and losses) on disposal.

There are **two methods for calculating amortisation** to be included in the tax computation:

(a) **Accounts basis.** Where the debits and credits are for trade purposes they will be treated as trading expenses or receipts of the trade. Thus **no adjustment to the accounting profit is required**.

(b) **4% straight-line basis.** The company can **elect** to have **the cost of the patent written off for tax at 4% straight line rather than claim the amount charged to the statement of profit or loss**. If a rate of less than 4% is used in the accounts, then you should elect to use the 4% rate.

When an intangible asset is **sold, the difference between the proceeds and tax written-down value will be taxed as a trade profit or loss. Tax written-down value will be net book value (NBV) unless the 4% alternate deduction has been claimed.**

1.2.3 Goodwill and customer-related intangibles

Amortisation of goodwill is not tax deductible and therefore any expense should be **added back** in an adjustment to profit.

On **disposal**, the company is **taxed on the difference between proceeds and cost**. A profit is taxed as trade income and a loss is treated as a non-trading loss; it can be offset against total profits of the current year, group relieved or carried forward.

1.2.4 Intangibles held for non-trade purposes

Essential reading

See Chapter 16 of the Essential reading, for the treatment of non-trading intangible assets.

The Essential reading is available as an Appendix of the digital edition of the Workbook.

1.2.5 Reinvestment relief for intangibles

It is also possible to **roll over** the gain on disposal of an intangible non-current asset.

The maximum income gain eligible for rollover is calculated as the **sale proceeds less original cost, not NBV**. Therefore, the amortisation charged to date cannot be deferred and must be charged immediately.

To be able to make a rollover claim the company needs to *buy a new* intangible non-current asset **in the period 12 months before to three years after disposal of the original** intangible non-current asset.

For **full** rollover relief of the eligible gain to be available, **all the proceeds must be reinvested** into another intangible non-current asset.

If the **proceeds are not fully reinvested**, then the **proceeds not reinvested become taxable now** (in addition to the amortisation charged to date) and the balance can be rolled over as for traditional rollover relief.

The amount deferred will be the **cost of Intangible 1 – cost of Intangible 2**

The deferred profit reduces the base cost of the replacement intangible asset.

Activity 2: Rollover of intangible profit

In June 2020 Sun Ltd sells patent rights which it acquired in May 2006.

Sale proceeds	£3,000,000
Original cost	£1,800,000
NBV in accounts	£890,000

Sun Ltd acquires another patent in June 2021.

Required

1   Assuming the new patent cost £3,500,000, calculate the following:

   (1)   The amount of gain that is available for rollover

   (2)   The amount taxable as trading income

   (3)   The base cost of the new patent

2   How would your answer to Requirement 1 differ if the new patent cost £2,500,000?

Solution

Exam focus point

Sale of an intangible and subsequent rollover relief was tested in Kitz Ltd Question 3 in the December 2019 exam. The examining team said that it was very poorly answered.

1.3 Research and development expenditure

1.3.1 Qualifying R&D

Additional tax relief is available to all companies for incurring expenditure on **qualifying R&D**. 'Qualifying' R&D is **revenue** expenditure on:

- **Staff costs**, including employer NIC and pension contributions but excluding benefits. If external workers are used, only 65% of the amounts paid will qualify.
- **Consumables and software, including fuel, power and water.**

Rent is not qualifying R&D expenditure. The definition does not cover expenditure incurred on acquiring rights (eg patents) arising from research and development.

Note that **100% FYA** can be claimed for **capital** expenditure on R&D – including laboratories and research equipment, but not land.

> **Exam focus point**
>
> R&D tax credits were tested in September 2015 Question 3 Cinnabar Ltd. The examining team commented that 'the majority of students were aware that directly related revenue expenditure qualifies for an additional [130%] deduction, but were rather vague in their explanations as to why items were or were not included'.

1.3.2 Relief for SMEs

A **small or medium-sized enterprise** (SME) can obtain **a 230% deduction for qualifying R&D expenditure.**

> **Exam focus point**
>
> It will be stated whether or not a company is a SME for R&D purposes in exam questions.
>
> Question 2 Mita in the March 2020 exam tested an explanation of the tax treatment of research and development expenditure incurred by a small enterprise and also on the acquisition of an intangible asset. The examining team stated 'many students displayed a surprising lack of technical knowledge, despite both being frequently tested areas.

1.3.3 R&D tax credits for SMEs

If a SME makes a **trading loss** it can claim a **tax credit** resulting in an immediate repayment.

The credit is **14.5% of the lower of**:

- **Unrelieved trading loss** (after a deemed current year claim and any actual carry back or group relief claims made)
- **230% of qualifying R&D expenditure**

> **Exam focus point**
>
> R&D tax credits were tested in June 2012 Question 5 Kurt Ltd. The examining team commented that 'the tax treatment of the expenditure on scientific research was explained well by the majority of candidates, many of whom were aware that there was a possibility of claiming a [14.5%] repayment. However, very few candidates attempted to evaluate whether or not the repayment should be claimed.

Activity 3: R&D Tax credits

Saturn Ltd is a small enterprise for the purposes of research and development. It was incorporated and started trading on 1 April 2020. During the year to 31 March 2021, it made a tax adjusted trading loss of £(100,000) before taking into account research and development expenditure of £30,000. It has no other income or gains.

Required

Explain the tax deductions and/or credits available in the year ending 31 March 2021 in respect of the R&D expenditure and comment on any choices available to Saturn Ltd.

Solution

1.3.4 R&D expenditure credits (RDEC) for large companies

A **large** company can claim an **'above-the-line' R&D expenditure credit (RDEC) of 13% of qualifying revenue expenditure incurred**.

The RDEC has **two** effects:

(a) It is treated as taxable income and therefore **increases the company's taxable income**.

(b) It **reduces the company's corporation tax liability**.

If the tax credit is greater than the corporation tax liability any excess can be paid to the company up to a maximum of the company's PAYE/NIC liability in respect of those employees involved in R&D activities for the relevant accounting period.

Any remaining balance can be carried forward and offset against the corporation tax liability of the future accounting periods or surrendered to another member of the group.

 Activity 4: RDEC for large companies

Innovative plc, a large company, spends £100,000 on qualifying R&D expenditure during the year to 31 March 2021. The company has taxable total profits of £2,135,000 before any deduction is taken for the R&D expenditure.

Required

Calculate the company's corporation tax liability for the year to 31 March 2021.

Solution

---

2 Chargeable gains for companies

PER alert

One of the competencies you require to fulfil Performance Objective 15 Tax computations and assessments of the PER is to prepare or contribute to the computation or assessment of tax computations for single companies, groups or other entities. You can apply the knowledge you obtain from this section of the text to help to demonstrate this competence.

2.1 Computing gains and losses

Companies do **not pay capital gains tax** (CGT). Their **gains are included in the taxable total profits** and are charged to corporation tax.

The calculation of the gain/loss is similar to that of an individual, except there is a **relief for inflation called indexation allowance, and no annual exempt amount** is available to a company.

Exam focus point

A non-UK resident company which disposes of UK land and buildings may be liable to UK tax on the gain in a similar way to a non-UK individual. However, the disposal by a non-resident company of a UK land and buildings is **excluded** from the Advanced Taxation (ATX – UK) syllabus.

2.1.1 Pro-forma chargeable gain computation

	£
Proceeds	X
Cost	
(including incidental costs of acquisition)	(X)
Unindexed gain	X

Indexation allowance	
Cost × Indexation Factor (to 3 d.p.)	(X)
Indexed gain	X

2.1.2 Indexation allowance

The **indexation allowance** is designed to give companies **relief for inflation** over their period of ownership of an asset. However, indexation was **frozen in December 2017** and so relief for inflation after this date will no longer be given.

The **indexation factor (IF)** is calculated by reference to **movements in the retail price index** (RPI) between the date of acquisition of an asset and the earlier of the date of disposal and December 2017.

Exam focus point

In your exam you will be given the relevant IF in the question and you will not be expected to calculate it from RPIs. You may be given the IF from the date of acquisition to the date of disposal **and** from the date of acquisition to December 2017. Remember that if disposal is after December 2017 you must use the IF up to December 2017.

Indexation is also given separately on any capital enhancement expenditure incurred prior to January 2018.

Remember that the indexation allowance **cannot increase or create a loss**.

Essential reading

See Chapter 16 of the Essential reading, for an example to recap the calculation of a chargeable gain.

The Essential reading is available as an Appendix of the digital edition of the Workbook.

2.2 Disposals of shares and securities

2.2.1 Share-matching rules

Different matching rules apply to companies. Shares should be matched in the following order:

(a) Acquisitions on the **same day**

(b) Acquisitions in **previous nine days**

(c) **FA 85 pool** (an indexed pool)

The examining team has stated that a detailed question will not be set on the pooling provisions. However, you are expected to understand how the pool works.

Essential reading

See Chapter 16 of the Essential reading, for an example of the share matching rules and a brief reminder of how the FA85 pool is constructed.

The Essential reading is available as an Appendix of the digital edition of the Workbook.

2.2.2 Reorganisations and takeovers

The rules on reorganisations and takeovers apply in a similar way for corporate shareholders as they do for individuals.

Essential reading

More information on this area can be found in Chapter 16 of the Essential reading.

The Essential reading is available as an Appendix of the digital edition of the Workbook.

2.3 Substantial shareholdings exemption (SSE)

PER alert

One of the competencies you require to fulfil Performance objective 17 Tax planning and advice of the PER is to mitigate and/or defer tax liabilities through the use of standard reliefs, exemptions and incentives. You can apply the knowledge you obtain from this section of the text to help to demonstrate this competence.

2.3.1 The exemption

Any gain on the disposal of **all or part of a substantial shareholding is exempt** and any **loss is not allowable**. This exemption is automatic and may not be disapplied.

Exam focus point

In the Advanced Taxation (ATX – UK) examination where you see a company disposing of shares you must first consider whether the SSE might apply. If the SSE does not apply then a gain must be calculated using the standard gain pro-forma.

2.3.2 Conditions

A shareholding is substantial if the investing company:

- Holds **at least 10% of the ordinary share capital**;
- Is entitled to at least 10% of the profits available for distribution; and
- Is entitled to at least 10% of the assets on a winding up.

The interests of other group companies may be aggregated (a group includes 51% subsidiaries for these purposes).

The substantial shareholding must have been held for a **continuous 12-month period during the six years prior to the disposal**.

This qualifying 12-month period can include the time when the assets owned by the company being sold were used within a trade carried on by the group, before being transferred to the company being sold.

The company invested in must be a **trading company or the holding company** of a trading group at the time of disposal however it is not usually necessary for the company invested in to continue to be a trading company after disposal.

Activity 5: Substantial shareholding exemption

Orange Ltd is considering disposing of a 7% shareholding in Lemon Ltd for £500,000. Orange Ltd acquired an 11% holding in Lemon Ltd on 1 May 2020 for £260,000 and Lemon Ltd is a trading company. Orange Ltd prepares its accounts to 31 March.

The indexation factor from May 2020 to March 2021 is 0.028.

Required

1 Calculate Orange Ltd's after-tax proceeds if the sale occurs on 31 March 2021.

2 What advice might you give the directors of Orange Ltd?

Solution

2.4 Replacement of business assets (rollover) relief

This is the **only relief available to companies**. It enables a gain on the sale of a qualifying asset to be rolled over into the cost of a replacement asset.

For companies the **indexed gain is deferred**.

The relief operates in the **same way as for individuals**, except that **goodwill is not a qualifying asset**.

A claim for the relief must be made by the later of four years of the end of the accounting period in which the disposal of the old asset takes place and four years of the end of the accounting period in which the new asset is acquired.

Essential reading

See Chapter 16 of the Essential reading, for a numerical example of rollover relief for companies.

The Essential reading is available as an Appendix of the digital edition of the Workbook.

3 Administration of corporation tax

3.1 Corporation tax self-assessment

> **PER alert**
>
> Some of the competencies you require to fulfil Performance Objective 16 Tax compliance and verification of the PER are to verify and question client submissions and ensure timely submission of all relevant information to the tax authorities by the due date, and to explain tax filing and payment requirements and the consequences of non-compliance. You can apply the knowledge you obtain from this section of the Workbook to help to demonstrate these competencies.

3.1.1 Notification of chargeability

Essential reading

See Chapter 16 of the Essential reading to recap the requirement to notify chargeability to corporation tax.

The Essential reading is available as an Appendix of the digital edition of the Workbook.

3.1.2 Filing

All companies must **file their return electronically** and include a self-assessment of any tax payable, usually **within 12 months after the end of the period of account**.

Companies are also required to file electronically a copy of their accounts in inline eXtensible Business Reporting Language (iXBRL).

Essential reading

See Chapter 16 of the Essential reading, for details of iXBRL and exceptions to the usual filing deadline.

The Essential reading is available as an Appendix of the digital edition of the Workbook.

3.1.3 Penalties

Penalties apply for:

- **Late filing** of corporation tax returns (see below)
- **Errors** in the return (see common penalty regime in Chapter 10 of this Workbook)
- **Failure to keep records: £3,000 per accounting period** (for time limit see the Essential reading for this Chapter)

The **penalty for late filing is £100, rising to £200 if the delay exceeds three months. These penalties become £500 and £1000 respectively for the third consecutive late filing.**

Tax geared penalties apply after six months (10% of the tax unpaid six months after the return was due) and 12 months (20% of the unpaid tax six months after the return was due).

> **Exam focus point**
>
> Sample question September/December 2017 question 3(b) Damiana tested filing dates for a long period of account and penalties for late filing. The examining team commented that 'surprisingly, this was not done at all well. Most candidates recognised that the long period would be split into two accounting periods for tax purposes, but fewer were able to state the correct split of the long period. Fewer still correctly identified the filing dates, with the most common error being to state the payment dates instead. The implications for a company in respect of late filing of returns elicited a number of answers stating that "penalties will arise" but candidates must be precise as to the nature and amounts of such penalties in order to gain marks in this type of question.

3.1.4 Compliance checks

HMRC may decide to conduct a **compliance check enquiry** on a return, claim or election that has been submitted by a company, in the same way as for individuals. The officer must give **written notice, usually within 12 months of the filing date**.

HMRC may correct **obvious errors on a return within nine months of when the return was filed**.

Essential reading

See Chapter 16 of the Essential reading, for the detail of the deadlines for a compliance check enquiry.

The Essential reading is available as an Appendix of the digital edition of the Workbook.

3.2 Payment of corporation tax

3.2.1 Companies which are not large

Companies which are **not 'large', calculate and pay their corporation tax (CT) liability nine months and one day after the end of the accounting period (AP)**.

For example, a non-large company with a year ended 31 March 2021 would pay its tax on 1 January 2022.

3.2.2 Quarterly instalments for large companies

A **large company** is one whose **augmented profits exceed £1,500,000**. Note **augmented profits are TTP plus dividends received from non-51% group companies**.

The £1,500,000 threshold is **reduced** in two circumstances:

(a) The limit is scaled down for a **short accounting periods**.

(b) The limit is **divided by the number of related 51% group companies including the company itself, at the end of the previous accounting period**. A 51% link must be established through companies and dormant companies are excluded.

For 12-month accounting periods, **four quarterly instalments are due in months 7, 10, 13 and 16 following the start of the AP, due on 14th of each month**.

Instalments are based on the **expected tax liability of the current accounting period**.

If the company has a short accounting period, instalments after the first instalment are at three-monthly intervals, but the final instalment is due on the 14th of the fourth month after the end of the accounting period.

The first and interim instalments are calculated as:

$$3 \times \frac{CT}{n}$$

Where CT is the corporation tax liability and n is the number of months in the accounting period.

The final instalment is the balance of corporation tax for the period.

Transitional relief is available for companies becoming large in an AP. **No quarterly payments are required if:**

(a) **Augmented profits are less than £10m, and**

(b) **The company was not large in the previous year.**

The requirement to pay by instalments is also waived if the corporation tax liability for a 12-month period is less than £10,000.

> ### Exam focus point
>
> Quarterly instalments are due on earlier dates for very large companies, however, these rules are not examinable in ATX – UK.

Activity 6: Quarterly instalments for a short accounting period

B plc has a 10-month accounting period to 31.10.20ˉ

Required

When will the corporation tax be due if the total liability is expected to be £4 million?

Solution

3.3 Interest and groups

3.3.1 Interest on underpaid and overpaid corporation tax

Interest runs from the due date on over/underpaid instalments. The position is looked at cumulatively after the due date for each instalment. HMRC calculate the interest position after the company submits its corporation tax return.

Companies which do not pay by instalments are charged interest if they pay their corporation tax after the due date, and will receive interest if they overpay their tax or pay it early.

Interest paid/received on late payments or overpayments of corporation tax is dealt with as investment income as interest paid/received on a non-trading loan relationship. For the purpose of the exam the assumed rate of interest on underpaid tax is 2.75% and the assumed rate of interest on overpaid tax is 0.5%.

3.3.2 Group payment arrangements

Where more than one company in a group is liable to pay their tax by instalments, arrangements may be made for the **instalments to be paid by one company (the nominated company) and allocated amongst the group.** These provisions were introduced because groups often have uncertainties over the tax liabilities of individual group members until all relevant group relief and other claims are decided upon following the end of the accounting period.

A group payment arrangement **mitigates the issue of the disparity between the interest rates on under- and overpaid tax.**

Chapter summary

```
┌─────────────────────────────────────────┐
│  Corporation tax for single companies    │
└─────────────────────────────────────────┘
              │
┌──────────────────────────────┐
│  Corporation tax computation  │
└──────────────────────────────┘
```

General rules

- UK resident companies chargeable on worldwide income and gains for accounting periods
- Pro-forma corporation tax computation:

	£	£
Adjusted profits	X	
Less capital allowances	(X)	
Trading profit		X
Investment income (NTLR credits – debits)		X
Overseas income (gross of foreign tax)		X
Miscellaneous income (eg non-trade IFA income)		X
UK rental income (accruals basis)		X
Chargeable gains (deduct capital losses b/f)		X
Total profits		X
Less losses relieved by deduction from total profits		(X)
Less qualifying charitable donations (paid basis)		(X)
Taxable total profits (TTP)		X
		—
Corporation Tax: 19% × TTP		X

- Long periods of account: 2 APs (12m and balance). Split TTP according to rules for each source of income
- Loan relationships: decide if trading or non-trading. NTLR items are net off to produce an overall credit (taxable) or debit (loss relief available)

Intangible non-current assets

- Patents and most intangibles:
  - Follow accounting treatment, or
  - Elect for 4% straight line amortisation
  - On disposal treat (proceeds–TWDV) as trading income
- Goodwill and customer-related intangibles:
  - Amortisation not deductible
  - On disposal, (proceeds–cost) = taxable trade income (if profit) or non-trade expense (if loss)
- Rollover
  - If purchase replacement intangible within 12m before/36m after sale, elect to defer profit
  - Maximum deferral = proceeds–cost
  - Tax any proceeds not reinvested immediately

Research and development

- 230% deduction for qualifying revenue expenditure for small or medium-sized companies
- If trade loss is created, a tax credit of 14.5% of the surrenderable loss can be claimed
- For large companies the RDEC applies: 13% of qualifying revenue expenditure is
  - Added to TTP and
  - Deducted from CT liability
  - Can be repaid subject to restrictions

Chargeable gains for companies

Computing gains and losses
- Gains part of TTP
- No annual exempt amount
- Indexation allowance = cost × IF (given in Q)
- Indexation frozen at December 2017
- Indexation can't create or increase a loss

Disposal of shares and securities
- Share matching rules:
  - Same day
  - Previous 9 days
  - FA85 indexed pool
- Takeovers = same treatment as for individuals

Substantial shareholding exemption (SSE)
- Gains and losses are exempt (automatic if conditions met)
- Investing company must hold at least 10% for 12m in last 6 years
- Investee company must be trade co or holding co of a trading group at time of disposal
- Can aggregate holdings of 51% group companies to achieve the 10%

Replacement of business assets (rollover) relief
- As for individuals except goodwill is not a qualifying asset
- Indexed gain is deferred

Corporation tax administration

Corporation tax self-assessment
- Notify within 3m of starting to trade, and within 12m of end of AP if no notice to file received
- File return and iXBRL accounts within 12m of end of PoA
- Late filing penalties for non-compliance
  - 1 day–3m £100
  - 3m–6m £200
  - 6m–12m 10% of unpaid CT 18m after AP end
  - > 12m+ 20% of outstanding CT 18m after AP end
- HMRC can correct obvious errors <9m and raise compliance check enquiries <12m

Payment of corporation tax
- Due date if not large: 9m 1d after end of AP
- Quarterly instalment payments (QIPs) required by:
  - Large companies (Augmented profits > £1.5m)
  - Augmented profits = TTP plus non-group dividends
  - Estimate current AP CT and pay on 14th of months 7,10,13 and 16 (12m AP)
- QIPs not required if:
  - Not large in previous AP and profits < £10m, or
  - CT liability < £10,000
- QIPs for short APs:
  - First and interim instalments are 3xCT/n (n= no of months of AP)
  - Final payment (balance of CT) due 14th of 4th month following end of AP

Interest and groups
- Interest runs from due date of QIPs (or due date for non-large cos)
- repayment interest taxable and interest on underpayment deductible (NTLR)
- Groups where > 1 co pay by instalments can enter group payment arrangement:
  - Nominated company pays instalments for the group and payments are allocated when liability is determined

Knowledge diagnostic

1. Computation of corporation tax

Companies pay corporation tax on their taxable total profits of each accounting period.

An accounting period cannot exceed 12 months in length. A long period of account must be split into two accounting periods, the first of which is 12 months long.

Tax rates are set for financial years.

There is a single rate of corporation tax which is applied to a company's taxable total profits to compute the corporation tax liability.

Taxable total profits are the total profits (income and gains) less some losses and qualifying charitable donations.

2. Loan relationships

A loan relationship arises when a company lends or borrows money. Trading loan relationships are dealt with as trading income. Non-trading loan relationships are dealt with as interest income.

3. Intangible fixed assets

Gains/losses arising on most intangible fixed assets are recognised for tax purposes on the same basis as they are recognised in the accounts.

No debits (amortisation or impairment) on goodwill are allowable for tax purposes except on disposal. On a disposal of goodwill, a credit is taxable as trading income but a debit is a non-trading debit.

There is a replacement of business assets relief for intangible fixed assets. However, relief is restricted to the gain based on original cost, not on the written-down cost.

4. Research and development

Companies can claim a deduction for the actual amount of revenue and capital expenditure on R&D. SMEs can obtain 230% relief for qualifying R&D expenditure. There is an 'above the line' R&D expenditure credit (RDEC) for large companies.

5. Chargeable gains for companies

Chargeable gains for companies are computed in broadly the same way as for individuals, but indexation allowance applies and there is no annual exempt amount.

The indexation allowance gives relief for the inflation element of a gain but is frozen at December 2017.

There are special rules for matching shares sold by a company with shares purchased. Disposals are matched with acquisitions on the same day, the previous nine days and the FA 1985 share pool.

Where a company owns shares in a trading company, there is an exemption on disposal if 10% or more of the shares are held.

Relief for replacement of business assets is available to companies to defer gains arising on the disposal of qualifying business assets.

6. Corporation tax administration

A company must notify HMRC within three months of starting to trade.

Corporation tax returns must usually be filed within 12 months of the end of an accounting period.

A compliance check enquiry into a return, claim or election can be started by an officer of HMRC within a limited period.

Large companies pay their corporation tax in quarterly instalments. Other companies pay their tax nine months and one day after the end of an accounting period.

Further study guidance

Question practice

Now try the following from the Further question practice bank (available in the digital edition of the Workbook):

- Fraser Ltd
- Melson Ltd
- Hogg Ltd

Further reading

There is a technical article on the ACCA website written by members of the ATX – UK examining team which is relevant to some of the topics covered in this chapter that you should read:

ACCA Technical article 'Corporation tax' found here:

https://www.accaglobal.com/uk/en/student/exam-support-resources/professional-exams-study-resources/p6/technical-articles.html

Activity answers

Activity 1: Single company corporation tax example

Lucky Ltd corporation tax computation for the five-month period ended 30 April 2021

	£
Operating profit	1,432,600
Advertising	0
Depreciation	14,700
Amortisation	9,000
Deduction for lease premium £46,800/12 × 5/12	(1,625)
Capital allowances (W1)	(435,867)
Trading profit	1,018,808
Interest income	700
Taxable total profits	1,019,508
Corporation tax £1,019,508 × 19%	193,707

Workings

1 *Capital allowances*

	Main pool £	Special rate pool £	Allowances £
Additions qualifying for AIA			
Integral features	206,000		
AIA	(206,000)		206,000
Transfer balance to special rate pool		0	
Computer	31,500		
Office equipment	264,500		
	296,000		
AIA (W2)	(210,667)		210,667
Transfer balance to main pool	85,333		
WDA 18% × 5/12	(6,400)		6,400
Addition qualifying for FYA			
Motor car	12,800		
FYA 100%	(12,800)		12,800
Transfer balance to main pool	0	—	
WDV carried forward	78,933	0	—
Total allowances			435,867

2 **AIA**

The AIA is reduced to £416,667 (£1,000,000 × 5/12) because Lucky Ltd's accounting period is five months long.

Note. The expenditure which is integral to the building is included in the special rate pool. It is beneficial to claim the annual investment allowance of £416,667 initially against this integral features expenditure, as it would otherwise only qualify for writing down allowance at the rate of 6%. The computer purchased on 19 August 2020 is pre-trading and is treated as incurred on 1 December 2020

Activity 2: Rollover of intangible profit

1   Profit per accounts on sale of patent rights:

	£
Sale proceeds	3,000,000
NBV	(890,000)
Accounting profit	2,110,000

All proceeds reinvested, so:	Income gain eligible for rollover	Amount taxable immediately
Proceeds	3,000,000	
Original cost	(1,800,000)	
Rollover relief	1,200,000	
Remaining accounting profit		910,000

Base cost of new patent: £3,500,000 − £1,200,000 = £2,300,000.

2   The accounting profit, as above, is £2,110,000.

Not all proceeds reinvested:	Gain eligible for rollover:	Amount taxable:
	£	£
Actual gain (proceeds − cost)	1,200,000	
Tax now proceeds not reinvested (3m − 2.5m)	(500,000)	
Rollover relief	700,000*	
Remaining accounting profit		1,410,000

*This is equal to the amount that the cost of the new asset exceeds the cost of the original asset (2.5m − 1.8m).

Base cost of new patent	£
Cost	2,500,000
Less income gain rolled over	(700,000)
	1,800,000

Activity 3: R&D Tax credits

Since Saturn Ltd is a small enterprise for the purposes of research and development, the expenditure of £30,000 will result in a tax deduction of £30,000 × 230% = £69,000. This will result in an increase in the loss of £69,000 which it must carry forward against total profits since it has no other income or gains in the current period (and has no previous accounting periods since this is its first accounting period).

Saturn Ltd can choose to claim a tax credit of 14.5% of its surrenderable loss, which is the lower of the trading loss (£169,000) and 230% of qualifying expenditure (£69,000), as an alternative to carrying the loss forward. This is therefore 14.5% × £69,000 = £10,005.

Saturn Ltd should consider claiming the 14.5% tax credit if cash flow is its main priority. Alternatively, if the company wishes to maximise the tax saved in respect of the expenditure, it should carry the loss forward. It will then save tax at 19% (provided it succeeds in generating TTP in the future).

Activity 4: RDEC for large companies

	£
Taxable total profit before R&D expenditure	2,135,000
Add RDEC £100,000 × 13%	13,000
Less R&D expenditure	(100,000)
Taxable total profit	2,048,000
Corporation tax £2,048,000 × 19%	389,120
Less RDEC £100,000 × 13%	(13,000)
Corporation tax payable	376,120

The tax saving using the RDEC is as follows:

	£
Corporation tax on additional income £13,000 × 19%	2,470
Less RDEC deducted from CT liability £100,000 × 13%	(13,000)
Corporation tax saving (10.53% of R&D expenditure)	10,530

Activity 5: Substantial shareholding exemption

1   The disposal does not meet the conditions for the SSE as Orange Ltd has not had a 10% holding in Lemon Ltd for a continuous 12-month period in the last six years. Consequently, a gain will arise.

	£
Proceeds	500,000
Cost (7/11 × 260,000)	(165,455)
Unindexed gain	334,545
Less indexation allowance (none as acquisition is post December 2017)	0
Gain	334,545
Corporation tax at 19% × 334,545	63,564
After tax proceeds (500,000 – 63,564)	436,436

2   Orange Ltd should wait until after 1 May 2021 to dispose of the shares. The conditions for the SSE would then be met and Orange Ltd would keep the full £500,000 disposal proceeds.

Activity 6: Quarterly instalments for a short accounting period

First and interim instalments are: 3 × £(4m/10) = £1.2 million

	£(m)
14.7.20	1.2
14.10.20	1.2
14.1.21	<u>1.2</u>
	3.6
14.2.21 (balance) (4th month after AP end)	<u>0.4</u>
	<u><u>4.0</u></u>

17

Losses for single companies

Learning objectives

On completion of this chapter, you should be able to:

	Syllabus reference no.
Remember the material already covered in Taxation (TX – UK) under the heading 'the use of exemptions and reliefs in deferring and minimising corporation tax liabilities'	A4(a) E6
Determine the tax treatment of non-trading deficits on loan relationships	A4(c)(ii)
Advise on the restriction of the use of losses on a change in ownership of a company	A4(c)(v)
Identify the restriction on carried forward trading losses and capital losses for companies with profits over £5 million	A4(c)(vi)

Exam context

In this chapter we will review how a company may obtain relief for trading losses, capital losses and property losses (which will be familiar to you from your Taxation (UK) studies), and also for deficits on non-trading loan relationships, which is new to you. Then we consider a restriction on the use of loss relief where there has been a change in ownership of the company. We look at the factors to take into account when deciding which loss relief to choose.

You are likely to come across company losses at some point in the exam, although the question may include group relief. Always look to see if any requirements are specified in the question, such as to claim relief as early as possible, and then consider how to optimise the relief. It may be more beneficial for a company to use a loss itself, via current year and prior year relief, than to surrender losses to other group members. This would particularly be the case if cash flow was an important issue for the company.

It is vital that you are able to distinguish between the different types of losses and deficits that a company may have, in order to relieve them against the correct income figures.

Chapter overview

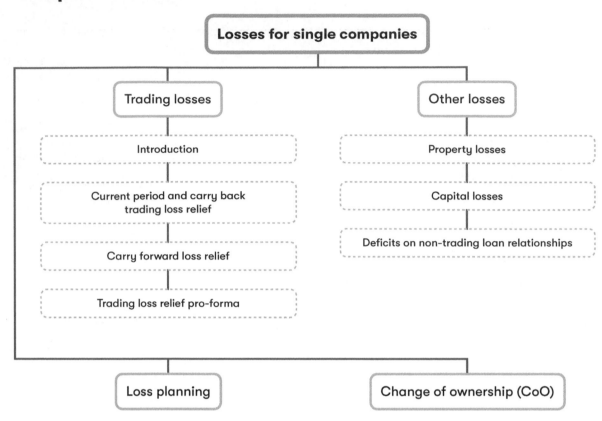

1 Trading losses

This section is assumed knowledge from Taxation (TX – UK).

1.1 Introduction

1.1.1 Available reliefs

The following reliefs are available for trading losses:

- **Current period and carry back against total profits**; and
- **Carry forward usually against total profits.**

These reliefs may be used in combination. The options open to the company are:

- Current-period relief only
- Current-period relief, then carry back relief
- Current-period relief, then carry forward relief
- Current-period relief, then carry back relief, then carry forward relief
- Carry forward relief only

1.1.2 Points to note

The **trading loss is computed after the deduction of capital allowances**, although the claim for capital allowances may be restricted if loss relief would be inefficient.

The trading income assessment for the loss-making period is **nil**.

The rules regarding the carry forward of trading losses changed with effect from 1 April 2017 and you will only be examined on the rules applying to trading losses incurred post 1 April 2017.

1.2 Current-period and carry back trading loss relief

1.2.1 Operation of the relief

Relief is claimed against the **total profits (before qualifying charitable donations**, QCDs) of the loss-making period. A **further claim** may then be made, if required, to set any remaining losses against the total profits (before QCDs) of the **preceding 12 months**. No carry back claim may be made without first relieving losses against profits (if any) of the current accounting period.

Losses used in this way must be relieved to the **fullest extent possible**, so QCDs may become unrelieved as a result of these claims.

If an accounting period falls only partly in the 12 months prior to the start of the loss-making period, its profits (before QCDs) must be apportioned to find the available profits against which the loss may be offset.

Essential reading

See Chapter 17 of the Essential reading for an illustration of carrying back to a non 12-month accounting period and an illustration of terminal loss relief (revised below).

The Essential reading is available as an Appendix of the digital edition of the Workbook.

1.2.2 Losses incurred in the final 12 months of trading

For losses incurred in the **final 12 months of trade,** the carry back period for loss relief is **extended to 36 months**. The carry back is on a **last in, first out basis** (ie most recent years first).

> ### Exam focus point
>
> In September 2016 Question 5 Cresco Ltd, candidates were required to show how a company could relieve trading losses incurred in its last few periods of account. This involved consideration of loss relief in an ongoing company, in addition to the availability of terminal loss relief. The examining team commented that: 'It is important in any question dealing with relief for losses that a well-considered and chronological approach is taken. Precise explanations of the reliefs are required in these sorts of questions. Well-prepared candidates were able to deal correctly with the earlier losses in accounting periods prior to the final period, and were aware that, on cessation, an extended three-year carry back is available, but almost all neglected to correctly calculate the loss which was available for this terminal loss relief. Nevertheless, those who adopted a sensible, logical approach scored well on this question part.'

1.2.3 Claim

Current period and prior year relief must be claimed. The deadline is two years from the end of the loss-making accounting period.

1.3 Carry forward loss relief

Unrelieved trading losses are **carried forward** and **claims may be made to set them against total profits of future accounting periods**. The claim may restrict the amount of loss that is relieved to prevent qualifying charitable donations becoming unrelieved.

1.3.1 Carry forward relief against total profits

If no current or carry back claims are made, or if losses remain after such claims then any carried forward losses will **automatically be carried forward** to the next accounting period.

A **claim** can then be made to **deduct all/part of the trade loss from the total profits of that accounting period**. Unlike a current year or carry back claim, a partial claim can therefore be made to preserve QCDs.

If the loss is not fully relieved it continues to be automatically carried forward and available for offset until it is fully relieved.

The claim to offset the carried-forward trade loss must be made within two years of the end of the accounting period **in which the loss is relieved**.

> ### Exam focus point
>
> Carried forward losses arising prior to 1 April 2017 **are not examinable** in Advanced Taxation (ATX – UK) as different rules apply to such losses.

1.3.2 Carry forward relief – potential restrictions

A **restriction** applies to the use **of trade losses carried forward against total profits in excess of a deduction allowance which is £5 million**. A company's **profits** (after the deduction of current year reliefs, including group relief and the deduction allowance) **can only be reduced by 50% using losses carried forward**. Finance Act 2020 extended these rules in order to **restrict the use of capital losses brought forward in addition to trading losses**. A **single £5 million deduction allowance** now applies to both trading losses and capital losses brought forward. A company must choose how this deduction allowance will be allocated between trading losses and capital losses brought forward.

A group of companies is only entitled to one deduction allowance of £5 million (which covers the offset of both trading losses and capital losses brought forward) and can allocate this to any company or companies in the group. For these purposes a group of companies means two or more companies where one company is the ultimate parent of each of the other companies and there is a 75% relationship between the ultimate parent and its subsidiaries.

Exam focus point

You are only expected to have an awareness of this restriction and will not need to apply this in your exam.

If a company's trade becomes **small or negligible** in an accounting period in which a trading loss arose, or from which a loss is carried forward, trading losses carried forward to future periods will **automatically be offset against future profits of the same trade, rather than against total profits**.

If a company's trade **ceases**, then its trading losses **cannot be carried forward against any future income**.

Essential reading

See Chapter 17 of the Essential reading for details of the restriction on losses where a trade has become negligible.

The Essential reading is available as an Appendix of the digital edition of the Workbook.

Activity 1: Trading loss relief

Bat Ltd had the following results in recent years:

	Y/e 30.6.19	Y/e 30.6.20	Y/e 30.6.21
	£	£	£
Trading profit/(loss)	15,000	(53,000)	20,000
Investment income	5,000	5,000	5,000
Capital gain/(loss)	3,000	(10,000)	7,000
QCD	(1,000)	(1,000)	(1,000)

Required

Show how Bat Ltd will utilise the loss, assuming it will make claims to utilise losses as early as possible, and show clearly any losses to carry forward.

Solution

1.4 Trading loss relief pro-forma

	2020	2021	2022
Trading income	X	nil	X
Other income and gains (net of capital losses)	X	X	X
Total Profits	X	X	X
Current period		(X)	
Carry back	(X)		
Carry forward (restrict to preserve QCDs)			(X)
Less QCDs	(X)	(X)	(X)
Taxable total profits (TTP)	X	X	X

2 Other losses

2.1 Property losses

All profits and losses on properties are **pooled** to give a property profit or loss (note that interest would be dealt with under the loan relationship rules).

A **property loss** can be set off against:

- **Current year total profits (automatic and to fullest extent possible)**
- Total profits of other group companies through **group relief** (see later)
- Any property loss not utilised in the above two claims is automatically carried forward to the next accounting period and a claim can be made to offset some, or all, of the loss against total profits of the next accounting period. As with trading losses, this claim can be restricted to preserve QCDs.

Note that property losses cannot be carried back.

2.2 Capital losses

Capital losses are **automatically offset against first available gains to the fullest extent possible**. They cannot be used against any other form of income and can never be carried back.

Any unutilised capital losses are then **automatically carried** forward to be offset against **gains of the next accounting period**. The amount of capital losses brought forward available for offset against chargeable gains in restricted to a maximum of the whole/ part of the £5 million deduction allowance plus 50% of the excess of chargeable gains for the period over that amount.

> ### Exam focus point
>
> The rules about the restriction of carried forward capital losses are complicated. As a result, you need only have an awareness of these restrictions in the ATX-UK exam. You will not be expected to apply them to a particular scenario.

If the company is in a chargeable gains group, consideration can be given to group allocation of gains and losses (see later).

2.3 Deficits on non-trading loan relationships

A **deficit** can be:

- Offset against **total profits of the current year**. The deficit is offset before current year or prior year trading loss relief and property business losses, and before relief for trading losses brought forward. **Claims to relieve only part of the deficit** (for example, to avoid wasting QCDs) **are possible.**
- Offset against **investment income** (non-trade loan relationship income) in the **previous 12 months (whole or partial claims are possible** and there is no requirement to offset the deficit in current year first as there is for a trade loss). The carried-back deficit relief is given after any current-period or brought-forward NTLR deficits or trading losses, and after QCDs.
- **Group relieved** against taxable total profits (TTP) of other group companies (see later).
- Any NTLR deficit left after the claims above is **automatically carried forward into the next accounting period, and a claim can be made to offset some, or all, of the deficit against the next period's total profits**. The deficit continues to be carried forward until it is fully utilised.

The deadline for current year and prior year claims is two years from the end of the deficit period. The deadline for carried-forward relief is two years from the end of the period where the loss is to be relieved.

3 Loss planning

> ### PER alert
>
> One of the competencies you require to fulfil Performance Objective 17 Tax planning and advice of the PER is to mitigate and/or defer tax liabilities through the use of standard reliefs, exemptions and incentives. You can apply the knowledge you obtain from this section of the text to help demonstrate this competence.

In a single-company loss question, the **best use of losses** will involve consideration of:

- **Timing of the loss offset** and thus **cashflow advantage** gained by relieving the loss as soon as possible – carrying back losses will generally result in repayments of corporation tax, and potentially higher tax savings due to falling rates of corporation tax in the UK.
- **Avoiding any QCDs being wasted** by restricting the use of brought-forward losses.
- Planning scenarios in the ATX exam will usually involve groups of companies; if this is the case, the planning position becomes more complex. We will consider group tax planning later in this Workbook.

Activity 2: Choice of loss relief

Monster Ltd has the following results:

Year ended 31 March

	2020	2021	2022	2023
Trading profit/(loss)	2,000	(500,000)	100,000	120,000
Chargeable gains	35,000	250,000	30,000	45,000
Qualifying charitable donations	30,000	20,000	20,000	20,000

Required

Recommend appropriate loss relief claims, stating by when the claims should be made, and compute the corporation tax for all years based on your recommendations, showing any unrelieved qualifying charitable donations. Assume the rate of corporation tax is 19% in financial years 2019 and 2020, and 17% in financial years 2021 and 2022.

Solution

4 Change of ownership

Loss relief for trading losses may be restricted where there is a **change in the ownership of a company and either:**

- A **major change in the nature or conduct of the trade (MCINOCOT) within any five-year period** (that begins no later than the change of ownership and no earlier than three years before the change of ownership); **or**
- After the change in ownership there is a **revival of activities which at the time of the change had been small or negligible.**

For example, if a company changes its ownership on 1 July 2021 and there is a MCINOCOT between 1 July 2018 and 30 June 2026, the carry back and carry forward of losses are restricted.

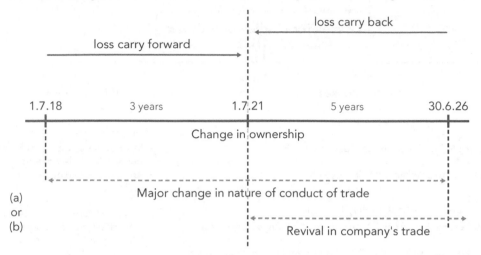

If the restriction applies:

*   Any losses incurred **before** the change in ownership **cannot be carried forward against post-acquisition profits; and**
*   Any losses incurred **after** the change in ownership **cannot be carried back against profits arising before the date of the change of ownership.**

Examples of a major change in the nature or conduct of the trade include:

*   Change in the nature of goods or services provided
*   Changes in the customer base
*   Changes in outlets or markets

However, changes to keep up with technology or rationalise the product range are unlikely to be regarded as major.

Exam focus point

These rules apply where there is **both** a change in ownership **and** a major change in the business of a company on or after 1 April 2017. Changes occurring prior to 1 April 2017 are **not examinable** in Advanced Taxation (ATX – UK).

Chapter summary

Losses for single companies

Trading losses

Introduction
- Options: carry forward, current period, carry back
- Can restrict CAs
- Only post-1/4/17 rules examinable in ATX

Current-period and carry-back trading loss relief
- Against total profits of current AP then carry back 12m against total profits
- Carry back extended to 36m (LIFO) for loss of final 12 months of trade
- No partial claims
- Can group relieve all/part of a current-period trade loss

Carry-forward loss relief
- Any losses remaining after other claims are automatically carried forward
- Claim to relieve all/part of trade loss against total profits of that AP (restrict claim to preserve QCDs)

Trading loss relief pro-forma

	2020	2021	2022
Trading income	X	nil	X
Other income and gains (net of capital losses)	X	X	X
Total profits	X	X	X
Current period		(X)	
Carry back	(X)		
Carry forward (restrict to preserve QCDs)			(X)
Less QCDs	(X)	(X)	(X)
Taxable total profits (TTP)	X	X	X

Other losses

Property losses
- Must offset vs total profits of current AP (fullest extent)
- Any loss remaining can be either:
  - Group relieved, or
  - Carried forward and claim to offset all/part against total profits of future APs

Capital losses
Set against current and future gains only (automatic)

Deficits on non-trading loan relationships
- Claim to set against total profit of current AP
- Carry back against NTLR income of previous 12m
- Group relief
- Carry forward and claim to offset all/part against total profits of future APs

Loss planning
- Consider:
  - Timing of relief
  - Cash flows (repayments of CT)
  - Unrelieved QCDs

Change of ownership (CoO)
- Trading losses cannot be CF or CB if a change of ownership and either:
  - MCINOCOT within any five year period beginning no later than the CoO and no earlier than three years before the CoO, or
  - Revival after CoO of activities which were small/negligible at time of CoO

Knowledge diagnostic

1. Trading loss relief

Trading losses may be relieved by deduction from current-period total profits, total profits of earlier periods or total profits of future periods.

Current-period trading loss relief and carry back trading loss relief are optional, but if claimed must be taken to the fullest extent possible against total profits, and so qualifying charitable donations may become unrelieved.

A claim for current period loss relief can be made without a claim for carry back. However, if a loss is to be carried back a claim for current-period relief must have been made first.

Trading losses in the last 12 months of trading can be carried back and deducted from total profits of the previous 36 months.

Unrelieved trading losses are carried forward and claims may be made to set them against total profits of future accounting periods. The claim may restrict the amount of loss that is relieved to prevent QCDs becoming unrelieved.

2. Other types of loss

Capital losses can only be set against capital gains in the current or future accounting periods.

Property business losses must be set off first against total profits in the current accounting period and then a carry forward loss relief claim can be made to set unrelieved losses against future total profits.

Deficits on non-trading loan relationships can be relieved by deduction from current-period total profits, carried back against non-trading credits of the previous 12 months or carried forward against total profits.

3. Restrictions on loss relief

If a company's trade has become small or negligible in an accounting period, it can only set carried-forward trading losses from that period against trading profits of the same trade.

Brought forward losses can only be relieved up to the allocated deduction allowance plus 50% of profits or gains in excess of this allowance. The deduction allowance is £5m per single company or group of companies.

If there is a change in ownership of a company, the carry forward of losses is restricted if there is also a major change in the nature or conduct of the trade within a five year period beginning no earlier than three years before the change in ownership.

4. Loss planning

When selecting a loss relief, consider the timing of the relief and whether relief for QCDs may be lost.

Further study guidance

Question practice

Now try the following from the Further question practice bank (available in the digital edition of the Workbook):

- Major Ltd
- Daley PLC

Activity answers

Activity 1: Trading loss relief

	Y/end 30.6.19	Y/end 30.6.20	Y/end 30.6.21
Trading profit	15,000	Nil	20,000
Interest income	5,000	5,000	5,000
Gains	3,000	–	–
Total profits	23,000	5,000	25,000
Less current and carry back relief	(23,000)	(5,000)	–
Less carry forward relief			(24,000)
Less QCD	–	–	(1,000)
Taxable total profits	–	–	–
Unrelieved QCD's	1,000	1,000	

Loss Memorandum

	£
Loss for y/end 30.6.20	53,000
Current year relief y/e 30.6.20	(5,000)
Carry back relief y/e 30.6.19	(23,000)
	25,000
Carry forward relief y/e 30.6.21	(24,000)
Trade loss to carry forward	1,000

Capital loss	
Loss for y/end 30.6.20	10,000
Used in y/end 30.6.21	(7,000)
Capital loss to carry forward	3,000

Remember that the current period and carry back relief claims cannot be restricted to preserve QCDs, whereas with carry forward relief the company can choose the amount of relief to avoid wasting QCDs. Capital losses can only be used against current or future chargeable gains and cannot be carried back.

Activity 2: Choice of loss relief

A current-period loss relief claim for the year ended 31 March 2021 will be against total profits of £250,000 and obtain relief quickly. This outweighs the fact that the claim will waste the QCDs of £20,000, so a current period claim should be made by 31 March 2023 (two years from the end of the loss-making period).

If a current-period loss relief claim is made, a carry back relief claim can also be made for the year ended 31 March 2020. This will be against total profits of (£35,000 + £2,000) = £37,000. This claim will waste QCDs of £30,000 and so would use £37,000 of loss to save tax at 19% on £7,000 (£35,000 + £2,000 – £30,000). A carry back claim should therefore not be made.

A carry forward relief claim will obtain relief in the year ended 31 March 2022 against total profits. The claim should be restricted to (£100,000 + £30,000 – £20,000) = £110,000 to keep £20,000 of total profit in charge to match the qualifying charitable donation. The remaining £(500,000 – 250,000 – 110,000) = £140,000 of the loss will be carried forward to the year ended 31 March 2023 to be set against total profits. This claim should be made in full, as it will not result in any qualifying charitable donations becoming unrelieved. These claims should be made by 31 March 2024 and 31 March 2025 respectively (two years from the end of the period in which the loss is relieved).

The corporation tax computations are as follows:

Year ended 31 March

	2020	2021	2022	2023
	£	£	£	£
Trading income	2,000	0	100,000	120,000
Chargeable gains	35,000	250,000	30,000	45,000
Total profits	37,000	250,000	130,000	165,000
Less current-period loss relief		(250,000)		
Less carry forward loss relief	-		(110,000)	(140,000)
Less qualifying charitable donations	(30,000)	0	(20,000)	(20,000)
Taxable total profits	7,000	0	0	5,000
CT at 19%/17%	1,330	0	0	850
Unrelieved qualifying charitable donations	0	20,000	0	0

18

Owner-managed business tax planning

Learning objectives

On completion of this chapter, you should be able to:

	Syllabus reference no.
Identify and advise on the taxes applicable to a given course of action and their impact	B1
Identify and understand that the alternative ways of achieving personal or business outcomes may lead to different tax consequences	B2
Advise how taxation can affect the financial decisions made by businesses (corporate and unincorporated) and by individuals	B3
Assess the tax advantages and disadvantages of alternative courses of action	B4
Understand the statutory obligations imposed in a given situation, including any time limits for action and advise on the implications of non-compliance	B5
Identify and advise on the types of investment and other expenditure that will result in a reduction in tax liabilities for an individual and/or a business	C1
Advise on legitimate tax planning measures by which the tax liabilities arising from a particular situation or course of action can be mitigated	C2
Advise on the appropriateness of such investment, expenditure or measures given a particular taxpayer's circumstances or stated objectives	C3
Advise on the mitigation of tax in the manner recommended by reference to numerical analysis and/or reasoned argument	C4
Be aware of and give advice on current issues in taxation	C6
Communicate advice, recommendations and information in the required format. For example, the use of: Reports, Memoranda, Letters and Meeting notes	D1
Present written information, in language appropriate to the purpose of the communication and the intended recipient	D2

	Syllabus reference no.
Communicate conclusions reached, together, where necessary with relevant supporting computations	D3
State and explain assumptions made or limitations in the analysis provided; together with any inadequacies in the information available and/or additional information required to provide a fuller analysis	D4
Identify and explain other, non-tax, factors that should be considered	D5

Exam context

A very common scenario that you will see in your exam is advising an owner-managed business. In this type of question, it is vital that from the start you recognise whether the business is a sole trader or partnership or a company. Many students see the word 'business' and simply assume it's a company. Sole traders and partners are liable for income tax on their profits whereas companies pay corporation tax – a mistake on interpreting the scenario early in the question can have disastrous consequences. The sections below take us through the journey of starting a business to eventual sale of the business and considers the tax issues we could see in the exam.

Chapter overview

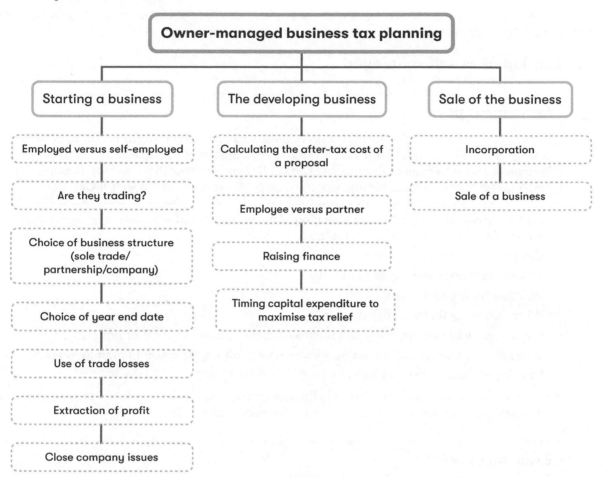

1 Starting a business

We start our planning chapter looking at some of the ideas which we might need to consider if we are advising a client who is about to start up their own business.

1.1 Employed vs self-employed

> ### Exam focus point
>
> A question could have us looking at an individual working with an already existing business asking us to consider whether the individual is an **employee** of the business thus paying **income tax** on employment income and **Class 1 NICs** or whether the individual is **self-employed** and thus paying **income tax** on trade profits and **Class 2 and 4 NICs**.

To determine whether an individual is **employed** or **self-employed** we saw earlier in the Workbook that we must consider the following factors:

- **Control** over how work is done
- Whether **provides own equipment**
- Whether **hires own helpers**
- What degree of **financial risk** is taken?
- What **degree of responsibility** for investment and management worker has?
- Whether and how far there is an **opportunity for profiting from sound management**
- **How many people** does worker work for?

If a contract is mentioned in the scenario then it has been held that a contract **of** service indicates **employment** but a contract **for** services indicates **self-employment**.

> ### Exam focus point
>
> In an exam question you will need to try to consider and **apply the factors** above to the scenario and then come to a **conclusion** based on the **big picture** of the factors

The table below sets out the main differences in tax which you may need to explain to the individual in the question. You will see that there are **tax advantages** to being treated as **self-employed** but, of course, self-employed individuals do **not** have the **protection offered to employees such as holiday pay, sick pay and requirement to give notice.**

	Employed	**Self-employed**
Pensions:	Personal/workplace	Personal only
NICs	Class 1	Classes 2, 4 (generally lower)
Expenses	Wholly, exclusively and necessarily	Wholly and exclusively (thus more expenses deductible)
Basis of assessment	Taxed under employment income on amounts received in the tax year	Taxed as trading income on CYB
Payment dates	Tax is collected under PAYE at the time of receipt of remuneration	Payments on account will be due on 31 January in the tax year and 31 July following the tax year, with a final payment on 31 January after the year of assessment (thus later)

Activity 1: Employment vs self-employment – Lucy

Assume that it is 1 March 2020.

Lucy is considering two work arrangements. She will start her chosen arrangement on 6 April 2020 and will continue with that arrangement for the whole of the tax year 2020/21.

Employment with Red plc

Lucy has been offered employment with Red plc. She would be paid a salary of £36,000 and would be required to work at Red plc's offices.

Lucy would travel from home to Red plc's offices by train and would buy an annual season ticket costing £1,500.

Self-employment

Lucy would work for a number of clients at their offices. She would receive fees of £36,000 from her clients in the year to 5 April 2021.

Lucy would travel from home to client offices in her own car. Her business mileage would be 4,600 miles during the year and she estimates this would actually cost 40p per mile.

Lucy would prepare accounts to 5 April 2021 and elect to use the cash basis and approved mileage allowances.

Required

Determine which of the work arrangements would result in Lucy having a higher amount of disposable income after deducting income tax, national insurance contributions and travel costs.

Solution

1.2 Are they trading?

We could see a scenario where an individual buys and sells assets (or provides a service for cash) and we're asked to determine whether they are **trading or not**. If they are **trading**, they will be liable to **income tax** on their trade profits and **Class 2 and 4 NICs**. If they **aren't trading**, we will need to consider whether there is any **capital gains tax** due on the sale of a capital asset.

To make this decision we use the badges of trade as we saw in Chapter 14 of the Workbook. The badges to consider are:

- **Subject matter**
- **Frequency of transactions**
- **Existence of similar trading transactions or interests**
- **Length of ownership**
- **The organisation of the activity as a trade**
- **Supplementary work and marketing**
- **Profit motive**
- **The way in which the asset sold was acquired**
- **Method of finance**
- **The taxpayer's intentions**

Exam focus point

In an exam question, these badges will not necessarily all point us in one direction, and we will need to conclude based on the **big picture** having **applied these badges to the scenario** we have in the question. The question could go on to ask us to calculate the tax due assuming the individual either is/isn't trading.

Question 3 Tomas in the March 2020 exam asked students to explain the difference in a taxpayer's total tax payable due to their profits being taxed as trading income rather than as chargeable gains. The examining team stated: 'When specific taxes are not mentioned in the question, students need to think broadly. Although the majority of students correctly identified the income tax implications, very few considered that there would also be NIC implications as well. In relation to the CGT implications, only a minority recognised that the items being sold constituted chattels under £6,000, and so were exempt. So the majority of students were only able to score two out of possible five marks. The question did ask for supporting calculations, but many students produced detailed, comprehensive income tax and CGT computations, in addition to explaining the implications. Calculations were only needed to support the explanation, and so need to only be brief. In particular, many students doing the computer based exam explained the position in the word processing document, referring the relevant numbers, and also produced comprehensive calculations in the spreadsheet, which did not gain them any additional marks.

Activity 2: Carrying on a trade

Martha has recently inherited a Rolls Royce Silver Phantom and, following installation of new leather seat coverings, has decided to start allowing friends to use it as their wedding car. She has initially been asking for a £100 contribution for use of the car and has started advertising the car's availability in local shops and on local Facebook groups. She believes she can start charging about £500 per use of the car. The car has currently been used only on six occasions over the last six months. Martha works full time as an estate agent.

Required

Discuss whether Martha's profits from her wedding car service will be liable to income tax.

Solution

1.3 Choice of business structure (sole trade/partnership/company)

A crucial decision to be made when starting a business will be the **choice of business structure** for our individual.

Do they use a more **flexible unincorporated entity such as a sole trader or partnership**? These are **more flexible** as there are fewer rules and regulations to follow and they offer **more confidentiality** as there's no requirement to file accounts at Companies House. In contrast, legally there is **no separate legal entity** and the individual has **unlimited liability** for the liabilities of the business.

Or, should the more **formal structure**, such as a company, be used? This will mean that the individual must follow **more rules and regulations and file accounts annually**. However, it can give a sense of **gravitas** to the business and provides the owner with the **separate legal entity** and benefit of **limited liability**.

Of course, these are not tax factors but syllabus area D5 states we should be able to identify and explain other, non-tax, factors that should be considered.

The differing tax position of unincorporated versus incorporated businesses is also vitally important. The following factors should be considered:

	Sole trader	Company
Profits	Pay income tax • Rates? • Limits? Opening year rules • Overlap profit	Pay corporation tax at 19%
Payment of tax	Payments on account	9 months and 1 day
Losses	Relief vs general income Carry forward relief Early year loss relief	Current and carry back relief Carry forward relief
Extract cash	Drawings	Salary

	Sole trader	Company
		Dividends • Consider implications to both company and individual
NIC	Classes 2 and 4	Class 1 – Employee – Employer

Activity 3: Choice of business structure

You should assume that today's date is 1 March 2021.

Hamish has a business idea, which he thinks will give rise to trading profits of £60,000 per annum. All of his expenses are tax deductible. He intends to start trading on 6 April 2021.

Hamish enjoys a lavish lifestyle and has significant expenses, so he wants to maximise his income from the business.

Required

Advise Hamish on how he should structure his business to best meet his needs. If he sets up as a company he will pay himself a salary of £8,788 and take the balance as a dividend.

(Assume FA 2020 rates continue to apply, and that Hamish will have no other taxable income in 2021/22.)

Solution

Exam focus point

In Question 1 Nelson in the December 2019 exam students were asked to compare the tax payable if an individual traded through a limited company compared to trading as an unincorporated trader. The tax payable if trading as an unincorporated trader was given in the question and did not need to be recalculated but despite this a number of students wasted time recalculating this figure and gained no marks for their efforts. The reminds us of the importance of correctly interpreting the requirement and planning before we start to write.

1.4 Choice of year end date

A new trader should consider which accounting date would be best. There are **several factors to consider** from the point of view of taxation.

- **If profits are expected to rise, a date early in the tax year** (such as 30 April) will delay the time when rising accounts profits feed through into rising taxable profits, whereas a date late in the tax year (such as 31 March) will accelerate the taxation of rising profits. This is because with an accounting date of 30 April, the taxable profits for each tax year are mainly the profits earned in the previous tax year. With an accounting date of 31 March, the taxable profits are almost entirely profits earned in the current year.

- If the accounting date in the second tax year is less than 12 months after the start of trading, the taxable profits for that year will be the profits earned in the first 12 months. If the accounting date is at least 12 months from the start of trading, they will be the profits earned in the 12 months to that date. **Different profits may thus be taxed twice**, and if profits are fluctuating this can make a considerable difference to the taxable profits in the first few years.

- **The choice of an accounting date affects the profits shown in each set of accounts**, and this may affect the taxable profits.

- **An accounting date of 30 April gives the maximum interval between earning profits and paying the related tax liability.** For example, if a trader prepares accounts to 30 April 2021, this falls into the tax year 2021/22 with payments on account being due on 31 January 2022 and 31 July 2022, and a balancing payment due on 31 January 2023. If the trader prepares accounts to 31 March 2021, this falls in the tax year 2020/21 and the payments will be due one year earlier (ie on 31 January 2021, 31 July 2021 and 31 January 2022).

- **Knowing profits well in advance of the end of the tax year makes tax planning much easier.** For example, if a trader wants to make personal pension contributions and prepares accounts to 30 April 2021 (2021/22), they can make contributions up to 5 April 2022 based on those relevant earnings. If they prepare accounts to 31 March 2021, they will probably not know the amount of their relevant earnings until after the end of the tax year 2020/21, too late to adjust their pension contributions for 2020/21.

- **However, a 31 March or 5 April accounting date means that the application of the basis period rules is more straightforward and there will be no overlap profits.** This may be appropriate for small traders.

- **With an accounting date of 30 April, the assessment for the year of cessation could be based on up to 23 months of profits.** For example, if a trader who has prepared accounts to 30 April ceases trading on 31 March 2021 (2020/21), the basis period for 2020/21 will run from 1 May 2019 to 31 March 2021. This could lead to larger than normal trading profits being assessable in the year of cessation.

- However, this could be avoided by carrying on the trade for another month so that a cessation arises on 30 April 2021 so that the profits from 1 May 2019 to 30 April 2020 are taxable in 2020/21 and those from 1 May 2020 to 30 April 2021 are taxable in 2021/22. Each case must be looked at in relation to all relevant factors, such as other income which the taxpayer may have and loss relief – there is no one rule which applies in all cases.

A question considering choice of year end date is covered in the Skills section after this chapter.

> ### Exam focus point
>
> December 2014 Question 2(a) part (iii) Piquet required candidates to identify two advantages of using a 30 April year end as opposed to a year end of 28 February. The examining team commented that 'many candidates were able to identify one advantage, but few were able to come up with two. This was disappointing as the choice of year end is a basic aspect of tax planning for the unincorporated trader and one that candidates should be confident of.'

This was also tested in March 2020 Question 3 Tomas where a taxpayer was considering adopting a 31 March or 30 April year end. This question also asked students to identify the taxpayer's basis periods and the examining team said that it was very surprising that very few candidates were able to do this. The examining team said 'a thorough knowledge of the opening and closing year basis period rules is essentially brought forward knowledge from TX. Both of these are frequently tested in ATX and students should ensure they have a sound knowledge of these rules.'

1.5 Use of trade losses

1.5.1 Choice of loss reliefs

When a business starts up often it incurs **losses** rather than profits in its first few years. If this is to be the case, then an important consideration will be the choice of business structure. Running the business as a **sole trade or partnership will allow more flexible use of any business losses**.

The table below compares the loss reliefs available to the different types of business:

Sole trader/Partners	Company
Optional:	**Optional:**
Current year – against **general income** (before PA)	**Current year** – against **total profits** (before QCD)
Prior year – against **general income** (before PA)	**Prior 12 months** – against **total profits** (before QCD)
All or nothing	All or nothing
Can do in any order	**HAVE TO DO CY FIRST**
May be restricted	
Automatic:	**Automatic:**
Carry forward – against future **trading income** of the same trade	**Carry forward** – a **claim** must then be made to offset some/all of loss against future **total profits**
Early trading loss relief	N/A
Losses which occur within the first 4 tax years against **general income** (before PA) of the previous 3 tax years on a FIFO basis	
Terminal loss relief	**Terminal loss relief**
Loss in the last 12 months (+ overlap profits)	Loss in the last 12 months
Against **trading income**	Against total profits (before QCD)
Previous three tax years LIFO basis	Previous three years LIFO basis

Note that running the business as a **sole trader** allows the owner to **offset the trade loss of the business against the owners own personal income** (such as property income, interest or dividend income.) In contrast, if the business is structured as a company then the trade loss can only be offset against the company's other income and gains and not against the owner's personal income.

Questions may require you to consider the best use of a loss and the tax savings this will generate. How you do this depends on the type of business you are advising and is considered in following sections.

1.5.2 Planning to use the loss as a sole trade/partnership

Many individuals will want the **cash flow advantage** of using their loss **as early as possible**. If this is the case, a prior year claim should be made, followed by a current year claim and finally a carry forward offset.

Other questions may want us to consider how to use the loss to save the **most tax** rather than get relief as quickly as possible. Here we will want to think about using the loss in the year that the individual is paying the **highest marginal rate of tax**. We can also consider **avoiding wasting the PA, savings starting and nil rate bands and dividend nil rate band**. In a year where the PA has been abated due to the individual having total income exceeding £100,000, the use of the loss can mean that the PA is no longer abated, and this can also generate tax savings.

Working at the margin to calculate the tax saved will be much more **time efficient** in your exam.

1.5.3 Planning to use the loss as a single company

If the company wants a **cash flow advantage**, then it should make a current year claim followed by a 12-month carry back and then finally carry forward the loss.

If the question wants us to consider **maximising the corporation tax saved**, then due to the flat 19% corporation tax rate this is normally simply 19% of the loss offset. However, we could consider whether any **QCDs were wasted** by a loss claim. Planning to use a loss in a corporate group can be more complex and this is covered in the Corporate tax planning chapter.

A question considering use of trade losses and the rate of tax saved is covered in the Skills section following this chapter.

> ### Exam focus point
>
> Question 1 Nelson in the December 2019 exam required an explanation of why a business owner had been advised to trade as an unincorporated business rather than through a company when trading losses were anticipated in the first couple of years of the business. The examining team said that 'many students wasted time and earned no marks by simply describing all the losses rules of companies and unincorporated businesses whereas what was needed was for students to apply their knowledge to the specific facts of the question.'

1.6 Extraction of profit

As a **sole trade/partnership** the individual and the business are one. The individual can therefore choose how much profit to extract from the business by way of **drawings** and these have **no tax consequence** as the profits of the business are taxed before drawings are deducted.

In contrast, if the business is set up as a **company**, the individual will be a separate entity to the company, and they will need to consider **how to extract their profits** from the company. The most common methods of profit extraction are for the individual to take a **salary (or benefits, or a bonus), dividend, loan interest, rental income or pension scheme contributions**. These different forms of extraction will have very different tax consequences for both the individual and the company which are summarised below:

Method	Company	Individual
Remuneration • Salary / bonus • Benefits	Deductible/Class 1 NICs Deductible/Class 1A NICs	Taxable/Class 1 NIC Taxable
Dividends	Not deductible	No tax if within dividend nil rate band. If in excess, tax at 7.5%/32.5% or 38.1% dependent on other taxable income No NICs
Loan interest	Deductible on accruals basis	Taxable as savings income if exceeds savings income nil rate band
Rental income	Deductible	Taxable as non-savings income

Method	Company	Individual
Pension contributions	Deductible	Tax free provided below AA

Activity 4: Extraction of profits

Sylvie is resident and domiciled in the UK and is 53 years old. She is a director and shareholder of Backwell Ltd and receives an annual gross salary of £50,000. She would like to extract an additional cash sum of £30,000, net of all taxes, from Backwell Ltd, to be paid on 31 March 2021. The additional sum will be extracted as either a bonus or dividend. She will not receive any other taxable income in the tax year 2020/21.

Required

Explain, with supporting calculations, the amount of any payments to be made by Backwell Ltd to HMRC in respect of each of the two ways for Sylvie to extract the additional £30,000 cash from the company.

Solution

Exam focus point

In Question 1 Nelson in the December 2019 exam students were asked to calculate the total tax payable if an individual incorporated their business and extracted profits as a mix of salary and dividends. The examining team stated 'Most students were able to calculate the corporation tax payable and recognised that employer's NIC would be both payable and tax deductible for corporation tax purposes if the owner took a salary from the company. Many students then successfully went on to calculate the income tax payable by the owner of the company, given the mix of dividends and salary. However most students failed to recognise that the owner would also have to pay employee's NIC on the salary from the company.'

1.7 Close company issues

It is very **likely** that a new start up company will **meet the definition of a close company** and so these questions could bring in close company knowledge, covered in Chapter 21 Close companies and investment companies later in this workbook.

Use your planning time to identify whether the company is close and then watch out for:

- **Loans from the close company to a shareholder**; or
- **Benefits provided to a shareholder who is not an employee.**

2 The developing business

2.1 Calculating the after-tax cost of a proposal

We may need to be able to advise an individual of the **after-tax cost of a proposal** in our exam. It will be important that the individual fully understands the cost of potential proposal in order that they can make an informed business decision.

The principle of an **after-tax cost is simply to add up the costs associated with a proposal and then, if they are all tax deductible, the tax saving associated with those costs is deducted to come down to an after-tax cost.**

For a sole trader we might consider:

	£
Costs of proposal	X
Any additional employer's NIC on costs of proposal	X
Total costs (reduction in trade profits)	X
Less income tax saving on costs (reduced profits) @ 20%/40%/45%	(X)
Less Class 4 NIC saved on costs (reduced profits) @ 9%/2%	(X)
After-tax cost	X

For a company we would instead consider the corporation tax saved on the total costs and there would be no Class 4 NIC consideration.

Activity 5: After-tax cost of employing a part-time employee

Ernest runs a successful unincorporated business, Gardening 4 You which makes taxable profits of £95,000 per annum. The business already has seven full-time staff and requires an additional part-time employee. Ernest also receives dividends of £32,000 per year.

The proposed remuneration package for the part-time employee includes:

- A salary of £14,000 per annum
- A mileage allowance of 50p per mile for the 50 miles of business driving the employee will be expected to drive each week while visiting clients. This will be for 46 weeks of the year.

This employment income will be the employee's only source of taxable income.

Required

Calculate the annual cost for Ernest, after income tax and NIC, of employing the part-time employee.

Solution

2.2 Employee vs partner

As our individual's business grows, it may well want to take on more staff. Some past exam questions have considered the individual wanting to bring their spouse in to the business and trying to decide whether to take them on as an **employee or to become a partnership and make them a partner**.

The question may give you specifics of how these arrangements will work and could ask you to calculate the tax consequences of this. Some key ideas to consider are given below:

	Employee	Partnership
Form of remuneration	Salary Possible benefits	Share of profit (which could include an entitlement to a salary as an appropriation of profit)
Tax consequences for the original sole trader	The salary and cost of providing any benefits will be extra costs for the sole trader thus reducing their taxable trading profits. In addition, employers NIC (and Class 1A on any benefits) will also need to be paid by the business. All these costs will reduce the taxable trade profits of the sole trader and thus reduce the amount on which income tax and Class 4 NICs are calculated.	The original sole trader will have a lower share of profits to be taxed. This will therefore save income tax and Class 4 NIC.
Tax consequences for the new employee/ partner	The new employee will pay income tax on any salary and/ or bonus and employee	The new partner will receive a share of the partnership profits and the opening year

	Employee	Partnership
	NIC on any cash benefits that they receive. Any non-cash benefits will have no NIC consequence for the new employee.	basis period rules will apply that profit to tax years.
What if the business makes losses?	The employee's salary and employer's NIC thereon will increase the size of the loss on which the original sole trader can claim loss relief. The new employee will still pay income tax and employee's NIC on the cash salary they receive and will not benefit from any loss relief as they are not entitled to a share of the loss.	The loss will be appropriated between the two partners using the profit-sharing agreement. Each partner will be able to use their share of the loss in whatever way they choose. There will be no Class 2 nor Class 4 NIC due.

A question considering taking on a new employee or partner is covered in the Skills section following this chapter.

Exam focus point

Calculations on whether to take on a new person as an employee or partner were tested in Question 4 Rosa in the December 2019 exam. The examining team said that there were some excellent answers to this part of the question and that 'students who did not do so well would have benefited from taking time to plan their answer before they began, thinking about which taxes affect which individual.'

2.3 Raising finance

As the business grows, the individual will need to **raise more finance**.

As an unincorporated business the following options are available:

- **Owner's own capital**
- **Bank overdrafts**
- **Bank loans**
- **Loans secured by mortgages of land**
- **Leasing and hire purchase arrangements**
- **Sale and leaseback arrangements**
- **Loans from private individuals**
- **Use of venture capital institutions such as business angels**

If the business is **incorporated**, in addition to the finance options stated above, the following options also become available:

- **Share issues** (including using EIS, SEIS schemes if the company qualifies)
- **Loan stock issues**

One of the main decisions for a company to make is whether to raise finance through debt or equity. As you will see in your financial management paper, equity finance is a more expensive source of finance for the business due to the risk taken by the investors. In contrast, debt is a cheaper source of finance as it is less risky for the investor.

In addition, the different sources of finance have different tax consequences for the business and the investor:

	Business	Investor
Debt	• Pays interest • Interest is tax deductible and thus saves IT (sole trader/ partnership) or CT (company) Cost to the business: Interest X Less tax relief on interest (X) Net cost X A company can also get a tax deduction for any capital costs to do with the loan.	If the investor is an individual: • Pays income tax on any interest in excess of the savings nil rate band If the investor is a company: • Pays corporation tax on the interest income accrued in the year
Equity	• Pays dividends • No tax relief Cost to the business: Dividend X	If the investor is an individual: • Pays income tax on any dividends in excess of the dividend nil rate band If the investor is a company: • No corporation tax on dividends received

An alternate financing decision, perhaps for a large piece of equipment, might be whether the equipment should be bought outright with the help of a loan or whether it should be leased. This is another decision that you will see in your financial management exam.

- If the asset is bought with a bank loan, then:
  - Capital allowances will be available on the cost of the equipment.
  - Interest on the loan will be tax deductible.
- If the asset is instead leased:
  - If the lease term is <5 years, then the lease payments will be tax deductible.
  - If the equipment is bought on hire purchase or leased under a long-term lease then the cash price of the equipment will qualify for capital allowances and the finance costs are tax deductible.

2.4 Timing capital expenditure to maximise tax relief

Once the business is established and is using the current year basis to calculate which accounting periods profits are taxed in which tax year, a question could ask you to consider the **impact of the timing of capital expenditure in terms of when tax relief is obtained**. This could involve consideration of the following factors:

- **Spend at the end of the accounting year**
  - This will allow tax relief for capital expenditure as quickly as possible after the capital spend.
- **Spread capital spending over accounting year ends if total qualifying spend will exceed the** annual investment allowance **(AIA)**
  - If a business plans to spend more than the AIA for its accounting period then in addition to trying to time that expenditure towards the end of the accounting year, the spend could be split across two accounting periods such that the AIA of each year could be used to increase the spend receiving 100% relief.
- **Consider claiming less than the maximum** capital allowances

- A sole trade/partnership could have profit levels which fluctuate causing the taxpayer to sometimes pay higher-rate/additional-rate tax and sometimes not. In order to avoid profits being taxed at the higher rates, capital allowance claims could be restricted to less than the maximum in years where profits are low in order that larger allowances can be claimed in year when profits are taxed at higher rates.

- Any business could consider reducing capital allowance claims in a year where the business makes a trade loss. This would reduce the size of the trade loss which could be useful if the only relief available is a carry forward relief. A larger capital allowance claim could then be made in future. years. (Note that for companies, with the flexibility available for their carried forward losses, this point is less relevant).

3 Sale of the business

3.1 Incorporation

As a business grows and becomes profitable, the owner may consider moving from an unincorporated to an incorporated business.

Why incorporate?

Advantages	Disadvantages
Limited liability to shareholders	Potential double capital gains charge on assets
Company has a more respectable image than a sole trader or partnership?	Trading losses restricted to set off against corporate profits
Retained profit subject to only CT not IT or NIC	No carry back of trading losses in opening years
Easier to dispose of shares than interest in a business	Statutory requirement for audits, keeping books, filing accounts. Increased disclosure due to published accounts
More generous pension provisions	Tax payment dates for a company and its employees are generally in advance of those for self-employed
Easier to obtain loan finance	

To achieve this the sole trader will incorporate their business by **selling all their assets to a company** (either newly incorporated or bought 'off the shelf'). In return for their business the individual will **receive consideration equal to the market value of the assets they have transferred, and this will include at least some shares in the company**.

We see all the different tax aspects of incorporation throughout this workbook but what we do here is bring all the different tax aspects together as you could see incorporation as a complete scenario in one of your exam questions. You will cover the VAT and stamp duty points in more detail later in this Workbook. They are included here for completeness.

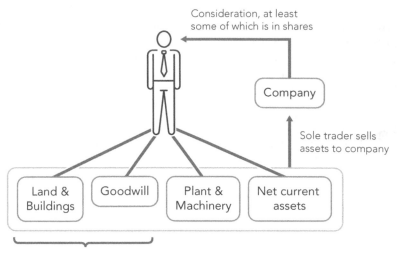

Sole trader ceases to trade:
- Closing year basis period rules, deduct overlap profits
- Stop paying IT and Class 2 and 4 NIC

Company starts to trade:
- Advise re filing CT returns and payment dates
- Probably a close company

Consideration, at least some of which is in shares

Company

Sole trader sells assets to company

Land & Buildings · Goodwill · Plant & Machinery · Net current assets

VAT: Transfer of a going concern. New commercial property and L&B OTT must have VAT charged unless purchaser OTT too. Cancel/transfer VAT registration number

Stamp: Company pays SDLT on MV of L&B transferred (no SD on new share issue)

If the ST business has a trade loss:
- Terminal loss relief is available
- Trade loss can be c/f to offset against future income from the company (loss relief on incorporation)
- CY and/or PY claim vs general income

- Sold with proceeds = MV
- Gives rise to gains
- Gains can be deferred through incorporation relief if conditions met (or gift relief if not)
- Gains charged immediately may qualify for BADR
- No BADR on GW if close company
- If an SBA asset is transferred (and incorporation relief applies) SBAs are claimed by the company with no adjustment to the seller's gains calculation. On subsequent disposal of the SBA asset by the company all the SBAs claimed to date are added to proceeds.

- Sold @ MV and balancing adjustments
- Can elect to transfer at TWDV

- Transfers @ MV
- Can elect to transfer at cost

Activity 6: Incorporation

You should assume that today's date is 1 September 2020.

Harry requires advice on the CGT and VAT implications of transferring his unincorporated sole trader business to a newly incorporated company, Sausages Ltd, and how he can obtain relief for his trade losses.

Harry:

- Has been in business as an unincorporated sole trader for many years

- Receives dividends of £3,000 each year

- Has no other source of income

- Is a higher-rate taxpayer for all relevant tax years

- Will transfer all the assets and liabilities of his business to Sausages Ltd on 1 October 2020

- Will make no other disposals for CGT purposes in the tax year 2020/21

- Will be the only director and shareholder of Sausages Ltd

Harry's unincorporated business:

- At 1 October 2019 Harry has trading losses brought forward of £70,000
- In the year ending 30 September 2020, Harry's business will have a taxable trading profit of £62,000, prior to the transfer to Sausages Ltd
- Is registered for VAT

The assets and liabilities to be transferred to Sausages Ltd:

	Cost	Value at 1 October 2020
	£	£
Goodwill	0	80,000
Workshop	50,000	110,000
Machinery	10,000	8,000
Inventory	2,000	2,000
Liabilities	n/a	(10,000)

Consideration to be paid by Sausages Ltd:

- 1,000 £1 ordinary shares in respect of 85% of the total value of the consideration for the business.
- The remainder of the consideration will be left on the loan account payable by Sausages Ltd to Harry.
- Harry will withdraw cash from the loan account to pay any CGT liability arising on the transfer of the business.

Sausages Ltd:

- Will pay Harry a salary of £70,000 per year, and dividends of £10,000 on 31 March each year
- Will not be regarded as a personal service company under the provisions of the IR35 legislation

Required

1   Explain how Harry can obtain relief for the trading losses of £70,000 brought forward in his unincorporated business at 1 October 2019.

2   Explain why the transfer of Harry's business to Sausages Ltd qualifies for incorporation relief, and, on the assumption that Harry does not elect to disapply this relief, calculate the balance on his loan account with Sausages Ltd after deducting the cash to be withdrawn to pay any CGT due.

3   Advise Harry of his administrative obligations under the VAT legislation, arising from the transfer of his business to Sausages Ltd, and whether or not he is able to transfer the VAT registration from his unincorporated business to Sausages Ltd.

   Note: This part of the question is included for completeness however, you may choose to leave it until after you have studied the VAT chapter. You can assume the transfer of a going concern rules will apply for VAT purposes, but are not required to discuss these rules.

Solution

Exam focus point

Question 1 Nelson in the December 2019 exam students were asked to explain the CGT implications of retaining personal ownership of a building when a sole trader incorporated his business. This meant that incorporation relief would not be available and there would be gains on the assets transferred to the company.

3.2 Sale of business

Once a business has run its course, our individual will want to **sell it on (or perhaps retire)**. A question could focus on the tax considerations of selling the business. The tax will be different dependent on whether we have an individual selling a sole trader business or whether we have the individual selling shares in the company they set up.

The tax situation is summarised in the diagrams following. Again, VAT and stamp duty are included for completeness but will be covered in detail later in this Workbook.

3.2.1 Sale of a sole trader business

Sole trader ceases to trade:
• Closing year basis period rules, deduct overlap profits
• Stop paying IT and Class 2 and 4 NIC

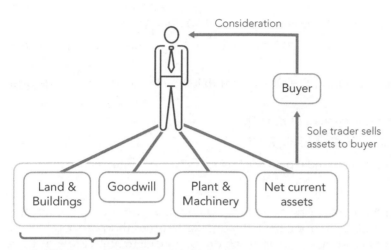

Consideration

Buyer

Sole trader sells assets to buyer

| Land & Buildings | Goodwill | Plant & Machinery | Net current assets |

• Sold with proceeds = MV
• Gives rise to gains
• SBAs claimed are added to disposal proceeds in gains calculation (if relevant)
• Gains may be taxed at 10% if BADR available
• Could also consider gift relief (if sale is for < MV)

• Sold @ MV and balancing adjustments

• Transfers @ actual proceeds

VAT: Transfer of a going concern. New commercial property and L&B OTT must have VAT charged unless purchaser OTT too. Deregister from VAT.

Stamp: SDLT paid by purchaser on MV of L&B.

IHT: Only an issue if the business if gifted, when gift is a PET. Consider availability of BPR.

If the ST business has a trade loss:
• Terminal loss relief is available
• CY and/or PY claim vs general income

3.2.2 Sale of shares in a company

Individual:
• CGT on share disposal
• 10% assuming BADR claim available
• Consider gift relief

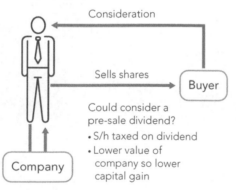

Consideration

Sells shares

Buyer

Could consider a pre-sale dividend?
• S/h taxed on dividend
• Lower value of company so lower capital gain

Company

Company:
• Continues trading
• CAs continue
• No disposals
• Trade losses stay in the company to be used in usual way

VAT: shares exempt

Stamp: Paid by purchaser at 0.5% of consideration for shares

Activity 7: Sale of a business

Amelia has carried on a business as a sole trader for many years, preparing accounts to 30 June annually. She anticipates no other taxable income in either 2021/22 or 2022/23. She has decided that she would like to cease trading and retire. She has two possible options for ceasing to trade:

Option 1: Cease to trade 31 January 2022, in which case the business will be sold to an unconnected person; or

Option 2: Continue to trade until 31 May 2022, when Amelia's daughter, Anna, will be able to take over the business.

Amelia's business:

- Has taxable trading profits of £50,000 for the year ended 30 June 2021
- Has budgeted tax-adjusted profits of £50,000 (before capital allowances) in the period ending 31 January 2022
- Has budgeted further taxable profits of £5,000 per month if Amelia continues to trade after 31 January 2022
- Has overlap profits from commencement of £15,000
- The TWDV on the main pool was £nil at 1 July 2021
- The market value of the assets in the main pool will be £4,000 at the date of cessation

Required

Advise Amelia, by reference to the increase in her trading income after tax and NIC, whether it would be beneficial for her to continue to trade until 31 May 2022, rather than ceasing to trade on 31 January 2022. You should assume any elections which are beneficial to Anna are made and support your advice with a brief explanation of the capital allowances in each case.

Note. Where necessary, you should assume that there are four weeks in each month of the years 2021 and 2022.

Solution

Exam focus point

The sale of shares in a newly incorporated company, in respect of which incorporation relief had been claimed, was tested in March 2020 Question 2 Mita. The examining team stated that 'despite the requirement only being to calculate the liability, a significant number of students also included explanations, which did not score marks. This was particularly noticeable among those who sat the computer based exam. Many included calculations in the spreadsheet, then explained the calculations in the word processing document, which was totally unnecessary, and just wasted time. The majority of students omitted to deal with the previously claimed incorporation relief, despite it being clearly flagged up in the question. It was also disappointing that many did not include gift relief, or business asset disposal relief, both of which were relevant. The different reliefs available to reduce, eliminate or defer capital gains are very frequently examined at ATX, and are regarded by the examining team as an extremely important part of the syllabus. It is therefore recommended that students take time within their revision to ensure they are familiar with the conditions required for the different relief, and then, precisely how they operate.'

Chapter summary

Owner-managed business tax planning

Starting a business

Employed versus self-employed

- Control of work
- Provision of own equipment
- Hire helpers
- Degree of financial risk
- Responsibility for investment and management
- Opportunity to profit from sound investment
- How many employers
- Contract of service – employment
- Contract for services – self-employment
- Employees
  - Can use personal or workplace pensions
  - Are liable to Class 1 NICs
  - Expenses deductible if incurred wholly, exclusively and necessarily in employment
  - Are taxed on employment income on amounts received in tax year
  - Have tax paid via PAYE
- Self-employed
  - Only personal pension available
  - Liable to Class 2 & 4 NICs
  - Expenses deductible if incurred wholly and exclusively for purposes of trade
  - Are taxed on trade profits using CYB rules
  - Pay tax through POA due 31 January and 31 July with balancing payment 31 January following the tax year

Are they trading?

- Use badges of trade
  - Subject matter
  - Frequency of transactions
  - Existence of similar transactions
  - Length of ownership
  - Organisation as trade
  - Supplementary work and marketing
  - Profit motive
  - Way in which asset sold was acquired
  - Method of finance
  - Taxpayer's intentions
- If trading – pay IT and Class 2 & 4 NICs on trade profits
- If not trading – consider CGT due

Choice of business structure (sole trade/partnership/company)

	Sole trader/ Partnership	Company
Profits	Pay income tax • Rates? • Limits? Opening year rules • Overlap profit	Pay corporation tax at 19%
Payment of tax	Payments on account	9 months and 1 day
Losses	Relief vs general income Carry forward relief Early year loss relief	Current and carry back relief Carry forward relief
Extract cash	Drawings	Salary Dividends • Consider implications to both company and individual
NIC	Classes 2 and 4	Class 1 – Employee – Employer

Choice of year end date

- If profits are rising a date early in the tax year delays the time when the profits are taxed
- Year end date affects overlap profits
- Knowing profits in advance of the end of the tax year makes planning easier

Starting a business continued

Use of trade losses

Sole trader/Partners	Company
Optional:	**Optional:**
Current year – against general income (before PA)	**Current year** – against total profits (before QCD)
Prior year – against general income (before PA)	**Prior 12 months** – against total profits (before QCD)
All or nothing	All or nothing
Can do in any order	**HAVE TO DO CY FIRST**
May be restricted	
Automatic:	**Automatic:**
Carry forward – against future **trading income** of the same trade	**Carry forward** – a **claim** must then be **made to offset some/all** of loss against future total profits
Early trading loss relief	N/A
Losses which occur within the first four tax years against **general income** (before PA) of the previous three tax years on a FIFO basis	
Terminal loss relief	**Terminal loss relief**
Loss in the last 12 months (+ overlap profits)	Loss in the last 12 months
Against **trading income**	Against total profits (before QCD)
Previous three tax years LIFO basis	Previous three tax years LIFO basis

Extraction of profit

Method	Company	Individual
Remuneration		
• Salary/ bonus	Deductible/ Class 1 NICs	Taxable/Class 1 NIC
• Benefits	Deductible/ Class 1A NICs	Taxable
Dividends	Not deductible	No tax if within dividend nil rate band. If in excess, tax at 7.5%/32.5% or 38.1% dependent on other taxable income No NICs
Loan interest	Deductible on accruals basis	Taxable as savings income if exceeds savings income nil rate band
Rental income	Deductible	Taxable as non-savings income
Pension contributions	Deductible	Tax free provided below AA

Close company issues
- A new start-up company will probably be a close company
- Once a close company is identified, watch for:
  - Loans from close company to a shareholder; or
  - Benefits provided to shareholders who are not employees

The developing business

Calculating the after-tax cost of a proposal

	£
Costs of proposal	X
Any additional employer's NIC on costs of proposal	X
Total costs (reduction in trade profits)	X
Less income tax saving on costs (reduced profits) @ 20%/40%/45%	(X)
Less Class 4 NIC saved on costs (reduced profits) @ 9%/2%	(X)
After-tax cost	X

Employee versus partner

See section *Employee versus partner* in the additional revision content

Raising finance

See section *Raising finance* in the additional revision content

Timing capital expenditure to maximise tax relief

- Spend at the end of the accounting year
- Spread spending over accounting years to avoid exceeding the AIA
- Sole traders and partnerships could consider claiming less than maximum capital allowances

Sale of the business

Incorporation

See section *Incorporation* in the additional revision content

Sale of a business

- Sale of a sole trader business
  - See section *Sale of a business* in the additional revision content
- Sale of shares in a company
  - See section *Sale of a business* in the additional revision content

Additional revision content

Employee vs partner

	Employee	Partnership
Form of remuneration	Salary Possible benefits	Share of profit (which could include an entitlement to a salary as an appropriation of profit)
Tax consequences for the original sole trader	Salary and cost of providing any benefits are extra reducing taxable trading profits. Employers NIC (and Class 1A on any benefits) will also need to be paid by the business. All these costs reduce the taxable trade profits of the sole trader and thus reduce the amount on which income tax and Class 4 NICs are calculated.	The original sole trader will have a lower share of profits to be taxed. This will therefore save income tax and Class 4 NIC.
Tax consequences for the new employee/partner	New employee pays IT on any salary and/ or bonus and employee NIC on any cash benefits received. Any non-cash benefits have no NIC consequence for the new employee.	The new partner receives a share of the partnership profits and the opening year basis period rules will apply that profit to tax years.
What if the business makes losses?	The employee's salary and employer's NIC thereon increase the size of the loss on which the original sole trader can claim loss relief. The new employee pays IT and employee's NIC on the cash salary they receive and will not benefit from any loss relief as they are not entitled to a share of the loss.	The loss will be appropriated between the two partners using the profit-sharing agreement. Each partner will be able to use their share of the loss in whatever way they choose. There will be no Class 2 nor Class 4 NIC due.

Raising finance

	Business	Investor
Debt	Pays interest Interest is tax deductible and thus saves IT (sole trader/partnership) or CT (company) Cost to the business: Interest X Less tax relief on interest (X) Net cost X A company can also get a tax deduction for any capital costs to do with the loan.	If the investor is an individual: • Pays income tax on any interest in excess of the savings nil rate band If the investor is a company: • Pays corporation tax on the interest income accrued in the year
Equity	Pays dividends No tax relief Cost to the business: Dividend X	If the investor is an individual: • Pays income tax on any dividends in excess of the dividend nil rate band If the investor is a company: • No corporation tax on dividends received

Incorporation

Sole trader ceases to trade:
- Closing year basis period rules, deduct overlap profits
- Stop paying IT and Class 2 and 4 NIC

Company starts to trade:
- Advise re filing CT returns and payment dates
- Probably a close company

VAT: Transfer of a going concern. New commercial property and L&B OTT must have VAT charged unless purchaser OTT too. Cancel/transfer VAT registration number

Stamp: Company pays SDLT on MV of L&B transferred (no SD on new share issue)

If the ST business has a trade loss:
- Terminal loss relief is available
- Trade loss can be c/f to offset against future income from the company (loss relief on incorporation)
- CY and/or PY claim vs general income

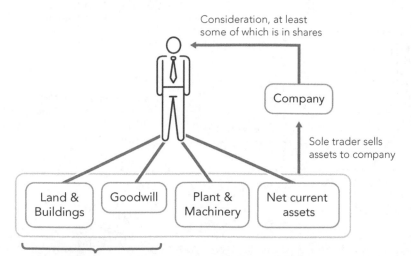

Land & Buildings
- Sold with proceeds = MV
- Gives rise to gains
- Gains can be deferred through incorporation relief if conditions met (or gift relief if not)
- Gains charged immediately may qualify for BADR
- No BADR on GW if close company
- If an SBA asset is transferred (and incorporation relief applies) SBAs are claimed by the company with no adjustment to the seller's gains calculation. On subsequent disposal of the SBA asset by the company all the SBAs claimed to date are added to proceeds.

Plant & Machinery
- Sold @ MV and balancing adjustments
- Can elect to transfer at TWDV

Net current assets
- Transfers @ MV
- Can elect to transfer at cost

Sale of a business – sale of a sole trader business

Sole trader ceases to trade:
- Closing year basis period rules, deduct overlap profits
- Stop paying IT and Class 2 and 4 NIC

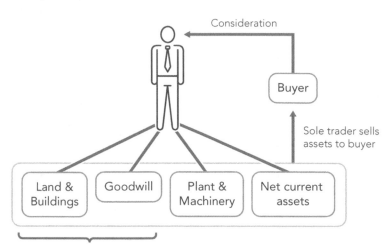

Consideration

Buyer

Sole trader sells assets to buyer

Land & Buildings | Goodwill | Plant & Machinery | Net current assets

- Sold with proceeds = MV
- Gives rise to gains
- SBAs claimed are added to disposal proceeds in gains calculation (if relevant)
- Gains may be taxed at 10% if BADR available
- Could also consider gift relief (if sale is for < MV)

- Sold @ MV and balancing adjustments

- Transfers @ actual proceeds

VAT: Transfer of a going concern. New commercial property and L&B OTT must have VAT charged unless purchaser OTT too. Deregister from VAT.

Stamp: SDLT paid by purchaser on MV of L&B.

IHT: Only an issue if the business if gifted, when gift is a PET. Consider availability of BPR.

If the ST business has a trade loss:
- Terminal loss relief is available
- CY and/or PY claim vs general income

Sale of a business – sale of shares in a company

Individual:
- CGT on share disposal
- 10% assuming BADR claim available
- Consider gift relief

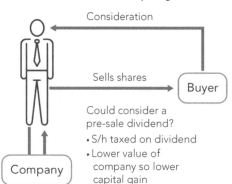

Consideration

Sells shares

Buyer

Could consider a pre-sale dividend?
- S/h taxed on dividend
- Lower value of company so lower capital gain

Company

VAT: shares exempt

Stamp: Paid by purchaser at 0.5% of consideration for shares

Company:
- Continues trading
- CAs continue
- No disposals
- Trade losses stay in the company to be used in usual way

Knowledge diagnostic

1. Employed vs self-employed

To determine whether an individual is employed/self-employed we consider: control, provision of own equipment, hire of helpers, financial risk, responsibilities, opportunity to profit and number of employers. A contract of service implies employment whereas self-employment uses a contract for services.

As an employee, an individual pays income tax on employment income and Class 1 employee's NIC. Whereas a self-employed individual pays income tax on trade profits and Class 2 and 4 NIC.

2. Badges of trade

To determine whether an individual is trading or not we use the badges of trade. It they are trading they pay income tax and Class 2 and 4 NIC. If they are not, we consider whether capital gains tax is due.

3. Sole traders

Sole trader and companies are taxed in different ways. Make sure you understand how their profits are taxed (including NICs), when they pay their tax, how they extract their profit from the business and what happens if they incur losses.

For a sole trader, choice of year end date creates tax considerations such as time between when the profits are made and when they are taxed and overlap profits.

4. Trade losses

Make sure you understand how trade losses can be offset for a sole trader and for a company. Be careful not to confuse the two. If losses are forecast, then a sole trader has more flexible loss relief available. They can offset their business trade loss against their own personal income and they also have the special opening year loss relief available.

When planning how to use a trade loss consider whether cash flow advantage is the key focus or whether it is tax saved. If cash flow advantage is important the loss should be used as quickly as possible. If it is tax savings which are important then consideration need be given to offsetting to save the highest marginal rate of tax while avoiding wasting the PA and savings and dividend nil rate bands. Offsetting the loss could also reinstate previously abated PA which would create further tax savings.

5. Extraction of profit

If the business is set up as a company, the choice of how profits are to be extracted has differing tax consequences. Make sure you can explain the consequences for both the individual and the company of extracting profit by way of remuneration, dividends, interest, rent or pension contributions.

A new small owner-managed company is likely to be a close company so make sure you look out for loans and/or benefits provided to shareholders.

6. Business development

It is important to be able to calculate the after-tax cost of a proposal. To do this we list all the costs associated with the proposal and then also the tax consequences of those costs need to be included.

You must be able to explain to a business owner the tax implications of taking on a new employee or bringing in a new partner.

You must be able to explain to a business owner the tax implications of how they can raise finance. Both consequences for the business and for the investor need to be known. Equity creates dividend payments for the company (which aren't tax deductible). The investor will be taxed on the dividends (if they are an individual). Debt creates interest payments for the business which will save tax. The investor will pay income tax on their interest income (if they are an individual).

Consider the timing of capital expenditure to maximise tax relief.

A question could focus on a business incorporating. Make sure you fully understand all the tax consequences of incorporation. Consider income tax, capital gains tax, corporation tax, VAT and stamp duty.

7. Sale of a business

Ensure you understand the ways in which a business can be sold – either by sale of a sole trade business or a share sale if the business is a company and the tax consequences of each of these.

Further study guidance

Question practice

Now try the following from the Further question practice bank (available in the digital edition of the Workbook):

- Gemma
- Ernie
- Norma
- Tax planning (although you will need to leave the VAT part until later)
- Financial planning

Further reading

There are two technical articles on the ACCA website written by members of the ATX – UK examining team which are relevant to some of the topics covered in this chapter that you should read:

- Taxation of the unincorporated business – the existing business
- Taxation of the unincorporated business – the new business

Activity answers

Activity 1: Employment vs self-employment – Lucy

> **Approach**
>
> You are expected to calculate the income tax and NIC liability for Lucy for each arrangement and then calculate her disposable income in each case, taking into account her travel costs.

Disposable income if Lucy is employee

Income tax	£
Employment income/net income	36,000
Less personal allowance	(12,500)
Taxable income	23,500

Income tax @ 20%	4,700

Class 1 NIC	£
Salary	36,000
Less employee's threshold	(9,500)
	26,500
Class 1 NIC @ 12%	3,180

Disposable income		£
Salary		36,000
Less:	Income tax	(4,700)
	Class 1 NIC	(3,180)
	Travel costs	(1,500)
		26,620

Disposable income if Lucy is self-employed

Income tax	£
Fees received	36,000
Less fixed rate mileage 4,600 @ 45p per mile	(2,070)
Trading income/net income	33,930
Less personal allowance	(12,500)
Taxable income	21,430
Income tax @ 20%	4,286

Classes 2 and 4 NIC	£	£
Class 2 NIC £3.05 × 52		159
Class 4 NIC		
Trading income	33,930	
Less lower limit	(9,500)	
	24,430	
Class 4 NIC @ 9%		2,199
Total NICs		2,358

Disposable income	
Fees received	36,000
Less: income tax	(4,286)
Classes 2 and 4 NICs	(2,358)
travel costs 4,600 @ 40p	(1,840)
	27,516

Lucy will therefore have a higher disposable income by £(27,516 – 26,620) = £896 if she undertakes the self-employed work arrangement.

Activity 2: Carrying on a trade

The tax treatment on the profit on the provision of the wedding car service will depend on whether it can be argued that Martha is carrying on a trade. If she is, then her profits will be subject to income tax.

In order to ascertain whether or not a trade is being carried on, a number of factors known as 'the badges of trade' must be considered. The most relevant factors in this care are:

- **Frequency of transactions**: Transactions will be interpreted as trading transactions where their frequency indicates the carrying on of a trade. As Martha intends to continue providing services of the wedding car and has already loaned it out on six occasions in the last six months this could indicate we have a trade.

- **Existence of similar transactions or interests**: if there is an existing trade, then a similarity to the transaction which is being considered may point to that transaction having a trading character. Martha's existing job as an estate agent is not similar to provision of a wedding car service and so this suggests it is not a trading transaction.

- **Way in which the assets were acquired**: As the car was received as an inheritance, rather than bought and financed with a loan, then the use of the car in a service is less likely to be considered a trade.

- **Supplementary work and marketing**: When work is done to make an asset more marketable, or steps are taken to find purchasers, the courts will be more ready to ascribe a trading motive. Martha has carried out supplementary work by having the seats recovered and by advertising the service it is more likely this will be considered a trade.

- **Taxpayer's intentions**: It does appear that Martha is intending to use the car to provide a service and her intention to increase the amount that she charges implies that she is trying to organise the business as a trade.

It would appear most likely that HMRC would consider that Martha is carrying on a trade with the provision of her wedding car. She will therefore be liable to pay income tax, Class 2 and Class 4 NICs based on the trade profits which she makes.

Activity 3: Choice of business structure

Option 1 – Hamish as sole trader

	£
Trading profit	60,000
Less: Income tax on trade profits (W1)	(11,500)
Class 2 NIC (W2)	(159)
Class 4 NIC (W2)	(3,845)
Net income from business	44,496

(W1) Income tax calculation

NSI

	£
Trade profits	60,000
PA	(12,500)
Taxable income	47,500
Tax: 37,500 @ 20%	7,500
10,000 @ 40%	4,000
47,500	11,500

(W2) NIC liabilities

	£
Class 2 NIC = 52 × £3.05	159
Class 4 NIC (50,000 – 9,500) @ 9%	3,645
(60,000 – 50,000) @ 2%	200
	3,845

Option 2 – Hamish forms a company ('Hamish Ltd') and pays himself a salary of £8,788 and the residue as a dividend

Hamish Ltd	£
Hamish Ltd profits	60,000
Salary to Hamish	(8,788)
Employer NIC on salary (below threshold)	Nil
Trading income (TTP)	51,212
CT liability in Hamish Ltd £51,212 × 19%	(9,730)
Maximum dividend payable to Hamish	41,482

Hamish

	£
Salary received	8,788
Dividend received	41,482
Less: Income tax (W3)	(2,751)
NIC on salary (below threshold)	Nil
NIC on dividend (N/A)	Nil
Net income from business	47,519

(W3) Income tax calculation	NSI £	Divs £
Salary	8,788	
Dividend received		41,482
PA	(8,788)	(3,712)
Taxable income	Nil	37,770

Tax:

		NSI	
2,000	@ 0% (dividend nil rate band)	0	
35,500	@ 7.5%	2,663	
270	@ 32.5%	88	
37,770			
Income tax payable		2,751	

Summary:

	£
Option 1	44,496
Option 2	47,519

Option 2 – Hamish should set up a company as this leaves him with £3,023 more money after tax than if he was a sole trader (£47,519 – £44,496).

Activity 4: Extraction of profits

Payment of bonus

Backwell Ltd will have to account for income tax and class 1 employee's and employer's national insurance under the PAYE regulations.

Sylvie will suffer deduction of income tax at the rate of 40%, and employee's NIC at the rate of 2% on the gross amount of the bonus. The gross amount payable will therefore need to be £51,724 (£30,000 × 100/ 58).

The total amount payable to HMRC by Backwell Ltd will be:

	£
Income tax on £51,524 at 40%	20,690
Employee's NIC on £51,724 at 2%	1,034
Employee's NIC on £51,724 at 13.8%	7,138
	28,862

Payment of dividend

No payments to HMRC will be required from Backwell Ltd.

Activity 5: After-tax cost of employing a part-time employee

	£
Salary	14,000
Mileage allowance £0.50 × 50 × 46	1,150
Class 1 employers NIC (W1)	735
Total additional expenditure	15,885
Less:	
Income tax higher rate saving (£15,885 × 40%)	(6,354)
Class 4 NIC saving (£15,885 × 2%)	(318)
Income tax personal allowance saving (W2) £6,942 × 40%	(2,777)
After-tax cost	6,436

Workings

1 *Class 1 NI employer's contributions*

	£
Salary £(14,000 − 8,788) × 13.8%	719
Mileage allowance £(0.50 − 0.45) × 50 × 46 × 13.8%	16
	735

2 *Personal allowance*

	Before	After
Basic personal allowance	12,500	12,500
Less: £(95,000 + 32,000 − 100,000) × 1/2	(12,500)	
Less: £(95,000 + 32,000 − 15,885 − 100,000) × 1/2		(5,558)
Personal allowance available	0	6,942

Tutorial note.

(1) The employment allowance would have already been used against the employer's NI contributions in respect of the existing employees.

(2) Only the excess mileage over 45p per mile is liable to Class 1 NIC.

(3) Ernest's (adjusted) net income before taking on the part-time employee was £127,000 so his personal allowance was reduced to £nil. After taking on the part-time employee his net income would have been reduced by the total additional expenditure of £15,885 thus entitling him to a personal allowance of £6,942. He would offset this against his non-savings (trading) income, saving income tax at a marginal rate of 40%.

BPP LEARNING MEDIA

18: Owner-managed business tax planning   **455**

Activity 6: Incorporation

1 *Reliefs available for the trading losses brought forward at 1 October 2019*

Trading losses brought forward are automatically offset against the first available future profits from the same trade. Harry will therefore offset £62,000 of the trading loss brought forward against the profit of his unincorporated business prior to its transfer to Sausages Ltd. £8,000 (£70,000 – £62,000) remains unrelieved.

However, as his business has been transferred to a company, Harry can relieve the remainder of the loss against his income from the company. The loss will be relieved against the first available income from the company, earned before unearned, which will be his salary of £35,000 (£70,000 × 6/12) in the tax year 2020/21. Harry qualifies for this relief as at least 80% of the consideration for the transfer of his business is in the form of shares. He must retain these shares until the end of 2020/21 in order to make this claim.

2 **Availability of incorporation relief and the balance on Harry's loan account**

Availability of incorporation relief

Incorporation relief will be available because:

- The business will be transferred as a going concern
- All the assets will be transferred; and
- The consideration includes shares.

Amount to be withdrawn from loan account

	£
Gain on goodwill	80,000
Gain on workshop (£110,000 – £50,000)	60,000
Total gains before relief	140,000
Less incorporation relief 85% × £140,000	(119,000)
Chargeable gains	21,000

	Gain eligible for BADR	Gains not eligible for BADR
	£	£
Gain attributable to the workshop (60/140 × 21,000)	9,000	
Gain attributable to the goodwill (80/140 × 21,000)		12,000
Less AEA (best use)	(300)	(12,000)
Taxable gains	8,700	0

Harry's CGT liability is £870 (£8,700 × 10%).

The funds left on loan account will initially be £28,500 (being 15% of the value of the net assets transferred, calculated as follows):

(15% × £190,000 (£80,000 + £110,000 + £8,000 + £2,000 – £10,000)).

The balance on Harry's loan account after deducting cash to be withdrawn to pay the CGT liability will be £27,630 (£28,500 – £870).

> **Tutorial note.** Goodwill is not a relevant asset for business asset disposal relief where it is transferred by an individual to a close company, and that individual is a related party to the close company, as is the case in this scenario.

There is no capital loss on the sale of the machinery as capital allowances will have been claimed.

3 The change in the legal status of the business from an unincorporated business to a company means that Harry is required to cancel the business's VAT registration. Sausages Ltd is required to register for VAT. The VAT registration number may be transferred from the business to Sausages Ltd, in which case Sausages Ltd will take over the rights and liabilities of the business in respect of VAT at the date of transfer.

Activity 7: Sale of a business

Cessation of trade 31 January 2022

The profits of the y/e 30 June 2021 of £50,000 will be taxed in the tax year 2021/22.

If Amelia ceases to trade on 31 January 2022, the profits of her final accounting period will also be taxed in this tax year. The tax liability in respect of the profits of the final accounting period will therefore be as follows:

	£
Tax-adjusted profit for the seven months ending 31 January 2022	50,000
Add: Balancing charge (£nil – £4,000)	4,000
Less: overlap profits	(15,000)
Taxable trading profit	39,000
Income tax (£39,000 × 40%)	15,600
Class 4 NIC (£39,000 × 2%)	780
Class 2 NIC (£3.05 × 7 × 4)	85
Total deductions	16,465

Income after tax and NIC is £33,535 (£50,000 – £16,465).

Cessation of trade on 31 May 2022

If Amelia continues to trade until 31 May 2022, the profits of her final accounting period will be taxed in 2022/23. The liability for this final period will therefore be:

	£
Tax-adjusted profit for the eleven months ending 31 May 2022 (£50,000 + 4 × £5,000)	70,000
Add: Balancing charge	Nil
Less: Overlap profits	(15,000)
Taxable trading profit	55,000
Income tax (Taxable income £42,500) (37,500 × 20% + 5,000 × 40%)	9,500
Class 4 NIC (£50,000 – £9,500) × 9% + (£55,000 – £50,000) × 2%	3,745
Class 2 NIC (£3.05 × 11 × 4)	134
Total deductions	13,379

Income after tax and NIC is £56,621 (70,000 – £13,379).

The increase in income after tax and NIC by continuing to trade until 31 May 2022 is £23,086 (£56,621 – £33,535). It is therefore beneficial for Amelia to continue to trade until that date.

Availability of capital allowances

No WDA is available in the final accounting period of a business. A balancing adjustment will, however, arise on the disposal of the assets. The sale proceeds will exceed the tax written down value of the assets at the start of the final period, so a balancing charge will arise.

If the sale is delayed until 31 May 2022, and the business is transferred to Anna, then as Amelia and Anna are connected persons, a succession election can be made to transfer the plant and machinery to Anna at its written down value at 31 May 2022 thereby avoiding the balancing charge.

Skills checkpoint 4

Owner-managed business tax advice

Chapter overview

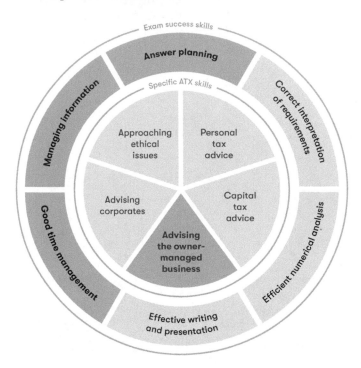

Introduction

The ATX exam could have a question which considers an owner-managed business (OMB).

In the Owner-managed business planning chapter, we have considered some of the types of scenarios that we could see in the exam. In this skills checkpoint we consider both the exam success skills and the specific ATX skills on owner-managed business tax advice that we shall need in order to be successful.

It is important that we use our exam technique skills to successfully interpret the requirement and apply our knowledge to the specifics from the scenario when we answer the question.

It is important that you refresh your memory using the **technical knowledge** presented in this Workbook before you attempt more exam standard questions.

Skills checkpoint 4: Owner-managed business tax advice

ATX Owner-managed business tax advice

The key steps in applying this skill are outlined below. They will be explained in more detail in the following sections, and illustrated by answering requirements from a past exam question.

STEP 1 Look at the mark allocation and calculate the amount of time available for the question.

STEP 2 Read the requirements and analyse them.

STEP 3 Read the scenario and highlight and/or make notes of the information that will enable you to answer the requirements.

STEP 4 Make a plan of the points that you need to cover in your answer, including what supporting calculations you will need to do.

STEP 5 Write up your answer using key words from the requirements as headings.

Exam success skills

The following illustration is based on a 16-mark extract from an exam question, Meg and Laurie, which appeared in the Sep/Dec 2017 sample questions.

- **Managing information.** In this question it is particularly important that you apply your technical knowledge to the specifics in the scenario. For example, knowing Meg and Laurie's taxable income in each relevant tax year will be important in determining the tax saving a loss offset will generate.

- **Answer planning: priorities, structure and logic.** It is important in the planning stage of this question that you think about how you are going to present your answer and your calculations.

- **Good time management.** ATX questions are usually divided into parts and sometimes sub-parts. You must make sure that you only spend about 1.95 minutes per mark in each part. In this question you need to make sure you leave at least half your time to answer (b)(ii).

Skill activity

STEP 1 Look at the mark allocation and calculate the amount of time available for the question.

Required

(a) (i) Calculate the taxable trading profit of MT Travel for each of the tax years 2020/21 and 2021/22 before considering relief for the anticipated trading loss of the tax year 2022/23.

3 marks

(ii) Identify and explain ONE practical tax disadvantage of MT Travel having a 31 March year end, rather than a 31 December year end.

2 marks

(b) (i) Calculate the allowable trading loss available to each of Meg and Laurie for the tax year 2022/23 if Laurie becomes an employee, or, alternatively, a partner in MT Travel on 1 April 2022.

3 marks

(ii) Advise Meg and Laurie of the alternative ways in which their respective trading losses as calculated in (b)(i) could be used depending on whether Laurie is taken on as an employee or as a partner, and state the rate at which income tax would be saved in each case.

8 marks

This is a 16-mark question and at 1.95 minutes per mark it should take 31 minutes. You will need to break your time down across each sub-requirement as follows:

- 6 minutes for (a)(i) and 4 minutes for (a)(ii)
- 6 minutes for (b)(i) and 16 minutes for (b)(ii)

You may prefer to spend 10 minutes or so at the start of the question reading and planning leaving the remaining 21 minutes to write up your answer – if you do so then make sure you leave plenty of time for (b)(ii), as at 8 marks it is half of this question.

STEP 2 Read the requirements and analyse them.

Required

(a) (i) Calculate[99] the taxable trading profit of MT Travel for each[100] of the tax years 2020/21 and 2021/22 before[101] considering relief for the anticipated trading loss of the tax year 2022/23.

3 marks

(ii) **Identify and explain**[102] **ONE practical tax disadvantage**[103] of MT Travel having a 31 March year end, rather than a 31 December year end.

2 marks

(b) (i) **Calculate**[104] the allowable trading loss available to **each**[105] of Meg and Laurie for the tax year 2022/23 **if Laurie becomes an employee, or, alternatively, a partner**[106] in MT Travel on 1 April 2022.

3 marks

(ii) **Advise**[107] **Meg and Laurie of the alternative ways in which their respective trading losses as calculated in (b)(i) could be used depending on whether Laurie is taken on as an employee or as a partner**[108], **and**[109] state the rate at which income tax would be saved in each case.

8 marks

The verbs here are to 'calculate', 'identify', 'explain' and 'advise'.

'Calculate' means to ascertain by computation or to make an estimate of or to evaluate or perform a mathematical process. The ACCA examiners have said that you should make sure you provide description along with numerical calculations.

'Identify' means to recognise and 'explain' means to make an idea clear, show how a concept is developed or give the reason for an event. The ACCA examining team say don't just provide a list of points- add some explanation to the points you're discussing.

[99] Verb - see ACCA guidance.

[100] So there are two calculations of trade profit here- one for each tax year

[101] Follow this advice- it's just a trade profit calculation we're being asked for.

[102] Verbs - see ACCA guidance.

[103] You only need ONE point here- there's no extra marks available for more. If you come up with several ideas pick your best. There will be 1 mark for identifying the disadvantage and then 1 mark for your explanation.

[104] Verb - see ACCA guidance.

[105] You will need to perform calculations of the allowable loss for BOTH Meg AND Laurie.

[106] So there are actually 4 calculations here - for EACH of Meg and Laurie we need to calculate their loss IF Laurie is an employee AND IF he is a partner - so 4 calculations here for 3 marks - we will need to be quick.

[107] Verb - see ACCA guidance.

[108] Make sure you use headings to talk about how Meg can use her loss and then discuss Laurie separately. Even if the loss is of a different amount the loss claims will be the same so you should be able to consider whether a different sized loss makes a difference as you work the detail.

[109] It's really important that when we advise on how the loss can be used that we apply our relief to the specifics of the question and state the rate at which IT will be saved.

'Advise' means to offer guidance or some relevant expertise to allow the recipient to make a more informed decision.

In (a)(i) it will be important that we clearly produce two calculations of taxable trading profit for each of the two tax years. As discussed above in (a)(ii) we will only need to pick one tax disadvantage of a 31 March year end rather than 31 December. The two marks will be for identifying **and** explaining it.

In (b)(i) we need to explain our calculations of the loss for each of Meg and Laurie for **each** of whether Laurie is an employee or partner – so we need four calculations.

In (b)(ii) we have we should make sure we consider the loss claims separately for Meg and Laurie. Even if the losses are of a different size then same claims are possible.

STEP 3 Read the scenario and highlight and/or make notes of the information that will enable you to answer the requirements.

You should assume today's date is 1 December 2021.

Meg is an unincorporated sole trader. She requires advice regarding a planned change of accounting date and bringing her husband into the business, either as an employee or as a partner.

Meg:

- Is 60 years old and is married to Laurie

- Owns an unincorporated sole trader business, MT Travel

- Has rental income of £8,600[110] each year in addition to any profits from MT Travel

> [110] If Meg makes a trade loss her other income is covered by the PA - no tax saving of loss offset!

MT Travel:

- Was set up by Meg on 1 January 2016[111]

- Has had accounts prepared to 31 December annually

> [111] So there will have been 3 months of overlap (1/1/16-5/4/16)

- Generated overlap profits of £7,400[112] on commencement

> [112] May need to use on change of accounting date basis period rules.

- Meg will change its accounting date to 31 March by preparing accounts for the 15 months ending 31 March 2022[113]

MT Travel – recent and forecast tax-adjusted trading profits:

	£
Year ended 31 December 2020	17,000
15 months ending 31 March 2022	9,000

Note. YE 31 December 2020 is taxed in 20/21. The 15 months ending 31 March 2022 will be taxed in 21/22 but will be 15 months, so deduct the 3 month overlap.

MT Travel – the future:

From 1 April 2022, Meg's husband, Laurie, will start to participate in the business.

Meg will either:

(a) employ Laurie part-time, paying him an annual salary of £12,000[114], the commercial rate for the work he will perform; or

(b) admit Laurie into the business as a partner[115], sharing profits and losses in the ratio 75% to Meg, and 25% to Laurie[116].

The business is expected to generate a tax-adjusted trading loss in the tax year 2022/23 of £20,000[117], before making any payment to Laurie.

The business is expected to become profitable again in the tax year 2023/24[118] and thereafter, but profits are not expected to exceed £30,000 per year for the foreseeable future.

Laurie:

- Is 63 years old

- Was employed for many years by Hagg Ltd, earning gross annual remuneration of £60,000[119], until 31 March 2021

- Has received annual dividends of £18,000[120] for many years. This is currently his only source of taxable income

STEP 4 Make a plan of the points that you need to cover in your answer, including what supporting calculations you will need to do.

You could use a mind map similar to the one below or alternatively you could use a bullet point list or simply annotate the question.

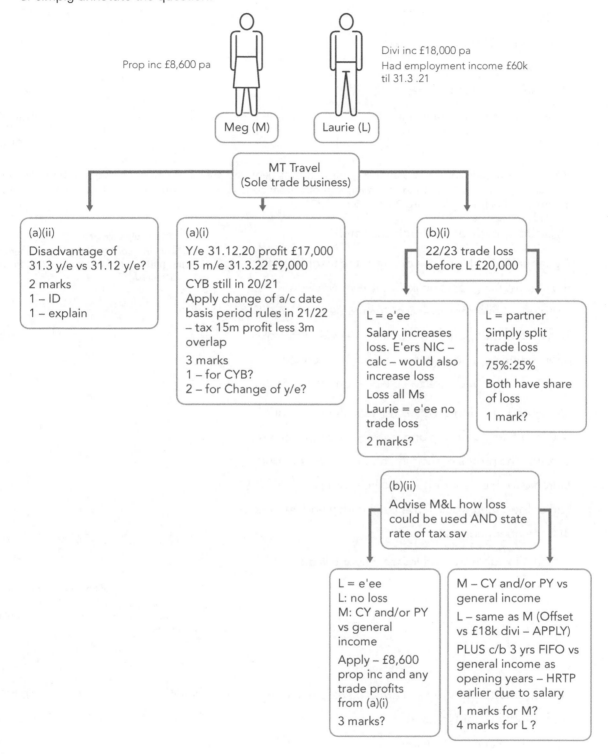

Prop inc £8,600 pa

Meg (M)

Divi inc £18,000 pa
Had employment income £60k
til 31.3 .21

Laurie (L)

MT Travel
(Sole trade business)

(a)(ii)
Disadvantage of
31.3 y/e vs 31.12 y/e?
2 marks
1 – ID
1 – explain

(a)(i)
Y/e 31.12.20 profit £17,000
15 m/e 31.3.22 £9,000
CYB still in 20/21
Apply change of a/c date
basis period rules in 21/22
– tax 15m profit less 3m
overlap
3 marks
1 – for CYB?
2 – for Change of y/e?

(b)(i)
22/23 trade loss
before L £20,000

L = e'ee
Salary increases
loss. E'ers NIC –
calc – would also
increase loss
Loss all Ms
Laurie = e'ee no
trade loss
2 marks?

L = partner
Simply split
trade loss
75%:25%
Both have share
of loss
1 mark?

(b)(ii)
Advise M&L how loss
could be used AND state
rate of tax sav

L = e'ee
L: no loss
M: CY and/or PY
vs general
income
Apply – £8,600
prop inc and any
trade profits
from (a)(i)
3 marks?

M – CY and/or PY vs
general income
L – same as M (Offset
vs £18k divi – APPLY)
PLUS c/b 3 yrs FIFO vs
general income as
opening years – HRTP
earlier due to salary
1 marks for M?
4 marks for L ?

STEP 5 Write up your answer using key words from the requirements as headings.

(a) (i) **Taxable trading profit**

	£
2020/21	
Year ended 31 December 2020	17,000
2021/22	
15 months ended 31 March 2022	9,000
Less: Relief for overlap profits	(7,400)
	1,600

Note. Present your answer to clearly lay out which tax year you are considering. As Meg has changed her accounting date to 31 March, all the overlap profits from commencement are relieved. This represents three months' profits from 1 January 2016 to 5 April 2016.

(ii) **Disadvantage of 31 March year end**[121]

A year end of 31 March means that the taxable profit for the current tax year is unlikely to be known with certainty until after the end of the tax year on 5 April. This means that payments to be made within the tax year – such as a payment on account or pension contributions – will have to be based on estimates.

A year end of 31 March gives the minimum interval between earning profits and paying the associated tax liability. The profits earned in January, February and March of any calendar year will be taxed one year earlier than they would have been if Meg had retained a 31 December year end.

[121] You would only need ONE disadvantage. A couple are given here to give you ideas of what you might have considered.

(b) (i) **Allowable trading losses if Laurie is an employee**[122]

[122] Note the use of headings - if Laurie is an employee and if Laurie is a partner - to make sure you show clearly what you are discussing.

	£
Tax adjusted trading loss in 2022/23 before any payment to Laurie	20,000
Add: Salary paid to Laurie	12,000
Employer's NIC (Note)	0
Allowable trading loss for Meg in 2022/23	32,000

Note. You mustn't forget to consider Class 1 NIC when you see an employee in a scenario! You need to pick this up at the planning stage.

Laurie[123] will not have an allowable trading loss in this case as the whole trade loss will be Meg's as the sole trader.

Note. Laurie's salary of £12,000 each year is an allowable expense for Meg's business. No Class 1 employer's national insurance contributions (NIC) will be payable in respect of this as they will be covered by the £4,000 annual employment allowance.

Allowable trading losses if Laurie is a partner

	Total	Meg	Laurie
	£	£	£
Tax-adjusted trading loss (allocated 75:25)	20,000	15,000	5,000

(ii) Loss relief available to Meg

In the tax year 2022/23 Meg has an allowable loss of £32,000, if Laurie is taken on as an employee, and £15,000, if Laurie becomes a partner.

Loss relief is available against Meg's total income of 2022/23 and/or 2021/22. In 2022/23 Meg's only income will be £8,600 rental income[124]. In 2021/22 her income will include a taxable trading profit of £1,600 (see part (a)(i)) in addition to the rental income of £8,600. In both these tax years her total income is covered by her personal allowance for the year, and therefore a loss relief claim will not result in any tax saving in either year.[125]

Alternatively, the full amount of the loss can be carried forward for relief against the first available future profits from the same trade, which are expected to occur in 2023/24. The maximum rate of relief will be 20% on the amount of Meg's taxable income (all non-savings), which falls within the basic rate band.

Loss relief available to Laurie

If Laurie becomes a partner in the business, he will have an allowable trading loss of £5,000 in 2022/23.

[123] An easy 1/2 mark if you remembered that you were asked about Meg AND Laurie!

[124] Note that it's important that we have application to the specifics from the scenario to score good marks here.

[125] Make sure you clearly state the tax saved with the loss claim - the question specifically asked for it so you must provide it.

His total income in each of the tax years 2022/23 and 2021/22 is £18,000, which is wholly dividend income, so he could relieve the loss in either year resulting in tax being saved at the rate of 7.5%[126] in respect of the dividends in excess of his personal allowance and dividend nil rate band.

As 2022/23 is the tax year of commencement[127] of business for Laurie, he can carry back the loss against his total income of the three tax years prior to the loss-making year on a first in, first out (FIFO) basis, giving relief first in 2019/20. Accordingly, he can offset the loss against his total income of 2019/20, when he was employed. This will result in a tax saving at the rate of 40%[128] as the loss will be relieved against his employment income, and Laurie was a higher rate taxpayer in 2019/20.

[126] Again, make sure you tailor specifically to the scenario - Laurie only has dividend income so show you know that.

[127] This special loss claim should have been spotted in your planning time.

[128] As specifically requested - make sure you state the rate of tax saved.

Examining team's comments and mark scheme

Examining team's comments

This question concerned an unincorporated business which was about to change its accounting date, and which was anticipating a trading loss in a future period.

The first part concerned the tax implications of a change of accounting date for an unincorporated business. Unfortunately, relatively few candidates appeared to be aware of the assessment rules on a change of accounting date, so this part was not done well. However, many candidates were able to identify and explain a disadvantage of choosing an accounting date which fell later in the tax year.

The second part of this question required a calculation of the loss available to the trader, and their spouse, on the basis that firstly, the spouse became an employee of the business, or, secondly, the spouse became a partner in the business. In general this was done well. Candidates were then required to go on and advise both taxpayers as to the reliefs available for their losses. The rules relating to trading losses are frequently examined, and while many candidates scored reasonably here, more precise answers would have scored higher marks. Candidates would do well to invest time at the revision stage of their studies to memorising the rules concerning relief for trading losses, and ensuring that they are able to recognise those rules which apply in a given scenario. In particular, they should be able to identify those which apply in certain situations only, such as the opening years of a business, which was applicable to just one of the partners here.

Those candidates who scored well on this particular part:

- Adopted a structured approach to outlining the reliefs for the trading loss separately for each of the individuals, and clearly stating the rate of tax saved, as required
- Didn't waste time considering irrelevant reliefs

Mark scheme   Marks

(a) (i)   Taxable trading profits   3

   (ii) Tax planning disadvantage   2

(b) (i)   Laurie as employee – loss available to Meg   2

                  – no loss available to Laurie   ½

       Laurie as a partner – split of loss in PSR   1

Max   3

   (ii) Loss relief available to Meg   5

       Loss relief available to Laurie   4½

Max   8

Exam success skills diagnostic

Every time you complete a question, use the diagnostic below to assess how effectively you demonstrated the exam success skills in answering the question. The table has been completed below for Meg and Laurie to give you an idea of how to complete the diagnostic.

Exam success skills	Your reflections/observations
Good time management	Did you leave about half of your time for (b)(ii) or did you overrun early in the question? It is important to keep moving and spend the right amount of time on each sub-requirement.
Managing information	Did you pick up on all the information you needed to satisfactorily answer the requirements? For example, did you correctly consider Meg and Laurie's income in different tax years to apply the saved tax rate as specifically asked in the question? Did you remember the overlap profits when using your change of year end basis period rules?
Correct interpretation of requirements	Have you fully answered each sub-requirement?
Answer planning	Did you pick up the tax technical points correctly and ensure you had planned to answer each part of the requirement? Did you brainstorm the different loss reliefs to make sure you got breadth in your answer? Did you spot the employer's NIC consideration if Laurie is employed?
Effective writing and presentation	Did you use headings/ subheadings to show clearly which part of the question or which tax year you were dealing with? Re-read your answer; does it make sense? Were your calculations clear?
Efficient numerical analysis	Did you pick up all the relevant information in the scenario, for example did you correctly identify Meg and Laurie's income in the relevant tax years to be able to work out the tax rate saved if the loss was offset?
Most important action points to apply to your next question	

Exam success skills	Your reflections/observations

Summary

Strong technical knowledge plays a vital role in exam success. However, it is important that you are able to apply that knowledge specifically to the scenario to ensure that you are gaining sufficient marks. It is also important that in your planning time that you brainstorm and make sure you get breadth in your answer; for example, did you spot the employer's NIC and did you consider all the relevant loss reliefs including the opening year loss claim for Laurie?

19 Corporate groups and consortia

Learning objectives

On completion of this chapter, you should be able to:

	Syllabus reference no.
Remember the material already covered in Taxation (TX – UK) under the heading of 'the effect of a group corporate structure for corporation tax purposes'	A4(a) E5
Advise on the allocation of the annual investment allowance between group or related companies	A4(e)(i)
Advise on the tax consequences of a transfer of intangible assets	A4(e)(ii)
Advise on the tax consequences of a transfer of a trade and assets where there is common control	A4(e)(iii)
Understand the meaning of consortium-owned company and consortium member	A4(e)(iv)
Advise on the operation of consortium relief	A4(e)(v)
Determine pre-entry losses and understand their tax treatment	A4(e)(vi)
Determine the degrouping charge where a company leaves a group within six years of receiving an asset by way of a no gain/no loss transfer	A4(e)(vii)
Determine the effects of the anti-avoidance provisions, where arrangements exist for a company to leave a group	A4(e)(viii)

Exam context

So far, we have studied the corporation tax rules for single companies. In this chapter we consider the extent to which tax law recognises group relationships between companies.

Companies in a group are still separate entities with their own tax liabilities but tax law recognises the close relationship between group companies. They can, if they meet certain conditions, share their losses and pass assets between each other without chargeable gains.

Consortium companies are companies which are controlled by several companies. They can also share their losses, but the rules are restricted to recognise the ownership shares of the controlling companies.

Groups and consortia are likely to be examined at most sittings. You must understand the difference between the definitions of a 75% group for group relief and a chargeable gains group, and understand the definition of a consortium. The question is likely to require a consideration of the various reliefs specifically available in group situations, with a view to minimising the group's tax liability.

Chapter overview

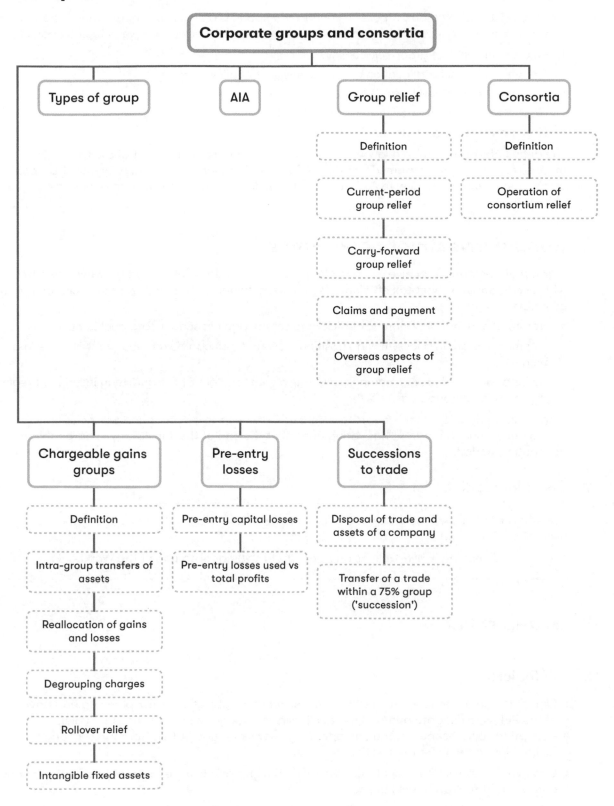

1 Types of group

A group exists for taxation purposes where one company is a subsidiary of another. Different tax consequences exist dependent upon the degree of control that exists between the companies.

There are four types of group relationship:

- Common control for allocation of annual investment allowance (AIA)
- 75% groups for group loss relief
- Consortia – not examined in Taxation (TX – UK)
- 75% groups for capital gains

The definitions of the group relationships (apart from consortia) and most of the tax implications of these relationships is assumed knowledge from the Taxation (UK) exam. However, there are certain aspects that are new to ATX, such as the implications of overseas companies in a group structure.

2 Annual investment allowance

A **group of companies receive a single AIA**. However, this can be **allocated between them in whatever manner is most tax efficient**. The following factors may be relevant in deciding how to allocate the AIA:

- Nature of expenditure (more tax efficient to set AIA against special rate pool items)
- If companies are in a loss-making position, how that loss can be relieved (AIA will make loss bigger)
- Lower augmented profits may possibly take a company out of the quarterly instalment regime, improving the group's cash flow

A group of companies for this purpose is defined in relation to a parent and will include subsidiaries where the parent has **voting control at the end of the subsidiary's chargeable accounting period**.

Essential reading

See Chapter 19 of the Essential reading for more detail on the definition of a group for the allocation of the AIA.

The Essential reading is available as an Appendix of the digital edition of the Workbook.

3 Group relief

PER alert

One of the competencies required to fulfil Performance objective 17 Tax planning and advice of the PER is to mitigate and/or defer tax liabilities through the use of standard reliefs, exemptions and incentives. You can apply the knowledge you obtain from this section of the text to help to demonstrate this competence.

Group relief allows UK resident members of a 75% group to transfer **current accounting period and brought forward** losses to each other.

3.1 Definition

> **Group relief group (75% group):** A 75% group is established where:
> - **One company is a 75% subsidiary of another**, or
> - **Both companies are 75% subsidiaries of the same parent company.**

For a company to be a 75% subsidiary, the parent must:
- Own at least 75% of the ordinary share capital
- Be entitled to at least 75% of the subsidiary's assets on a winding up, and
- Be entitled to at least 75% of the subsidiary's income on a distribution

Any **sub-subsidiaries** are only 75% group members if the **ultimate parent's effective interest is at least 75%**. Overseas resident companies can help to establish a group, but generally cannot participate in group relief.

Essential reading

See Chapter 19 of the Essential reading for an example of a group structure and all the relevant group relationships.

The Essential reading is available as an Appendix of the digital edition of the Workbook.

3.2 Current-period group relief

3.2.1 Operation of the relief

A company with a **current period loss** may transfer **all or part** of this loss to another member of the 75% group.

The company with the loss is referred to as the **surrendering company**. The following types of loss can be surrendered:
- **Trade losses**
- **Non-trading deficits on loan relationships**
- **Excess qualifying charitable donations***
- **Excess management expenses (investment companies)***
- **Excess property losses***
- **Excess non-trading losses on intangible fixed assets***

Any amount of the loss can be surrendered, and there is **no need to offset trading losses or non-trade loan relationship deficits against the surrendering company's own profits first**. The remaining types of loss marked with an asterisk (*) above, may **only be surrendered to the extent that they exceed the surrendering company's own profits of the accounting period** (the 'excess' amount).

The company receiving the loss is referred to as the **claimant company**.

The claimant company sets the loss against its **taxable total profits** of the **same** period as the surrendering company's loss-making period.

These taxable total profits must be reduced by its own current period losses and losses brought forward, even if it does not claim loss relief against total profits for those losses. Group relief is given before relief for any losses carried back.

Essential reading

See Chapter 19 of the Essential reading for an example of available profits and losses.

The Essential reading is available as an Appendix of the digital edition of the Workbook.

3.2.2 Corresponding accounting periods

If the accounting period of a surrendering company and a claimant company are **non-coterminous**, both profits and loss must be **time-apportioned**, so that only the results of the **corresponding period** may be offset. Apportionment is on a time basis.

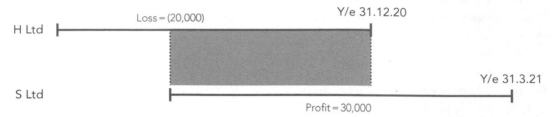

The maximum group relief in the overlapping period is the lower of:

9/12 × £(20,000) and

9/12 × £30,000

ie £15,000

Note that the remaining £5,000 loss could be surrendered to S Ltd in its year ended 31.3.20.

Similar provisions also apply when a company either **joins or leaves a group**; the relevant profit and surrenderable loss for the period a company **joins** a group runs from the **date of the share acquisition**.

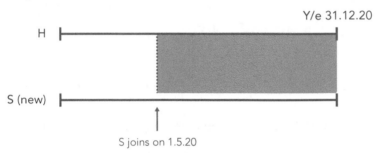

Group relief would only be available for the post-acquisition period, so both the loss and profit would be time apportioned by 8/12.

When a company **leaves** a group, the group relief group is deemed to end when **'arrangements' are in place for the subsidiary to be sold**. 'Arrangements for sale' generally means that negotiations have taken place and an offer has been accepted.

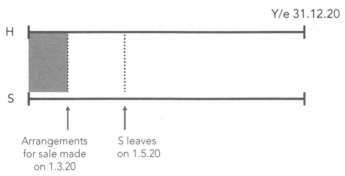

Group relief would only be available until arrangements for sale were in place, ie until 28 February.

3.2.3 Planning considerations and exam approach – group relief

> **Exam focus point**
>
> **ACCA's article Corporation tax – group relief for Advanced Taxation (ATX – UK),** written by a member of the Advanced Taxation (ATX – UK) examining team, considers a number of group relief tax planning issues that could be introduced in an exam question.

When **planning** where to use the available group losses, the following considerations are relevant:

- **Removing** companies from the **quarterly instalment regime** to delay payment of corporation tax and **improve the cash flow** position of the group
- Using losses **as early as possible** to obtain a **cash flow advantage** – consider a current year and carry back claim within the surrendering company to generate refunds of corporation tax
- **Avoiding unrelieved QCDs**

In the exam we suggest the following approach to a group planning scenario:

(a) **Identify what group relationships exist** in the group structure
(b) **Set out income/qualifying charitable donations** (QCDs) of each company
(c) Leave **gaps** for loss reliefs (current year and carry back, carry forward, group relief)
(d) Put losses/excess qualifying charitable donations in **loss memo**
(e) **Discuss options for loss and recommend appropriately**

Activity 1: Current-period group relief tax planning

K plc has one 75% subsidiary, L plc. The results for the group are as follows:

	Y/e 31/3/21	Y/e 31/3/21	Y/e 31/3/20
	K plc	L plc	L plc
	£	£	£
Trading profit/(loss)	(4,000)	(20,700)	0
Non-trading loan relationship income	10,000	2,900	6,200
Chargeable gain	15,000	0	15,000
QCDs	(2,000)	(3,200)	(1,000)

Required

What are the options for L plc to use its loss, assuming it does not want to carry the loss forward? Consider which option would be most beneficial.

Solution

BPP LEARNING MEDIA

3.3 Carry forward group relief

3.3.1 Operation of the relief

A company with a **loss carried forward** may transfer **all or part of this loss** to another member of the 75% group.

A company can surrender **any amount of carried forward**:

- **Trading losses**
- **Property losses**
- **NTLR deficits, and**
- **Management expenses**

To other group companies under **carry forward group relief**. However, unlike current period-group relief, these can **only** be surrendered if the company **cannot deduct them from its own total profits for the current period.**

The claimant company must use its own losses to the fullest extent possible in working out the available taxable total profits to receive the carry forward group relief. Carry forward group relief is given after all other reliefs for the current period but before any relief for any losses carried back.

Activity 2: Carry forward group relief

X plc has one 75% subsidiary, Y plc. The results for the group for the year ended 31 March 2021 are as follows:

	X plc	Y plc
	£	£
Trading profit	45,000	62,000
Trading loss carried forward at 1 April 2020	(4,000)	(150,000)
Non-trading loan relationship income	5,000	6,000
Non-trading loan relationship debit brought forward at 1 April 2020	(500)	(4,000)
Chargeable gain	15,000	20,000

Required

What is the maximum carry forward group relief that X plc can claim from Y plc?

Solution

3.3.2 Overlapping accounting periods

Losses surrendered under carry forward group relief must be set against profits of an **overlapping accounting period.** This is similar to the rules about corresponding accounting periods discussed earlier in this chapter.

The **overlapping period** is the period which **falls within both of the following:**

- The accounting period to which the **surrendering company has carried forward the loss,** and
- The accounting period in which the **claimant company will offset the loss**

3.4 Claims and payment for group relief

Claims for group relief must be made within **two years of the end of the claimant company's profit-making accounting period.** If the surrendering company is also claiming current-period or carry back relief, the group relief claim must be submitted first.

Intra-group payments for losses are ignored for corporation tax purposes.

3.5 Overseas aspects of group relief

75% UK subsidiaries of a holding company that is resident anywhere in the world can transfer trading losses to each other.

Group relief extends to **UK branches of overseas companies,** as long as the profits of the branch are within the scope of UK corporation tax.

4 Consortia

4.1 Definition of a consortium

> **Consortium:** A relationship where **two or more companies own 5%–74.99% of the shares in another company.**

A consortium is established in the following circumstances:

- **Two or more** companies (the **'consortium members'**) together **own at least 75%** of the ordinary share capital of another company (the **'consortium company'**).
- **Each** consortium member has **at least 5%** of the share capital, together with the same rights to profits and assets in a distribution.
- **No individual consortium member owns more than 75%** of the consortium company.

A and B are the consortium members (CM)

C is the consortium owned company (CC)

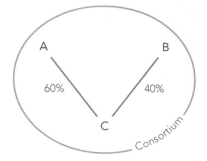

4.2 Operation of consortium relief

Losses can flow **between the consortium company and its consortium members in either direction** (but **not between the consortium members**). Losses can also be surrendered to and from any 90% trading subsidiaries of a consortium company to the members of the consortium.

However, the **maximum consortium relief** claim is the **lower** of:

- The **consortium member's 'result'**, and
- The **consortium members percentage interest in the consortium company multiplied by the consortium company's 'result'**.

Thus a 20% consortium member could claim up to 20% of a consortium company's losses (subject to its available TTP) or could cover up to 20% of a consortium company's TTP with its losses.

The losses which can be offset through consortium relief are the **same as those which can be group-relieved** and this includes carried-forward losses.

If the consortium company (or its 90% subsidiary) is the surrendering company, losses are deemed to be relieved in the surrendering company (even if no claim is actually made) before any remaining loss can be consortium-relieved up to a consortium member.

 ### Activity 3: Consortium relief

S Ltd is owned by the following companies:

A Ltd   30%

B Ltd   30%

C Ltd   20%

D Ltd   20%

S has a trading loss of £1 million, and a chargeable gain of £200,000. A Ltd has profits of £500,000.

Required

What is the maximum consortium relief claim possible by A Ltd?

Solution

Activity 4: Consortium relief – loss in consortium member

S Ltd is owned by the following companies:

A Ltd   30%

B Ltd   30%

C Ltd   20%

D Ltd   20%

S has a trading profit of £400,000, and a chargeable gain of £100,000. A Ltd has a trading loss of £100,000.

Required

What is the maximum consortium relief claim possible by S Ltd?

Solution

5 Chargeable gains groups

5.1 Definition

KEY TERM

Chargeable gains group: Established when:

- An ultimate parent company **owns ≥75%** of a subsidiary's share capital, rights to profits and assets, or
- **Two subsidiaries are owned ≥75% by the same parent company.**

Sub-subsidiaries are included if the ultimate parent has an **effective interest of at least 50%.** Chargeable gains groups can be **established through companies resident anywhere in the world. It is also extended to UK branches of overseas companies** (if the asset remains in the UK tax net).

5.2 Intra-group transfers

Capital assets are automatically transferred between group members at a **no gain/no loss price (NG/NL)** (ie indexed cost).

If an SBA asset is transferred between group members the transferee is treated as if it had always owned the asset. The transferee claims SBAs based on the original eligible cost and the transferor does not add SBAs claimed to date to their disposal proceeds. On a subsequent sale of the SBA asset by the transferee, all the SBAs claimed to date (by both the transferor and transferee) are added to the proceeds in the transferee's gains calculation.

Intangible fixed assets are also transferred on a **'tax-neutral'** basis, ie at tax written-down value.

5.3 Reallocation of gains and losses

Any part of a gain or loss arising in an accounting period can be transferred between group companies. The election must be made within two years of the end of the accounting period of the company within which the relevant disposal took place.

This enables two tax planning opportunities:

- Chargeable gains and capital losses within a group can be '**matched**', or offset, to minimise corporation tax for the group. However, remember that if a company has large capital losses brought forward that the amount available for offset against gains is restricted to the 'part of the £5 million deduction allowance allocated to that company and capital losses' plus 50% of the gains in excess of that amount. You only need an awareness of this restriction in your ATX exam.

- **Gains arising in companies which pay by quarterly instalments can be reallocated to smaller companies**, in order to reduce the instalments and improve the group's cash flow.

5.4 Degrouping charges

5.4.1 Circumstances where a degrouping charge may arise

A **degrouping charge** may arise where an asset has been transferred on **a no-gain, no-loss (NG/NL) basis** between companies in a chargeable gains group, and within **six years of the transfer, shares in the recipient company are sold**, such that it leaves the gains group, whilst **still owning the asset** transferred to it.

> **Exam focus point**
>
> Be careful when deciding whether the degrouping charge applies. It applies where there is a **sale of the shares in the company,** as a result of which the company leaves the group. It does **not apply where a company simply sells its assets** to another company.

5.4.2 Calculation and taxation

The **degrouping gain (or loss)** is calculated by assuming the recipient company disposed of, and immediately reacquired, the asset at the date of the NG/NL transfer for its market value at that time. In other words, it **is the gain or loss avoided by the application of the NG/NL rule.**

The degrouping gain (or loss) is **added to (or deducted from) the proceeds received on the sale of the shares that led to the recipient company leaving the group.** If the relevant conditions are met, the **substantial shareholdings exemption** may apply to this share disposal, and this would also exempt the degrouping charge from tax.

> **Exam focus point**
>
> The degrouping charge was tested in December 2012 Question 1 Flame plc group. The examining team commented that: 'The degrouping charge was done well on the whole. Those candidates who did not do so well were divided into two groups. The first group missed the degrouping charge altogether. The second group of candidates knew that there would be a degrouping charge somewhere in the answer and earned most of the marks available for saying why and for calculating it. However, they did not know which of the two possible transactions (a sale of a group company's shares or a sale of its assets) would give rise to the charge, and either put it into the wrong section of the report or put it into both sections. This was not particularly costly but would have been in a different question which was only concerned with one of these two transactions. Candidates must know their stuff; degrouping charges only occur on the sale of a company, ie on the sale of shares, and not on the sale of assets.'

5.5 Rollover relief

A chargeable gains group is treated as one unit for the purpose of rollover relief. This means that if one company generates a gain on a qualifying asset, and another invests in a new qualifying asset within the usual reinvestment period, the gain can be deferred. This requires a joint election, and must involve a purchase of a new asset from outside the group.

Activity 5: Chargeable gains groups

Ibiza Ltd owns 90% of Benidorm Ltd. These shares were purchased for £300,000 in February 2008. In June 2015 Ibiza Ltd transferred a building to Benidorm Ltd for £100,000. On this date its market value was £360,000 and it had cost Ibiza Ltd £150,000 in April 2000.

Assume the following indexation factors:

April 00 to June 15 is 0.468

June 15 to December 17 is 0.114

June 15 to July 20 is 0.127

February 08 to December 17 is 0.316

February 08 to July 20 is 0.332

Required

1 What are the tax implications of the transfer of the building?

2 If Benidorm Ltd sells the building for £400,000 to a third party in July 2020, what is the capital gain arising?

3 Or if Ibiza Ltd sold its shares in Benidorm Ltd in July 2020 for £500,000, what are the tax implications?

Solution

5.6 Intangible fixed assets

Essential reading

See Chapter 19 of the Essential reading, for the implications of the transfer of intangible fixed assets within a chargeable gains group.

The Essential reading is available as an Appendix of the digital edition of the Workbook.

6 Pre-entry losses

KEY
TERM

> **Pre-entry losses:** A loss that was generated by a company before it was acquired by a new group.

6.1 Pre-entry capital losses

If a subsidiary (Company A) is **acquired** which has **capital losses brought forward** (ie losses crystallised on disposals that happened prior to the acquisition date**), such losses cannot be used to shelter gains on assets transferred from other group companies and then sold to crystallise a gain**. Such losses can only be used against:

- Gains on Company A's own assets, which were either disposed of before it joined the group or owned at the date of joining and subsequently sold, or
- Assets acquired by Company A from third parties post-acquisition, used in Company A's existing trade, and then subsequently sold.

Where they are allowed to be offset, pre-entry capital losses are used in priority to any other loss.

6.2 Pre-entry losses against total profits

6.2.1 Restriction on carry forward group relief following change of ownership

There is a **restriction on the use of carry forward group relief** where there has been a **change in ownership** of a company (Company A) such that Company A joins a group relief group. Company A's carried forward losses arising **before** it joined the group **cannot be surrendered to other group companies, broadly for five years following the change in ownership**. There is, however, no restriction on other group companies surrendering losses to Company A.

6.2.2 Offset of pre-entry trading losses against chargeable gains

If a subsidiary (Company A) is acquired which has trading losses carried forward that could be offset against total profits, then use of these **'pre-entry' losses** is **restricted** where there has been a **change in ownership** of Company A, and a **chargeable gain is transferred** to Company A by another gains group company (either by NG/NL transfer with A then selling the asset or by electing to transfer the gain to A).

If the gain accrues in A within **five years of the change in ownership**, then A **cannot relieve the gain by using its own trading losses carried forward at the date of change in ownership.**

7 Successions to trade

7.1 Tax implications of the disposal of the trade and assets of a company

Generally, if a **trade is transferred from one company (Company A) to another (Company B),** that is treated as a **cessation** of the trade by Company A and a **commencement** of the trade by Company B. Any trading losses brought forward by Company A are extinguished and cannot be utilised by Company B. In addition, balancing adjustments may arise on assets qualifying for capital allowances. Gains would be calculated on any chargeable assets transferred, and there may be VAT and stamp tax implications of the sale/purchase of the assets (see later).

7.2 Transfer of a trade within a 75% group ('succession')

KEY TERM

> **Succession:** The transfer of a trade between companies which are under the same (75%) ownership.

If, however, the **transfer of the trade amounts to a 'succession'**, it is **treated as continuing** for certain specific purposes. A succession to trade occurs if a trade carried on by one company (the predecessor, ie Company A) is transferred to another company (the successor, ie Company B) in **substantially the same ownership.** Broadly, this means that the same person or company has a **75% interest** in both the predecessor and successor.

If the conditions for a succession are met:

- An **accounting period ends** on the date of transfer.
- Company A may claim capital allowances in the final accounting period **as if no transfer had taken place.** Company B **automatically** takes over the unrelieved expenditure and is entitled to capital allowances thereon in the period in which the transfer takes place.

- Company **B is entitled to relief for carried-forward trading losses not utilised** by Company A (subject to the restrictions explained below).
- **Only trading losses are transferred with the trade;** all other losses remain with Company A.

Restriction on the carry forward of transferred losses

If selling company (company A) has had:

(a) A **change of ownership,** and

(b) **Sells its trade within the period three years before to five years after the change of ownership**

then for a **five-year period from the change of ownership** the acquiring company (Company B) can **only use Company A's carried-forward losses against profits of the trade transferred** (not total profits) and cannot group relieve them

BPP
LEARNING
MEDIA

Chapter summary

Corporate groups and consortia

Types of group

- Common control for allocation of AIA
- Group relief groups
- Consortia
- Chargeable gains groups

AIA

- One AIA available per group
- Parent company plus subsidiaries where parent has voting control
- Group decides how to allocate AIA
- Consider nature of expenditure and whether the AIA would create a loss

Group relief

Definition
- 75% ownership and effective interest
- UK resident companies only to participate in GR
- NR companies can establish the group

Current-period group relief
- Surrendering company can surrender any amount of current period:
  - Trading loss
  - Deficits on NTLR
  - Excess QCDs
  - Excess management expenses (of investment companies)
  - Excess property losses
- Claimant company:
  - Must be able to use surrendered amounts in current period
  - Deemed offset of claimant's own losses first to establish available profits
  - Offset is against TTP

Carry-forward group relief
- Surrendering company can surrender carried forward:
  - Trading loss
  - Deficits on NTLR
  - Property losses
  - Management expenses
  - IFA losses
- Can only be surrendered if surrendering company cannot use vs own profits
- Claimant company:
  - Must use its own losses to the fullest extent in working out available TTP to receive carry forward group relief

Claims and payment
- Claim within 2 years of end of claimant's profit-making period
- Intra-group payments for GR are ignored for CT

Overseas aspects of group relief
- 75% UK subs of non-resident parent can surrender losses to each other
- Can surrender to/from UK branches of non-resident group members

Consortia

Definition
- Each investing company (Consortium member or CM) owns ≥5% of a company (consortium company or CC) and together own ≥75%
- No one CM owns ≥75% of CC

Operation of consortium relief
- Relief only for UK companies
- maximum relief is lower of:
  - CM results
  - CMs interest in CC's trading profit or loss

Chargeable gains groups

Definition
- 75% ownership and 50% effective interest of ultimate UK holding company
- UK resident companies or assets chargeable to UK CT
- NR companies can establish the group

Intra-group transfers of assets
Automatically NG/NL

Reallocation of gains and losses
- Can elect for gains and losses to be treated as made by any group member
  - Ensure gains made by co with capital losses
  - Reallocate gains where tax would be paid by quarterly instalments

Degrouping charges
- Arises when subsidiary leaves a group within 6 years of acquiring an asset via a NG/NL transfer, and still owns the asset
- Charge is the gain not charged at the date of the intra-group transfer
- Charge is added to the proceeds on disposal of the shares (could be exempt via SSE)

Rollover relief
Group treated as carrying on one trade for rollover relief

Intangible fixed assets
- Transfers within gains group are tax-neutral, ie at TWDV
- Group-wide IFA rollover is available
- Degrouping charges apply as per tangible assets, but are charged on the company leaving the group
  - Can be transferred to another group member
  - Can be deferred via rollover relief
- No IFA degrouping charge if share sale qualifies for SSE

Pre-entry losses

Pre-entry capital losses
Pre-entry capital losses of the joining company cannot be used to shelter gains transferred to the company by members of its new group

Pre-entry losses used vs total profits
- Pre-entry brought forward losses of a joining company cannot be group relieved for 5 years
- Also cannot be used against gains transferred in from new group members for 5 years

Successions to trade

Disposal of trade and assets of a company
- Cessation of trade for one company, commencement for the other
  - Trading losses are lost
  - CA balancing adjustments and gains can arise
  - May be VAT and stamp tax implications

Transfer of a trade within a 75% group ('succession')
- Not treated as a cessation of trade
  - Trading losses ONLY are transferred to the successor company
  - If ownership changes following the succession, transferred losses can only be used against profits of the transferred trade

Knowledge diagnostic

1. AIA within a group

A group of companies is only entitled to a single annual investment allowance (AIA) which can be allocated between the companies as they think fit. A similar rule applies to companies under common control.

2. Group relief and consortia

Group relief is available where the existence of a group or consortium is established through companies resident anywhere in the world.

A surrendering company can surrender any amount of its current period trading loss but a claimant company can only claim an amount up to its available taxable total profits.

Carried forward losses may also be surrendered under group relief.

Within a consortium there is some scope for loss relief.

3. Chargeable gains groups

Within a chargeable gains group, assets are automatically transferred at no gain/no loss.

A degrouping charge arises if a company leaves a group within six years of acquiring an asset from another group member.

Gains and losses can be transferred between group companies.

Rollover relief is available in a chargeable gains group.

Restrictions apply to the use of pre-entry losses within chargeable gains groups.

4. Successions

A succession occurs when a trade carried on by one company is transferred to another company in substantially the same ownership. In this case losses may be carried forward, subject to certain restrictions, and balancing adjustments do not arise for capital allowances purposes

Further study guidance

Question practice

Now try the following from the Further question practice bank (available in the digital edition of the Workbook):

- Hawthorn Ltd, Linden Ltd and Maple Ltd

Further reading

There are two technical articles on the ACCA website written by members of the ATX – UK examining team which are relevant to some of the topics covered in this chapter that you should read:

- Corporation tax – group relief
- Corporation tax – groups and chargeable gains

Activity answers

Activity 1: Current-period group relief tax planning

L plc can either (1) make a current current-year and 12-month carry back claim to use the loss itself or (2) can group relieve the loss to K plc in the current year.

Current-year and carry back claim:

Y/e 31/3/21	£
Trade profit	0
Non-trading loan relationship income	2,900
Total profits	2,900
Less current year trade loss relief	(2,900)
Qualifying charitable donations (£3,200 wasted)	(0)
Taxable total profits	0

Trade loss left to carry back £17,800 (20,700 − 2,900).

There would also be £300 of excess QCDs in y/e 31/3/21 which could be group relieved to K to generate a tax saving of £57 (300 × 19%).

Y/e 31/3/20	£
Trade profit	0
Non-trading loan relationship income	6,200
Gains	15,000
Total profits	21,200
Less trade loss carried back	(17,800)
Less qualifying charitable donations	(1,000)
Taxable total profits	2,400

Remaining trade loss £0 (17,800 − 17,800).

This will generate a tax rebate of £3,382 (17,800 × 19%).

Total tax saving is £3,439 (£57 + £3,382)

Group relief

L plc can surrender losses under group relief as follows:

	£
Current year trading loss	20,700
Excess qualifying charitable donations £(3,200 − 2,900)	300
Total losses available for group relief	21,000

K plc has the following available taxable total profits:

	£
Non-trading loan relationship income	10,000
Chargeable gain	15,000
	25,000
Less current year trading loss	(4,000)
	21,000
Less qualifying charitable donations	(2,000)
Available taxable total profits	19,000

	£
Maximum group relief that K plc can claim from L Ltd (lower of £21,000 and £19,000)	19,000

K plc must take account of its current year trading loss in working out available taxable total profits, even if it does not actually make a claim for current year relief.

The group relief claim will save £3,610 (19,000 × 19%) of corporation tax this year.

Conclusion

The immediate tax savings are better if the group makes a group relief claim from L plc to K plc. This also has the advantage that not all of the trade loss is utilised in this claim, leaving £2,000 of trade loss (assuming the QCDs are group relieved first) to carry forward to be utilised in the next accounting period and achieving further tax savings. It does, however, not have the cash flow advantage of the tax rebate from the carry back claim.

Activity 2: Carry forward group relief

Y plc can surrender its carried-forward trading loss and its non-trading loan relationship debit under carry forward group relief as follows:

	£
Carried-forward trading loss	150,000
Carried-forward non-trading loan relationship debit	4,000
Less: amount which could be used against own current-period total profits £(62,000 + 6,000 + 20,000)	(88,000)
Loss available for carry forward group relief	66,000

X plc has the following available taxable total profits:

	£
Trading income	45,000
Non-trading loan relationship income	5,000
Chargeable gain	15,000
	65,000
Less: Carried-forward trading loss	(4,000)
Carried-forward non-trading loan relationship debit	(500)
Available taxable total profits	60,500

	£
Maximum group relief that X plc can claim from Y plc (lower of £66,000 and £60,500)	60,500

Activity 3: Consortium relief

£240,000

Lower of:

(1) A Ltd's profit = £500,000

(2) 30% of S Ltd's loss (after deemed current year offset): 30% × £(1,000,000-200,000) = £240,000

Activity 4: Consortium relief – loss in consortium member

£100,000

Lower of:

(1) A Ltd's loss = £100,000

(2) 30% of S Ltd's TTP = 30% × £(400,000 + 100,000) = £150,000

Activity 5: Chargeable gains groups

1   Building automatically transferred at NG/NL = cost + indexation to date of transfer

ie 150,000 + (0.468 × 150,000) = £220,200

Benidorm Ltd has a base cost for the building of £220,200 for a future disposal.

2   A gain arises when building is sold to a third party outside the 75% group.

	£
Proceeds	400,000
Cost (from requirement 1)	(220,200)
Indexation allowance	
0. 114 × £220,200	(25,103)
Gain	154,697

3   Degrouping charge as Benidorm Ltd leaves the group within six years of the original transfer.

	£
Proceeds (MV at date of transfer)	360,000
Cost	(150,000)
Indexation allowance 0.468 × 150,000	(70,200)
Degrouping charge	139,800

This is added to the consideration Ibiza receives on the sale of Benidorm Ltd, giving rise to a capital gain of:

	£
Proceeds	500,000
Degrouping charge	139,800
Less cost	(300,000)

Less indexation allowance

0.316 × £300,000   (94,800)

                                                                                  245,000

Assuming Benidorm Ltd is trading, this gain on the sale of shares will be exempt under the substantial shareholding rules.

20

Administration, winding up and purchase of own shares

Learning objectives

On completion of this chapter, you should be able to:

	Syllabus reference no.
Identify and evaluate the significance of accounting periods on administration or winding-up	A4(b)(iii)
Conclude on the tax treatment of returns to shareholders after winding up has commenced	A4(b)(iv)
Advise on the tax implications of a purchase by a company of its own shares	A4(b)(v)

Exam context

In this chapter, we look at some of the consequences of placing a company into administration or liquidation.

Companies' lives regularly come to an end – either because the individuals owning the shares wish to retire, and cannot find a buyer for their business, or the company's trade is transferred (maybe to another group member), or perhaps because it has got into financial difficulty and is insolvent. If there is any value in the company to distribute to its shareholders, this should be done in a tax-efficient way.

Similarly, if a shareholder wishes to withdraw their investment from a company, and cannot find a willing buyer for their shares, this can be achieved by having the company repurchase those shares.

If the exam includes a question which involves the purchase by a company of its own shares you must be careful to consider whether the capital treatment will apply, and if so, whether it is beneficial. You must be prepared to advise whether any variation to a suggested purchase would be beneficial.

We are typically advising the shareholders, rather than the company itself, in these scenarios; so personal tax issues will be relevant (as well as some administrative issues for the company).

Chapter overview

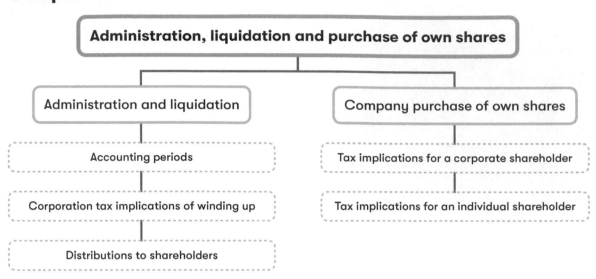

1 Administration and liquidation

Tax planning after liquidation proceedings commence is limited. Companies in voluntary liquidation should use the pre-liquidation period for tax planning. Companies in compulsory liquidation will not be able to do this.

1.1 Accounting periods

1.1.1 Accounting periods in administration

A company may be placed in administration in an effort to avoid liquidation. In such cases, the following rules apply relating to when an accounting period will be deemed to end.

An **accounting period ends and a new one begins when a company goes into administration**. Thereafter, future tax accounting periods follow the **original accounting dates**, until the company either **leaves administration or goes from administration into liquidation** – these events also bring an **accounting period to an end**.

Essential reading

See Chapter 20 of the Essential reading for further information and examples of accounting periods when a company goes from administration to liquidation and *vice versa*.

The Essential reading is available as an Appendix of the digital edition of the Workbook.

1.1.2 Accounting periods in liquidation

An **accounting period ends and a new one begins when winding up commences,** ie upon the appointment of a liquidator.

Then an accounting period ends **only every 12 months until winding up is complete**. Note that a **cessation of trade and a set of accounts being prepared after the company has gone into liquidation do not trigger the end of a tax accounting period**.

Activity 1: Accounting periods in liquidation

Taylor Ltd has a December year end and ceased trading 5 July 2020.

The members passed a resolution to wind up the company on 18 October 2020 and the winding up was completed 2 February 2022.

Required

Show the accounting periods from 1 January 2020 to the completion of the winding up.

Solution

1.1.3 The importance of accounting periods

The **date on which an accounting period ends will affect the accounting periods into which income and capital profits and losses fall**. This may prevent relief being obtained in the most beneficial way. For example trading losses of the current year or carried back can be set against other income or gains, whilst trading losses carried forward can sometimes only be set against trading profits, for example if the company's business has become small or negligible in the loss making period. Capital gains may therefore be taxable if made after trade ceases even though there may be unrelieved trading losses.

1.2 Corporation tax implications of winding up

1.2.1 Events in a winding-up

A **company has to pay corporation tax on the profits arising during the winding up. All assets will be disposed of**, including chargeable assets and trading assets such as stock and machinery. Therefore, **trading profits/(losses) and chargeable gains may aris**e. Any assets passed up to the shareholders as a **'distribution in specie'** are **deemed to be sold at market value**.

1.2.2 Corporation tax implications of asset sales and trade cessation

The following tax issues arise as a result of the liquidation process:

Event/issue	Corporation tax implications
Disposal of chargeable assets (including L&B)	Chargeable gains/capital losses arise
Disposal of trading inventory	Trading profits/losses arise
Disposal of plant and machinery	Balancing adjustments arise on all capital allowance pools on cessation of trade
Disposal of intangible assets	Trading profits/losses arise
Trading losses (c/yr and b/fwd)	• No carry forward after cessation of trade • Both current period and brought forward losses can be used to shelter the above gains/profits • Terminal loss relief available (carry back three years on cessation vs TTP) • Planning point: the company should attempt to sell assets standing at a gain prior to trade cessation, in order to shelter the gains with trade losses
Group implications	If a parent company is put into liquidation, this 'severs' the group relief group as it loses beneficial ownership of its assets (the shares in its subsidiaries). Group relief is no longer possible between any group members. The chargeable gains group, however, continues unaffected.

1.3 Tax consequences of distributions to shareholders

PER alert

One of the competencies you require to fulfil Performance objective 17 Tax planning and advice of the PER is to assess the tax implications of proposed activities or plans of an individual or entity with reference to relevant and up-to-date legislation. You can apply the knowledge you obtain from this section of the text to help to demonstrate this competence.

1.3.1 Pre- and post-liquidation distributions

Distributions to shareholders made **after winding up has commenced** are treated as **capital disposals** of shares for the shareholder. If a company has distributable reserves, it may prefer to pay these out as a dividend **prior to the appointment of a liquidator**, as such payments would be taxed as **dividends** in the normal way.

Essential reading

See Chapter 20 of the Essential reading for further information about distributions made outside of a formal winding-up.

The Essential reading is available as an Appendix of the digital edition of the Workbook.

1.3.2 Tax considerations for individual shareholders

A **pre-liquidation distribution** will be charged to income tax as a **dividend**. This is liable to income tax, subject to the nil rate band and personal allowance, at the dividend rates (7.5, 32.5 or 38.1%).

A **post-liquidation distribution** is liable to **capital gains tax**, subject to the annual exempt amount, at 10% or 20%, depending on the availability of business asset disposal relief (BADR) and the basic rate band.

BADR will be available despite the fact that the company may have ceased trading, provided that the individual had held their shares, which qualified for BADR, for two years before the company ceased to trade and the distribution is happening within three years of cessation of the trade.

1.3.3 Tax considerations for corporate shareholders

A **pre-liquidation distribution** would **not be liable to tax on a corporate shareholder**, as dividends are not liable to corporation tax.

A **post-liquidation distribution** may also be **exempt** from corporation tax, but only if the conditions for the **substantial shareholding exemption** are met. Otherwise, any gain on the disposal of the shares will be liable to corporation tax at 19%.

Activity 2: Distributions on a winding up

Bruce Ltd is a family-run business owned by father and son. The father wishes to retire and the son does not want to continue in business. They both want to realise cash from the company, so it was put into liquidation with net assets as follows:

	£
Building	150,000
Inventory, cash, receivables	80,000
	230,000
Payables	(35,000)
	195,000

The share capital is split as follows:

Father holds 75,000 shares costing £37,500 in July 1987

Son holds 25,000 shares costing £20,000 in September 1992

In December 2020 the net assets are distributed to father (an additional-rate taxpayer) and son (a higher-rate taxpayer).

Required

1 Calculate the taxable gains arising on both father and son, assuming that neither has any other chargeable disposals in 2020/21. Explain the tax rate applicable to the gains.

2 Discuss whether a pre-liquidation dividend may be beneficial.

3 What difference would it make if the 25,000 shares held by the son were instead held by a company?

Indexation factors:

Sept 92 – Dec 17 = 0.995

Sept 92 – Dec 20 = 1.157

Solution

---

2 Company purchase of own shares

 PER alert

One of the competencies you require to fulfil Performance objective 17 Tax planning and advice of the PER is to review the situation of an individual or entity advising on any potential tax risks and/or additional tax minimisation measures. You can apply the knowledge you obtain from this section of the text to help to demonstrate this competence.

2.1 Tax implications for a corporate shareholder

A **repurchase of its own shares** by a company from a **corporate shareholder** will always be treated as a **capital disposal** of shares. Therefore, a chargeable gain or loss will need to be computed based on the repurchase price paid by the company.

The gain may be exempt from corporation tax if the conditions for the substantial shareholding exemption are met.

2.2 Tax treatment for an individual shareholder

The repurchase of shares from an individual may be treated as either a:

- **Distribution** (the **default** treatment for individual shareholders), or
- **Capital disposal** (compulsory if certain conditions are met)

2.2.1 Purchase of own shares – income treatment

Unless the conditions for the capital treatment to apply are met, the shareholder will be treated as receiving a **distribution** (charged to income tax as a dividend).

The amount charged to income tax will be:

	£
Proceeds = amount paid by company	X
Less: original subscription price when shares were *first issued*	(X)
Amount taxed as a dividend	X

Any difference between the original subscription price and the amount paid by this shareholder is then charged to capital gains tax – this would usually be an allowable capital loss.

2.2.2 Purchase of own shares – capital treatment

The repurchase of shares **must** be treated as a **capital disposal** if **all** of the following conditions are satisfied:

(a) The company repurchasing the shares is an **unquoted trading company** (or the unquoted parent company of a trading group).

(b) The repurchase must **benefit the trade**. Examples of this test being satisfied are:
  - A dissident or disruptive shareholder is bought out
  - A proprietor wishes to retire
  - An outside investor wishes to withdraw his investment
  - A shareholder dies and the personal representatives do not wish to retain the shares

(c) The vendor must be **UK resident** at the date of the repurchase.

(d) The vendor must have held the shares for either:
  - **Five years**, or
  - Three years if they were inherited; the ownership period of the deceased can be included

(e) The vendor, together with their associates, must **reduce their interest in the company by at least 25%,** ie their ordinary shareholding must be less than 3/4 of what is was prior to the repurchase.

(f) The vendor must be unconnected after the repurchase – this means **not holding more than 30%** of the company or any of its group members.

Note. That if **any** of the above conditions is **failed**, the **income treatment will apply.**

Exam focus point

The period of ownership will often be an essential point in an exam question. For example, you may be given a scenario where the purchase can be timed either before the five-year deadline, or after it, and asked to show the taxation consequences in each case.

Activity 3: Repurchase of own shares

Greg owns 16,000 of the 40,000 shares in Thomas Ltd. Greg subscribed for the shares at £3.40 each in May 2003. He is not an officer or employee of Thomas Ltd.

Greg has always lived in the UK; has taxable income of £126,000 in 2020/21 which includes £17,000 dividend income; and uses his annual exempt amount every year.

On 31 July 2020 he will be selling some, or all, of his shares to the company for £38.60 per share.

Required

1   Assuming that Greg sells all of his shares back to the company, advise Greg on the tax treatment of the proceeds he will receive in respect of the sale of his shares to Thomas Ltd. Prepare a calculation of the net (after tax) proceeds from the sale based on your conclusions.

2   If Greg were to sell 4,500 of his shares back to Thomas Ltd, and these shares were subsequently cancelled, would the substantial reduction in shareholding test be met?

Solution

2.2.3 Other issues

An **application for clearance** from HMRC may be obtained in order to ensure that a repurchase is treated as capital.

Capital treatment may also apply if a repurchase is made in order to settle an IHT liability arising on a death. The normal capital conditions do not then need to be satisfied.

Chapter summary

Administration, liquidation and purchase of own shares

Administration and liquidation

Accounting periods
- New AP when administration or liquidation start
- Subsequently – accounting date (administration) or anniversary of winding up commencement (liquidation)
- AP ends when administration/liquidation end

Corporation tax implications of winding up
- Co remains liable to CT on profits arising during winding up
- Assets sold, or are deemed sold at market value
  - Gains on L&B
  - BA/BC on P&M
  - Profit on inventory
- Trade losses:
  - No c/fwd past trade cessation
  - Offset vs gains if same AP
  - TLR – c/b 3 years

Distributions to shareholders
- Pre-liquidation = taxed as dividend
  - No tax for corporate s/h
  - IT @ 7.5%, 32.5% or 38.1% for individual s/h (subject to DNRB)
- Post-liquidation - taxed as a capital receipt (gain or loss arises)
  - CT for corporate s/h (SSE may apply to exempt gain)
  - CGT for individual @ 10%/20% (possible BADR to tax at 10%)

Company purchase of own shares

Tax implications for a corporate shareholder
- Always treated as a capital receipt
  - CT on any gain arising
  - Possible SSE to exempt gain

Tax implications for an individual shareholder
- Default is distribution
  - Distribution = proceeds minus original subscription price
  - Original subscription price becomes proceeds in CGT comp
  - Distribution liable to IT as a dividend
- Mandatory capital treatment if conditions met (Normal CGT disposal)
- Conditions:
  - Unquoted trade co
  - repurchase benefits trade
  - Vendor UK Res
  - Shares held ≥ 5 years (3 if inherited)
  - Vendor holding reduced by ≥25%
  - Vendor holds ≤30% afterwards

Knowledge diagnostic

1. Administration and liquidation

A new accounting period (AP) begins when a winding up commences. Thereafter APs are for 12 months until the winding up is complete. Distributions made during a winding up are capital. There are special rules in respect of accounting periods when companies go into administration.

2. Company purchase of own shares

A purchase of a company's own shares may be taxable on the vendor shareholder as the receipt of an income distribution or (if certain conditions are satisfied) as capital proceeds.

Further study guidance

Question practice

Now try the following from the Further question practice bank (available in the digital edition of the Workbook):

- Clarke Ltd

Activity answers

Activity 1: Accounting periods in liquidation

1.1.20–5.7.20	To the date trade ceased
6.7.20–17.10.20	Commencement of winding up brings an AP to an end
18.10.20–17.10.21	AP cannot exceed 12 months
18.10.21–2.2.22	AP ends when winding up complete

Activity 2: Distributions on a winding up

1

	Father	Son
	£	£
Gains on disposal of shares		
Consideration 195k × 75%/25%	146,250	48,750
Cost	(37,500)	(20,000)
	108,750	28,750
Less AE	(12,300)	(12,300)
Taxable gains	96,450	16,450

Both will be taxed at 10% CGT due to the availability of business asset disposal relief

2 **Pre-liquidation dividend**

Dividends will be taxable on both individuals on dividend in excess of the £2,000 nil rate band (assuming no other dividends currently received):

- Father will be taxed at 38.1%
- Son will be taxed at 32.5%

Thus, it is not tax efficient to take a dividend.

3 If a company owned 25,000 shares rather than the son then the substantial shareholding exemption would be available as Bruce Ltd had been a trading company and the investing 'company' has held more than 10% of the shares for a continuous 12-month period in the last six years. Consequently, there would be no corporation tax.

Pre-liquidation dividend would not be taxable on company and so either option would be tax free.

If the conditions for the SSE were not met (for example a 12-month ownership period did not exist/<10% shares held/Bruce Ltd was not a trading company) then a pre-liquidation dividend would be preferable to avoid paying corporation tax on the gain.

Activity 3: Repurchase of own shares

1

	£
Distribution method	
Proceeds 16,000 × £38.60	617,600
Less subscription cost 16,000 × £3.40	

	£
	(54,400)
Net distribution	563,200
Tax on £(150,000 − 126,000) = £24,000 @ 32.5%	7,800
Tax on £(563,200 − 24,000) = £539,200 @ 38.1%	205,435
	213,235
Net cash 617,600 − 213,235 =	404,365

An amount equal to original subscription price is proceeds in a gain calculation:

	£
Proceeds	54,400
Less cost	(54,400)
Gain	0

The above is the case unless the shareholder satisfies a number of conditions to allow sale to be treated as capital gain. Greg is selling all of his shares, which means that he satisfies the requirements of holding less than 30% after the repurchase and of his shareholding reducing by at least 25%. He is also UK resident and has held his shares for five years. However, it is uncertain from the information in the question whether Thomas Ltd is a trading company, and if so, whether the repurchase of Greg's shares benefits the trade. If these conditions are met, the capital method will automatically apply:

	£
Capital method	
Proceeds	617,600
Less cost	(54,400)
	563,200
CGT @ 20% (already used AE, business asset disposal relief not available due to Greg not working for Thomas Ltd and investors' relief not available as shares subscribed for prior to 17/3/16)	112,640
Net cash 617,600 − 112,640 =	504,960

2   Greg's shareholding before the repurchase is (16,000/40,000) = 40%.

After the repurchase, Greg will still hold (16,000 − 4,500) = 11,500 shares, and the company's revised number of ordinary shares in total after the cancellation is (40,000 − 4,500) = 35,500.

Greg now holds 11,500/35,500 = 32.4% of the ordinary shares. This is 80.9% of his previous shareholding, and therefore the substantial reduction test is not met. Also, the requirement to be unconnected after the repurchase is failed, as he still holds >30% of the shares in the company.

The repurchase of 4,500 shares would therefore be treated as an income distribution.

21

Close companies and investment companies

Learning objectives

On completion of this chapter, you should be able to:

	Syllabus reference no.
Identify and calculate corporation tax for companies with investment business	A4(b)(i)
Apply the definition of a close company to given situations	A4(b)(ii)
Conclude on the tax implications of a company being a close company or a close investment holding company	A4(b)(ii)

Exam context

Companies with investment business are any companies that make investments, for example in shares, and collect the income from them. Expenses of managing those investments are generally deductible for corporation tax purposes.

A close company may have any type of business, but it needs special tax treatment because it is under the control of a few people who might try to take profits out of it in non-taxable forms.

You may be asked about how a company with investment business can deduct management expenses. Questions involving planning for families may include a consideration of close companies. The rules for treating benefits as distributions are fairly straightforward, but you must be careful not to overlook the disallowance of the expenses in the corporation tax computation. The tax charge for loans to participators is a significant cost of making any such loan, even though it is recovered when the loan is repaid or written off.

Chapter overview

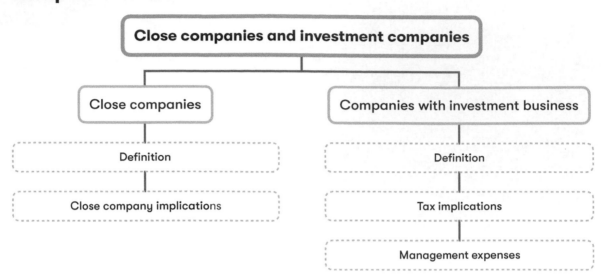

1 Close companies

Owner-managed and family-owned companies could easily be used for tax avoidance. Special rules apply to these 'close' companies to counteract this.

1.1 Close company definition

KEY TERM

> **Close company:** Any **UK resident company** that is **controlled** by either:
> - **Five or fewer shareholders**, or
> - **Any number of shareholding directors**

This definition will apply to most private companies, for example where a married couple own all the shares. The shares owned by 'associates' are combined before determining the level of control exercised by the five largest participators, or by the directors.

1.1.1 Associates

Associates include:

- Relatives (not in-laws):

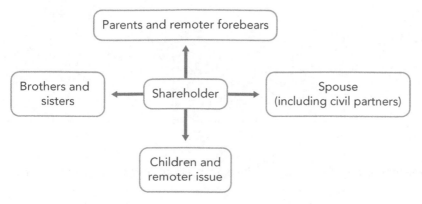

- Business partners
- Trustees of any trust if the shareholder (or their associate) was the creator

Activity 1: Close company example

Nelson Ltd is owned by the following:

	%
Paul	18
Sarah (Paul's wife)	3
Holly	8
Guy	7
Joe	7
Matthew	7
Shaun (Matthew's brother-in-law)	6
Jacky	5
Josh (Jacky's son)	4
Other shareholders (1% each)	35
	100

BPP LEARNING MEDIA

Paul, Holly, Guy and Joe are directors.

Required

Comment on whether Nelson Ltd is a close company.

Solution

1.1.2 Exceptions

A subsidiary is only a close company if its parent is close. Non-UK resident companies are not close companies.

> **Exam focus point**
>
> Identifying a close company was tested in December 2013 Question 2 Forti Ltd group. The examining team commented that: 'This was intended to be a relatively straightforward requirement, which then required some thought if a very good mark were to be obtained. However, the majority of candidates simply did not know the rules, such that the performance in this part of the question was poor. On the whole, candidates focused on the owners of the company and knew the rules had something to do with five shareholders and any number of directors. However, the key to the rules is who controls the company as opposed to who owns it.'

1.2 Close company implications

The rules on loans and benefits from close companies are intended to deter shareholders from using the obvious ways of extracting value from their company without paying tax.

1.2.1 Loans to participators

Loans advanced to a shareholder, which are **not repaid before the end of the company's accounting period**, will create a **'penalty tax'** liability on the company at **32.5% of the amount of the outstanding loan**.

The tax is due on the **normal due date(s) for payment of CT for the accounting period**, eg for companies which are not large nine months and one day after end of the accounting period, **but need not be paid if the loan has been repaid by this date**.

'Loans' include debts owed to the company, debts of the participator that have been assigned to the company, and overdrawn directors loan accounts.

1.2.2 Loans repaid or waived

Where the loan is **repaid by the shareholder**, the **penalty tax is repayable**. The repayment is due nine months and one day following the end of the accounting period in which the loan is repaid.

> ### Exam focus point
>
> If a loan made during an accounting period is to be repaid during the next accounting period, repayment before the due date for payment of the corporation tax will avoid the need for the penalty tax charge to be paid. Later repayment will defer the refund date for a year.
>
> In Question 1 Nelson in the December 2019 exam students were asked to explain the tax implications of a loan to a shareholder from a close company and it subsequently being repaid. The question specifically told students not to explain any matters relating to employment income but the examining team said that 'many students went on to discuss these matters, again wasting their valuable time and earning no marks. Once again these students would have benefitted from spending their time to ensure they were clear on the requirement and planning their answer, before they began to write.'

If the loan is **written off** the company will receive a **repayment of any penalty tax paid**. Therefore, it is only a cash flow issue for the company. However, the **shareholder is deemed to receive a dividend equal to the amount of loan written off**. The charge as a dividend overrides any employment benefit that may have otherwise arisen.

Essential reading

See Essential reading for Chapter 21 for details of interest payable to/from HMRC on penalty tax charges.

The Essential reading is available as an Appendix of the digital edition of the Workbook.

1.2.3 Excepted loans

Penalty tax does not apply where:

(a) The loan is less than £15,000;

(b) It is made to a full-time director or employee; and

(c) The borrower (together with associates) does not own more than 5% of the ordinary shares. If this limit is exceeded when a loan is already in place, the loan is deemed to have been made when the interest goes over 5%.

Loans are also excepted if they relate to the individual acquiring goods or services from their employer on credit, on normal commercial credit terms which are less than six months.

1.2.4 Other items treated as a distribution

Where a **benefit is provided to a shareholder** or one of their associates and it is not caught under the normal employment income benefit rules, it will be treated as a **distribution**, ie disallowed in the corporation tax computation and taxed on the shareholder as a dividend. **The amount of the deemed distribution is the amount that would otherwise be taxed as earnings.**

Activity 2: Loans to participators

Hoddle Ltd (a close company) makes a loan at commercial rates to Glen (a shareholder in the company) of £65,000 on 1 May 2018. On 1 May 2019 Glen repays £20,000. On 1 May 2020 the company waives the balance. Hoddle Ltd has a 31 December year end and is not a large company. Assume Glen has taxable income of £40,000 in 2020/21 which includes £1,000 of dividend income. Also assume that the rules and rates for 2020/21 have always applied.

Required

What are the tax implications for both Hoddle Ltd and Glen?

Solution

Activity 3: Close companies – benefits to participators

Dash and Violet are both shareholders of Incredibles Ltd, a close company. Dash is an employee of the company but Violet is not.

They are both provided with newly registered identical company cars, both with a list price of £20,000, hybrid petrol engines with CO_2 emissions of 48g/km and an electric range of 80 miles.

Required

Calculate and explain the amounts Dash and Violet will be taxed on for their cars, and explain the tax implications for Incredibles Ltd of the expenses incurred

Solution

2 Companies with investment business

2.1 Definition

Investment company: A company whose business consists **wholly or mainly in making investments** and gets the **principal part of its income from investments**.

2.2 Tax implications

Rules are **identical to trading companies except that expenses incurred in managing the investments** ('management expenses') **are automatically deducted from total income**. Interest on a loan taken out by an individual to invest in a *close* investment holding company is not qualifying loan interest for the purpose of the interest being deductible in the income tax computation.

2.3 Management expenses

Common expenses that would be classified as management expenses include:

- Commissions
- CAs on plant used for purpose of management of investment activities unless otherwise available (eg against rental income)
- Reasonable salaries and redundancy payments
- Unavoidable expenses of management, eg rent, audit fees

Expenses relievable elsewhere, eg rental expenses are not included as management expenses.

Interest paid on loans taken out to fund investment activities is relieved as a debit on a non-trading loan relationship in the normal way.

To the extent that management expenses cannot be relieved against income of the current accounting period the excess may be carried forward and a claim can be made to offset some or all of the expenses against the total profits of that next accounting period.

Alternatively, excess management expenses can be used within a group relief claim (see Chapter 19).

Illustration 1: Corporation tax computation for an investment company

TC Ltd, a non-close company with wholly investment business, has the following results for the year ended 31 March 2021.

	£
Rental income	150,000
Building society interest	8,000
Chargeable gains	100,000
Management expenses:	
Property management	40,000
General	50,000
Capital allowances:	
On property	800
General	1,000
Qualifying charitable donations	47,000

Unrelieved management expenses carried forward at 1 April 2020 amounted to £60,500. TC Ltd wishes to make a claim wholly to relieve these in the current accounting period.

Required

Compute the corporation tax payable.

Solution

		£	£
Rents			150,000
Less:	Capital allowances	800	
	Property management expenses	40,000	
			(40,800)
Property income			109,200
Interest income			8,000
Chargeable gains			100,000
Total profits			217,200
Less:	General management expenses	50,000	
	General capital allowances	1,000	
	Management expenses brought forward	60,500	–
			(111,500)
			105,700
Less qualifying charitable donations			(47,000)
Taxable total profits			58,700
Corporation tax payable £58,700 × 19%			11,153

Chapter summary

Close companies and investment companies

Close companies

Definition
- UK company controlled by either:
  - Five or fewer shareholders
  - Any number of directors
- Include shares owned by associates when determining level of control

Close company implications
- Benefits provided to shareholders
  - If employee – taxed under employment income
  - if not employee - treated as dividend (valued at equivalent employment benefit)
- Loans to shareholders:
  - Co pays penalty tax at 32.5% due on normal due date for CT
  - Penalty tax refunded if loan repaid or written off
  - If loan written off, taxed on shareholder as a deemed dividend
  - Loan excluded if ≤ £15,000, to full-time worker with under 5% shareholding

Companies with investment business

Definition
Income derived from making investments, eg interest, rental income, dividends

Tax implications
- Charged to CT as normal
- Interest on loans to acquire shares in close investment co = not qualifying interest for IT relief

Management expenses
- Automatically offset vs current period total profits
- Excess can be carried forward or group relieved

Knowledge diagnostic

1. Close companies

A close company is one which is controlled by either five or fewer participators, or by its directors.

The rules on loans and benefits from close companies are intended to deter shareholders from using these ways of extracting value from their company without paying tax.

2. Companies with investment business

A company that generates income from investments can usually deduct the expenses of managing their investments for corporation tax purposes.

Excess management expenses can be either carried forward, or group relieved.

Further study guidance

Question practice

Now try the following from the Further question practice bank (available in the digital edition of the Workbook):

- Huis Ltd and Beauvoir Ltd
- Landscape Ltd

Activity answers

Activity 1: Close company example

The five largest shareholders and their associates are:

	%
Paul and wife (18 + 3)	21
Jacky and son (5 + 4)	9
Holly	8
Guy	7
Joe	7
Total	52

Company is controlled by five shareholders so Nelson Ltd is a close company.

The fact that the company is not controlled by its directors is irrelevant; only one of the two tests needs to be met for the company to be close.

Activity 2: Loans to participators

Penalty tax due by Hoddle Ltd based on the loan outstanding on 1 October 2019: £45,000

ie £45,000 × 32.5% = £14,625 due 1.10.19.

Waiver on 1 May 2020:

The penalty tax of £14,625 will be refunded to the company on 1.10.2021 (nine months and one day following end of AP of waiver).

Glen will be deemed to receive a dividend in 2020/21 of £45,000.

Taxed as dividend income.

	£
Dividend	45,000
Dividend nil rate band (2,000 −1000) = 1,000 × 0%	0
£44,000 × 32.5%	14,300
Higher rate tax due 31.1.22	14,300

Activity 3: Close companies – benefits to participators

A hybrid- electric car with emissions up to 50g/km and an electric range of 80 miles has a percentage of 3% for the car benefit.

Dash will be taxed under employment income as a taxable benefit of 20,000 × 3% = £600. Violet will be taxed on £600 as above, but this will be treated as a dividend received.

Incredibles Ltd will get no CAs or running costs as allowable expenses on Violet's car as she is not an employee.

Incredibles Ltd will pay Class 1A NIC on Dash's benefit at 13.8% which will be corporation tax deductible. This will not be required on Violet's car.

Input VAT on both cars will not be recoverable due to the private use.

22

Overseas aspects of corporation tax

Learning objectives

On completion of this chapter, you should be able to:

	Syllabus reference no.
Assess the impact of the OECD model double tax treaty on corporation tax	A4(d)(i)
Evaluate the meaning and implications of a permanent establishment	A4(d)(ii)
Identify and advise on the tax implications of controlled foreign companies	A4(d)(iii)
Advise on the tax position of overseas companies trading in the UK	A4(d)(iv)
Calculate double taxation relief	A4(d)(v)
Advise on the tax treatment of an overseas branch	A4(e) (ix)

Exam context

A question on the overseas aspects of corporation tax could require you to advise on the tax consequences of relationships with overseas companies. This could involve a discussion of the merits of trading through a permanent establishment (eg a branch) or subsidiary, and could extend to the anti-avoidance controlled foreign company rules where the subsidiary is resident overseas but controlled by UK shareholders. Double tax relief is an important consideration; the relief is the lower of the UK corporation tax and the foreign tax paid.

Chapter overview

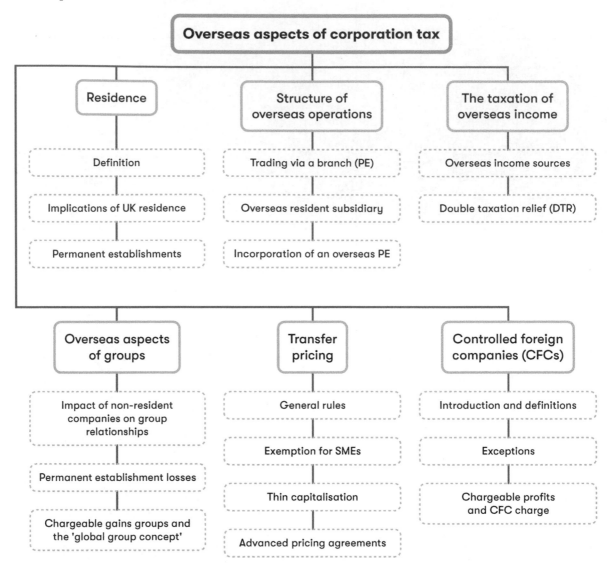

1 Residence

1.1 Definition

A company is **UK resident** if it is either:

- **Incorporated in UK**; or
- **Controlled and managed from UK** (on day to day basis) – this is usually determined by where the board of directors meet

1.2 Implications of UK residence

UK resident companies are taxable on **worldwide income**. **Non-resident companies** are **only liable to UK corporation tax if they are trading in the UK through a permanent establishment** (PE), and only the profits of the PE are taxable.

1.3 Permanent establishments

A **PE** is a **fixed place of business** through which the business of the enterprise is wholly or partly carried on. It includes a branch, office, factory, workshop, mine, oil or gas well, quarry and construction project lasting more than 12 months. It does not include use of storage facilities, maintenance of a stock of goods and delivery of them or a fixed place of business used solely for purchasing goods or any ancillary activity.

1.3.1 Overseas PE of a UK company

A company may be subject to **overseas tax as well as to UK corporation tax on the same profits usually if it has a PE in that overseas country**. Double taxation relief (see below) is available in respect of the overseas tax suffered.

1.3.2 UK PE of an overseas resident company

A **non-UK resident company will be chargeable to corporation tax if it carries on a trade in the UK through a PE.**

The profits of such a company which are chargeable to corporation tax, whether or not they arise in the UK, are:

- Any trading income arising directly or indirectly from the PE
- Any income from property or rights used by, or held by or for, the PE (other than dividends from UK companies)
- Any chargeable gains arising from the disposal of assets situated in the UK

> ## Exam focus point
>
> In the March 2020 exam, Question 2 Mita had a UK resident company which traded through an overseas PE and students were asked to explain why the company's profits were subject to UK corporation tax. The examining team said 'this elicited some intriguing answers. The company was clearly stated as being UK resident, and the overseas PE as being just that ie not a subsidiary, yet a significant minority of students thought the company was a controlled foreign company, which was clearly incorrect, and then went on to waste time talking about the CFC exemptions. A good number of others thought that the company would be liable to UK tax because its parent company was UK resident. Clearly there appeared to be a significant misunderstanding of these overseas issues. Questions have been frequently set on corporate overseas issues in the past, and students would be well advised to practice a broad range of these.'

Essential reading

See Chapter 22 of the Essential reading for further information about calculating the chargeable profits of overseas companies trading in the UK.

The Essential reading is available as an Appendix of the digital edition of the Workbook.

2 The structure of overseas operations

If a UK company wishes to expand its trade overseas, it has two main choices – trading via a **branch (PE)** or setting up a **foreign subsidiary**. We will now look at the tax implications of these options.

PER alert

One of the competencies you require to fulfil Performance objective 17 Tax planning and advice of the PER is to assess the tax implications of proposed activities or plans of an individual or entity with reference to relevant and up-to-date legislation. You can apply the knowledge you obtain from this section of the Workbook to help to demonstrate this competence.

2.1 Trading via a branch (PE)

If the overseas PE makes profits, these will be **chargeable to UK corporation tax as trading income of the UK company. UK capital allowances are available** in the usual way on assets owned by the PE. The profit will probably have also been liable to overseas tax – therefore double tax relief is available to reduce the UK tax charge.

Losses of an overseas PE are normally **netted off against the UK company's trading income**, and if an overall loss arises, the usual trading loss reliefs are available.

However, UK companies can make an **irrevocable election to exempt from corporation tax the profits and losses of all their overseas branches**; if made, the election must apply to **all** the UK company's PEs, and so this election will probably not be beneficial if either:

- A company has **loss-making overseas branches** as the election will prevent these losses being eligible for relief, or
- The overseas tax rates are fairly high, such that the UK tax charge after DTR is minimal

Essential reading

See Chapter 22 of the Essential reading for some further information about overseas trades and for an example of the overseas branch exemption.

The Essential reading is available as an Appendix of the digital edition of the Workbook.

Exam focus point

The rules regarding the exemption of overseas PE profits are complex, especially where small companies are concerned. The examining team has stated that these more complex aspects are not examinable. In any examination question, it should therefore be assumed that the exemption option is available for all overseas PEs.

2.2 Overseas resident subsidiaries

Profits are not charged to UK CT. The **non-resident subsidiary will pay foreign tax** and remit its profits to the UK parent by way of dividends. **Overseas dividends are not taxable for the UK parent.**

Losses are not available to set against UK profits since the losses arose in a non-UK company.

> ### Exam focus point
>
> Taxable overseas dividends will not be examined in Advanced Taxation (ATX – UK).

2.3 Incorporation of an overseas permanent establishment

When an overseas branch becomes profitable, and if the overseas tax rate is lower than that of the UK, consideration should be given to either **making the election to exempt all branch profits and losses,** or **converting the PE into a non-resident subsidiary,** via incorporation.

Essential reading

See Chapter 22 of the Essential reading for the tax implications of incorporating an overseas PE.

The Essential reading is available as an Appendix of the digital edition of the Workbook.

3 The taxation of overseas income

As we have seen, **UK resident** companies are liable to corporation tax on their **worldwide income. Overseas income may have suffered tax already,** and there are various ways of mitigating the effect of double taxation. The method used will depend on the terms of the double taxation treaty (if any) that exists between the UK and the overseas tax jurisdiction.

3.1 Overseas income sources

Taxable overseas income is usually included **gross of foreign tax within TTP.** The types of overseas income liable to UK tax include:

- Trading income of an overseas PE (where no exemption election has been made)
- Interest income from overseas securities
- Income from overseas possessions, for example property income derived from overseas land and buildings
- Chargeable gains on the disposal of overseas assets

3.2 Double taxation relief (DTR)

3.2.1 DTR methods

Relief for foreign tax can be given in one of three ways:

(a) **Exemption method** – under a treaty between UK and the overseas country, income is only taxed in one country.

(b) **Credit relief** – income is taxed in both countries, but a tax credit is given in the UK. This method may be specified in a treaty, or may be available for use 'unilaterally' by the UK company if no treaty exists. See below.

(c) Unilateral expense relief (outside of syllabus).

Only (a) and (b) are used under the OECD Model Agreement.

3.2.2 Credit relief

The **gross overseas income is included within TTP** and charged to corporation tax in the usual way. Then **DTR reduces the UK corporation tax liability,** and is restricted to **lower** of:

- **Foreign tax suffered on the overseas income**
- **UK corporation tax on the overseas income**

DTR is calculated separately for each source of overseas income.

3.2.3 Allocation of losses and QCDs

For the purpose of calculating DTR, qualifying charitable donations (QCDs) and losses can be offset in the way that is most **beneficial** to the company (ie avoids wasting DTR where possible). In order to achieve this:

(a) Set off against **UK income first**, then

(b) Any remaining qualifying charitable donations/losses should be allocated to the foreign source which suffers the **lowest rate** of **foreign tax**

Activity 1: Unilateral double tax relief with multiple overseas income sources

Kairo plc is a UK resident company with five UK resident subsidiaries and two overseas branches, one in Atlantis and one in Utopia. The company produced the following results for the year to 31 March 2021.

	£
UK trading profits	10,000
Profits from overseas branch in Atlantis (before overseas tax of £6,000)	40,000
Profits from overseas branch in Utopia (before overseas tax of £110,000)	250,000
Qualifying charitable donations	(15,000)

Required

Compute the UK corporation tax liability, assuming an election has not been made to exempt the profits of overseas PEs.

Solution

Where a company can specify the amount of relief to claim (for example, brought-forward losses or group relief), it is possible to select an amount such that the corporation tax after double taxation relief becomes nil.

See Chapter 25 Corporate tax planning for an illustration of how to perform this calculation.

4 Overseas aspects of groups

4.1 Impact of non-resident companies on group relationships

The group relief rules allow **groups and consortia to be established through companies resident anywhere in the world.** However, **group relief and consortium relief can normally only take place between companies within the charge to corporation tax.** Group and consortium relief therefore applies to:

- Companies resident in the UK
- Companies resident overseas but operating in the UK through a PE – only the results of the PE (ie those within the scope of corporation tax) may be classed as available losses/ available profits

4.2 Permanent establishments

Losses incurred by permanent establishments are not always available for group relief.

Essential reading

See Chapter 22 of the Essential reading for detail of the loss relief aspects of PEs.

The Essential reading is available as an Appendix of the digital edition of the Workbook.

4.3 Gains groups – the global group concept

As with group relief groups and consortia, a gains group can be established through companies resident anywhere in the world. Thus, a non-UK parent company with two 75% UK resident subsidiaries would form a gains group.

The global group concept means that instead of looking at the residence of a company one needs to look at whether the company is subject to UK corporation tax on any of its chargeable gains. Provided the assets transferred do not result in a potential leakage of UK corporation tax, no-gain/no-loss transfers will be possible within a worldwide (global) group of companies.

The global group concept applies to the transfer of the whole or part of a trade and extends to certain intra-group transfers of assets and to transfers of assets where one company disposes of the whole or part of its business to another company as part of a scheme of reconstruction or amalgamation.

5 Transfer pricing

5.1 General rules

Anti-avoidance legislation exists to prevent companies under common control structuring their transactions to **shift profits (or losses) from one company to another,** in order to **reduce the tax burden** on the group. This could be achieved by shifting profits from a UK company (taxed at 19%) to a subsidiary company in a lower tax jurisdiction. An illustration of this is given below together with a diagram summarising the position.

If H (a UK resident company) bought goods for £10,000 and sold them to a third party for £20,000, a profit of £10,000 would arise in H, which would be liable to corporation tax (at 19%) of £1,900.

However, the transaction could be rearranged as follows:

- Sell to subsidiary S (in a lower taxed country, for example with a corporate tax rate of 10%) for £14,000
- Subsidiary sells to third party for £20,000.

Only £4,000 profit now arises in H, saving UK corporation tax of (19% × £6,000) = £1,140, and incurring only 10% tax (£600) in the subsidiary. H is said to have gained a 'tax advantage' as a result of this transaction.

The legislation requires **UK taxable profit to be computed as if the transaction had arisen at arm's length**. The TTP of H Ltd will be adjusted upwards by £6,000. S's profit has been overstated by £6,000 (due to lower than market value cost of sales), however a corresponding 'downwards' transfer pricing adjustment is only allowed if S is within the charge to UK corporation tax.

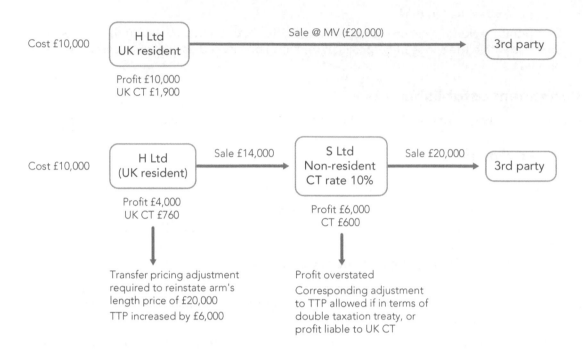

The transfer pricing rules apply to transactions between two persons if either:

(a) One person directly or indirectly participates in the management, control or capital of the other; or

(b) A third party directly or indirectly participates in the management, control or capital of both.

5.2 Exemption for SMEs

> **Small and medium-sized enterprises (SMEs):** A company with less than 250 employees, and either turnover of not more than €50m or a balance sheet total of not more than €43m.

Small and medium-sized enterprises (SMEs) are **normally exempt** from transfer pricing requirements **unless one of the parties is resident in a non-qualifying territory** (eg one without a double tax treaty with the UK).

5.3 Thin capitalisation

The same rules apply where a company makes **non-commercial loans** (ie at non-commercial rates) to another connected company, so that **profits can be shifted via the payment of interest** (aka **'Thin Capitalisation'**).

Again, profits are adjusted to the **arm's length amounts**. Therefore, if a commercial lender would not have lent the money (for example due to existing high gearing), the whole interest charge would be disallowed in the debtor company.

5.4 Advanced pricing agreements

Transfer pricing adjustments are self-assessed. It is possible for a company to enter into a voluntary 'advanced pricing agreement' with HMRC to ensure that its transfer pricing policy is acceptable to HMRC.

6 Controlled foreign companies

6.1 Introduction and definitions

6.1.1 Aims of the legislation

The controlled foreign company (CFC) rules focus on the artificial diversion of income profits (not gains) from the UK.

Where a **CFC has 'chargeable profits'** and the **CFC is not covered by one of the exemptions**, those **chargeable profits are apportioned to the CFC's UK corporate shareholders**.

6.1.2 Definition of a CFC

Controlled foreign company (CFC): A company which:

- Is **resident outside the UK**; and
- Is **controlled by persons resident in the UK**.

Essential reading

See Chapter 22 of the Essential reading for a more detailed definition and example of what makes a company a CFC.

The Essential reading is available as an Appendix of the digital edition of the Workbook.

6.2 Exceptions

Profits do not need to be apportioned if:

(a) **Exempt period exemption** – a 12-month exemption from the CFC charge applies when a non-UK resident company is acquired by a UK resident person.

(b) **Tax exemption** – the local tax paid is at least 75% of the amount of tax the CFC would have paid in the UK if it were UK resident.

(c) **Excluded territories exemption** – the CFC is resident in one of the territories specified.

(d) **Low profits exemption** – CFC's profits <£500,000 and its non-trading income <£50,000.

(e) **Low profit margin exemption** – CFC's accounting profits are no more than 10% of its expenditure.

6.3 Chargeable profits and CFC charge

6.3.1 CFC chargeable profits

Chargeable profits are those income profits (not gains) of the CFC which have been artificially diverted from the UK. No profits will become chargeable if any of the following conditions are met:

- The CFC's profits are **not derived from tax planning schemes.**
- **None of the company's assets or risks are managed from the UK in the accounting period.**
- **The CFC is not reliant on UK management** - it has the commercial capability to trade without UK managerial involvement.

6.3.2 CFC charge

Chargeable profits of a CFC are apportioned to UK resident companies (not individuals) entitled to at least 25% of those profits.

The apportioned profit does **not** form part of taxable total profits and so the tax is shown **separately** to the tax on TTP. Corporation tax will be due on the apportioned profit at 19% and a deduction for DTR will be available.

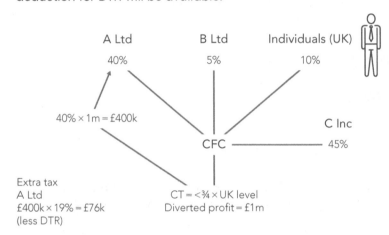

Activity 2: CFC charge

Ribbon Inc is owned 75% by Jenkins Ltd and 25% by Jack. Both Jenkins Ltd and Jack are UK resident. Ribbon Inc is a non-UK resident company such that it is a controlled foreign company. None of the CFC exemptions apply to Ribbon Inc.

In the year to 31 March 2020, Ribbon Inc had chargeable profits of £650,000. It paid income tax in its own country at the rate of 8%.

Required

Show how the profits of Ribbon Inc will be apportioned to Jenkins Ltd and the CFC charge on Jenkins Ltd.

Solution

Chapter summary

Overseas aspects of corporation tax

Residence

Definition
Incorporated or managed and controlled from the UK

Implications of UK residence
- UK resident company taxed on worldwide income
- Non-UK resident company only taxed on profits of UK PEs

Permanent establishments
- Fixed place of business in a country
- Overseas PEs of UK resident companies – liable to UK CT (DTR available)
- UK PEs of non-UK resident companies – liable to UK CT on trading profits, income derived from trading assets, and gains on UK assets used in the PE

Structure of overseas operations

Trading via a branch (PE)
- Taxed on 100% of profits
- Losses can be offset as trading losses
- UK co can make irrevocable election to exempt all overseas PEs profits and losses from UK tax

Overseas resident subsidiary
- No UK tax on profits or dividends
- No UK relief for losses incurred

Incorporation of an overseas PE
- Transfer of assets at market value gives rise to profits/gains
- Gains can be deferred under branch incorporation relief until:
  - Assets are sold within 6 years, or
  - UK co sells shares in overseas co
- EU PEs have different rules - transfers at NG/NL if some conditions met

The taxation of overseas income

Overseas income sources
- UK Co taxed on all overseas income, eg PE profits, interest, gains
- All overseas income grossed up for overseas withholding tax (WHT)

Double taxation relief (DTR)
- Exemption, credit relief, or expense relief (expense relief not in syllabus)
- Credit relief DTR is the lower of:
  - UK tax on overseas income
  - Overseas tax suffered
- Allocate losses and QCDs to UK income first, then overseas source with lowest rate of overseas tax

Overseas aspects of groups

Impact of non-resident companies on group relationships
- Non-resident companies can link any type of group together
- Loss relief only between UK companies or UK PEs of non-resident companies

Permanent establishment losses
UK loss relief depends on the availability of loss relief overseas

Chargeable gains groups and the 'global group concept'
NG/NL rule applies if the asset stays within the charge to UK CT

Transfer pricing

General rules
- Anti-avoidance legislation
- Transactions between companies under common control adjusted to arm's-length values

Exemption for SMEs
Rules do not apply to SMEs unless transaction with entity in non-qualifying territory

Thin capitalisation
Disallow interest on excessive loans if UK company highly geared

Advanced pricing agreements
Voluntary agreement with HMRC to approve transfer prices in advance

Controlled foreign companies (CFCs)

Introduction and definitions
- Anti-avoidance legislation aimed at preventing profits being diverted from the UK to a tax haven
- A CFC is a non-resident company under the control of UK resident 'persons'

Exceptions
- Exemptions apply for:
  - Exempt period of 12m after UK company acquires existing non-resident company
  - Overseas tax ≥ 75% of UK equivalent
  - CFC resident in an excluded territory
  - CFC profits < £500,000 and non-trading income < £50,000
  - Low margin – CFC's profit < 10% of operating expenditure

Chargeable profits and CFC charge
- No chargeable profits if:
  - No profits derived from tax planning schemes
  - No assets or risks managed from the UK, or
  - CFC capable of self-management if UK managerial involvement stopped
- If chargeable profits arise:
  - Apportion profits to UK corporate shareholders with ≥ 25% shareholdings
  - Charge to corporation tax (not part of TTP)
  - DTR available for overseas tax paid

Knowledge diagnostic

1. Company residence

Company residence is important in determining whether its profits are subject to UK tax.

A non-resident company is liable to UK corporation tax if it carries on trade in the UK through a permanent establishment.

2. Overseas expansion

A UK resident company intending to do business abroad must choose between a permanent establishment and a subsidiary.

An irrevocable election can be made to exempt profits and losses of all overseas branches from UK corporation tax.

3. Double taxation relief

A company may obtain DTR for overseas tax. The allocation of qualifying charitable donations and losses can affect the relief.

Double tax relief (DTR) is the lower of the UK tax on overseas profits and the overseas tax on overseas profits.

4. Overseas aspects of groups

The group relief rules allow groups and consortia to be established through companies resident anywhere in the world.

5. Corporate anti-avoidance legislation

The transfer pricing legislation prevents manipulation of profits between members of a group which can occur when a company chooses to buy and sell goods at a price which is not a market price.

Chargeable profits of a controlled foreign company (CFC) are apportioned to UK resident companies entitled to at least 25% of those profits and are subject to a CFC charge.

Further study guidance

Question practice

Now try the following from the Further question practice bank (available in the digital edition of the Workbook):

*   Exotica Inc and Willow Ltd

Activity answers

Activity 1: Unilateral double tax relief with multiple overseas income sources
Kairo plc – corporation tax year to 31 March 2021

	Total	UK	Atlantis	Utopia
	£	£	£	£
Total profits	300,000	10,000	40,000	250,000
Less: QCDs (W)	(15,000)	(10,000)	(5,000)	–
Taxable total profits	285,000	Nil	35,000	250,000
Corporation tax @ 19%	54,150		6,650	47,500
Less DTR (W)	(53,500)		(6,000)	(47,500)
Corporation tax	650		650	–

Working

The DTR is the lower of:

Atlantis: UK tax £6,650

Overseas tax £6,000 (Rate of overseas tax = 15%), ie £6,000

Utopia: UK tax £47,500

Overseas tax £110,000 (Rate of overseas tax = 44%), ie £47,500

Note. The Atlantis branch profits suffer the lower rate of overseas tax so the qualifying charitable donations remaining after offset against the UK income are allocated against the Atlantis branch income in preference to the Utopia branch income.

Activity 2: CFC charge

	£
Chargeable profits of Ribbon inc	650,000
Apportioned to Jenkins Ltd (75%)	487,500

Jenkins Ltd's CFC charge

Tax on apportioned profits	£
£487,500 × 19%	92,625
Less creditable tax (8% × £650,000) × 75%	(39,000)
CFC charge	53,625

23

Value added tax

Learning objectives

On completion of this chapter, you should be able to:

	Syllabus reference no.
Remember the material already covered in Taxation (TX – UK) under the headings:	
'the VAT registration requirements'	A6(a) F1
'the computation of VAT liabilities'	A6(a) F2
'the effect of special schemes'	A6(a) F3
Advise on the value added tax (VAT) implications of the supply of land and buildings in the UK	A6(a)(i)
Advise on the VAT implications of partial exemption	A6(a)(ii)
Advise on the application of the capital goods scheme	A6(a)(iii)

Exam context

VAT is a very important tax for businesses and there are few small enough to remain unregistered. You may be required to advise on almost any aspect, such as registration, including group registration.

A question may require you to consider the effect of following a particular course of action, for example commencing to make exempt supplies may lead to a greater than expected VAT cost as the partial exemption rules result in the disallowance of a proportion of input tax.

Chapter overview

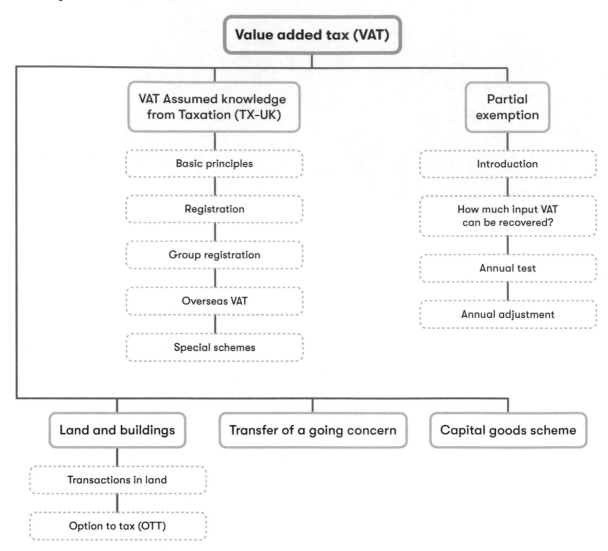

1 VAT assumed knowledge from Taxation (TX – UK)

All of the basics of Value Added Tax (VAT) are assumed knowledge from your Taxation (TX – UK) studies.

Essential reading

Included here are some summaries of key points which you should remember however, see Chapter 23 of the Essential reading for more detailed revision of your VAT assumed knowledge including Activities for you to test your understanding.

The Essential reading is available as an Appendix of the digital edition of the Workbook.

1.1 Basic principles

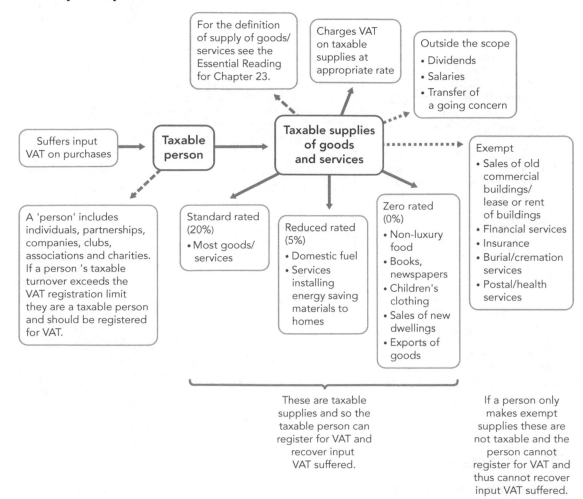

Once registered for VAT, a VAT return must be filed quarterly.

Output VAT due on sales	X
Less: Input VAT recoverable on purchases	(X)
Net VAT due to HMRC	X

The VAT return is due with payment of VAT by one month and seven days after the end of the VAT period.

Exam focus point

Due to the Coronavirus outbreak, the UK government allowed deferral of VAT payments due in the period 30 March to 30 June 2020. The ACCA examining team have stated that where relevant, you are to assume that the taxpayer has NOT opted to defer such payments.

1.2 Registration

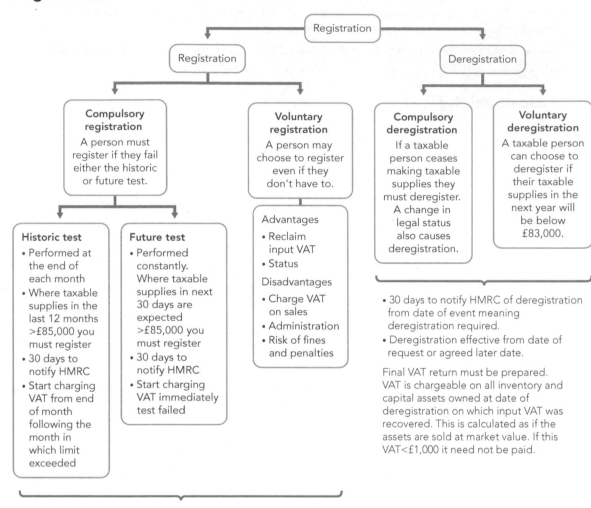

Once registered, charge output VAT on taxable supplies, recover input VAT suffered on purchases and submit VAT returns, usually quarterly.

1.3 VAT group registration

1.3.1 Effect of group registration

Allows groups to nominate **one entity** in the group to **prepare VAT returns for entities with the registration** (the 'representative member').

Intra-group transactions are **disregarded** for VAT purposes.

Administratively easier. Any VAT balances from individual entities are adjusted through inter-entity accounts.

All members of group registration are **jointly and severally liable** for the VAT liability.

1.3.2 Who can form a group?

The holding entity must **control subsidiaries** (ie by voting power) and the entities within the group registration must have **a fixed establishment in the UK**. The **holding** entity can be a **company, sole trader or partnership** but the **rest of the group members must be corporate**. The holding entity must control the UK company(/ies) that they wish to form a group with.

Subsidiaries under common control of an overseas company may also apply for group registration.

The inclusion of an exempt entity in the group VAT registration could result in the whole group becoming partially exempt (if not de minimis).

1.3.3 Election needed

Entities must **elect to form a VAT group**, it is not automatic, and not all eligible entities need to be included.

> ### Exam focus point
>
> In the exam, questions will often focus around practical application as to which group companies should or should not be included in a VAT group.

1.4 Overseas VAT

When a business starts to **trade overseas** consideration will need to be given as to the VAT rules. This will vary depending on whether the business is trading **within the European Union (EU) or outside it.**

1.4.1 Overseas VAT outside the EU

Sales/Exports

Purchases/Imports

HMRC holds goods at point of entry into UK

Input VAT paid on value of goods imported

Input VAT deductible on next VAT return

1.4.2 Overseas VAT within the EU

The UK officially left the EU on 31 January 2020. However, for exams in the period 1 June 2021 to 31 March 2022, it will be assumed that the EU rules continue to apply.

Sales/Dispatches

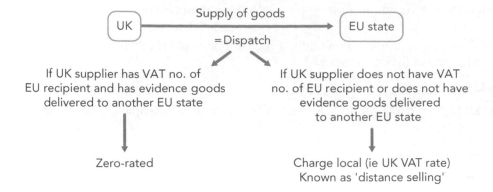

Purchases/Acquisitions

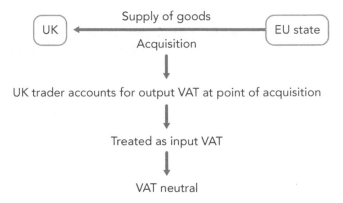

1.5 Special schemes

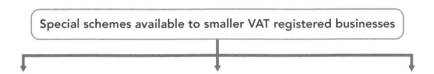

Cash accounting	Annual accounting	Flat-rate scheme
Available to trader with annual taxable turnover (VAT excl) not expected to exceed £1,350,000 in following 12 months with VAT returns and payments up to date	Available to traders with taxable turnover not expected to exceed £1,350,000 in the following 12 months with payments up to date	Available to traders with taxable turnover not expected to exceed £150,000 in next 12 months
VAT can be accounted for on the basis of cash paid and received rather than using tax points (tax points are an excluded topic at ATX but were covered in TX)	One annual return due within two months of year end	VAT due = flat % × Total (VAT incl) turnover

Cash accounting	Annual accounting	Flat-rate scheme
Advantages (a) Cash flow; and (b) Automatic impairment loss (bad debt) relief	Payment of 90% of previous year's VAT liability due in nine equal instalments (end of months 4–12); balance due with return	Flat % depends on trade sector. (1% reduction in first year of VAT registration)
Trader must cease to use the scheme as soon as revenue is expected to exceed £1,350,000 in following 12 months	Advantages (a) Less frequent submission of returns so less likelihood of default (b) Ability to manage cashflow more accurately (c) Avoids quarterly calculations for partial exemption purposes and input VAT recovery	There is no recovery of input VAT
	Disadvantages (a) Need to monitor future taxable supplies to check limit not exceeded (b) Timing of payments have less correlation to turnover (and thus cash received) by business (c) Payments based on prior year may not reflect current year turnover	The scheme removes the need to calculate and record output and input VAT. However, VAT at 20% is still treated as being charged where supply is to a VAT registered business, and a VAT invoice must still be issued.
	Can't be used by a company in a group VAT registration	Simplifies VAT calculation for very small businesses
		Advantage (a) Reduction in VAT admin
		VAT due may/ may not be lower dependent on the specific figures and this is not intended to be an advantage of the scheme
		A flat rate of 16.5% for businesses with no, or only a limited amount of, purchases of goods. In the exam you will not be expected to determine whether this rate applies but a question could be set applying this rate.
		If 16.5% rate applies, it is usually not advantageous to use the flat-rate scheme unless input VAT is very low

2 Partial exemption

2.1 Introduction

A trader may only recover the VAT on supplies made to them if it is attributable to their taxable supplies. **Where a person makes a mixture of taxable and exempt supplies, they are partially exempt. In this case, not all their input tax may be recoverable because some of it is attributable to their exempt supplies.**

2.2 How much input VAT can be recovered?

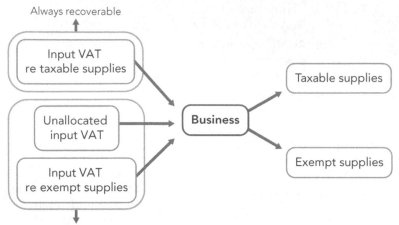

If the business passes one of three tests (known as *de minimis* tests or partial exemption tests), **it can recover all its input VAT:**

(a) Total input VAT ≤£625/month; **and**

(b) Exempt supplies ≤50% of total supplies.

OR

(a) Total input VAT – input VAT re taxable supplies ≤£625/month; **and**

(b) Exempt supplies ≤50% of total supplies.

OR

	✔ Recover	✘ Recover
Input VAT re taxable supplies	X	
Input VAT re exempt supplies		X
Unallocated input VAT		
Input VAT × Taxable supplies/Total supplies*		
Balance	$\underline{X}$	$\underline{X}$
	X	X[#]

*Round 'Taxable supplies/ Total supplies' up to nearest %.

[#] If ≤£625/month **and** ≤50% × total input VAT can recover **all** input VAT!

An alternative method of attributing input tax ('special' method) may be agreed in writing with HMRC.

Activity 1: Partial exemption

Sue makes the following supplies in the quarter ended 31 October 2020.

	£
Taxable supplies (excl. VAT)	28,000
Exempt supplies	6,000
	34,000

Sue analyses her input tax for the period as follows.

	£
Wholly attributable to: taxable supplies	1,500
exempt supplies	900
Non-attributable (overheads)	1,200
	3,600

Required

How much input tax is available for credit on Sue's VAT return assuming that she uses the percentage for the return period, where relevant?

Solution

2.3 Annual test

The annual test gives a trader the option of applying the *de minimis* test once a year instead of every VAT return period.

To use the annual test, **the trader must satisfy the following conditions:**

(a) Have been *de minimis* **in the previous partial exemption year**

(b) **Consistently apply the annual test throughout any given partial exemption year** (ie does not switch between the quarterly tests and the annual test in the year)

(c) Have reasonable grounds for **not expecting to incur more than £1 million input tax in its current partial exemption year**

If these conditions are satisfied, the trader can opt to treat himself as *de minimis* in the current partial exemption year. The trader can therefore recover input tax in full in each VAT return period without needing to see if one of the *de minimis* tests is satisfied for each VAT return period. This means that there is provisional recovery of all input tax in the year which will give a cash flow benefit and an administrative time saving.

At the end of the year, the trader must review their *de minimis* status using the *de minimis* tests applied to the year as a whole. If **one of the tests is failed**, the trader must carry out an **annual adjustment** as described below and which will result in a repayment of part of the input VAT previously recovered in full.

> ## Exam focus point
>
> The annual test for partial exemption was tested in June 2015 Question 3(c)(ii) Nocturne Ltd. The examining team commented that this part of the question was 'not done well. The problem here was that the majority of candidates addressed the annual accounting scheme rather than the subject of the question. This was unfortunate and meant that very few candidates did well on this part of the question.'

If the trader does not use the annual test, they must apply the *de minimis* tests for every VAT return period.

Tests 1 and 2 are simple to apply because they do not require the trader to make a calculation of residual VAT.

Test 3 is more complicated as it requires the calculation of residual VAT, usually using the standard method explained earlier in this chapter.

2.4 Annual adjustment

An annual adjustment is made with the *de minimis* tests applied to the year as a whole.

If **Tests 1 or 2 passed** for the year, **the trader will not need to pay back any of their already reclaimed input VAT and does not need to carry out a partial exemption calculation.**

If Tests 1 or 2 are failed, the trader will need to carry out a **full partial exemption calculation for the year to determine whether Test 3 is passed**. If it is, **the trader will not need to pay back any of their already reclaimed input VAT.**

The result for the year is compared with the total of results for the individual VAT periods and any difference is added to or deducted from the input tax either on the return for the last period in the year or on the return for the first period after the end of the year, at the option of the trader.

Essential reading

See Chapter 23 of the Essential reading for an Illustration showing the annual adjustment.

The Essential reading is available as an Appendix of the digital edition of the Workbook.

3 Land and buildings

3.1 Transactions in land

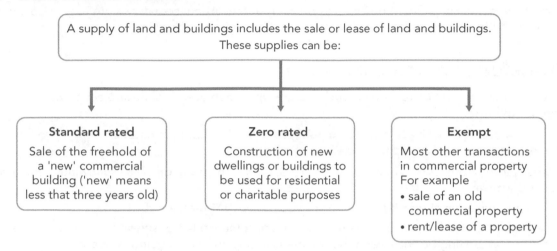

In an exam scenario, if we see a business buying a new commercial property, we know that they will suffer input VAT on their purchase and we shall need to see whether this input VAT can be recovered.

For a trader **using the building in their trade** recovery of input VAT will depend on whether their trade is making taxable supplies. If they **make 100% taxable supplies all of their input VAT suffered can be recovered**. If their business is **partially exempt they will recover their input VAT using the capital goods scheme** as explained later in this chapter.

If a **new commercial building** is bought as an **investment property and rented out,** then the owner of the building is using the building to make an **exempt supply**. On first principles this means that the **input VAT suffered cannot be recovered**. However, as explained below, the business can make an **option to tax (or 'waive the exemption') on the building**. This will ultimately mean that **input VAT suffered on the purchase of the building and its ongoing running costs can be recovered**.

3.2 Option to tax (OTT)

The owner of land or a commercial building may **elect** to **treat sales and leases of these assets as a taxable rather than exempt supply**. This is known as **waiving the exemption** or the **option to tax** the building.

A typical scenario where this would be useful would be where a business buys a new commercial property (thus suffering input VAT) and decides to rent the property out (thus making an exempt supply of the building).

On first principles, the input VAT suffered on purchase and any input VAT on ongoing costs associated with the property cannot be recovered as the building is being used to make an exempt supply.

However, if an **option to tax is made** it will mean that:

- The owner can **recover input VAT suffered on purchase and ongoing running costs of the property.**
- **VAT will need to be charged on the rent and any future sale of the property.**
- The **VAT status of the rental tenants and any future purchaser of the property must therefore be considered before the decision to opt to tax is made**. The option will increase the rental cost for any non-VAT registered tenant or tenants making exempt/ partially exempt supplies.

An option to tax is made on an **individual building** rather than on all the buildings owned by a person. If made, the option applies to the **whole** of the building.

The option to tax is made by the owner of the land or commercial building and **does not transfer to any new owner on a future sale of the asset**. Once made the election can be revoked:

- During a six-month 'cooling off' period

- Where no interest has been held in the property for over six years; or
- Where more than 20 years have elapsed since the election first had effect.

VAT consequences on the sale of land and buildings (and those included in the sale of a business as a whole) can be significant and it is important that the VAT consequences are fully understood. These will be further considered in Chapter 25 on Corporate tax planning.

4 Transfer of a going concern

When the assets of a **VAT-registered business are sold, each asset will be subject to VAT at the appropriate rate**.

When, however, the business is sold as **a going concern** the supply of assets is deemed to be **outside the scope of VAT** and thus **no VAT is chargeable**.

In order for the transfer of a going concern (TOGC) rules to apply, **all** of the **following conditions must be satisfied**:

- The **purchaser** must also **be** (or immediately become) **VAT registered**
- The assets are to be used by the purchaser in the **same kind of business** (whether or not as part of an existing business) and the business is transferred as a **going concern**
- If only **part** of the business is transferred, that **part is capable of separate operation**
- There is **no significant break in trading**

Where land and buildings are included in the transfer and ordinarily they would be standard rated (new commercial property or OTT) then VAT must be charged on these assets. This can be avoided, however, if the purchaser opts to tax these buildings too.

> **Exam focus point**
>
> The sale of the trade and assets of a business is a **common exam scenario** and you should make sure you can fully explain the VAT points.

These points will be further considered in Chapter 25 on Corporate tax planning.

5 Capital goods scheme

The scheme mainly affects partially exempt businesses and enables the amount of VAT recovered to be adjusted for each year's use.

The CGS applies to:

(a) **Computers**, boats and aircraft **costing £50,000 or more**, which are dealt with over **five VAT years**, and

(b) **Land and buildings costing £250,000 or more**, which are dealt with over **ten VAT years**.

Where an asset under the capital goods scheme is purchased, **initial recovery of input VAT is based on the asset's initial use**:

- Wholly taxable business - 100% of input VAT is recoverable
- Partially exempt business - input VAT recovery is based on its use in the quarter of purchase and then adjusted at the end of the VAT year. The input tax recovered for the first year as adjusted at the year end is the initial recovery
- Wholly exempt business - no input VAT may be recovered initially

For each subsequent VAT year over the recovery period of five or ten years an adjustment is made to the VAT recovery.

> **Formula to learn**
>
> **Adjustment = Original input VAT/ 10 or 5 intervals x (taxable % usage now – original taxable % use)**

The adjustment is made in the second VAT return following the end of the VAT year.

If the asset is sold before the end of the recovery period, **two** adjustments are needed:

(a) The **normal adjustment** for the VAT year of sale as if the proportion of use for the period from the start of the year until the date of sale had applied for the whole VAT year

(b) An additional adjustment ('**sale adjustment**') for each remaining VAT year of recovery calculated using 100% if VAT is charged on the sale or 0% if it is an exempt sale

Exam focus point

The capital goods scheme (and the 'sale adjustment' in particular) was tested in Hyssop Ltd in the September/ December 2015 hybrid paper. The Examining team commented that it was not done particularly well. They stated that the capital goods scheme is not easy to explain and that many candidates were unable to organise their thoughts and provide a coherent explanation of the implications of the disposal of the building. They went on to say that candidates would help themselves if they told the story from the beginning and explained how to apply this further in the context of the question.

The capital goods scheme was also tested in Question 4 Rosa in the December 2019 exam. The examining team said 'some students spent time writing everything they knew about the capital goods scheme when only the implications upon disposal were required. Only knowledge which addresses the question requirements will earn marks.'

Activity 2: Capital goods scheme

Zoran Ltd purchased a computer for £100,000 + 20% VAT on 1 July 2020. It used it 58% for taxable use in the quarter of purchase and 60% for taxable purposes in the year to 31 December 2020.

The taxable use in the year to 31 December 2021 was 50%. The computer was sold on 10 May 2022. The taxable use in the period 1 January 2022 to 10 May 2022 was 50%.

Required

Calculate the initial input recovery and adjustments required for all other years.

Solution

Chapter summary

```
┌─────────────────────────────┐
│     Value added tax (VAT)    │
└─────────────────────────────┘
```

```
┌──────────────────────────────────────────────┐
│   VAT Assumed knowledge from Taxation (TX-UK)  │
└──────────────────────────────────────────────┘
```

Basic principles

- VAT charged on taxable supplies made by a taxable person
- Taxable supplies can be standard rated (20%), reduced rated or zero rated
- Exempt supplies are not taxable supplies
- Returns usually filed quarterly and due (with payment) by one month and 7 days after quarter end

Registration

- Compulsory registration
  - Must register if taxable supplies in last 12 months >£85,000 (historic test); or
  - Must register if taxable supplies in next 30 days >£85,000 (future test)
  - 30 days to notify HMRC (either test)
  - Start charging VAT from end of month following month limit exceeded (historic) or date test failed (future)
- Voluntary registration
  - Allows input VAT to be recovered and gives company status
  - VAT charged on sales, administration and exposure to interest and penalties
- Compulsory deregistration
  - Required if cease making taxable supplies or change in legal status
- Voluntary deregistration
  - If taxable supplies in next year <£83,000
  - On deregistration a final VAT return is prepared. VAT is chargeable on all inventory and capital assets owned on which input VAT recovered although need not be paid if <£1,000

Group registration

- Holding entity (co/ST/p'ship) must control (by votes) subsidiary cos and must have fixed establishment in UK
- Subsidiaries controlled by an overseas company can also form a group
- Group nominates a representative member who prepares one VAT return for entire group
- Intra group transactions disregarded for VAT
- All members of group jointly and severally liable for VAT
- A VAT group may contain exempt entities thus making the whole group partially exempt
- Individual entities can opt out of group registration

Overseas VAT

- Outside EU:

Zero-rated

HMRC holds goods at point of entry into UK

↓

Input VAT paid on value of goods imported

↓

Input VAT deductible on next VAT return

Special rules where trader is approved under duty deferment scheme or goods held in HMRC warehouse

- Within EU: Acquisitions and despatches

If UK supplier has VAT no. of EU recipient → Zero-rated

If UK supplier does not have VAT no. of EU recipient → UK VAT at applicable rate

UK trader accounts for output VAT at point of acquisition

↓

Treated as input tax (provided tax invoice issued by supplier)

↓

VAT neutral

VAT Assumed knowledge from Taxation (TX-UK) continued

Special schemes

- Cash accounting
  - Annual taxable turnover in next 12 m ≤ £1,350,000
  - Tax point becomes date cash received/paid
  - Cashflow advantage and automatic impairment loss relief
- Annual accounting
  - Annual taxable turnover in next 12 m ≤ £1,350,000
  - One annual return due within two months of year end
  - 90% of previous year's VAT due in nine monthly instalments (m 4–12) with balance due with return
  - Less frequent preparation of return, easier cashflow management
- Flat rate scheme
  - Annual taxable turnover in next 12 m ≤ £150,000
  - VAT due = flat rate % × total (VAT incl) turnover
  - No recovery of input VAT
  - Simplifies admin for very small businesses

Partial exemption

Introduction

A partially exempt trader may not be able to recover all their input VAT

How much input VAT can be recovered?

- If a business passes one of three tests it can recover all its input VAT
  - Test 1: Total input VAT ≤ £625/m AND exempt supplies ≤ 50% of total supplies; or
  - Test 2: Total input VAT – input VAT re taxable supplies ≤ £625/m AND exempt supplies ≤ 50% of total supplies; or
  - Test 3:

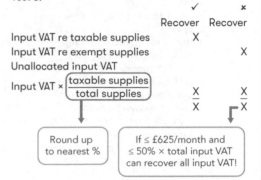

	✓ Recover	✗ Recover
Input VAT re taxable supplies	X	
Input VAT re exempt supplies		X
Unallocated input VAT		
Input VAT × $\dfrac{\text{taxable supplies}}{\text{total supplies}}$	$\dfrac{X}{X}$	$\dfrac{X}{X}$

Round up to nearest %

If ≤ £625/month and ≤ 50% × total input VAT can recover all input VAT!

Land and buildings

Transactions in land

- New commercial property (<3 yrs old) – standard rated supply
- Construction of new buildings for residential/charitable purposes – zero-rated supply
- Most other transactions (eg sale of old commercial property, rent/lease) – exempt supply

Option to tax (OTT)

- Owner of a commercial property can opt to tax their property
  - Useful for landlord renting building thus making an exempt supply
  - OTT means input VAT on purchase and ongoing costs can be recovered but VAT must be charged on rent and future sale of building
  - Consider VAT position of tenants and future owners

Transfer of a going concern

- Normally when VAT registered business sold – VAT is charged on all the individual assets
- If business is sold as a going concern and conditions are met it becomes a transfer of a going concern and becomes outside the scope of VAT
- Conditions
  - Purchaser is (or becomes) VAT registered
  - Same kind of business carried on
  - No significant break in trading

Capital goods scheme

- Applies to partially exempt business which acquires computers costing > £50k and/or land/buildings costing > £250k
- Computers dealt with over 5 years and land/buildings over 10 years
- In VAT year of purchase, input VAT recovered based on use of asset for quarter of purchase, adjusted at end of VAT year
- For each subsequent VAT year there's an adjustment if taxable use changes
- Adjustment = Original input VAT/10 or 5 × (taxable % usage now – original taxable % use)
- Adjustment made in second VAT return following end of VAT year
- On sale before end of recovery period two adjustments needed:
  - Normal adjustment as if item used whole year
  - Additional sale adjustment for each remaining VAT year of recovery calculated using 100% taxable use for taxable supplies (or 0% for an exempt supply) in each of those years

Knowledge diagnostic

1. Basics

VAT is charged on turnover at each stage in a production process, but in such a way that the burden is borne by the final consumer.

VAT is charged on taxable supplies of goods and services made by a taxable person in their business.

Some supplies are taxable (either standard-rated, reduced-rated or zero-rated). Others are exempt.

VAT is charged on the VAT-exclusive price. Where a discount is offered for prompt payment, VAT is chargeable on actual amount received for the supply.

2. Registration

A trader becomes liable to register for VAT if the value of taxable supplies in any period up to 12 months exceeds £85,000 or if there are reasonable grounds for believing that the value of the taxable supplies will exceed £85,000 in the next 30 days. A trader may also register voluntarily.

3. Recovery of input VAT

VAT incurred on goods and services before registration can be treated as input tax and recovered from HMRC subject to certain conditions.

Not all input VAT is deductible, eg VAT on most motor cars.

If fuel is supplied for private purposes all input VAT incurred on the fuel is allowed and the business will normally account for output VAT using a set of scale charges.

Relief for VAT on impairment losses (bad debts) is available if the VAT has been accounted for, the debt is over six months old (measured from when the payment is due) and has been written off in the trader's accounts.

4. Returns and administration

VAT is accounted for on regular returns which are usually filed online within one month plus seven days of the end of the VAT period. Extensive records must be kept.

VAT is administered by HMRC and the Tax tribunal hears appeals.

A default occurs when a trader either submits their VAT return late or submits the return on time but pays the VAT late. A default surcharge is applied if there is a default involving late payment during a default surcharge period.

There is a common penalty regime for errors in tax returns, including VAT. Errors in a VAT return up to certain amounts may be corrected in the next return.

Default interest is charged on unpaid VAT if HMRC raise an assessment of VAT or the trader makes a voluntary payment before the assessment is raised. It runs from the date the VAT should have been paid to the actual date of payment but cannot run for more than three years before the assessment or voluntary payment.

5. Overseas VAT

Imports from outside the EU are subject to VAT and exports to outside the EU are zero-rated. Taxable acquisitions from other EU states are also subject to VAT and sales to registered traders in other EU states are zero-rated.

International services between VAT registered businesses require the customer to account for both output and input tax under the reverse charge rules. Output tax on other international services is usually accounted for by the supplier in the usual way.

6. Special schemes

Special schemes include the cash accounting scheme, the annual accounting scheme and the flat rate scheme. These schemes make VAT accounting easier for certain types of trader usually with relatively low turnover.

7. Partial exemption

A trader making both taxable and exempt-supplies may be unable to recover all their input tax.

A partially exempt trader can recover all input VAT attributable to taxable supplies and the proportion of their unallocated input VAT that relates to their proportion of supplies which are taxable. Their remaining input VAT is irrecoverable unless it meets one of three de minimis tests.

8. Land and buildings

Transactions in land may be zero-rated, standard-rated or exempt. Sales of new commercial buildings (<3 years old) are standard-rated and sales of old commercial buildings and rent/ lease of buildings are an exempt supply.

An option to tax can be made on a commercial building which makes the supply of the building become taxable. This allows the owner to recover input VAT relating to the building, but VAT must be charged on future rent and sale of the building.

9. Transfer of a going concern

On the sale of a business VAT must be charged on all the assets at the appropriate rate unless the conditions are met for a transfer of a going concern. If the TOGC conditions are met the transfer becomes outside the scope of VAT and no VAT needs to be charged.

10. Capital goods scheme

The capital goods scheme (CGS) allows HMRC to ensure the VAT claimed on the purchase of certain capital items accurately reflects the taxable use to which they are put over a period of time.

Further study guidance

Question practice

Now try the following from the Further question practice bank (available in the digital edition of the Workbook):

- VAT groups
- Stewart Ltd

Activity answers

Activity 1: Partial exemption

Test 1

Total input VAT is = £1,200 per calendar month, more than £625 per calendar month.

Proportion of exempt supplies = 17.6%

Test 1 failed as only one part of test satisfied.

Test 2

	£
Total input VAT for period	3,600
Less wholly attributable to taxable supplies	(1,500)
	2,100

Monthly average = £700 per calendar month, more than £625 per calendar month.

Proportion of exempt supplies = 17.6%

Test 2 failed as only one part of test satisfied.

Test 3

	£
Wholly attributable to taxable supplies	1,500
Partly attributable to taxable supplies	
28,000/(28,000 + 6,000)	
ie 82.35% rounded up to 83% × £1,200	996
	2,496
£(900 + (1,200 − 996)) = 1,104	
Exempt input tax is *de minimis* (W)	1,104
Input tax recoverable	3,600

ie all input tax is recoverable

Working

Monthly average = £368 ie not more than £625

Proportion of total = 30.7% ie not more than 50%.

Both parts of Test 3 satisfied so Test 3 passed.

Activity 2: Capital goods scheme

For the first VAT year to 31 December 2020 the recovery (after the annual partial exemption adjustment) is £100,000 × 20% = £20,000 × 60% = £12,000.

For the second VAT year to 31 December 2021 the adjustment is £20,000 × (− 10%) (ie 50% − 60%) × 1/5 = (£400), payable to HMRC.

For the third VAT year to 31 December 2022 there are two adjustments:

(1) £20,000 × (– 10%) 1/5 = (£400), payable to HMRC

(2) £20,000 × 40% (ie 100% – 60%) × 2/5 = £3,200

The net adjustment for the third VAT year to 31 December 2022 is £3,200 – £400 = £2,800 recoverable from HMRC.

Stamp taxes

Learning objectives

On completion of this chapter, you should be able to:

	Syllabus reference no.
Identify the property in respect of which stamp taxes are payable	A5(a)(i)
Advise on the stamp taxes payable on transfers of shares and securities	A5(b)(i)
Advise on the stamp taxes payable on transfers of land	A5(b)(ii)
Identify transfers involving no consideration	A5(c)(i)
Advise on group transactions	A5(c)(ii)

Exam context

Stamp taxes will make up a minor part of a question but must not be overlooked as they can be a significant cost in many transactions.

Chapter overview

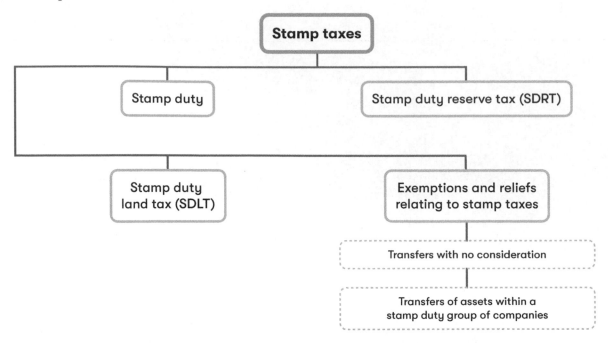

1 Stamp duty

Stamp duty applies to **transfers of shares and securities** which are effected by a paper **stock transfer form.** It is **payable** by the **purchaser.**

Stamp duty applies at the **rate** of **0.5%** of the **consideration** unless the transfer falls within one of the **specific exemptions** (see the section on exemptions later in this chapter). The duty is rounded up to the nearest £5.

> **PER alert**
>
> Two of the competencies you require to fulfil Performance Objective 15 Tax computations and assessments of the PER are to prepare or contribute to the computation or assessment of tax computations for individuals and to prepare or contribute to the computation or assessment of tax computations for single companies, groups or other entities. You can apply the knowledge you obtain from this section of the text to help demonstrate these competences.

2 Stamp duty reserve tax (SDRT)

Stamp duty reserve tax (SDRT) is applicable to **transfers of shares and securities** which are effected by an **electronic paperless transaction.** It is **payable** by the **purchaser.**

Most of these transactions are made through **an electronic system** called **CREST.** Some shares are held outside CREST ('Off Market') but may still be transferred electronically, for example if they are held by a nominee such as a bank.

SDRT applies at the **rate** of **0.5%** of the **consideration** unless the transfer falls within one of the **specific exemptions** (see the section on exemptions later in this chapter).

3 Stamp duty land tax (SDLT)

Stamp duty land tax (SDLT) applies to **land transactions in England and Northern Ireland.**

> **Exam focus point**
>
> There are similar taxes called Land and Buildings Transaction Tax (LBTT) on land transactions in Scotland and Land Transaction Tax (LTT) on land transactions in Wales. LBTT and LTT are excluded from the Advanced Taxation (ATX – UK) syllabus.

A land transaction is a **transfer of land** or an **interest in,** or **right over, land. SDLT is** generally **payable** based on the **consideration for the land transaction.** It is **payable** by the **purchaser.** The **amount of the charge to SDLT** depends on whether the land is **residential** (eg houses, flats) or **non-residential** (eg shops, warehouses, factories).

> **Exam focus point**
>
> The charge to stamp duty land tax on residential property and the treatment of leases are excluded from the Advanced Taxation (ATX – UK) syllabus.

The following rates of SDLT apply to non-residential property:

Non-residential	Rate (%)
Up to £150,000	0
£150,001 – £250,000	2
£250,001 and above	5

Formula provided

The thresholds and rates of SDLT for non-residential property will be shown in the Tax Rates and Allowances available in the exam.

 ## Activity 1: Non-residential property (1)

Raymond buys a freehold shop in England in November 2020 for £145,000.

Required

Calculate the stamp duty land tax due

Solution

 ## Activity 2: Non-residential property (2)

Klear plc buys a freehold factory in Northern Ireland in August 2020 for £350,000.

Required

Calculate the stamp duty land tax due.

Solution

4 Exemptions and reliefs relating to stamp taxes

4.1 Transfers with no consideration

Stamp taxes are charged on the **consideration** passing under the document or transaction. If there is **no consideration**, there is **an exemption from stamp taxes**. Examples include:

- **Gifts** (except a gift of land to a connected company)
- A **transfer on divorce**, annulment of marriage or judicial separation
- **Variations** of a **will** or **intestacy** made within two years of death for no consideration
- Transfers to **charities** if the shares or land is to be used for charitable purposes

If **land is transferred** to a **company**, for example on **incorporation**, SDLT is payable on the **market value** of land.

4.2 Transfers of assets within a stamp duty group of companies

Relief from **stamp duty** and **SDLT** is given for **transfers of assets** between **companies within a stamp taxes group**. There is no direct relief for stamp duty reserve tax so the transaction must be made by using a stock transfer form and a claim made for stamp duty relief.

There are **two conditions** which must be met to attract the relief, namely that:

- The effect must be to transfer the **beneficial interest** in property from one company to another; and
- **One company must be the parent of the other company** or **both companies must have a common parent company.**

One company is regarded as the parent of another if:

- The company has beneficial ownership of at least 75% of the ordinary share capital, ie if all the issued share capital of a company, other than fixed rate preference shares; and
- The company has at least a 75% interest in dividends and assets in a winding up; and
- There are no 'arrangements' for a non-group person to acquire control of the transferee company but not the transferor company.

For indirect holdings, it is necessary to reduce the degree of ownership at each level to the appropriate fraction in determining whether the 75% test is met (as for corporation tax group relief).

This relief is something which you should consider if there's a transfer of shares or buildings in a corporate group scenario and we will see its application in Chapter 25 on Corporate tax planning.

Activity 3: Stamp duty relief

Allegri Ltd owns 90% of the ordinary share capital of Byrd Ltd, which in turn owns 85% of the ordinary share capital of Corelli Ltd. Shares are transferred from Corelli Ltd to Allegri Ltd under an instrument executed on 1 June 2020.

Required

Is stamp duty relief available?

Solution

SDLT relief is withdrawn where **land has been transferred from one group company to another** and **within three years of the transfer** the **transferee company leaves the group** whilst still owning the land. Note that the **transferor** company leaving the group does not cause the SDLT relief to be withdrawn as the land is still held by the transferee company and so it is still within the group.

> ### Exam focus point
>
> SDLT on groups was tested in June 2015 Question 2(a) Helm Ltd group. The examining team commented that 'the stamp duty land tax aspects of the question were not handled well with very few candidates recognising that the inter group exemption that was available when the trade and assets of Aero Ltd were transferred to Bar Ltd would be withdrawn due to the sale of Bar Ltd within three years'.

Chapter summary

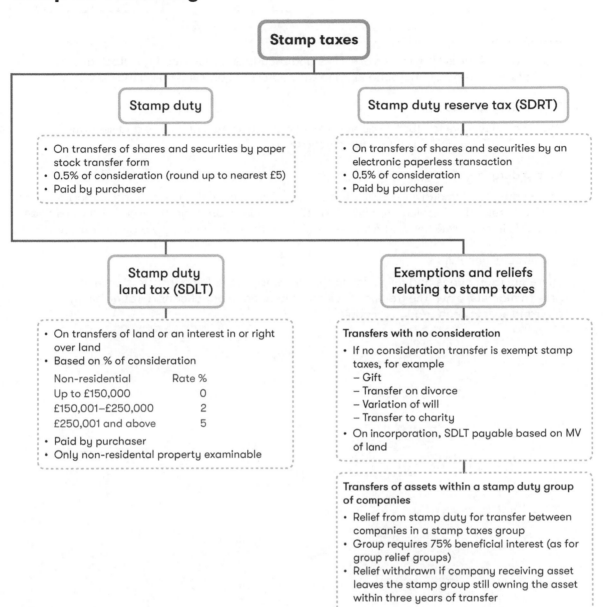

Stamp taxes

Stamp duty
- On transfers of shares and securities by paper stock transfer form
- 0.5% of consideration (round up to nearest £5)
- Paid by purchaser

Stamp duty reserve tax (SDRT)
- On transfers of shares and securities by an electronic paperless transaction
- 0.5% of consideration
- Paid by purchaser

Stamp duty land tax (SDLT)
- On transfers of land or an interest in or right over land
- Based on % of consideration

Non-residential	Rate %
Up to £150,000	0
£150,001–£250,000	2
£250,001 and above	5

- Paid by purchaser
- Only non-residental property examinable

Exemptions and reliefs relating to stamp taxes

Transfers with no consideration
- If no consideration transfer is exempt stamp taxes, for example
  - Gift
  - Transfer on divorce
  - Variation of will
  - Transfer to charity
- On incorporation, SDLT payable based on MV of land

Transfers of assets within a stamp duty group of companies
- Relief from stamp duty for transfer between companies in a stamp taxes group
- Group requires 75% beneficial interest (as for group relief groups)
- Relief withdrawn if company receiving asset leaves the stamp group still owning the asset within three years of transfer

Knowledge diagnostic

1. Stamp duty

Stamp duty applies to transfers of shares and securities transferred by a stock transfer form. It is 0.5% of the consideration (rounded up to the nearest £5) and is paid by the purchaser.

2. Stamp duty reserve tax

Stamp duty reserve tax (SDRT) applies to electronic transfers of shares and securities. It is 0.5% of the consideration and is paid by the purchaser.

3. Stamp duty land tax

Stamp duty land tax (SDLT) applies to the sale of land, or of rights over land, in England and Northern Ireland. It is calculated based on the consideration using the rates and thresholds available in the Tax Rates and Allowances given in the exam and is paid by the purchaser.

4. Exemptions and reliefs

There are exemptions and reliefs for stamp taxes, for example on transfers of securities traded on growth markets, when the transfer does not involve payment of consideration, such as a gift, and on transfers between group companies.

Further study guidance

Question practice

Now try the following from the Further question practice bank (available in the digital edition of the Workbook):

- Dan

Activity answers

Activity 1: Non-residential property (1)

His stamp duty land tax is £145,000 × 0% = £0.

Activity 2: Non-residential property (2)

Its stamp duty land tax is:

	£
£150,000 × 0%	0
£100,000 (£250,000 – 150,000) × 2%	2,000
£100,000 (£350,000 – 250,000) × 5%	5,000
£350,000	7,000

Activity 3: Stamp duty relief

Relief is available, since Allegri Ltd owns indirectly 76½% (ie 90% × 85%) of the ordinary share capital of Corelli Ltd.

25 Corporate tax planning

Learning objectives

On completion of this chapter, you should be able to:

	Syllabus reference no.
Identify and advise on the taxes applicable to a given course of action and their impact	B1
Identify and understand that the alternative ways of achieving personal or business outcomes may lead to different tax consequences	B2
Calculate the receipts from a transaction, net of tax and compare the results of alternative scenarios and advise on the most tax-efficient course of action	B2(a)
Assess the tax advantages and disadvantages of alternative courses of action	B4
Understand the statutory obligations imposed in a given situation, including any time limits for action and advise on the implications of non-compliance	B5
Advise on legitimate tax planning measures, by which the tax liabilities arising from a particular situation or course of action can be mitigated	C2
Advise on the mitigation of tax in the manner recommended by reference to numerical analysis and/or reasoned argument	C4
Communicate advice, recommendations and information in the required format: for example, the use of Reports, Letters, Memoranda and Meeting notes	D1
Present written information, in language appropriate to the purpose of the communication and the intended recipient	D2
Communicate conclusions reached, together where necessary, with relevant supporting computations	D3

	Syllabus reference no.
State and explain assumptions made or limitations in the analysis provided; together with any inadequacies in the information available and/or additional information required to provide a fuller analysis	D4
Identify and explain other, non-tax, factors that should be considered	D5

Exam context

We are going to be looking at specific tax planning issues relating to companies and groups of companies. In the exam you can expect to see at least one question involving a company or group of companies, and you are expected to be able to provide appropriate tax advice that will minimise their tax liabilities. This may well involve the use of losses and double taxation relief.

Of particular importance to companies is the availability of the substantial shareholdings exemption. You must be aware of the conditions that need to be met, and be able to apply those conditions to facts given in the question. This will be relevant for any company considering the disposal of shares.

Chapter overview

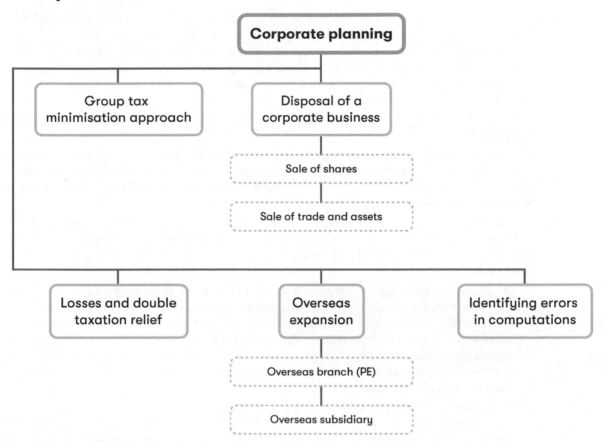

1 Group tax minimisation approach

A scenario with a corporate group and multiple different types of losses to deal with can be a daunting examination question. The method below may help you structure your answer.

(a) **Draw out a group structure** and work out the **number of related 51% group companies** as well as **identifying any group relief and gains groups**. Note any **non-coterminous year ends or any companies being bought or sold during the year** as these will all need more careful consideration when deciding how any losses can be used.

(b) **Divide the £1,500,000** (quarterly instalment threshold) by the **number of related 51% group companies**.

(c) Set out a **table with a column for each company** within the group and enter the results from the question. Remember that capital losses brought forward have lost any flexibility and must now remain in the same company. The capital losses carried forward can only be offset against net gains in that same company.

(d) Next any brought-forward (non-capital) losses need to be identified and considered in addition to any current year losses. This is where a **neatly presented loss memo** will help maximise your marks. When thinking about how to use losses the following points can help you to score marks:

(i) **Any capital losses within companies can only be offset against capital gains.** Thus, consider moving current year capital losses and gains around the group to match the losses and gains together. Think about which companies the net gains should be left to arise in (for example, those with available capital losses brought forward although be aware that large brought forward losses could be restricted as covered earlier in this workbook), and whether group rollover relief can be utilised to reduce the amount immediately chargeable.

(ii) If any companies within the group are currently paying tax through quarterly instalments, consider transferring any net gains to other group companies or allocating group trade losses through group relief to these companies **in order to bring their TTP down to below the threshold and remove them from the quarterly instalment paying regime**.

(iii) If you are given information about prior years do remember to consider a current year and 12-month carry-back trade loss claim – remember a **carry-back claim generates a cashflow advantage**.

(iv) If any claims **waste QCDs** ensure you note this in your answer as some of your loss claim will now not be saving tax.

(v) Generally, it is easier to consider **allocating capital gains and losses around the group before considering any group relief claims and then finally dealing with any consortium relief claims** at the end of the question. While this may not give you a perfect solution every time the structure will give you a process to follow and will allow you to access the easier marks rather than getting caught up in the tougher areas such as consortium relief.

(e) Finally, do try to make a **reasoned recommendation** as to how the losses can best be utilised. **Only quantify the tax saving if the question requires it**.

Activity 1: Alpha Group

Alpha Ltd is a UK resident company. It has a 31 March year end. It owns the following UK subsidiaries:

Bravo Ltd	Acquired 1/1/1990	March year end	100%
Charlie Ltd	Acquired 30/4/2007	December year end	80%
Delta Ltd	Acquired 1/4/2020	March year end	80%

Alpha Ltd also has one overseas trading subsidiary, which does not have any UK permanent establishments.

Charlie Ltd owns 80% of Echo Ltd which it acquired before it joined the Alpha Ltd group.

The most recent results for the group are as follows:

Alpha Ltd	YE 31/3/21 Trading loss	£(140,000)
	Trading loss b/f	£(100,000)
Bravo Ltd	YE 31/3/21 property income	£100,000
	Capital gain 1/2/21	£120,000
Charlie Ltd	YE 31/12/20 Trading income	£510,000
Delta Ltd	YE 31/3/21 Trading profit	£150,000
	UK property income	£50,000
	Capital loss bf at 1/4/20	£(30,000)
	Trading loss b/f	(200,000)
Echo Ltd	YE 31/12/20 Trading loss	£(10,000)
	Capital loss 30/9/20	£(40,000)

Bravo Ltd's gain arose on the sale of a factory used in its trade for £500,000. Shortly after Bravo Ltd sold its factory, Alpha Ltd acquired a new office building for £440,000.

There has been no major change in Delta Ltd's trade since it was acquired.

Alpha Ltd would like the group to utilise its losses for the benefit of the group as soon as possible.

Required

You are required to calculate the TTP for each company assuming beneficial claims and elections are made. Explain your treatment of the losses in the group.

Solution

2 Disposal of a corporate business

If a corporate group wants to divest itself of one of its trading subsidiaries, there are two main ways of achieving this – a **sale of the shares** in the subsidiary (which is usually the most straightforward method), or a **sale of its trade and assets**, followed by a **solvent liquidation or the payment of a dividend** to the holding company. The following table shows the tax implications of each of these routes, along with the **tax implications of the transfer of a trade within a 75% group**:

	Sale of a company to a third party	Sale of a company's trade to a third party	Transfer of a company's trade within a 75% group
Gains arising	(a) Possible degrouping charge (b) Possible gain on sale of shares by parent (unless substantial shareholdings exemption applies)	(a) Sale of individual *chargeable* assets giving rise to gains and losses in the company whose trade is sold (b) Possible relief if proceeds reinvested in qualifying assets (group-wide rollover relief)	No gain/no loss rules will apply to capital assets

	Sale of a company to a third party	**Sale of a company's trade to a third party**	**Transfer of a company's trade within a 75% group**
Unrelieved trade losses	C/f in company sold **unless** new owner makes **major** changes to nature/conduct of trade (eg customer base, geographic location, type of business)	Lost	Transferred with the trade and c/f trade loss reliefs can be used (eg to offset vs acquirer's total profits or group relieved.) If selling company has had: (a) A change of ownership (CoO); and (b) Sells its trade within 3 yrs before or 5 yrs after CoO Then for a 5 yr period from CoO the acquirer can only use seller's c/f losses vs profits of trade transferred (not total profits) and can't group relieve them
Unrelieved capital losses	C/f in company sold = pre-entry for new group	Remain with transferor	Remain with transferor
Capital allowances	No effect – company is continuing	Transferred at MV (BC may arise) For SBA assets - the seller adds SBAs claimed to date to disposal proceeds in gains calculation and buyer claims SBAs based on original eligible cost	Automatically transferred at TWDV For SBA assets - seller does not add SBAs claimed to date to proceeds in gains calculation. The buyer claims SBAs and, on subsequent disposal, adds all SBAs (of both seller and buyer) to its disposal proceeds
VAT	Exempt supply	Transfer of business as a going concern – outside scope if transferee is/becomes registered	Transfer of business as a going concern – outside scope if transferee is/becomes registered
Stamp duty	½% on value of consideration paid by the purchaser	Up to 5% on value of land and buildings paid by purchaser	No stamp duty with transfers in a 75% group (unless transferee sold within three years of transfer)

To recommend a route, it is necessary to consider the after-tax disposal proceeds in the parent company.

With a sale of trade and assets, consider the tax implications of each asset being sold, the impact on TTP, and then multiply by the rate of corporation tax (19%). Deducting this corporation tax from the proceeds of the sale of assets will give you the amount of cash distributable to the parent company (and any other shareholders).

> ### Exam focus point
>
> Question 3 Kitz Ltd in the December 2019 exam tested a sale of shares. The examining team said that while many students spotted the SSE few identified the degrouping charge despite there being clues in the question. They also noted 'this question specifically asked for no calculations and yet a significant number gave calculations. Even if workings were correct, there were no marks awarded when they were specifically not asked for. Once again students are wasting their limited exam time earning no marks.'

Activity 2: Sale of shares vs trade and assets

Skye Ltd has owned 100% of Moonshine Ltd since January 2019. The shares cost Skye Ltd £100,000.

Skye Ltd has been approached with two separate offers for the sale of Moonshine Ltd as follows:

Offer 1 – Sale of shares, we have been offered £580,000 for the whole share capital.

Offer 2 – Sale of trade and assets of the business.

We have been offered £616,000 for the company's trade and assets as follows.

This will leave Moonshine Ltd with net current liabilities of £20,000 which it will pay out of the sale proceeds.

Both companies are trading companies.

	Offer	Cost	TWDV
	£	£	£
Premises	483,200	392,000	N/A
Plant and machinery	36,800	64,000	52,000
Goodwill	96,000	Nil	
	616,000		

Required

Calculate the after-tax proceeds in respect of each of the two offers. Assume indexation allowance on premises is £50,930. Recommend which offer should be accepted.

Solution

3 Pre- or post-liquidation distributions

Where the liquidation is not a result of insolvency, tax planning for the distribution of assets is very important.

Distributions before winding up commences		Distributions after winding up commences	
Treated as a normal **dividend**		Treated as a **capital disposal**	
Individual shareholder		**Individual** shareholder	
Income tax	Effective rate	Capital gains tax	Effective rate
BRT	7.5%	BRT (No BADR)	10%
HRT	32.5%	HRT/ART (No BADR)	20%
ART	38.1%	BADR*	10%
Corporate shareholder:		**Corporate** shareholder:	
No CT – dividends are exempt		Gain chargeable to CT unless SSE applies	
		*Disposal must be within three years of cessation	

The position for corporate shareholders

If the SSE applies, a corporate shareholder would generally be indifferent between pre- and post-liquidation distributions, as no corporation tax would be suffered either way.

However, the receipt of a pre-liquidation distribution, if from a non-group company, may affect the obligation to pay by quarterly instalments (whereas a post-liquidation distribution qualifying for the SSE would have no impact on TTP or augmented profits).

If the SSE is not applicable, then a pre-liquidation distribution will be preferable as no corporation tax will be due.

The position for individual shareholders

The choice of whether to pay a pre-liquidation distribution depends on **two main factors**:

(a) The **availability of capital losses, annual exempt amount and business asset disposal relief** to mitigate/exempt their gains

(b) The **rate of tax they would pay on a pre-liquidation (dividend) distribution**

A basic-rate taxpayer would probably benefit from a small amount of pre-liquidation distribution, to use up any available dividend nil rate band (DNRB) and the 7.5% rate payable on dividends (as compared to a CGT rate of 10% on amounts above the annual exempt amount) A higher- or additional-rate taxpayer would (subject to the DNRB) invariably be better off with a post-liquidation payout, as the applicable marginal rate of tax on a gain is lower than that on a dividend.

A mixture of personal and corporate shareholders

It is not possible to discriminate between shareholders; if a dividend is declared it must be paid to (and taxed on) all those entitled to it.

Illustration 1: Sale of trade and assets – liquidation decision

Using the data in the previous Activity, assume that Moonshine had significant non-trading activities and that therefore the share disposal would not qualify for the SSE.

Required

Explain why Offer 2 is now more attractive to Skye Ltd, and whether the sale proceeds should be extracted as a pre- or post-liquidation distribution.

Solution

As SSE no longer applies, the disposal of shares gives rise to a chargeable gain in Skye Ltd, and corporation tax thereon will be:

£(580,000 – 100,000) × 19% = £91,200

After-tax sale proceeds are now £488,800

The sale of trade and assets of Moonshine Ltd for £616,000 gave rise to net cash of £572,997.

If this were paid to Skye Ltd as a **pre-liquidation** distribution (up to Moonshine Ltd's distributable reserves), no corporation tax would arise. A liquidator would be appointed to distribute the remaining cash as a capital distribution, and a capital gain or loss would be calculated by deducting the base cost of £100,000.

4 Losses and double taxation relief

Where a company can specify the amount of relief to claim (for example, brought-forward losses or group relief), it is possible to select an amount such that the corporation tax after double taxation relief becomes nil.

In order to achieve this, it is necessary to use an amount of loss relief to leave sufficient TTP to give a corporation tax charge equal to the amount of foreign tax suffered.

Activity 3: DTR and group relief

Sherman Ltd, a UK resident company which is part of a large group of companies, has trading profits of £850,000 for y/e 31 March 2021.

Sherman received £150,000 from a foreign property subject to 18% withholding tax.

Sherman also paid a qualifying charitable donation of £100,000.

Required

Calculate the maximum loss that can be surrendered to Sherman Ltd by the other group companies if relief in respect of the tax suffered overseas is not to be wasted.

Solution

5 Overseas expansion

As we saw in Chapter 22, when a UK company is looking to **expand overseas**, it must decide between setting up an **overseas branch** or a **subsidiary**. The **election to exempt the profits of all overseas PEs is irrevocable** and would **exclude the company from relieving any of the losses of its overseas PEs against UK profits in future**. This **election** cannot be made on a PE-by-PE basis, or even a country-by-country basis, and **applies to all (current and future) PEs**.

If the election is not to be made, then each expansion opportunity must be considered separately. The decision between setting up a PE or subsidiary will depend on the following factors:

- The **overseas tax rate**: if it is **higher** than in the UK, then the decision will probably not greatly impact the overall tax charges (as both a PE or a subsidiary are likely to be taxed in the destination country, and DTR would cover the UK corporation tax on the PE profits). If the overseas tax rate is **lower** than in the UK, using a subsidiary would mean that any profits are only taxed overseas and the lower tax rate can be taken advantage of (subject to CFC rules). If a branch is used, DTR would not fully cover the UK tax charge on profits and so an overall 19% tax rate would apply.

- **Rules for deductibility of expenses**: for example, capital allowance regimes will be different across the world; if the destination country's regime is more generous than that of the UK (or if more expenses were deductible than in the UK), a subsidiary would be able to benefit from the additional allowances to reduce tax in the earlier years of trading.

- The **likelihood of losses**: If losses are likely to arise in early trading periods, using a PE would give the UK group access to those losses to minimise UK corporation tax (via current year offset, carry back or group relief). Losses of overseas subsidiaries cannot be used as group relief.

> ### Exam focus point
>
> A discussion of the advantages and disadvantages of making an election to exempt the profits of an overseas PE from UK corporation tax was tested in March 2020 Question 2 Mita. The examining team stated 'that most students were able to list two or three of these, but very few got all four.'

Activity 4: Branch vs subsidiary

The SJA Group is a UK-based group of very profitable companies. The directors wish to expand overseas to the country of Overlandia, where the corporation tax regime is very similar to that of the UK. However, the tax authorities of Overlandia tax the profits of branches of overseas companies at a rate of 15%, and Overlandian companies at a rate of 12%. Loss relief is given to Overlandian resident companies (against current and future total profits), but is not permitted for Overlandian PEs of overseas resident companies.

In the first year of trading, the directors of SJA Ltd anticipate losses within the Overlandian branch of £100,000, followed by profits of £250,000 in Year 2.

Required

Recommend whether a branch or subsidiary structure should be used based on the information for Years 1 and 2.

Solution

6 Identifying errors in computations

Occasionally in questions, you may be presented with draft computations provided by a client, or by a tax junior in your firm. It will probably be your task **to analyse the computations given to you, and to identify and correct any errors made**. You looked at the methods and approach to spotting errors within Chapter 13 (Capital tax planning), so the approach will not be repeated here.

From a corporation tax perspective the following would be common mistakes to watch out for:

- Adjusting profits for **private expenses of the owner**, or **restricting capital allowances for private use**
- **Awarding indexation allowance for periods after December 2017**
- Awarding the **substantial shareholdings exemption when it is not due** (or vice versa)
- **Awarding CGT reliefs that are only available to individuals** – eg PPR, business asset disposal relief, investor's relief
- **Failing to gross up overseas income correctly**
- **Charging dividends to corporation tax**

VAT and stamp taxes may also have been incorrectly applied to a transaction: remember the following when reviewing calculations:

- VAT only applies to **commercial property** that is either '**new**' or has been **opted to tax**. VAT never applies to residential property.
- **Unless the VAT is irrecoverable, figures should be shown in corporation tax computations** (eg capital allowances, adjustment of profits, and chargeable gain computations) **NET of VAT**
- It is always the **purchaser** who **suffers stamp taxes**, and the rates are different for shares and property.

Illustration 2: Errors in a draft gain computation

A client has prepared the following calculation of after-tax proceeds on the sale of a building by a subsidiary and the payment of a dividend of those proceeds to the parent company:

	Notes/workings	£
Sale proceeds (June 2020)		150,000
Cost (June 2008)		(100,000)
Gain before indexation		50,000
Less: rollover relief:	£130,000 reinvested in goodwill by another group member on 21/5/21	(30,000)
Amount not reinvested	£(150,000 – 130,000)	20,000
Indexation allowance June 2008-December 2017	0.283 × £50,000	(14,150)
Chargeable gain		5,850
Corporation tax at 19%		(1,112)
Cash available for distribution to parent company		4,739
Corporation tax on dividend at 19%		(900)
Cash available in respect of the building sale		3,839

Required

1 Identify any errors and any further information that you would need to verify that the calculation was correct.

2 As far as possible, prepare a revised computation of the after-tax proceeds available on disposal of the building.

Solution

1 Errors noted:

- Rollover relief should be applied, where available, to the indexed gain for companies (as opposed to the unindexed gain as per the draft computation). However, no rollover relief will be available in this case as goodwill is not a qualifying asset for rollover relief for a company.

- Indexation allowance should be applied to cost of the asset, not to the gain.

- The cash available for distribution should be *proceeds* minus tax, not the gain minus the tax.

- Dividends are not taxable on the parent company.

Further information required:

- Is there any reinvestment around the group that qualifies for rollover relief in the period June 2019 to June 2023?
- Are any capital losses available in the group to shelter the gain?
- Were any disposal costs, enhancement expenditure or costs of acquisition incurred?
- Was the acquisition in June 2008 from a gains group member or a third party?

2

	Notes/workings	£
Sale proceeds (June 2020)		150,000
Cost (June 2008)		(100,000)
Gain before indexation		50,000
Indexation allowance June 2008—December 2017	0.283 × 100,000	(28,300)
Chargeable gain		21,700
Corporation tax at 19%		4,123
Cash available for distribution to parent company	150,000 – 4,123	145,877
Corporation tax on dividend		Nil
Cash available in respect of the building sale		145,877

Chapter summary

Corporate planning

Group tax minimisation approach

- Establish group relationships
- Reallocate chargeable gains/ capital losses
- Consider relief for losses (current year and brought forward):
  - Reduce quarterly instalments
  - Avoid wasting QCDs and DTR
  - Earlier loss relief is better for cash flow
  - Be aware of restrictions, eg different AP dates, joiners and leavers

Disposal of a corporate business

Sale of shares
- Losses continue subject to major change rules
- Chargeable gain on shares arises in parent company
- Consider whether SSE applies to the disposal
- Degrouping charges may arise (intra group transfer to departing company < 6yrs ago) – CT if no SSE
- Stamp duty payable by buyer
- No VAT on shares

Sale of trade and assets
- Company (sub) is selling each asset for market value
- Chargeable gains/trade profits/balancing adjustments arise
- Consider mitigation – rollover/ losses?
- Losses not transferred except under successions rules (common 75% ownership of selling/buying co)
- SDLT payable by buyer on any L&B
- VAT should be TOGC if conditions met – special treatment of L&B if new or 'opted'

Losses and double taxation relief

- When using b/f losses and group relief, avoid wasting DTR if possible
- Only use enough loss such that UK CT = overseas tax suffered

Overseas expansion

Overseas branch (PE)
- UK CT on profits
- Relief in UK for losses incurred
- UK capital allowances
- DTR available for overseas tax suffered
- Exemption election available:
  - Exempts all overseas PEs from UK CT
  - Irrevocable once made
  - Lose UK loss relief

Overseas subsidiary
- No UK CT on profits or dividends
- No UK loss relief or CAs
- If overseas tax rate <UK rate, start overseas operation as a PE then incorporate once profitable

Identifying errors in computations

- Review for obvious mistakes
- Re-work computation in full if required by question
- Remember to explain errors
- Common CT errors:
  - Application of rules for individuals to chargeable gains computations and reliefs
  - Private use adjustments made in adjustment of profits or CA computations
  - Incorrect application of VAT to a transaction or figure
  - Charging dividends to CT

Knowledge diagnostic

1. Group tax minimisation

Group tax planning requires careful thought so don't be in a rush to start writing. You need to be able to identify the relevant group relationships and know how they impact on the tax planning opportunities available, and use all types of losses in the most beneficial way.

2. Disposal of a corporate business

In considering whether a trade and assets deal or a share deal is more beneficial to the selling party, it is important to analyse all the tax implications. One vital factor will be the availability of the substantial shareholdings exemption.

Transfers of trade between members of a 75% group will usually have no immediate tax consequences.

The decision about whether to extract value from a company before or after the appointment of a liquidator will depend on its shareholders – whether they are companies or individuals, and their marginal rates of tax on both income and gains

3. Losses and DTR

When using losses that allow a company to specify an amount to use, it is possible to preserve DTR by leaving an appropriate amount of the overseas income within the charge to corporation tax.

4. Overseas expansion

The key elements of overseas expansion decisions will be whether losses are likely to arise, and what the overseas tax rate is.

5. Identifying errors in computations

In order to be able to identify errors in computations, it is necessary to have a very detailed knowledge of the computational rules that apply to each relevant calculation. Questions will not test mathematical mistakes, only errors in application of tax legislation.

Further study guidance

Question practice

Now try the following from the Further question practice bank (available in the digital edition of the Workbook):

- Hulse Finds
- Daniel

Further reading

There are several technical articles on the ACCA website written by members of the ATX – UK examining team which are relevant to some of the topics covered in this chapter that you should read (if you haven't already read them):

- Corporation tax
- Corporation tax – group relief
- Corporation tax – groups and chargeable gains

Activity answers

Activity 1: Alpha Group

	Alpha Ltd YE 31/3/21	Bravo Ltd YE 31/3/21	Charlie Ltd YE 31/12/20	Delta Ltd YE 31/3/21	Echo Ltd YE 31/12/20
	£	£	£	£	£
Trading profit		–	510,000	150,000	
UK property income		100,000		50,000	
Capital gain (W1)					60,000
Less: Capital loss b/f					(40,000)
		–	–	–	–
TTP		100,000	510,000	200,000	20,000
B/f loss claim				(200,000)	
Group relief					
From E Ltd			(10,000)		
From A Ltd – current period		(35,000)	(105,000)		
From A Ltd		(25,000)	(75,000)		–
Revised TTP		40,000	320,000		20,000

Loss memo:

Alpha Ltd Trading loss	£
Trading loss (current year)	140,000
To C Ltd: cap 9/12 × £140,000 (note)	(105,000)
	35,000
To B Ltd (unrestricted)	(35,000)
	–
Trading loss b/f	100,000
To C Ltd: cap 9/12 × 100,000	(75,000)
To B Ltd (balance)	(25,000)
	–

Group relationships

At the end of the previous accounting period, there are five companies under common control: Alpha, Bravo, Charlie and Echo, and the overseas subsidiary. Delta joined the group in the current accounting period and so is not a related 51% group company for this accounting period. Hence the limit for paying tax by quarterly instalments is (£1,500,000/5) = £300,000.

Alpha, Bravo, Charlie and Delta form a group for loss relief purposes as Alpha Ltd owns at least 75% of each. Echo Ltd cannot be in the group as Alpha Ltd's indirect interest is less than 75% at 64% (80% × 80%).

Echo and Charlie Ltd form their own group for loss relief purposes thanks to Charlie Ltd owning at least 75%.

All the companies form a chargeable gains group as Alpha Ltd has a direct interest of at least 75% and an indirect interest of more than 50% in Echo Ltd.

Working

Chargeable gains

The gain in Bravo Ltd can be rolled over using the acquisition of a property by Alpha Ltd. £60,000 of gain remains chargeable representing the proceeds not reinvested (£500,000 – £440,000).

The gain can be transferred to Echo Ltd (or the current year capital loss in Echo could have been transferred to Bravo Ltd) in order to reduce the gain to £20,000.

Delta Ltd's capital loss brought forward is pre-entry as it arose before the company joined the Alpha Ltd group therefore cannot be used.

Loss relief

Delta Ltd should make a claim to relieve its brought-forward losses against its TTP. Note that as they are losses brought forward, they could not be group relieved as they are deemed to be offset against Delta's own profit first.

Group relief

Echo Ltd has a trading loss of £10,000 and this can be group relieved to Charlie Ltd to utilise the loss as soon as possible.

The current period and brought-forward losses of Alpha Ltd can be group relieved to Bravo Ltd or Charlie Ltd (Delta has no remaining TTP and Echo is not in Alpha's group relief group). As Charlie Ltd pays tax by quarterly instalments, as much loss as possible should be surrendered to Charlie Ltd, as the tax saving will be generated at an earlier point in time.

Charlie Ltd has a 31 December year end. The profits available for group relief are £510,000 × 9/12 = £382,500. The maximum loss available in Alpha Ltd is £140,000 × 9/12 = £105,000 (current year) and £100,000 × 9/12 = £75,000 brought forward.

Loss relief to Bravo Ltd is unrestricted as Alpha and Bravo have the same year end. All remaining losses should therefore be surrendered to Bravo Ltd.

Activity 2: Sale of shares vs trade and assets

Sale of share capital:

Due to substantial shareholdings exemption gain on disposal of shares will be exempt.

After-tax proceeds will be £580,000.

Sale of trade and assets:

	£
Sale proceeds	616,000
Less: Corporation tax (W1)	(23,003)
Repayment of liabilities	(20,000)
After-tax proceeds	572,997

The cash within Moonshine Ltd could be paid as a pre- or post-liquidation distribution (subject to distributable reserves) with no tax implications for Skye Ltd.

Offer 1 should be accepted as it results in the higher after-tax sale proceeds.

Workings

1 **Corporation tax**

	£
Gain on sale of premises (W2)	40,270
Balancing allowance on plant and machinery (36,800 – 52,000)	(15,200)
Profit on sale of goodwill	96,000
	121,070
CT @ 19%	23,003

2 **Gain on sale of premises**

	£
Proceeds	483,200
Cost	(392,000)
IA	(50,930)
	40,270

No SBAs would have been available on these premises as (due to the availability of indexation allowance) it must have been constructed prior to 29 October 2018.

No capital loss on plant and machinery due to balancing allowance.

Activity 3: DTR and group relief

Corporation tax computation for y/e 31.3.2021

	Total	UK	Overseas income
	£	£	£
Trading profit	850,000	850,000	
Overseas income (150,000 ×100/82)	182,927		182,927
Less qualifying charitable donation	(100,000)	(100,000)	–
Taxable total profits	932,927	750,000	182,927

DTR is the lower of:

(1) Foreign tax 18% × £182,927 = £32,927

(2) UK tax on overseas income 19% x £182,927 = £34,756

Therefore, in order not to waste the double tax relief the UK tax on the overseas income must be at least £32,927.

Sherman Ltd can choose to offset the qualifying charitable donation and the group relief in the most tax-efficient manner. Accordingly, the qualifying charitable donation and group relief will be deducted first from the UK profits, reducing these to zero. It should then be used to reduce the overseas income to the amount that results in the UK corporation tax being equal to the tax suffered overseas.

The overseas income should not be restricted to below £173,300 (£32,927/19%).

The maximum loss that should be surrendered to Sherman Ltd is:

	£
UK profits less qualifying charitable donation	750,000
Overseas income (£182,927 – £173,300)	9,627
Maximum loss to be surrendered to Sherman Ltd	759,627

Activity 4: Branch vs subsidiary

	Overlandian branch	Overlandian subsidiary
Year 1 – Loss of £(100,000)	Relief will be available against UK profits, saving UK CT at 19% = £19,000	No relief available as no profit to offset against in Year 1. Group relief to UK companies is not available.
Year 2 – Profit of £250,000	Overseas tax will be at 15% = £37,500 Profit will be taxable in the UK: CT at 19% = £47,500 Less: DTR (37,500) Additional UK tax 10,000	Profit (after loss relief for b/f loss of £100,000) = £150,000 Overlandian tax at 12% = £18,000 No further UK tax will arise on distributing profits, unless CFC rules apply
Total tax suffered by group	£(37,500 + 10,000 – 19,000) = £28,500	£18,000

Based on these figures, the subsidiary option would be recommended based on the lowest tax charge. However, if timing is important, the £19,000 of UK tax relief of the branch option would be beneficial.

The optimal position would probably be achieved by incorporating the branch at the end of Year 1 (to benefit from the UK loss relief in Year 1, and minimise the tax on the Year 2 profit).

Skills checkpoint 5
Corporate tax advice

Chapter overview

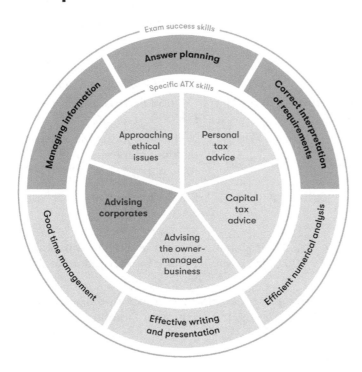

Introduction

The Advanced Taxation exam could contain a question involving a company or group of companies, that has either carried out or is considering a range of transactions. Your task will be to analyse the taxation implications of those transactions, in a set of structured requirements.

This may involve more than one tax (for example, VAT and stamp taxes issues may well arise on corporate transactions, and companies may also need to consider employment taxes). It is important to be methodical in dealing with corporate questions; to be able to analyse the information given to determine the relevant syllabus areas and to identify any tax planning opportunities that may arise.

This skills checkpoint focuses on a group of companies that is proposing to sell one if its subsidiaries – but the principles and approach to this question can be applied to a range of corporate scenarios.

In this skills checkpoint we will focus on three general exam success skills and the specific ATX – UK skill on corporate tax advice. Once you are familiar with these skills, you can then use them to tackle further corporate tax advice questions. Make sure that you refresh your memory using the technical knowledge presented in this Workbook before you attempt more exam standard questions.

Skills checkpoint 5: Corporate tax advice

ATX corporate tax advice

The key steps in applying this skill are outlined below. They will be explained in more detail in the following sections, and illustrated by answering requirements from a past exam question.

STEP 1 Look at the mark allocation and calculate the amount of time available for the question.

STEP 2 Read the introduction to the question, then read the requirements and think how you might answer them.

STEP 3 Now go back to the scenario in the question and highlight the information that will enable you to answer the requirements. Highlight important facts such as dates of transactions and ownership percentages.

STEP 4 Make a plan of the points that you need to cover in your answer, including what supporting calculations you will need to do. A group structure diagram may help you to understand the group relationships and their relevance to the scenario.

STEP 5 Write your answer.

Exam success skills

The following illustration is based on a 30-mark part of a 35-mark exam question, Grand Ltd, which appeared in the Sep/Dec 2018 sample questions.

- **Correct interpretation of requirements.** Make sure you pay attention to the verbs in the requirements ('explain' means the examiner is requesting a narrative answer), and any specific instructions (for example, to ignore a particular tax, or that calculations are/are not required).

- **Managing information.** The information in this question is spread across several sections, and you needed to identify how each fact given was relevant to the requirements.

- **Answer planning.** A group structure diagram, annotated with dates, would have helped to identify the group relationships and ownership periods to help arrive at the correct technical analysis.

Skill Activity

STEP 1 Look at the mark allocation and calculate the amount of time available for the question.

Prepare the memorandum as requested in the email from your manager. The following marks are available:

(i)	Offer A – in respect of a sale of the company's shares.	**(8 marks)**
(ii)	Offer B – in respect of a sale of the company's trade and assets.	**(11 marks)**
(iii)	Offer B – value added tax (VAT).	**(7 marks)**

Professional marks will be awarded for the approach taken to problem solving, the clarity of the explanations and calculations, the effectiveness with which the information is communicated, and the overall presentation and style of the memorandum and notes.

(4 marks)

The mark allocation for the question is 30 marks (including 4 skills marks) – this gives you 58.5 minutes of total time for the question. The requirements give you a breakdown of the marks available – 8 marks (16 minutes) for part (i), 11 marks (21 minutes) for part (ii) and 7 marks (14 minutes) for part (iii). There are also 4 skills marks available; this gives you an extra 8 minutes to think about the structure, language and presentation of your answer. It is particularly important in Question 1 of Section A to ensure that you focus on producing a document that is fit for presentation to the relevant recipient, be that a client or your manager.

It is worth spending approximately a quarter to a third of your time on reading and planning and the rest of the time writing up your answer.

For 8 marks in part (i) you have about 16 minutes so spend 2 minutes reading the question, 3 minutes planning what you need to write and then the remaining 11 minutes producing an answer.

For 11 marks in part (ii) you have about 21 minutes. This time should be split approximately as follows:

- Reading the question – 3 minutes
- Planning your answer – 3 minutes
- Writing your answer – 15 minutes

Part (iii) is worth 7 marks, giving you approximately 14 minutes; this should be 2 minutes each for reading and planning, with 10 minutes of writing time.

STEP 2 Read the introduction to the question, then read the requirements and think how you might answer them.

Prepare the memorandum as requested in the email

from your manager. The following marks are available:

(i) Offer A – in respect of a sale of the company's

shares. **(8 marks)**

(ii) Offer B – in respect of a sale of the company's

trade and assets. **(11 marks)**

(iii) Offer B – value added tax (VAT). **(7 marks)**

Professional marks will be awarded for the approach

taken to problem solving, the clarity of the explanations

and calculations, the effectiveness with which the

information is communicated, and the overall

presentation and style of the memorandum and notes.

(4 marks)

Note. The following indexation factors should be used, where necessary: November 2013 to December 2017 0.103 ; February 2014 to December 2017 0.094

In this particular question (and in many Section A

questions), the detailed requirements were to be found

in the 'body' of the question (in this case, in an email

from your manager). The 'requirements' section merely

specifies the format of your answer (memorandum), the

sections to be prepared, and the marks for each section

(from which you can allocate your 58.5 minutes

between the requirements). It also gives indexation

factors – which indicates that there will almost certainly

be some chargeable gains to compute.

The email mentioned in the requirement contained this detail.

The memorandum should cover the following:

(i) Offer A – in respect of a sale of the company's shares[129]:

- An **explanation**[130] of **whether or not**[131] tax relief will be available in respect of the capital loss arising on the sale of the shares

- An explanation of the **tax implications**[132] of Colca Ltd leaving the Grand Ltd group whilst still owning the Atuel building. This explanation should **not include any calculations**[133]

- A calculation of the expected **post-tax proceeds**[134]

(ii) Offer B – in respect of a sale of the company's trade and assets:

- A calculation of the **expected post-tax proceeds**[135]. For this purpose you should ignore any chargeable gains or allowable losses arising on the sale of the items of machinery

- In relation to the sale of the items of machinery, an **explanation**[136] as to whether or not they will result in chargeable gains or allowable capital losses **and**[137] of the availability of rollover relief

- An explanation of the companies to which Colca Ltd can **transfer any capital losses**[138] arising on the assets sold

(iii) Offer B – value added tax (VAT):

In respect of offer B: an explanation as to **whether or not Colca Ltd should charge VAT**[139] on the sale of its buildings and/or its machinery.

[129] So this is a sale of shares vs sale of T&A which is a really common exam scenario and it's really important that you understand the difference and don't confuse them!

[130] Explain: narrative answer required.

[131] You can infer from this that relief might not be available - you need to work out why.

[132] No specified tax, so need to consider a range of taxes.

[133] Follow this instruction to avoid wasting time.

[134] Post-tax proceeds = proceeds minus any taxes payable.

[135] Same calculation but selling assets this time. It's a really common mistake that students think this is the sale of 1 asset (the business), whereas in fact it's the sale of all the assets separately, each for their market value. What are the CT implications of the sale of each asset?

[136] Explain again, so a narrative answer. Do chargeable gains/losses ever arise on machinery?

[137] The word 'and' gives you an extra 'job' to do. What types of P&M qualify for rollover?

[138] Transfer capital losses = gains group members

[139] Are these items (buildings and machinery) taxable supplies?

STEP 3 Now go back to the scenario in the question and highlight the information that will enable you to answer the requirements. Highlight important facts such as dates of transactions and ownership percentages.

You should assume that today's date is 4 September 2021.

Extract from the email from your manager – dated 3 September 2021

    (a) Grand Ltd group of companies

Grand Ltd has two wholly owned subsidiaries, Colca Ltd and Sautso Ltd[140], and also owns shares in a number of other companies. All of the group companies are UK-resident trading companies[141], which prepare accounts to 31 March each year. All supplies made by the group are subject to VAT at the standard rate[142]. Sautso Ltd has been a member of the Grand Ltd group for many years.

[140] Group structure - needed for parts (i) and (ii).

[141] Relevant to SSE.

[142] Relates to (iii).

Sale of Colca Ltd

Grand Ltd purchased the whole of the ordinary share capital of Colca Ltd for £800,000 on 1 November 2013[143]. The value of Colca Ltd has fallen and the company is to be sold on 1 December 2021[144]. Two separate offers have been received: offer A and offer B.

[143] Base cost and acquisition date - relevant for share sale.

[144] Date of disposal - relevant to reliefs.

Offer A – in respect of a sale of the company's shares

- The purchaser will pay £730,000[145] for the whole of the ordinary share capital of Colca Ltd. This amount will be reduced by any tax liabilities payable by Colca Ltd arising as a result of the company being sold.

[145] Sale proceeds for (i).

Offer B – in respect of a sale of the company's trade and assets

- The purchaser will pay £695,000[146] for the trade and assets of Colca Ltd.

[146] Total sale proceeds for sale of trade and assets (ii).

Colca Ltd – expected asset values on 1 December 2021[147]

[147] MV at disposal = proceeds in any necessary gain computations

	£
Oribi building	410,000
Atuel building	230,000
Items of machinery	25,000
Net current assets (at cost)	30,000
	695,000

There is further information[148] in respect of these assets in the attached schedule from Bryce.

[148] May affect our calculations or explanations.

The value of Colca Ltd's goodwill[149] is negligible and should be ignored for the purposes of this work.

[149] So in this question we won't worry about a gain on GW.

Please prepare a memorandum for the client file.

Note. When calculating the post-tax proceeds in respect of the two offers, you should assume that tax relief at the rate of 19%[150] will be obtained in respect of any allowable capital losses

[150] May increase post-tax proceeds.

Schedule of information from Bryce

Colca Ltd – details of assets

Colca Ltd uses both the Oribi and Atuel buildings in its trade.

	Oribi building	Atuel building	Machinery
Date of purchase	1 February 2014	1 April 2019	N/A
Purchase cost (note a)	£320,000 (note b)	£255,000 (note c)	(note d)
VAT option to tax made?	No (note e)	No	N/A

Notes.

(a) Are these the correct figures for 'cost' in the gains computations?

(b) On 1 December 2013, Colca Ltd sold a machine for £74,000 resulting in a chargeable gain of £17,000. This gain was rolled over[151] against the purchase of the Oribi building.

[151] Rollover relief reduces base cost of new asset.

(c) Colca Ltd purchased the Atuel building from Sautso Ltd for £255,000, its market value at that time. As Colca Ltd and Sautso Ltd are both 100% subsidiaries of Grand Ltd, the transfer of the building took place at no gain, no loss. [152]Sautso Ltd had purchased the Atuel building, new and unused, for £340,000[153] on 1 January 2019.

(d) All of the items of machinery are moveable[154]. The sale of the machinery will give rise to a balancing charge of £12,100.

(e) So only VAT if sale is new commercial building as no OTT made?

Most of the items of machinery are worth less than their original cost. However, a small number of items are particularly specialised, such that their current market value exceeds their original cost[155].

[152] So we need to work out the NG/NL transfer price for the sale in part (ii). If Offer A (sale of shares) happens, a degrouping charge will arise if the transfer was less than 6 years ago. How is this calculated and charged?

[153] This gives the base cost of the building and the purchase would have been standard-rated for VAT (commercial property <3 years old).

[154] Therefore chattels rules apply, and not 'fixed' for rollover relief.

[155] Possible gains on sale of these items.

STEP 4 Then make a plan of the points that you need to cover in your answer, including what supporting calculations you will need to do. A group structure diagram may help you to understand the group relationships and their relevance to the scenario.

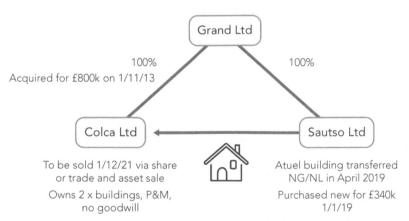

(i) Consider whether SSE applies (would make a capital loss not allowable).

Explain degrouping charge – how it's calculated (based on MV at transfer) BUT NO CALCULATIONS and what happens to it (add to share sale proceeds). SDLT to consider (intra-group transfer and now asset leaving group). Calculate post-tax proceeds: share sale proceeds – any taxes identified.

(ii) Calculate gains / losses on each building, and effect on TTP. Tax these and the balancing charge.

Deduct the CT from the sale proceeds.

Discuss machinery – some items increased in value – chargeable?

Rollover – no as not fixed.

Gains group members (75% subs)

(iii) VAT – if TOGC no output tax – are conditions met?

Building <3yrs old included in TOGC?

STEP 5 Write your answer.

(a) **Memorandum**[156]

Client Grand Ltd group[157]

Subject Sale of Colca Ltd

Prepared by Tax senior

Date 4 September 2021

(i) **Offer A – in respect of a sale of the company's shares**[158]

Tax relief available in respect of the capital loss on the sale of the shares

The capital loss on the sale of the shares will not be allowable for tax purposes due to the automatic application of the substantial shareholding exemption (SSE).

The SSE applies because[159]:

- Colca Ltd is a trading company; and

- Grand Ltd will have owned at least 10% of the ordinary share capital of Colca Ltd for at least 12 months in the six years prior to the sale of the company.

The tax implications of Colca Ltd leaving the Grand Ltd group whilst owning the Atuel building

Degrouping charge[160]

- The sale of the Atuel building by Sautso Ltd to Colca Ltd took place at no gain, no loss because the two companies were members of a chargeable gains group. This resulted in a base cost in the building for Colca Ltd equal to Sautso Ltd's cost plus indexation allowance up to December 2017.

- Colca Ltd will leave the Grand Ltd group within six years of purchasing the building from Sautso Ltd, such that a degrouping charge will arise. Colca Ltd will be deemed to have sold the building for £255,000, its market value as at 1 April 2019.

[156] Format and presentation of answer = skills marks

[157] Make sure you break the memo down into sub-sections matching up to the requirements to make it really clear what we're discussing in our answer - the Examination team frequently say that students' answers are often unclear as to which point they are discussing.

[158] The SSE and DGC are frequently examined topics and it's vital that you understand the rules around them and can apply them in questions like this.

[159] Using the word 'because' here demonstrates the application of knowledge, and is more time-efficient than stating all the conditions and then explaining why they're met.

[160] The degrouping charge discussion was worth 2.5 marks, with a further 3.5 for the stamp duty land tax implications of degrouping. Link this back to the requirement asking for 'tax' implications - it's more than just corporation tax.

This deemed disposal results in a capital loss. However, this loss merely increases Grand Ltd's cost of the shares in Colca Ltd. This in turn will increase the capital loss on the sale of the shares, which is not allowable due to the SSE (as noted above).

Tutorial notes:

(a) There was no need to calculate the capital loss in respect of the degrouping charge because it merely increases the capital loss on the sale of Colca Ltd, which is not allowable under the SSE.

(b) Colca Ltd will also be deemed to have purchased the building for £255,000, such that this will be its base cost in the building when calculating the chargeable gain or allowable loss arising on any future disposal of the building.

Stamp duty land tax (SDLT)

• There was no SDLT liability when Colca Ltd purchased the Atuel building from Sautso Ltd because both companies were 75% subsidiaries of Grand Ltd.

• However, Colca Ltd will leave the Grand Ltd group within three years of purchasing the building, such that it will have to pay the SDLT which would have been due at the time of purchase if the group exemption had not been available.

Post-tax proceeds

	£
Sale proceeds	730,000
Less: SDLT payable by Colca Ltd in respect of the Atuel building (W)	(2,250)
Post-tax proceeds	727,750

Working

SDLT payable by Colca Ltd in respect of the Atuel building

£	£
150,000 × 0%	0
100,000 × 2%	2,000
5,000 × 5%	250
255,000	2,250

(ii) Offer B – in respect of a sale of the company's trade and assets

Post-tax proceeds[161]

[161] Note the verb here was 'calculate' so a wholly numerical answer is given.

	£
Sale proceeds	
Trade and assets	695,000 (note)
Tax liability/credit in respect of:	
Chargeable gain on the Oribi building (£78,518 (W1) × 19%)	(14,918)
Plant and machinery balancing charge (£12,100 × 19%)	(2,299)
Allowable loss on the Atuel building (£110,000 (W2) × 19%)	20,900
Post-tax proceeds	698,683

Note. Remember that method marks will be available here so even if your tax calc figures are wrong you must have the confidence to bring them together to try to calculate the post-tax proceeds.

Workings

(a) Sale of the Oribi building

	£
Proceeds	410,000
Less: cost (£320,000 – £17,000)	(303,000)
Less: indexation allowance (£303,000 × 0.094)	(28,482)
Chargeable gain	78,518

(b) Sale of the Atuel building

	£
Proceeds	230,000
Less: cost (original cost to Sautso Ltd)	(340,000)
Allowable loss	(110,000)

Tutorial note: Colca Ltd has a base cost in the Atuel building equal to the cost of the building to Sautso Ltd plus indexation allowance up to December 2017. However, the indexation allowance has to be excluded[162] from the base cost when calculating a capital loss because indexation allowance cannot be used to increase the allowable loss.

[162] This is a very technical point, not needed to score a good mark.

Chargeable gains and allowable capital losses on the sale of the machinery[163]

[163] This is a tricky, rarely examined topic, and was worth 4 marks.

- The items of machinery will not be exempt under the wasting chattels rule because they qualify for capital allowances.

- However, any item where both the cost and the proceeds are less than £6,000 will be exempt.

- In respect of the chargeable items of machinery (where the cost or the proceeds is at least £6,000):

    - An item sold at a loss will not result in an allowable capital loss. This is because Colca Ltd will have received capital allowances equal to the fall in value of the item.

    - An item sold at a profit will result in a chargeable gain. Rollover relief will not be available because the items are moveable as opposed to fixed.

Transfer of capital losses to group members[164]

[164] This should have been an easy section as it is brought forward knowledge from TX. Note that they have not just dealt with the two 100% subsidiaries, but mentioned other shareholdings - we know that Grand Ltd does own some other shares, but the question does not specify the % ownership.

- The whole or part of any capital loss can be transferred to Grand Ltd, Sautso Ltd and any other member of the Grand Ltd chargeable gains group.

- This group consists of Grand Ltd, its directly held 75% subsidiaries, their directly held 75% subsidiaries and so on.

- Each company is an effective 51% subsidiary of Grand Ltd.

    (iii)   Offer B – value added tax (VAT)

BPP LEARNING MEDIA

Colca Ltd should not charge VAT on the sale of its business if the sale is a transfer of a going concern (TOGC). This requires all of the following conditions to be satisfied:[165]

- The business of Colca Ltd is transferred as a going concern.

- The purchaser will use the assets to carry on the same kind of business as Colca Ltd.

- There is no significant break in trading.

- The purchaser is VAT registered or will become registrable as a result of the purchase.

However, even where the sale of the business qualifies as a TOGC, VAT must still be charged on the sale of any building included as part of the sale if either:[166]

- An option to tax has been made in respect of the building, or

- The building is a commercial building which is less than three years old

No option to tax has been made in respect of either of the buildings to be sold by Colca Ltd.

However, the Atuel building[167] is a commercial building which will be less than three years old on 1 December 2021, such that the sale of this building will be a standard rated supply and VAT must be charged unless the purchaser opts to tax the building.

Examining team's comments and mark scheme

Examining team's comments

Marks were available for professional skills in Question 1. In this case candidates were required to provide a memorandum for a client file, including explanations and calculations of the outcome of two alternative strategies for the sale of a wholly owned subsidiary company. Candidates should keep two things at the back of their minds while addressing this type of requirement: Firstly, that explanations contained in the notes must be concise, but comprehensive enough to be understandable by another member of staff who may subsequently need to consult them. Secondly, the computations should be presented in a logical, structured way, such that they are easy to follow. Candidates who scored well, structured their answer according to the matters to be addressed, wrote concisely in short, clear paragraphs, provided easy to follow calculations, and demonstrated a logical thought process in addressing each of the issues.

This question required advice on the corporation tax consequences of disposing of a wholly-owned subsidiary company by either selling all of the shares, or, alternatively, selling the trade and assets, together with the value added tax (VAT) implications if the sale of trade and assets route is chosen. [...] The sale of shares versus sale of trade and assets decision is one which is regularly tested, so a well-prepared candidate should have been familiar with the main issues which they needed to discuss. Additionally, there are significant differences, practically and commercially, between selling shares in a company, and selling its trade and assets, which are reflected in the approach taken for tax purposes. If candidates are not familiar with a scenario, they should take time to think about the reality of the situation, which will often give them pointers as to the tax treatment. More generally, many candidates need to spend more time ensuring they are familiar with key areas relating to chargeable gains for companies – the substantial shareholding exemption (SSE), calculation of indexation, conditions for rollover relief and chattel exemptions in particular.

The use of subheadings, taken from the issues in the manager's email, provides a useful structure in this type of question, which all candidates should consider adopting.

The first part of the question, which was worth 8 marks, required candidates to explain whether or not tax relief would be available for a loss on the sale of the shares, the implications of the subsidiary leaving the group with a building which had recently been transferred to it by another group member, and a calculation of the after-tax proceeds. It was disappointing to see that a significant number of candidates did not mention that the SSE applied in this case, and so wasted time describing reliefs for the capital loss which were not relevant. Awareness of SSE and when it applies is fundamental at ATX. In any question concerning a corporate disposal of shares, the candidate's first thought should be to consider the application of SSE. There will be marks for considering this, and for demonstrating knowledge of the conditions, which will allow a decision to be made as to whether or not it applies. A few candidates did consider it, but concluded that it did not, or need not, apply where there is a loss, so, again wasted time with unnecessary calculations and discussion of reliefs.

The majority of candidates recognised that the company leaving the group with an asset that had been transferred to it within the last three years would give rise to a degrouping charge (and cited the six-year time limit), but only very few also recognised that there would also be stamp duty land tax implications. A small minority of candidates confused the implications of a share sale with those of a trade and asset sale, and so included calculations of the gains/losses on the individual assets in addition to, or instead of, the shares. This confusion then continued into the second part of the question, meaning that relatively few marks were available. As stated above, a few moments spent thinking about the reality of the different scenarios should have enabled a candidate to at least set off in the right direction.

The second part of the question concerned the disposal of the trade and assets of the company, as an alternative to the sale of shares. This part was worth 11 marks and, on the whole, was done better than the sale of shares, with the majority of candidates calculating a correct, or nearly correct, gain/loss on the two buildings, and, pleasingly, identifying the balancing charge on the machinery. The most common errors in this part were to treat the whole business as a single asset, and calculate just a single gain/loss by reference to the total costs and proceeds, and to calculate an indexation allowance to increase an unindexed capital loss. It was also pleasing to see that most candidates did try and address all parts of this requirement, but in a significant number of cases they were let down by their lack of detailed knowledge in relation to capital gains tax exemptions and reliefs, in this case the chattels exemptions (wasting chattels and £6,000 rule), and the precise requirements for rollover relief (moveable plant and machinery doesn't qualify).

The third part of the question concerned charging VAT on the sale of the building and machinery if the company decides to sell the trade and assets. This was worth 7 marks. Most candidates picked up a few marks here in relation to the buildings, and consideration of their age and the option to tax. However, very few picked up a key issue, embedded in the facts of this scenario, that transferring the trade and assets would constitute the transfer of a going concern, such that the transaction would be outside the scope of VAT, apart from, potentially, the buildings. Candidates at ATX should not rely on always been prompted in relation to the issues being tested, with a direct reference to the issue. They are encouraged to spend a little time thinking about the reality of the situation, so as to be able to identify the aspect(s) of a tax which may be relevant.

Overall, candidates who prepared satisfactory answers to Question 1:

- Appeared to have practised similar questions
- Read the requirements very carefully
- Applied their knowledge well to the scenario

- Produced concise explanations and clearly laid out computations

Mark scheme   Marks

(i) Offer A
Calculation of post-tax proceeds

Loss on sale of the shares	1	
Leaving the Grand Ltd group:	3	
Degrouping charge		
Stamp duty land tax	2½	
	3½	
Max	10	8

(ii) Offer B
Calculation of post-tax proceeds

Oribi building chargeable gain	1½	
Plant and machinery balancing charge	2	
Atuel building allowable loss	1	
Plant and machinery chargeable gains/allowable losses	1½	
Capital gains group	4	
	2	
Max	12	11

(iii) Transfer of a going concern

Rules in relation to buildings	4	
	4	
Max	8	7

Problem solving

Clarity of explanations and calculations	1	
Effectiveness of communication	1	
Overall presentation and style	1	
	1	
Max	4	4

Exam success skills diagnostic

Every time you complete a question, use the diagnostic below to assess how effectively you demonstrated the exam success skills in answering the question. The table has been completed below for Grand Ltd to give you an idea of how to complete the diagnostic.

Exam success skills	Your reflections/observations
Good time management	Did you fit in the whole question, including reading and planning? Were you disciplined in breaking down your exam time according to the marks for each part of the question?
Managing information	Did you link the information in the exhibit (the information from Bryce) to the relevant calculations in part (ii)?
Correct interpretation of requirements	Were you happy with the difference between the parent company selling shares, or the subsidiary selling its assets? Did you pay attention to the verbs and specific instructions

Exam success skills	Your reflections/observations
	not to perform calculations in certain sections?
Answer planning	Did your group structure help to identify gains group members, and the dates of the transactions to establish the availability of SSE and the relevant time periods for degrouping charges and 'new' commercial property? Were you able to tick off each 'job' as you completed it?
Effective writing and presentation	Did you follow the required format (a memo?) Did you use subheadings to communicate which part of which requirement you were answering?
Efficient numerical analysis	There were relatively few calculations in this question. Calculating chargeable gains accurately was tricky in this question due to the no gain no loss transfer and the rollover relief, but you need to ensure you can do this. After-tax proceeds calculations are very commonly tested; think about them in terms of cash flows (with tax savings being a positive cash flow).
Most important action points to apply to your next question	

Summary

Corporate scenarios in ATX are generally transactions based rather than compliance focused. Taking a moment to look at the 'big picture' of the company or companies, the proposed transactions and relevant dates should enable you to identify what the important issues are and what taxation issues will be relevant to the taxpayer (and therefore to your answer). Analysing the requirements to identify when and when not to perform calculations will save you valuable time in the exam.

Make sure you can distinguish between taxes and reliefs relevant to companies and to individuals – the SSE was a vital factor in part (i) of this question but would never be relevant for an individual selling shares!

Appendix 1:
Tax Tables

Supplementary information

(a) You should assume that the tax rates and allowances for the tax year 2020/21 and for the financial year to 31 March 2021 will continue to apply for the foreseeable future unless you are instructed otherwise.

(b) Calculations and workings need only be made to the nearest £.

(c) All apportionments may be made to the nearest month.

(d) All workings should be shown.

Tax rates and allowances

The following tax rates and allowances are to be used in answering the questions.

Income Tax

		Normal rates	Dividend rates
Basic rate	£1 – £37,500	20%	7.5%
Higher rate	£37,501 – £150,000	40%	32.5%
Additional rate	£150,001 and over	45%	38.1%

Savings income nil rate band	Basic rate taxpayers	£1,000
	Higher rate taxpayers	£500
Dividend nil rate band		£2,000

A starting rate of 0% applies to savings income where it falls within the first £5,000 of taxable income.

Personal allowance

	£
Personal allowance	12,500
Transferable amount	1,250
Income limit	100,000

Where adjusted net income is £125,000 or more, the personal allowance is reduced to zero.

Residence status

Days in UK	Previously resident	Not previously resident
Less than 16	Automatically not resident	Automatically not resident
16 to 45	Resident if 4 UK ties (or more)	Automatically not resident
46 to 90	Resident if 3 UK ties (or more)	Resident if 4 UK ties
91 to 120	Resident if 2 UK ties (or more)	Resident if 3 UK ties (or more)
121 to 182	Resident if 1 UK tie (or more)	Resident if 2 UK ties (or more)
183 or more	Automatically resident	Automatically resident

Remittance basis charge

UK resident for:	Charge
Seven out of the last nine years	£30,000
12 out of the last 14 years	£60,000

Car benefit percentage

The relevant base level of CO_2 emissions is 55 grams per kilometre.

The percentage rates applying to petrol-powered motor cars (and diesel-powered motor cars meeting the RDE2 standard) with CO_2 emissions up to this level are:

51 grams to 54 grams per kilometre	13%
55 grams per kilometre	14%

A 0% percentage applies to electric-powered motor cars with zero CO_2 emissions.

For hybrid-electric motor cars with CO_2 emissions between 1 and 50 grams per kilometre, the electric range of a motor car is relevant:

Electric range

130 miles or more	0%
70 to 129 miles	3%
40 to 69 miles	6%
30 to 39 miles	10%
Less than 30 miles	12%

Car fuel benefit

The base figure for calculating the car fuel benefit is £24,500.

Company van benefits

The company van benefit scale charge is £3,490, and the van fuel benefit is £666.

Individual savings accounts (ISAs)

The overall investment limit is £20,000.

Property income

Basic rate restriction applies to 100% of finance costs relating to residential properties.

Pension scheme limits

Annual allowance	£40,000
Minimum allowance	£4,000
Threshold income limit	£200,000
Income limit	£240,000
Lifetime allowance	£1,073,100

The maximum contribution that can qualify for tax relief without any earnings is £3,600.

Approved mileage allowances: cars

Up to 10,000 miles	45p
Over 10,000 miles	25p

Capital allowances: rates of allowance

Plant and machinery

Main pool	18%
Special rate pool	6%

Motor cars

New motor cars with CO_2 emissions up to 50 grams per kilometre	100%
CO_2 emissions between 51 and 110 grams per kilometre	18%
CO_2 emissions over 110 grams per kilometre	6%

Annual investment allowance

Rate of allowance	100%
Expenditure limit	£1,000,000

Commercial structures and buildings

Straight-line allowance	3%

Cash basis accounting

Revenue limit	£150,000

Cap on income tax reliefs

Unless otherwise restricted, reliefs are capped at the higher of £50,000 or 25% of income.

Corporation tax

Rate of tax: Financial year 2020	19%
Financial year 2019	19%
Financial year 2018	19%
Profit threshold	£1,500,000

Value added tax (VAT)

Standard rate	20%
Registration limit	£85,000
Deregistration limit	£83,000

Inheritance tax: nil rate bands and tax rates

Nil rate band	£
6 April 2020 to 5 April 2021	325,000

Nil rate band	£
6 April 2019 to 5 April 2020	325,000
6 April 2018 to 5 April 2019	325,000
6 April 2017 to 5 April 2018	325,000
6 April 2016 to 5 April 2017	325,000
6 April 2015 to 5 April 2016	325,000
6 April 2014 to 5 April 2015	325,000
6 April 2013 to 5 April 2014	325,000
6 April 2012 to 5 April 2013	325,000
6 April 2011 to 5 April 2012	325,000
6 April 2010 to 5 April 2011	325,000
6 April 2009 to 5 April 2010	325,000
6 April 2008 to 5 April 2009	312,000
6 April 2007 to 5 April 2008	300,000
6 April 2006 to 5 April 2007	285,000
Residence nil rate band	175,000
Rate of tax on excess over nil rate band – Lifetime rate	20%
– Death rate	40%

Inheritance tax: taper relief

Years before death	Percentage reduction
More than 3 but less than 4 years	20%
More than 4 but less than 5 years	40%
More than 5 but less than 6 years	60%
More than 6 but less than 7 years	80%

Capital gains tax

		Normal rates	Residential property
Rates of tax:	Lower rate	10%	18%
	Higher rate	20%	28%
Annual exempt amount			£12,300

Capital gains tax: business asset disposal relief (formerly entrepreneurs' relief) and investors' relief

Lifetime limit - business asset disposal relief	£1,000,000
- investors' relief	£10,000,000
Rate of tax	10%

National insurance contributions

Class 1 Employee	£1 - £9,500 per year	Nil
	£9,501 - £50,000 per year	12%
	£50,001 and above per year	2%
Class 1 Employer	£1 – £8,788 per year	Nil
	£8,789 and above per year	13.8%
	Employment allowance	£4,000
Class 1A		13.8%
Class 2	£3.05 per week	
	Small profits threshold	£6,475
Class 4	£1 - £9,500 per year	Nil
	£9,501 - £50,000 per year	9%
	£50,001 and above per year	2%

Rates of interest (assumed)

Official rate of interest	2.25%
Rate of interest on underpaid tax	2.75%
Rate of interest on overpaid tax	0.50%

Standard penalties for errors

Taxpayer behaviour	Maximum penalty	Minimum penalty – unprompted disclosure	Minimum penalty – prompted disclosure
Deliberate and concealed	100%	30%	50%
Deliberate but not concealed	70%	20%	35%
Careless	30%	0%	15%

Stamp duty land tax

Non-residential properties

Up to £150,000	0%
£150,001 – £250,000	2%
£250,001 and above	5%

Stamp duty

Shares	0.5%

Index

BPP LEARNING MEDIA

Bibliography

Brown v Burnley Football and Athletic Co Ltd 1980   [1980] 53 TC 357

Cape Brandy Syndicate v CIR 1921   [1921] 1 KB 64

CIR v Fraser 1942   [1942] 24 TC498

Croydon Hotel & Leisure Co v Bowen 1996   [1996] STC (SDC) 466

Donald Fisher (Ealing) Ltd v Spencer 1989   [1989] STC 256

Horton v Young 1971   [1971] 47 TC 60

Law Shipping v CIR 1923   [1923] 12 TC 621

Lawson v Johnson Matthey plc 1992   [1992] STC 466

Mitchell v B W Noble Ltd 1927   [1927] 11 TC 372

Odeon Associated Theatres Ltd v Jones 1971   [1971] 48 TC 257

Pickford v Quirke 1927   [1927] 13 TC 25

Ricketts v Colquhoun 1925   [1925] 10 TC 118

Samuel Jones & Co (Devondale) Ltd v CIR 1951   [1951] 32 TC 513

Strong and Co v Woodifield 1906   [1906] AC 448

Wisdom v Chamberlain 1969   [1969] 45 TC 92

Tell us what you think

Got comments or feedback on this book? Let us know.
Use your QR code reader:

Or, visit:
https://bppgroup.fra1.qualtrics.com/jfe/form/SV_9TrxTtw8jSvO7Pv